RIGHTS AND LAW – ANALYSIS AND THEORY

Richard,
      with thanks for
perceiving many stimulating
      discussions.

                  Andrew

Rights and Law
Analysis and Theory

ANDREW HALPIN

·H A R T·
PUBLISHING

OXFORD
1997

Hart Publishing
Oxford
UK

Distributed in North America by
Northwestern University Press
625 Colfax, Evanston IL
60208-4210 USA

Hart Publishing is a specialist legal publisher based in Oxford, England.
To order further copies of this book or to request a list of other
publications please write to:

Hart Publishing, 19 Whitehouse Road, Oxford, OX1 4PA
Telephone: +44 (0)1865 434459 or Fax: (0)1865 794882 or 434459

Payment may be made by cheque payable to 'Hart Publishing' or by
credit card.

British Library Cataloguing in Publication Data
Data Available
ISBN 1–901362–14–0 (hardback)
1–901362–15–9 (paperback)

Typeset in 10pt Sabon
by SetAll, Abingdon
Printed in Great Britain on acid-free paper
by Biddles Ltd. Guildford and King's Lynn

Preface

I hope that this book will be read by those with a variety of interests in law and legal theory, in human rights, political theory and moral philosophy. It does not presume to cater comprehensively for any of these interests, but does provide within a range of studies what should relate to each of them, connected by their concerns with rights. Although it is possible to locate particular interests with particular parts of the book, those seeking a direction to the work as a whole will find it expounded in part 2 of chapter I, and two basic issues that thread their way through the book are picked out for treatment in chapter X.

Much of this book was written for a doctoral thesis at Oxford. I am grateful for the inspiring supervision provided by John Finnis and Joseph Raz. At the examination of the thesis I benefited from the comments of Colin Tapper and Neil MacCormick, the latter kindly offering further comment as the project progressed towards a book.

In the Law Faculty at Southampton I have been fortunate to find a number of colleagues whose own interests have intersected or met some of the issues addressed in this book. I am grateful to all of my colleagues at Southampton for contributing to a friendly and stimulating workplace, and for specific discussions with Jenny Steele, Christine Chinkin, Jonathan Montgomery, Kit Barker and Sebastian Poulter.

Further afield, I am grateful for comments I have received on particular topics from Richard Youard, David Feldman, Yasuo Hasebe and David Humphris-Norman.

The production of the manuscript was greatly eased by the assistance of Darren Elliott, and the chores of proof reading by Roger Whitney. To all stages of the production process Marion Dalton has contributed her efficient and helpful labours. Richard Hart has combined qualities to transcend the conventional image of a publisher.

To Dorit, to Rafael, Daniel and Avital, and to my Parents, I am grateful for more than I can encapsulate here.

The material used in four of the chapters is substantially the same as that previously published in articles in (1985) 44 *Cambridge Law Journal* 435 (ch II), (1996) 16 *Oxford Journal of Legal Studies* 129 (ch III), (1991) 10 *Law and Philosophy* 271 (ch IV), and, (1994) 53 *Cambridge Law Journal* 573 (ch VII).

Abbreviations for works that are frequently cited are introduced within the footnotes of each chapter. The footnotes for each chapter constitute a separate system, with the exception of the footnotes for chapter IX, which run on from those for chapter VIII.

Contents

Part 1
Introduction

I
Analysis and General Theory

1 INTRODUCTION

If the literature on rights is burgeoning then it is also the case that some strange mutations are being harvested from it. One can find "right" being used to signify some position of benefit or advantage that has been determined as applying to a particular individual, but one can also find it employed to signify a claim to such a position that has yet to be determined, and even to signify a claim for such a position that has failed to be established:[1]

"[Rights] encompass even those claims that lose, or have lost in the past, if they continue to represent claims that muster people's hopes and articulate their continuing efforts to persuade."

Such flexibility in the use of language could appear more than strange in other contexts. Suppose such a widening of the term were to be applied to "graduate", we should find ourselves awarding degrees not only to those who had passed their final examinations, but also to those who had merely sat the examinations (without engaging in the chore of marking them), and even to those whose examinations had been marked and found to have failed (at least so long as they expressed an intention of taking a resit). In the context of rights, do we find a richer diversity of meaning for the language we use, or should we conclude that the language of rights has been debased to the point of being incapable of expressing any distinctive sense from which a proper inference can be drawn, or with which a meaningful point can be made?[2]

There is also to be found within the literature the proclamation of new strains of rights which are alleged to have some superiority over the traditional varieties:[3]

". . .the received ideas about the nature of rights . . . cannot readily inform the existing sorts of communal existence, much less the ones to which we aspire."

---

[1] Martha Minow, "Interpreting Rights" (1987) 96 *Yale Law Journal* 1860 at 1867.

[2] It is a commonly expressed anxiety that looseness of rights-talk can lead to the invocation of rights being rendered worthless – eg L.W. Sumner, *The Moral Foundation of Rights* (Oxford, Clarendon Press, 1987) ch 1, particularly at 8-9. For some actual examples of loose talk, see John Finnis, "Some Professorial Fallacies about Rights" (1972) 4 *Adelaide Law Review* 377.

[3] Roberto Unger, "The Critical Legal Studies Movement" (1983) 96 Harvard Law Review 561 at 598. For further discussion, see ch VII.

Though even amongst those committed to the cultivation of these new strains, there remains disagreement as to which variety is the most fruitful.[4]

But the great number of enterprises concerning rights is not limited to those who are endeavouring to cultivate them (whether old or new varieties). There are those whose purpose is to spray the whole field of rights with a defoliant to prevent the harvesting of any crop whatsoever. The chemical make-up of the defoliant varies. In some cases it is ideological:[5]

> "It is not just that rights-talk does not do much good. In the contemporary United States, it is positively harmful. . . . People need food and shelter right now, and demanding that those needs be satisfied. . . strikes me as more likely to succeed than claiming that existing rights to food and shelter must be enforced."

In other cases it is analytical:[6]

> "What, to my mind, is at the crux of the matter is the enterprise of stating the law as it is. . . On this view one can state the content of a legal system without recourse to the concept of a legal right at all. . ."

Any full discussion of rights needs to be capable of meeting these expressions of dissent.

2 THE ROUTE FROM ANALYSIS TO THEORY

The discussion of rights in this book was provoked by the assumption that there must be some connection between the analysis of legal rights and the general theory of law, and the observation that whatever the connection might be, it seemed to be largely neglected from both sides. The underlying assumption amounts to saying that neither those who endeavour to construct an analysis of legal rights nor those who embark upon the enterprise of general legal theory can achieve their particular objective without reaching an intersection with the other objective – and if they wish to see their narrower concerns fully

---

[4] A.C. Hutchinson and P.J. Monahan, "The Rights Stuff: Roberto Unger and Beyond" (1984) 62 *Texas Law Review* 1477 sets out to improve upon the approach to rights in Unger above n3.

[5] Mark Tushnet, "An Essay on Rights" (1984) 62 *Texas Law Review* 1363 at 1386, 1394.

[6] Richard Tur, "The Leaves on the Trees" [1976] *Juridical Review* 139 at 139. Tur proceeds to allow the use of a right as "an auxiliary concept" in some circumstances, but it is clear that this is not intended to affect the dispensability of rights, as maintained both here and in "The Notion of a Legal Right: A Test Case for Legal Science" [1976] *Juridical Review* 177.

Tur follows Kelsen in dispensing with rights. See Hans Kelsen, *The Pure Theory of Law*, translated by Max Knight (Berkeley and Los Angeles, CA, University of California Press, 1967) 127ff; Kelsen's *General Theory of Law and State* (Cambridge, MA, Harvard University Press, 1945) 75ff allows a possible but not necessary, secondary role for rights in the form of a power to determine whether a duty will be enforced (contrast Hart's position discussed in ch III, which makes this role primary) – a position also found in *General Theory of Norms* (Oxford, Clarendon Press, 1991) 136-7. I have suggested grounds for reinstating the concept of a right through a consideration of the general structure of Kelsen's system of legal norms in "The Limitations of a Legal System" [1981] *Juridical Review* 29.

realised that they must turn to participate to some extent in that other objective.

This may seem little more than a platitudinous assertion that legal theory must take account of rights, as a rallying call to muster forces against the ranks of scepticism in a battle that has already been fought and won too many times by both sides. Or it may strike the more suspicious reader as the introduction of yet another stratagem by which legal theory is to be harnessed to the unbroken will of political outlook whilst the ineffectual reins are placed in the hands of analysis.

Either of these responses should be discouraged at the outset by pointing to the precise scope of the analysis of legal rights as envisaged at this point, and to the nature of the consequent contrast with general legal theory.

By the analysis of legal rights I wish to refer initially to the task of providing a conceptual classification by which accepted legal materials can be organised and clarified, and from which looser and misleading statements about a person's legal position can be dispelled. The scope of this task does not extend to providing a platform for campaigns to instate a contentious position within the law, nor is it troubled by more abstruse points on the nature of the positions that are to be sorted out within its classification. And in these respects we may see a sharp contrast with the concerns of general legal theory.

First then, we may characterise this analysis of legal rights as being concerned with accepted legal material, whilst general legal theory extends to a concern with what the law ought to be and also deals with the preliminary task of proposing models of appropriate techniques to discover what the law is where the law is unclear. In other words, general legal theory encompasses both an epistemological apparatus and a critical apparatus, for which an analysis of legal rights finds no need, its concern being merely to classify the material that may be the product of an epistemological apparatus or may be fed in to a critical apparatus, without expressing any concern over whence the material came or how it might be evaluated.

Secondly, it is characteristic of such an analysis of legal rights to be concerned with the immediate practical consequences of legal material, whereas general legal theory finds a proper concern with the broader implications of the existence of legal material. In essence, we may express this distinction as being between the practical task of advising the individual what the law says he may or may not do, and the more theoretical objective of examining the social function of law, exactly how it relates to the society in which it is practised. This concern of general legal theory may be found in providing what we may style as a political apparatus, in the sense of providing a means of understanding the political significance and outworking of law. And again, an analysis of legal rights finds no need for this, for its concern to classify legal material proceeds irrespective of how that material is regarded as cohering with other elements that together sustain a society.

The disdain by the analysis of legal rights for the epistemological, political, and critical apparatuses of legal theory exhibits in general a technical rather than theoretical emphasis. This is not to say that the analysis is lacking in profundity, but is to point out that it is geared towards the immediate technical function of the law, to instruct what may or may not be done, rather than the deeper theoretical issues that motivate the discussions of general legal theory.

In order to explore the relationship between this sort of analysis of legal rights and the general theory of law, I shall use the work of Hohfeld as a point of departure. His work is particularly appropriate for this purpose since he has acquired a preeminence for his analysis of legal rights but also explicitly disavows the need to attend to general legal theory – the very need which it is my purpose to maintain. I shall move in the direction of those who have acquired a preeminence in discussing rights from the perspective of general legal theory – Dworkin, Rawls and Nozick, but who, astonishingly, omit consideration of Hohfeld's analysis from their theories. In their major works which have been applauded for the contribution they make to our understanding of rights within general legal theory, Rawls makes no reference to Hohfeld while Dworkin and Nozick each makes a single reference. But, as we shall see, in doing so each betrays a misunderstanding of Hohfeld's analysis.

There are a number of reasons for choosing to explore this subject. Doubtless many connections between different areas of jurisprudence remain unexplored, or at least not opened up to the full flow of traffic that they are capable of supporting. Why pick upon this one as the route for a major highway? The answer is not simply that we can expect a great deal of commerce to flow in both directions between key locations within jurisprudence, though this itself provides good reasons. The further reasons concern the particular territory over which the route has been mapped, for this is remarkably rugged and the successful construction of a highway here will teach us much about the techniques of road building which can then be employed to open up routes elsewhere.

Put more prosaically, the discussion of a number of issues within this subject is intended to achieve three things: a contribution to improving the technical achievements of an analysis of legal rights, particularly through demonstrating the points at which the technical objectives of this analysis must have recourse to issues of general legal theory; a clarification of how certain issues of general legal theory are inextricably linked to the technical concerns of an analysis of legal rights, with the aim of setting further discussion of those issues on firmer ground; and more obliquely, the enunciation of some general principles of the methodology of jurisprudence, which will emerge from the techniques that will be employed in relation to the particular objectives that are being pursued here.

It is necessary to expand the scope of this project in one respect and to limit it in others. The expansion of the project takes the form of widening the terms of the study by omitting the restriction to *legal* rights and theory. Although legal rights remain the core area of study, it is necessary to expand the project to rights in general in order to even adequately deal with this core area. There are a number of reasons for taking this approach. First, the predominant view within the literature is to treat legal rights and other rights together, so that it is impossible to effectively isolate legal rights as a discrete area of study. (It is commonly accepted that the same *concept* of a right applies equally to legal and moral orders,[7] but this is not universally accepted.[8] There is also controversy over whether any dividing line at all can be drawn between moral and legal rights.[9]) Secondly, and more particularly, the contribution of Hohfeld to the analysis of legal rights has been widely discussed in relation to non-legal rights. Thirdly, even within the more specialist literature on legal rights, there is not a consistency in attributing the epithet to a particular grouping of rights, so that a very real danger of question begging arises if we attempt to limit the scope of our study by an initial restriction to legal rights.

Some limitation on a project of this nature is necessary. I seek to limit it by selecting for discussion those issues which most readily demonstrate the underlying relationship of interdependence between analysis and general theory that I am attempting to demonstrate.

Even so, there is much that a study of this kind could reach towards that I have held back from. I hope, nevertheless, that what is undertaken is sufficient to provide assistance in tackling other subjects that are not pursued here. For example, I have held back from direct discussion of human rights, though much of what follows (particularly in chapters V, VI, VIII and IX) may be regarded as having significant repercussions for this subject. Similarly, there is often material that clearly relates to our understanding of judicial reasoning and the role of precedent (notably in chapters V and VI). Again, I hope that what is found here may be regarded as illuminating in pursuing these subjects further – but that work is not undertaken here.

The various chapters that follow may be treated as a number of self-contained studies on various aspects of rights. However, it should be possible to discern a sense of direction that links them together.

Chapters II–IV deal primarily with three of the ideas contained in Hohfeld's analysis: privilege or liberty, power, and claim. (Immunity is not given separate detailed treatment here, on the grounds that this would not make any significant contribution to our present concerns, and as will subsequently emerge, due to Hohfeld's portrayal of immunity/disability as the negation of

---

[7] Alan White, *Rights* (Oxford, Clarendon Press, 1984) at 18–9.

[8] Michael Perry, "Taking Neither Rights-Talk nor the `Critique of Rights' Too Seriously" (1984) 62 *Texas Law Review* 1405 is introduced with a distinction between moral and legal rights, but it is interesting to note that the distinct subject matter of moral rights collapses subsequently when an argument is mounted from the perspective of the courtroom (at 1414).

[9] Frequently discussed in relation to Ronald Dworkin's denial of the dividing line in *Taking Rights Seriously* (London, Duckworth, 1977), eg by Joseph Raz, who treats this aspect of Dworkin's theory of rights as "The Natural Law Thesis", in "Professor Dworkin's Theory of Rights" (1978) 26 *Political Studies* 123 at 133, 136–7. For further discussion, see ch IX.

liability/power being more accurate than his portrayal of privilege/no-right as the negation of duty/right.) In each of these studies there is an attempt to sharpen Hohfeld's analysis, and also to open it up to broader theoretical concerns.

The broader concerns of general legal theory are met in chapters V–VII and taken further in chapters VIII–IX (chapter V performing something of a pivotal role between analysis and general theory). These concerns are approached using the analytical insights gained from earlier studies, with the aim not merely of enriching our understanding of general theory but also of bringing those analytical insights themselves to completion.

3 CONCEPTUAL ANALYSIS

(1) The Directions of Conceptual Analysis

It is understandable that concepts, terms/labels,[10] and categories should be regarded as interchangeable. The term that is used to label the idea that constitutes the concept is also employed for the category whose members comprise all the instantiations of that concept. In short, the one word covers all three. As with "law", which is a term that may express a concept as well as a member of the category of phenomena that are regarded as instantiating that concept.[11]

As a starting point I want to suggest that we need to clarify the differences between, and hence the possible relationships between, terms/labels, concepts, and categories. There are two preliminary stages that I shall adopt in order to carry out this objective. First, I shall favour at a more elementary level "term" over "label", so as to be able to convey those instances where terms that may be used as labels are being employed for a different purpose, or indeed are being employed simultaneously for different labels. Secondly, I shall abandon "category" at this level, so as to avoid the confusion that can arise between categories and sub-categories, where one person's category is another person's sub-category; and also, so as to avoid the presupposition that conceptual analysis is identical to establishing clear taxonomies of phenomena. Instead, I shall refer at the elementary level to a field of enquiry. It will

---

[10] I use "term" in a broader sense than "label", so that all labels are terms but not all terms are labels. The need to make the distinction should become apparent shortly, but for the moment the distinction is immaterial. It is also worth mentioning that "term" used in this way bears its looser meaning of a word that is used to express something, rather than its more technical meaning of a word used in a definite or precise sense (see entries IV.13.b and IV.13.a in the OED).

[11] The example is found in Brian Bix, "Conceptual Questions and Jurisprudence" (1995) 1 *Legal Theory* 465 at 465-6 – hereinafter, Bix. A slightly different version of Bix's article appears in the introductory section to his book, *Jurisprudence: Theory and Context* (London, Sweet & Maxwell, 1996) – page references prefixed by B are to this book. Bix states *inter alia*, "Conceptual claims. . . are assertions. . . about labels. . . that often also serve as categories. . .".

then be possible subsequently to identify categories of phenomena within that field should it be considered appropriate to do so.

Within this initial part of our consideration of conceptual analysis my principal aim is then to demonstrate the different relationships that may exist between terms, concepts, and fields of enquiry. In particular, I shall suggest that the direction taken between these three critically determines the purpose(s) that a conceptual analysis can effectively perform.

We start as we must do, with a field of enquiry. The failure to identify our field of enquiry means that we cannot be sure of engaging in meaningful discussion with others, since there is always a danger that we are investigating different fields of enquiry. Even though the field of enquiry may be identified by a particular term, we cannot simply assume that identifying the field of enquiry with a term guarantees a common field of enquiry with those whose field is identified by the same term. This is so because the common usage of a term is frequently capable of conveying different meanings, so that theorist$_1$ in investigating field "X" with meaning$_1$ is involved in a totally different enterprise to that engaged in by theorist$_2$ who is investigating field "X" with meaning$_2$.[12]

This is not to preclude the possibility of a full scale investigation into the richness of linguistic usage of a particular term. However, if this is our objective then we need to identify our field of enquiry as encompassing all the usages of that particular term. Otherwise, we must specify what we are taking the term to convey. This point may be made as a general principle of conceptual analysis:

(A) A field of enquiry must be specified in such a way that it is possible to identify its members that are the subject of the theoretical investigation.

It does not follow from this that all the members of the field will be known to the theorist – but it will be possible to identify any new discovery as a fit subject for that particular investigation, or not.[13] Nor does it follow from the ability to identify members of a field of enquiry that everything is known about them. Even if we can identify what is and what is not "municipal, institutional law", it does not follow that we understand what municipal, institutional law is. Many can identify a modern motor car without having the foggiest idea of the workings of the internal combustion engine. Indeed, it is

---

[12] This general point applies across the three principal purposes for conceptual analysis in Bix's classification. Bix himself points out the "unresolvable disagreement" that occurs when two theorists are apparently debating the nature of law but have separately identified law with a different significant feature that the term is capable of conveying. (Bix, 472-473 – in Bix's illustration at n22, the contrast is between a feature of guiding human behaviour preferred by Hart, and a feature of justifying state coercion selected by Dworkin.) This will apply equally where a different understanding of linguistic usage is taken, or where different criteria for an evaluative test are associated with the term. In his own introduction to legal theory, Bix is forced to limit the term "law" to "municipal, institutional law." (Bix, B7 n1.)

[13] Of course it is possible that the discovery of a phenomenon that does not fit into any established field of enquiry will cause theorists to reconsider what field of enquiry they should be investigating.

difficult to justify engaging in conceptual analysis unless it does bring about some greater understanding of the members of the field of enquiry that we are investigating.[14] It is perhaps worth reiterating this as a second general principle:

(B) *The possibility of identifying members of a field of enquiry is not to be equated with an understanding of them.*

The way is clearly being prepared for locating conceptual analysis at a secondary phase in providing us with understanding of the members of the field of enquiry that we have identified. But there seems an obvious objection to this where the field of enquiry is itself conceptual. Suppose we are investigating *the idea* of justice?

This seems to locate our conceptual analysis at the first phase, since the process of specifying our field of enquiry involves identifying concepts of justice – and so appears to amount to conceptual analysis. However, this argument betrays a misunderstanding which can be cleared up by noting more carefully what exactly is the nature of our enquiry.

If we are merely enquiring into the idea of justice as a matter of historical record – perhaps tracing the development of concepts of justice from classical times to the present day, then no conceptual analysis is required: the concepts of justice that we identify as members of our field of enquiry do not require analysing, but recording.

It is unlikely that such a relatively straightforward enquiry would be undertaken for the simple reason that the ideas of justice over the centuries are not themselves so clear as to limit our interest to merely documenting them. There is much controversy over, for example, Aristotle's concept of corrective justice.

However, once we recognise that our enquiry will extend beyond mere documentation so as to embrace the conceptual analysis of the ideas of justice over the centuries, then it is apparent that we are actually engaging in conceptual analysis at the second phase *after* we have specified our field of enquiry. The field of enquiry is in fact the historical sources for the idea(s) of justice, and conceptual analysis then comes in to provide different ways of representing the historical material, with the aim of improving our understanding of it.

The point can be illustrated by means of the specific example of Aristotle's concept of corrective justice. The phrase "Aristotle's concept of corrective justice", if it does not refer to a clearly recognisable concept on which no further analysis is required, is in fact a conventional truncation for the more accurate description of what we are examining: "Aristotle's thoughts on corrective justice as found in his extant writings". The process of conceptual

---

[14] If the confusion that presently dims our understanding is solely along the lines of whether *a* is an X with properties p_1 or a Y with properties p_2, and all that can be understood about X or Y is conveyed by p_1 or p_2, then conceptual analysis within the field of X or Y has no part to play. We simply need better empirical information about *a*.

analysis within this field of enquiry may even cause us to doubt that Aristotle's thoughts on corrective justice can be coherently reduced to a single concept: perhaps there are two distinct concepts of corrective justice that Aristotle covers by the same term.[15]

More generally, we can say that investigations in fields of enquiry that are conceptual in nature still require us to abide by principle (A) above, in specifying our field of enquiry and identifying its members before we can engage in conceptual analysis that permits us to hold meaningful discussion with others. The general point can easily be lost here precisely because of the solecism of describing the field of enquiry as a single concept.[16]

Whether the field of enquiry is loosely identified by a particular term whose common usage may be ambiguous, or even more loosely identified with a particular idea which on closer examination is seen to represent a collection of disparate thoughts on a particular subject, if conceptual analysis is to prove helpful in increasing our understanding within that field of enquiry,[17] we must as a preliminary specify more carefully our field of enquiry in accordance with principle (A). This then suggests a third general principle which encapsulates an appropriate progression for the theorist to follow, if conceptual analysis is to be employed in increasing our understanding in a way that can be meaningfully communicated with others:

(C) *The proper progression in undertaking conceptual analysis with a view to increasing understanding of a particular matter is: specifying the field of enquiry; proposing concepts that assist in the understanding of that field; finding appropriate terms with which to label the proposed concepts.*

I shall have more to say below on the actual exercise of conceptual analysis, and the task of labelling concepts with appropriate terms. However, it is important to note here that the direction of the route between field of enquiry, concept and term that is proposed in principle (C) is not the only possible

---

[15] Compare the suggestion that John Stuart Mill in *On Liberty* was actually dealing with two concepts of liberty.

[16] This solecism is also evident in a manner of describing conceptual theory that has been made popular by John Rawls (*A Theory of Justice* (Oxford, OUP, 1972) at 5-6), and Ronald Dworkin (*Taking Rights Seriously* (London, Duckworth, 1977) at 134-5, 226; *Law's Empire* (London, Collins, 1986) at 70-1, 74) in talking of conceptions of a concept. Again the singular concept is used to refer to the field of enquiry (the concept of justice) – and the conceptions to refer to different viewpoints or different theorists' attempts at conceptual analysis within that field. The phrase is for that reason unhelpful. There simply does not exist within (say) western thought a single concept of justice. There is thinking about justice which encompasses a number of ideas, some varying slightly, some widely diverging; some transparently coherent, others muddled or inconsistent. To say that we wish to examine western thinking on justice as our field of enquiry, and to be able to identify what falls within that field of enquiry, as, eg, thinking on the principles that govern fair relations or conduct between people (cp Rawls: "principles for assigning basic rights and duties and for determining. . . the proper distribution of the benefits and burdens of social cooperation" – at 5), is far from identifying *a concept* of justice.

[17] We should not ignore the possibility that all conceptual analysis capable of assisting our understanding has already been undertaken – in which case, the following is redundant, because we have already properly matched the field of interest with the appropriate concept(s) and terms and hence it does not matter if we approach the subject matter through the term or the concept.

route to take. In understanding legal materials, in particular, a different route is frequently taken. This is because the starting point is necessarily ordained by the legal materials themselves, and they do not invariably commence by clearly indicating a field of enquiry. Frequently, the starting point is a bald term.

Take, for example, the use of the term "intention" within the definition of murder in the English criminal law. The mere mention of this term is not sufficient to indicate a field of enquiry. Neither common usage nor previous legal usage is capable of marking off unequivocally a field of applications for this term, as the vacillations of the English appellate courts in the last twenty or so years have demonstrated. Conceptual analysis within this area must accordingly not simply increase our understanding of what the term is taken to apply to but must also set the boundaries of what is covered by the term.

Now there may prove to be common features between the former role of conceptual analysis in increasing understanding within an established field of enquiry, and this role of setting the boundaries of the field of enquiry. Nevertheless, this latter role poses an additional issue for the theorist in determining what the scope of the field of enquiry will be by the concept that is proposed. And this issue cannot be addressed by bearing in mind the desire to increase understanding, because selecting the concept will affect what it is that we are seeking understanding of. This then opens up a further desideratum for conceptual analysis in finding a concept that satisfies one or more criteria for what that field of enquiry should be, whilst leaving to the theorist an element of discretion in selecting the criteria.

To continue with the example of "intention", since the term does not itself mark off a field of applications, the theorist[18] must decide what criteria should be acknowledged in selecting a concept that will set the scope of the field. That is not to say the theorist enjoys complete licence – selecting criteria that defeated any intelligible purpose for the term within the context it is found in would be pointless. But there may exist a number of competing purposes for the term in that context: providing a definition of murder that is compatible with common morality, or popular sentiment; providing a definition of murder that clearly distinguishes the offence from manslaughter; providing a definition of murder that is capable of including a particularly heinous form of killing (eg, a case involving a terrorist bombing), or that is capable of excluding a less heinous form of killing (eg, mercy killing); and so on. And different choices from among this number will provide different criteria which may then influence what concept of intention is proposed.

This more obviously provides the opportunity for normative criteria to enter the selection of the proposed concept, and at the very least necessarily provides the theorist with a discretion which falls outside the desideratum of

---

[18] The same function is performed by the judge who is faced by a legal provision containing such a term. A point that has implications for our understanding of the judicial interpretation of the law.

advancing understanding found in principle (C). We may attempt to capture this in a further general principle:

(D) *Where the progression involved in a case of conceptual analysis is constructed so as to commence with a term, followed by proposal of a concept, leading to the specification of the field of enquiry, then the role of conceptual analysis must be expanded to take into account the selection of appropriate criteria that will affect which concept is proposed.*

(2) Virtuous Stipulation

Although I have suggested that there are two quite distinct ways in which conceptual analysis works, indicated by principles (C) and (D) above, I want now to consider generally the part played by stipulation within conceptual analysis without for the moment bringing this distinction to bear on our discussion. A fundamental point to clarify is what the stipulation actually affects. We commonly talk of "stipulative definitions" – but what exactly is being defined on such occasions? A further pertinent question to pose is – why do we need to stipulate in the first place?

Again, it may be helpful to keep in mind the trio of term, concept, and field of enquiry. Do we define a term or do we define a concept? Must there exist some recognisable defect in the prevailing terminology or array of concepts, before any resort to stipulation is justified? Does the particular field of enquiry that is involved have any relevance to these issues?

As a way of approaching these questions we can note the evident virtue that a stipulative definition possesses when we are suffering from a battery of inconsistencies in previous approaches to the subject. Joseph Raz has put this forward in relation to his stipulating an approach to "moral individualism".[19]

However, in offering a stipulative definition there is the danger that we may move from the virtuous provision of a firm path with which our reader may negotiate the bogs of inconsistency, to the vice of leading our reader on a selective route of the scenery that is the most attractive to our own viewpoint. Raz himself has recognised this in commenting on the dangers of stipulating a definition of rights, concluding with the observation that, "The definition may advance the case of one such theory, but if successful it explains and illuminates all."[20]

The very activity of stipulating a definition of a term presumes some background practice that we are stipulating against. This may be the use of the term either in colloquial speech or in learned discourse, and the stipulated definition of the term may then be contrasted with an analysis of earlier usage of that term.[21]

[19] *The Morality of Freedom* (Oxford, Clarendon Press, 1986) at 198.
[20] *ibid.* at 165–6.
[21] Neil MacCormick notes this contrast in "Rights, Claims and Remedies" (1982) 1 *Law and Philosophy* 335 at 347-8 n17.

The current usage (whether colloquial or learned) may be inconsistent but discretely coherent: the inconsistency comes from one participant employing the term in one sense and another participant responding with another sense. A rigorous analysis of usage would detect these different senses for the term, say: S1, S2, S3, S4. On the other hand, current usage may in addition, or as an alternative, to being inconsistent, be incoherent – ie at least some of the different uses of the term make no sense. Incoherence may arise through internal contradiction; or, by the definition being applied uniformly to both example and counterexample; or, by being so vague as to be incapable of setting apart the phenomena it purports to identify from other phenomena.[22] In the case of incoherence a rigorous analysis would discard the use of the term as unworkable.

Stipulation may accordingly be a necessary device to rescue us from the inconsistency or incoherence that a rigorous analysis of current usage reveals. Alternatively, the task of hacking through the thicket of current usage may be too daunting and stipulation is happily employed so that we can safely proceed along the path of coherence and consistency that we ourselves have provided, rather than wasting our energy on the thicket that has grown over other people's labours. In such a case, the stipulator may at least gain our sympathy and avoid our suspicion if he is prepared to defend his stipulation against any senses that others may extract from the thicket of current usage rather than merely use his stipulation to avoid further discussion.

The essential point to be made here is that the virtuous stipulation of the definition of a term is not opposed to analysis of current usage of that term, nor indeed to the more fundamental pursuit of analysis of the phenomena to which the term is applied. It is in the nature of a virtuous stipulation to enrich our understanding of these phenomena. And in order to facilitate the detection of virtue and vice, it is worth specifying some of the features of virtuous stipulation in a further general principle (the first two features may be regarded as the normal[23] threshold features which call for some stipulation to be made):

(E) *A stipulative definition may be regarded as virtuous if it possesses an appropriate combination of the following features –*
(i) *avoidance of incoherence, and/or*
(ii) *avoidance of inconsistency;*
(iii) *breadth of coverage: Does our stipulation permit us to accommodate a*

---

[22] The possibility of incoherence within ordinary usage should not be underestimated and it would be presumptuous to assume that learned discourse is immune from it. The recognition of incoherence within ordinary usage places a fundamental reservation upon any "ordinary language" analysis. I have touched upon this in relation to the analysis of intention in the English criminal law in "Good Intentions" (1987) 137 *New Law Journal* 696 at 698.

[23] But see also features (iii)-(v), which may indicate stipulation is called for not because of the inconsistency or incoherence found within current usage but due to its impoverished state.

sufficient number of phenomena within our analysis, or does it artificially restrict the scope of our analysis?[24]

(iv) depth of coverage: Does our stipulation permit us to explore significant subtleties within the phenomena, or is this hindered by it?

(v) correlation with current usage: Can we either accommodate current usage with our stipulation or reject it as inferior to what we have stipulated?[25]

(vi) fit with other schemes: Does our stipulation provide us with a scheme of analysis that is compatible with other schemes of analysis; so that the concepts within one scheme can be clearly distinguished from and (where appropriate) related to the concepts of another, so that there is no unnecessary duplication between schemes? – and, so that

*(vii) any intelligible issue can be discussed – ie **we do not stipulate any intelligible issue out of our scheme of analysis without being able to demonstrate that there is a suitable location for discussing it elsewhere.***[26]

How then does the practice of virtuous stipulation relate to the questions we raised at the beginning of this section? We have, I think, said enough on why the need for stipulation may arise. But so far we have been content to talk rather loosely of the stipulative definition of terms, without seeking to understand what exactly is defined by a stipulative definition and bringing to bear on this the points raised in the earlier part of this section.

We have noted the easy interchangeability of terms(/labels), concepts, and fields of enquiry(/categories). What implications does this have for stipulation? The simple statement that the stipulation defines the term becomes more complicated precisely because the term can be used to represent different things.

A term may be used to represent a concept or the phenomena that are regarded as instantiating that concept. A term may also be used to represent a field of enquiry identified with what is covered by existing linguistic usage of that term. There is no reason why the last possibility should be specifically

---

[24] Notice that the accommodation of phenomena within the analysis may be satisfied as much by indicating why a particular phenomenon is not to be given a particular status as by indicating why it is. So, for example, this aspect of virtue would be found in a stipulation which informed us why animals were not to be regarded as possessing rights, but would be absent from a stipulation which prevented the question of animals' rights arising by restricting the investigation *ab initio* to the rights of man. As to the further impact upon the virtue of our stipulation raised by the question whether issues of animal welfare are being denied a hearing by failing to treat them as rights of the animals, see feature (vii).

[25] Accommodation may be possible in the case of an impoverished current usage (see (iii) & (iv)), which can be improved on by stipulation. But where current usage is unworkable as inconsistent and/or incoherent (or, at least, so confusing as likely to be so) (see (i) & (ii)), then rejection will be appropriate.

[26] So, for example, we could maintain the virtue of a stipulation which denied the possibility of talking of the rights of works of art if we could show that any intelligible issue on the conservation of works of art could be discussed in terms of the rights of men to enjoy them. The possibility of doing this explains how we can draw the line between attributing rights to men but not to works of art, or trees (*pace* Richard Tur, "The Leaves on the Trees" [1976] *Juridical Review* 139 at 150); and I would suggest that this feature of virtuous stipulation is the key to clarifying the discussion on animal/foetus/children's rights.

conceptual. The word constituting the term in question may be applied in a fairly unarticulated manner in popular usage to all manner of things: sensations, visual images, social practices or institutions, etc. So "law" may express a concept of law, the phenomena that are regarded as instantiating that concept; and may also express everything to which the word "law" has been applied, including social practices, social institutions, feelings of compulsion, etc – notwithstanding the lack of conceptualisation that may have accompanied the use of the term.

The scope for unvirtuous stipulation may be greater than we first imagined. If by stipulating a definition for a term we are indicating how that term is to be exclusively understood, and that term is used to represent or label a concept, then we are limiting our understanding of that concept to the sense stipulated. If, however, that term is used to represent a field of enquiry, then we are shutting off our enquiry to deal only with what falls under the sense stipulated. Vice is to be detected not only where a slick stipulation takes our audience to our favoured concept away from the path of a rival concept, but also where our audience is cocooned into the belief that the world only holds what can be recognised as instantiations of our favoured concept.

(3) Relationships Between Concepts

Further reflection on the connections between concepts and a field of enquiry, which may easily be obscured by the same term being employed to refer to both, reveals a number of different relationships that may hold between different concepts. There are three basic possibilities.

First, there is the possibility of *conflicting concepts*, where each equally claims comprehensive sway over a particular field of enquiry, and the two are incompatible. So, for example, the *Caldwell* concept of recklessness in the English criminal law conflicts with the *Cunningham* concept of recklessness, since the latter requires awareness of risk by the particular defendant, which is not required by the former. The conflict occurs within the field constituted by the offence of criminal damage, so that the House of Lords in *Caldwell* was forced to overrule a previous precedent that had adopted the *Cunningham* approach for this offence.[27]

However, in the wider field constituted by all criminal offences, the relationship between the two concepts was not so simple. Even in *Caldwell* itself it was recognised that *Cunningham* recklessness would still apply to some offences other than criminal damage.[28] This gives rise to the second possibil-

---

[27] [1981] 1 All ER 961, at 965–7 overruling *Stephenson* [1979] 2 All ER 1198.

[28] Exactly which offences became a troubling question – see, eg, *Parmenter* [1991] 4 All ER 698. The picture became even more confused when *Caldwell* was deposed from holding exclusive sway over even those offences to which it did apply – see *Reid* [1992] 1 All ER 793, *Adomako* [1994] 3 All ER 79.

ity, where the concepts though potentially conflicting may coexist if it is recognised that each applies to a separate part or category within the field of enquiry. We might call this a relationship between *subconcepts* so as to indicate their holding sway within their own subdivisions of a field of enquiry.

One of the perplexing issues in the current English criminal law is delineating the proper scope for each of the numerous concepts of recklessness that now exist, and it would not be appropriate to hold these up as paragon illustrations of subconcepts. Perhaps a more effective illustration is furnished by Hohfeld's analysis of rights. Hohfeld stipulates four distinct categories: (1) where A is entitled to some behaviour of B; (2) where A is entitled to behave in a particular way himself; (3) where A is entitled to change the position of entitlement of himself and/or another; (4) where A is entitled to maintain his position of entitlement against change by another.[29] Hohfeld's four concepts of rights – claim-right, privilege/liberty, power, immunity, respectively – coexist as subconcepts within the field of enquiry constituted by positions described as rights in practical legal discourse, because each subconcept is allocated an exclusive category within that field.

The third possibility is that of *complementary concepts*. These do not need to be kept apart in separate categories in order to coexist within a field of enquiry. For although they differ, there exists no conflict due to the fact that neither concept purports to hold exclusive sway within the field. This possibility may be related to the observation made in principle (B), that identifying members of a field should not be confused with understanding everything about them. It follows that identifying members of a field as instantiations of a particular concept is not necessarily to exclude the possibility of further enlightenment by identifying those members also as instantiations of a different concept.

This possibility is illustrated by a view taken of the relationship between the ideas of natural law and legal positivism. According to this viewpoint, within the field of enquiry constituted by what is commonly referred to as municipal, institutional law, a concept of law along the lines of the regulation of social conduct which derives its authority from settled Natural Law precepts which ensure human flourishing, is compatible with a concept of law along the lines of the regulation of social conduct which derives its authority due to its being traceable to a recognised positive source; and our understanding of municipal, institutional law is enriched by the insights offered by both of these concepts.[30]

[29] *Fundamental Legal Conceptions*, W.W. Cook (ed.), (New Haven, CT, Yale University Press, 1919) – discussed in detail in ch II.

[30] John Finnis, "Comment [on Positivism and the Foundations of Legal Authority]" in Ruth Gavison, (ed.), *Issues in Contemporary Legal Philosophy* (Oxford, Clarendon Press, 1987) 62 at 69–70 – see also his *Natural Law and Natural Rights* (Oxford, Clarendon Press, 1980) at 16–9; and see further his "The Truth in Legal Positivism" in Robert George (ed.), *The Autonomy of Law* (Oxford, Clarendon Press, 1996). Cp Joseph Raz, *The Authority of Law* (Oxford, Clarendon Press, 1979) at 157–9.

Whether we do treat these concepts as complementary or conflicting depends on how exclusively we regard the claims of Natural Law and Legal Positivism in their accounts of municipal, institutional law.[31] Nevertheless, the illustration serves to make the point that two concepts which appear to contradict each other may in fact coexist if neither is purporting to provide exclusive illumination on the phenomena under investigation.[32]

These observations merit another general principle:

(F) The stipulative definition of a term cannot be fully comprehended or assessed before we take into account how that term relates the concept we are proposing to the field of enquiry we are investigating, and how that concept relates to other possible concepts within that field. In particular, we need to be able to clarify the relationship between such concepts so as to distinguish conflicting concepts, subconcepts, and complementary concepts.

The general point to note here is that the process of stipulation, although carried out on a term, effectively sets boundaries on concepts and/or fields of enquiry. We may reasonably talk of a stipulated concept or a stipulated field of enquiry as indicating the product of stipulating a term in particular circumstances. It is only when we have explored all the ramifications of a stipulation in accordance with the above principle that we will be in a position to assess its virtue.

However, an ancillary point needs to be made here on virtuous labelling. For given the possible ambiguity that we have detected where the same term may act as a label both for a field of enquiry and for concepts within that field, there is an obvious possibility that a flaw in stipulating the definition of a term can be traced directly to such ambiguous use of the term.

This is worth making as a separate point because it may be the case that our concerns over a theorist's stipulation do not affect the concept that emerges from that stipulation but rather the label the theorist has chosen for that concept, and it is easy to lose the exact focus of our criticism.

The point can be simply illustrated by considering the virtue of Hohfeld's stipulation of his subconcept (2), "privilege", within the field of enquiry constituted by positions described as rights in practical legal discourse. There is to be found a strong preference for replacing "privilege" with "liberty" as the label for (2).[33] But this changing of labels has nothing to do with the virtue of Hohfeld's stipulated concept.[34] If we recognise the virtue within our con-

---

[31] For a portrayal of conflicting concepts, see Barney Reynolds, "Natural Law versus Positivism: The Fundamental Conflict" (1993) 13 *Oxford Journal of Legal Studies* 441.

[32] Bix makes a similar point (at 474–5) in suggesting that both Fuller's and Hart's concepts of law are "valuable and useful". However, by suggesting the two concepts can be regarded as "incompatible" yet "not inconsistent", Bix is eliding the crucial point about exclusivity within a field of enquiry. Within the common field of enquiry of municipal, institutional law, if both concepts purport to exclusively identify what is law, then they are incompatible *and* the analyses they provide are inconsistent.

[33] eg Glanville Williams, "The Concept of Legal Liberty" (1956) 56 *Columbia Law Review* 1129.

[34] Walter Wheeler Cook in his "Introduction", above n29 at 11 – "mere question of phraseology".

ceptual analysis of rights in practical legal discourse of distinguishing between the subconcepts (1), (2), (3) and (4), that is one thing. What we call these sub-concepts is another.

So to argue that Hohfeld's subconcepts impoverish our analysis of rights because they forbid us from exploring these phenomena in sufficient depth[35] would be to challenge his stipulation, but to argue that "privilege" bears a confusing connotation different from that for which Hohfeld uses it is not to challenge his stipulation but his labelling.[36] The confusion between the two arises because it is easy to come out with the loose criticism, "Hohfeld's privilege is inadequate", which may convey either.[37]

This leads us to consider principles of good practice in bestowing labels. It would be wrong to regard this in the same way as virtuous stipulation, for we have seen that the stipulation and the labelling may be quite separate. However, we can regard this as ancillary to virtuous stipulation, for we have also seen that poor labelling is likely to conceal any virtue that the stipulation may possess.[38] The main features of good labelling appear in the following general principle:

(G) In allocating a label to a concept the following objectives should be kept in mind-

(i) avoidance of ambiguity: Is the term we use as a label to be found elsewhere serving a different function?

(ii) compatibility with current usage: Can the term we use as a label be readily understood without jarring with current usage of that or similar terms?

(iii) clear indication of technical restrictions where necessary: Given that nevertheless we shall frequently find ourselves employing terms that are popularly employed but with a more restrictive technical meaning – Can we readily see how the term used as a label differs from its popular usage?

(4) Analytical and Normative Approaches

There is to be found within the literature[39] a recognition of two different kinds of approaches to rights. The one, dubbed normative, seeks to establish a justification for the acceptance of a particular set of substantive rights; the other, dubbed analytical, seeks to establish the logical form or necessary

---

[35] I argue this in relation to Hohfeld's privilege in ch II.

[36] Williams, above n33, prefers a different label but does not challenge Hohfeld's concept of a privilege.

[37] Of course, it would also be possible for the critic to be suggesting both; and in the case where poor labelling confuses the stipulator himself, the one is likely to lead to the other.

[38] So I W Sumner in his *The Moral Foundation of Rights* (Oxford, Clarendon Press, 1987) at 19-20 insists on relabelling Hohfeld's subconcept (1) as a "claim" rather than a "right" so as to avoid what he considers would otherwise be an unvirtuous stipulation that "arbitrarily closed some important questions about the univocity and complexity of rights".

[39] For example, MacCormick above n21 at 356; Jules Coleman, *Markets, Morals and the Law* (Cambridge, Cambridge University Press, 1988) at 33–4.

features of rights. Naturally there may be some connection between the two,[40] and we might raise the anxiety that it would be possible to stipulate a definition for rights so that the ensuing logical form supported a particular normative approach.[41]

Bix has suggested that an evaluative element may enter conceptual analysis in one of two ways: because the theorist is setting his own agenda for what counts as important, or because the theorist is establishing an evaluative test, within two of the three principal purposes Bix suggests for conceptual analysis.[42]

The relationship between a normative role for concepts and the analysis of concepts is an important one. Critically because the use of analysis to produce normative consequences naturally attracts the suspicion that the analysis has been skewed to provide the desired normative result, whilst concealing the evaluative assumptions on which it is based. We should accordingly endeavour to clarify as far as possible what forms this relationship can take.

One point that has already emerged from the general principles proposed above is that if we are using conceptual analysis to bring out something that is important to understand within our field of enquiry then this is a valuable role in itself.[43] This gives us an evaluation of the conceptual analysis, but does not call for an evaluative role to be *played by* the conceptual analysis.

However, it is when the theorist's choice of an important feature is made exclusive in determining what is to be identified as falling within a field of enquiry that the role of the analysis changes, and may be regarded as unvirtuous. It is now performing an evaluative role in prescribing what counts as important.[44]

Another point already noted is that in some cases an evaluative role may be forced on the conceptual analysis because of the situation in which the theorist is placed. The conceptual analysis is linked to a term which may be employed to serve a number of competing objectives, and the analysis will determine which of those objectives is promoted. This has been distinguished as broadening the role of the theorist, in performing analysis *and* prior to that adopting criteria appropriate to the objective selected.[45] This has not been castigated as unvirtuous – so long as the additional aspect alongside the conceptual analysis is recognised and made explicit.

---

[40] Coleman, above n39 at 34, extends analytical to cover working out the content of rights derived from the foundational theory which is the focus of the normative approach. Although this is undeniably analytical in the broad sense, it is not clear it is thus to be regarded as part of the analytical approach to rights for there is nothing intrinsically pertaining to rights in this form of analysis.

[41] The anxiety is expressed by MacCormick, above n21 at 356.

[42] Bix, 469; 472-3; 473, 477. At 471 Bix suggests that there may not be a hard and fast distinction, between these two purposes. Bix's other purpose is tracking linguistic usage.

[43] See principle (E): (iii), (iv) & (vii).

[44] See principle (F) and surrounding text. It is submitted that it is when this exclusive role is taken on that any distinction between Bix's purposes of stating what is important and applying an evaluative test does dissolve – but not when the former is being used in a non-exclusive way.

[45] See principle (D).

One way of looking at the conceptual analysis of rights is to view the theorist's task as that of finding a way to handle the term "right". Given that the term may serve a number of objectives, the theorist will have to select an objective, and appropriate criteria. It is possible to regard Hohfeld's analysis in this way: selecting as the objective for the term, expounding legal materials for the practitioner, and adopting criteria of intelligibility, consistency, etc.[46]

Neither of these two possibilities gives us a case of a virtuous conceptual analysis performing an evaluative role. In the first case it is not virtuous, and in the second case the evaluation of the objective selected and its appropriate criteria is made prior to the performance of the conceptual analysis.[47] A third possibility to consider is where the concept that the most virtuous form of conceptual analysis can provide contains an evaluative element which can only be further explicated by filling out that evaluative element, but there does not exist an accepted standard by which to do this. Here the evaluative role arises not from the analysis of the concept but from the existence of value pluralism relating to an element found within the concept as analysed. This value pluralism may be moral (as with dishonesty) or aesthetic (as with art), but it exerts an external influence over the use of a concept rather than being the product of conceptual analysis. It is this possibility that is captured by Gallie's "essentially contested concept",[48] but what is contested is not strictly what the concept should be but what value should be selected to fill out an element found within the concept.[49]

---

[46] This is explored further in ch II. An alternative objective would be to employ "right" as a means of social change – an example of which is considered in ch VII. It should be stressed that simply making explicit the objective selected in a case falling under principle (D) does not guarantee that all subsequent conceptual analysis will prove virtuous – the demands of principles (E)–(G) are still to be met.

[47] Though the descent to vice is an easy one, by not acknowledging the objective selected. A vice that is perhaps most prevalent in the judicial pretext of simply declaring the ordinary meaning of the term.

[48] One way of regarding the divergent views on rights is to consider right as an "essentially contestable concept" in the sense propounded by W.B. Gallie, "Essentially Contested Concepts" (1956) 56 *Proceedings of the Aristotelian Society* 167. Gallie's suggestion that certain concepts are doomed to be the subject of irresolvable conflict has been widely received (for further bibliographical detail, see Horacio Spector, *Autonomy and Rights* (Oxford, Clarendon Press, 1992) at 6 n10). However, the impediment to further theoretical advances that the assumption of essential contestability may bring has been noted (in relation to the political concept of power) by John Gray, "Political Power, Social Theory, and Essential Contestability" in David Miller and Larry Seidentop (eds.), *The Nature of Political Theory* (Oxford, Clarendon Press, 1983). Neil MacCormick, *Legal Right and Social Democracy* (Oxford, Clarendon Press, 1982) at 160 argues that "in relation to their substance, rights belong to the class of essentially contested concepts". Torben Spaak, *The Concept of Legal Competence* (Aldershot, Dartmouth, 1994) at 143, 152 n7 goes further in regarding this to apply also to the form of a right. It is submitted that Spaak's approach would lead to precisely those dangers that Gray notes, and a major burden of what follows is to reject essential contestability for rights. MacCormick's approach limited to the substance of the rights is perhaps best not regarded as an issue of essential contestability of the concept. Having clarified the concept, we should be in a better position to identify what exactly are the substantial issues that are being contested.

[49] There are allusions to this in the conclusion of Gallie, above n48. At 197, he links "clarification . . . of an appraisive concept" to fulfilling "recognized standards", and distinguishes this from other processes of conceptual clarification.

In conclusion, the appearance of a proper evaluative role for conceptual analysis has been discredited by a fuller understanding of what conceptual analysis itself involves. That is not, of course, to say that conceptual analysis has no part to play in serving normative purposes, but rather to emphasise that these normative purposes should be recognised rather than concealed in a confused portrayal of what conceptual analysis involves.

Quite apart from the general charge of vice that can be made whenever a stipulation is engineered to support a particular normative viewpoint rather than to enrich our investigation, the contrived stipulation is self-defeating. This follows from the *justificatory* nature of the normative approach – in essence stipulation cannot justify.

No matter how sophisticated or extensive is our argument, if by the end of it we have stipulated a definition of right so that a particular set of substantive rights must necessarily be accepted within our theory (eg, those rights which can be exercised by all citizens; or, those rights which find constitutional support) then what we have done is to start with the field of phenomena usually referred to as rights, then we have stipulated a category within that field of phenomena, and finally we have labelled that category as rights. But it is clear that the label rights that we finish with has nothing to do with the label that was broadly applied to the field of phenomena that we started with – though unfortunately the same term is used for both. And as we have seen, confusion springs from employing the same term to label a stipulated category as is used to cover a field of phenomena.

Once the confusion is dispelled then we must admit that we cannot import into our stipulated category the exclusive enjoyment of connotations associated in general with the field of phenomena, for these connotations belong to the broad use of the term as employed to cover the field of phenomena and not to the term as label for the stipulated category. For example, if the field of phenomena labelled rights bears a connotation of entitlement, and we then stipulate as a category those members of the field which enjoy constitutional support, and then label this category as rights, it is false to conclude that we find within our stipulated category the only things that can be accepted as entitlements. The correct conclusion is that we find within our stipulated category what we have stipulated to be within it: the only things that can be accepted as entitlements enjoying constitutional support.

Of course the strength of the illusion that we have somehow necessarily established a particular set of substantive rights (constitutional rights) would be dissipated if only we had chosen a different label for our stipulated category. If we had labelled it in accordance with the scheme of good practice for labelling (notably feature (i)) and chosen a distinct label, such as "constitutionally supported rights", then the illusion would never have got off the ground because it would have been apparent that we had simply demarcated a particular category of phenomena, rather than demonstrated that the members of this category possessed (exclusively) a special status that we had in mind prior to the stipulation. By employing the label, we would only have been able to say that members of this category are "constitutionally supported rights" rather than that they are *the rights*.

This denunciation of a bogus normative approach would not be so straight-forward if the approach made a stronger stipulation by exclusively stipulat-ing the falsely borrowed connotation from the field of phenomena within the stipulated category itself. Suppose the category had been stipulated exclusively as containing not only constitutional entitlements but also on the basis that only constitutional entitlements were to be recognised as entitlements. This would then be established within our theory, but if we then claim to have *justified* the acceptance of constitutional entitlements as the only set of enti-tlements (and thence as having established a particular set of substantive rights), the claim would be palpably false, for we have done nothing more than construct a tautology, which justifies nothing.

There is nothing more revealing in the foregoing than the simple observa-tion that in order to justify the acceptance of something there must be some criterion of justification existing independently of the thing sought to be justified. And this requirement of an external criterion cannot be satisfied by the illusion that it is inherent within the thing to be justified through a manip-ulation of terminology; nor by the brazen stipulation of the criterion within the thing sought to be justified. The defence of wearying the reader with such a protracted treatment of this simple point must rest upon the discovery that the evasion of the point is correspondingly elaborate in those theories of rights which falsely purport to establish a normative approach by stipulating an ana-lytical approach.[50]

---

[50] For illustrations, see chs VII and IX.

Part 2
Analysing Rights

II

Rights and Liberties and Hohfeld's Fundamental Conceptions

1 INTRODUCTION

If Jurisprudence strikes the law student as a miry bog, the analysis of a legal right ought, at least, to provide a path through the marshland. The disparate rumours of such a path may have a greater tendency to lead him into the middle of the bog than bring him safely to the other side.

It is characteristic of this area of legal theory that the attempt by Hohfeld to provide a precise analysis of legal rights has itself fallen victim to misunderstanding and misrepresentation. The supporters of Hohfeld readily concede that the mastery of his analysis is a difficult discipline,[1] but the prize should be reward enough: a clear understanding of the concept of a legal right. Its value is freely acknowledged among Hohfeld's antagonists:[2]

> "The chief attribute of scientific progress is greater clearness of distinction. In this the law has been the most backward of sciences, and it is really astonishing, when one stops to consider the fundamental importance of ultimate categories in legal reasoning that the insufficiency of our technical apparatus, in a scientific sense, had not long before impressed itself."

Hohfeld claimed to have identified the eight fundamental legal conceptions, and as such to have provided a technical apparatus for legal analysis: the atomic elements into which all legal material can be reduced. In this chapter, I shall commence with an introduction to the nature of Hohfeld's conceptions. I shall argue that six of Hohfeld's conceptions are reducible, in terms of the other two, and cannot therefore maintain their position as fundamental conceptions. I shall further suggest that, as a result, Hohfeld's conceptions do not provide us with the required technical apparatus to analyse with accuracy legal material.

---

[1] Arthur Corbin, "Foreword" to Walter Wheeler Cook (ed.), *Fundamental Legal Conceptions as Applied in Judicial Reasoning* by Wesley Newcomb Hohfeld (New Haven, CT, Yale University Press, 1964) (hereinafter, FLC) at iii.

[2] Albert Kocourek, *Jural Relations*, 1ed. (Indianapolis, IN, The Bobbs-Merrill Co., 1927) (hereinafter, Kocourek).

2 HOHFELD'S FUNDAMENTAL LEGAL CONCEPTIONS

Hohfeld provides us with eight conceptions which he claims to be both fundamental and legal. We can clarify the alleged nature of these conceptions by examining further the two attributes he gives them. The first attribute, "fundamental", is not given a clear definition by Hohfeld but may be regarded as possessing three features:

   (i)   comprehensive;
   (ii) sufficient;
   (iii) irreducible.

The conceptions are comprehensive in that all legal positions may be expressed in them. They are "the legal elements that enter into all types of jural interests."[3]

Furthermore, the conceptions are sufficient: all legal positions may be expressed adequately in them alone. They are referred to as "the lowest generic conceptions to which any and all 'legal quantities' may be reduced."[4]

Thirdly, they are irreducible. This is to say that the conceptions cannot be broken down into anything more basic, and, as a result, they can only be expressed in terms of their relations to each other. They are "the basic conceptions of the law", "the lowest common denominators of the law". "The strictly fundamental legal relations are, after all, *sui generis*. . ."[5].

There is little room for disagreement with the way that Hohfeld uses the term, "fundamental". His exposition of the second attribute, "legal", is more tendentious, and contestable. The meaning Hohfeld gives to this attribute rests on two preliminary distinctions, made by him before presenting his conceptions.

The first distinction is between legal conceptions and non-legal conceptions.[6] Hohfeld points out reasons why these have been confused: in early law the legal phenomenon is associated with the physical phenomenon by which it is made manifest; the same word is often used for both phenomena. The principal target that Hohfeld selects is "property". This may be used to refer to the physical object owned, or to refer to the legal interest of the owner. Confusing the two uses leads to transferring the unity of the object owned to the legal interest, and speaking of the *right* of property. As we shall see, Hohfeld considers the legal interest should be viewed as an aggregate of legal relations and thus more properly be referred to as the *rights* of the owner.[7]

---

[3] FLC, 27.
[4] FLC, 64.
[5] FLC, 27, 64 and 36.
[6] FLC, 27ff.
[7] FLC, 28, 96.

Once the legal interest is separated from the thing over which it is exercised, it can be confined to an abstract existence. From this viewpoint, Hohfeld can mock the distinction between corporeal and incorporeal property. All property is incorporeal since all legal interests are abstract.[8] Hohfeld adduces other examples of the confusion that prevails between legal and non-legal conceptions, notably contract, which is used to refer to both the agreement between the parties (non-legal) and the contractual obligation (legal).

The second preliminary distinction is between operative facts and evidential facts.[9] The former, by satisfying a legal rule, bring about a change in a legal relation; the latter are grounds for inferring other facts, which may be evidential or operative. To the casual reader of Hohfeld's condensed prose, this distinction is not obviously linked to his subsequent analysis of legal rights. However, Hohfeld uses it to make two important points. In the case of a written contract, the document is, at the time of writing, an operative fact which brings about the contractual relation between the parties. But, later, it becomes an evidential fact from which may be inferred the operative fact that a piece of paper existed by which a contractual obligation arose. This point serves to prevent the legal obligation from being identified with the document. Also, the point is made that generic terms, such as possession, are often applied to certain types of operative facts, and these terms are confused with the legal relations brought about by the operative facts.

Both preliminary distinctions, accordingly, have the function of clarifying a legal relation as something abstract, which is quite separate from the mental or physical phenomena through which it arises, or over which it is exercised. In this sense, Hohfeld refers to a legal relation as being "purely legal".[10]

To the extent that Hohfeld considers that a legal right is abstract, his notion will not be challenged. A right is a concept, and concepts are generally regarded as being abstract. But Hohfeld's use of "purely legal" goes beyond this. Legal relations are presented solely in terms of these fundamental abstract conceptions. He not only identifies abstract legal conceptions: he identifies legal interests with these abstract conceptions alone.

This is ironic when Hohfeld's stated intent is that "the emphasis is to be placed on those points believed to have the greatest practical value."[11] It is as though the author of a textbook for medical practitioners were to start in an introductory chapter by identifying medicine as being concerned with the concept of health, and then to deny that medicine had anything to do with bodies. We should not expect the author to be able to maintain this dichotomy between the abstract and the physical in subsequent chapters, when it came to dealing with the actual practice of medicine. Hohfeld's relegation of the

---

[8] FLC, 30.
[9] FLC, 32ff.
[10] FLC, 27.
[11] *ibid.*

term "legal" to a purely abstract existence can be challenged when it comes to examining practical legal situations.

The eight conceptions spring from Hohfeld's dissatisfaction with the common tendency to assume that all legal relations can be reduced to rights and duties.[12] Out of the ambiguity of the single solecistic pair of concepts, Hohfeld brings four distinct pairs. In place of the vague concept of a right, we have the concepts:[13] right, privilege, power and immunity – together with their correlatives: duty, no-right, liability, disability. Each concept is also the jural opposite of another concept. They can be presented in Glanville Williams' famous table, with their jural correlatives vertically above or below and their jural opposites diagonally opposite, as follows.

A right is a legal claim of one person that another person acts or omits to act in a certain way.[14] The position of the other person is described by saying that he has a duty.

A privilege describes the position of a person who is free to do, or refrain from, some act, without transgressing a legal obligation to another person.[15] The position of the other person is described as having a no-right.

A power is the legal ability of one person to change the legal situation of another.[16] The position of the other person is described as having a liability.

An immunity describes the position of a person who is free to enjoy a legal relation without it being changed by another person.[17] The position of the other person is described as having a disability.

Each fundamental legal conception may be contrasted with its opposite. The presence of the one indicates the absence of the other, with regard to a particular act or omission. If A has a right that B does *x*, then A does not have a no-right that B does *x*; if B has a liberty (or privilege) with respect to A to do *y*, then B does not have a duty to A not to do *y*; and so on.

Finnis has drawn attention to three cardinal features of Hohfeld's analysis,[18] failure to respect any one of which is a sure means of confusion and misunderstanding. We shall cover Finnis's points here in a slightly different

---

[12] FLC, 35.

[13] "Right" is sometimes given the alternative title of "claim," or "claim-right". Most authors prefer "liberty" to "privilege". I retain "privilege" in the text of this chapter to make it easier to follow Hohfeld's own discussion, but the reader should understand "liberty" as a synonym for "privilege" throughout.

[14] FLC, 38.

[15] FLC, 38ff.

[16] FLC, 50ff.

[17] FLC, 60ff.

[18] John Finnis, "Some Professorial Fallacies about Rights" (1971-2) 4 *Adelaide Law Review* 377 at 379ff.

presentation,[19] and append a further important feature of Hohfeld's analysis. The cardinal features are then as follows.

(1) Each legal relation is concerned with one activity, or omission, of one person.
(2) Each legal relation regards an activity, or omission, with respect to two, and only two, persons.
(3) The analysis of a legal relation ignores the question of sanctions.
(4) The analysis is concerned with the effect of all laws on a particular activity or omission. It is not concerned with presenting the material of a particular law.

Features (1) and (2) indicate that the currency of Hohfeld's analysis is the bipartite relation concerned with one activity or omission. The position of each party is described by a fundamental legal conception, which is the correlative of that describing the position of the other party. It is important to stress that the correlative conceptions refer to the one activity or omission. "Any given single relation necessarily involves two persons. Correlatives in Hohfeld's scheme merely describe the situation viewed first from the point of view of one person and then from that of the other."[20]

Any legal interest can be broken down into an aggregate of legal relations. So, Hohfeld takes the interest of property and reduces it to a complex aggregate of rights, privileges, powers and immunities – together with their correlatives.[21] Hohfeld believes that to talk of the right of property is an oversimplification which leads to error: "the tendency – and the fallacy – has been to treat the specific problem as if it were far less complex than it really is."[22]

When an analysis is made in terms of legal relations, any sanction is ignored, as stated in feature (3). It should be noted that the existence of legal sanctions is not being denied by Hohfeld. He does not find it necessary to bring them into the analysis of a legal relation; but rather indicates that the application of a sanction may itself be separately analysed in terms of legal relations.[23]

Feature (4) stresses the point that the fundamental legal conceptions are meant as "mental tools for the comprehending and systematizing of our complex legal materials."[24] The legal relation does not present the raw material

[19] Features (1) and (3) correspond to Finnis's axioms (1) and (3). Finnis only deals with the first four of Hohfeld's fundamental legal conceptions in his paper. His axiom (2), that A's claim-right is never that A do or omit something but that B do or omit something, is based on the otherwise impossible situation of having a claim-right without a correlative. Feature (2) generalizes this point for all of Hohfeld's conceptions.

[20] Wheeler Cook, FLC "Introduction" at 10. See Finnis above n18, for a critical account of eminent examples of failing to respect this point.

[21] FLC, 96–7.

[22] FLC, 26.

[23] This is most clearly stated at FLC, 41, n39, where Hohfeld criticizes Gray for confusing a householder's privilege of ejecting a trespasser with the potential rights, etc. which may arise in an action by the trespasser for assault. Cp FLC 102, where the duty of Y to return X's horse is treated quite separately from his prior duty not to take it, which has been transgressed.

[24] FLC, 67.

of the legal sources, statute or whatever, but the net effect of that material on the two persons and one activity in question. It is not, therefore, necessary for a particular legal relation, as such, to appear in any source of law. It may be the result of applying a number of laws to a particular situation; it may be the result of discovering that a law does not apply to a particular situation.

In order to challenge Hohfeld's analysis, it is necessary to deny his eight conceptions the attributes, "legal" and "fundamental". It is not enough to produce other legal conceptions to compete with Hohfeld's. These contenders might have some value, but they can always be criticised for not presenting the law in its fundamental conceptions, and for so proving to be "a serious obstacle to the clear understanding, the orderly statement, and the correct solution of legal problems."[25]

3 OPPOSITES

Hohfeld's analytical framework has an apparently symmetrical foundation in the eight conceptions arranged as correlatives and opposites. But there is a crack in the foundation. The symmetry is broken in Hohfeld's explanation of his conceptions, and can be traced to his ambiguous use of "opposite".

Opposite is itself an ambiguous term. At the dining table, we make a distinction between the person sitting directly opposite another and the person sitting diagonally opposite him. If we turn from the diners to the food, the different uses of opposite can be further illustrated. The vegetables may be assessed as "fresh or stale". Or, with regard to a gourmet concern for eating vegetables picked on the same day, the option may be simply, "fresh or not fresh". Yet another possibility is to query whether the vegetables are "fresh or frozen". Each of the three pairs of options provides us with a different opposite to "fresh": "stale", "not fresh", "frozen".

Differing types of opposites were noted by Aristotle who gave as four paradigms: half, double; good, bad; blindness, sight; sitting, not sitting.[26] I shall not attempt an exact taxonomy of opposites here, but it is worth pointing out, for our present purposes, that there are not only different types of opposites, but also that different opposites can exist in relation to the same term. And if a limited classification of opposites can help to make this clear, we should return to the vegetables paradigm, and note that in relation to "fresh": "stale" is an opposite of *extreme*; "not fresh" is an opposite of *negation*; and "frozen" is an opposite of *alternative*.[27]

---

[25] FLC, 26.

[26] *Organon* 11ᵇ 15ff. The paradigms represent: "correlatives"; "contraries"; "privatives and positives"; "affirmatives and negatives." Elsewhere, Aristotle lists six types of opposites – *Metaphysica*, 1018ᵃ 20ff.

[27] The classification is limited, in that, for example, it does not deal with the spatial opposites of the dining table mentioned above. However, it does provide us with three distinct types of verbal opposites which will be helpful when dealing with Hohfeld's analysis.

An opposite of extreme involves the utmost progression or regression of a common quality. An opposite of negation simply involves the absence of the term. An opposite of alternative involves the presence of another term which is mutually exclusive with the first term, without the relationship of common quality existing in an opposite of extreme.

4 HOHFELD'S PRIVILEGE – AS OPPOSITE OF DUTY

Kocourek criticized Hohfeld for being inconsistent in his use of opposite, and himself suggested other possible opposites for Hohfeld's conceptions. The charge of inconsistency concerns a vacillation between opposite in the sense of negation and some other sense of opposite.[28] Unfortunately, Kocourek does not recognise an opposite of negation and, through indulgence in logical surrealism, concludes that the negation of a duty is no more a privilege than an elephant – since the negation of one thing involves the presence, or possible presence, of everything else in the universe.[29] Taking opposite to have some sense other than negation, Kocourek posits other opposites for Hohfeld's conceptions, including the suggestion that right should be considered to be the opposite of duty.[30] In doing this, Kocourek strays beyond the confines of Hohfeld's analysis.[31] Kocourek thus concludes "that 'privilege' (liberty) and 'duty' are neither opposites nor negations",[32] but it is a conclusion reached with little reference to Hohfeld's use of these terms.

Hohfeld's inconsistency in his use of opposite can be pinpointed to his illustration of the privilege of the landowner to enter his own land. Concerning this case, he states:[33]

> "As indicated in the above scheme of jural relations, a privilege is the opposite of a duty . . .
>
> X . . . himself has the *privilege* of entering the land; or, in equivalent words, X does not have a duty to stay off. The privilege of entering is the negation of a duty to stay off. . . . when it is said that a given privilege is the mere negation of a *duty*, what is meant, of course, is a duty having a content or tenor precisely *opposite* to that of the privilege in question . . . X's privilege of entering is the precise negation of a duty to *stay off*."

[28] Kocourek, 364-5.
[29] Kocourek, 367 and 378; cp W.J. Kamba, "Legal Theory and Hohfeld's analysis of a legal right" [1974] *Juridical Review* 249 at 256. Kocourek confuses the two propositions: $(\exists)\sim m$, "there is something which is not an m"; and, $\sim m$, "not an m." Put less formally, it is the distinction between: "Alice has a pet which is not a dog"; and, "Alice has not got a dog."
[30] Kocourek, 364-5.
[31] This is aided by a truncated statement of Hohfeld's view of opposite. At 364, Kocourek refers to Wheeler Cook's Introduction (FLC 10, n13) where he states that opposites look at "two different situations from the point of view of the same person." Kocourek ignores the continuation: "*i.e.* in one situation he has, for example, a right, in the other, no-right."
[32] Kocourek, 365.
[33] FLC, 38–9. Original emphasis.

The first thing to note is that Hohfeld is not simply switching from privilege
to duty in order to reach his opposite. He also changes the content governed
by the legal concept from the positive action of entering to the negative action
(or rather, omission) of staying off the land. Hohfeld openly admits this in his
text, but it is not evident in the general table of fundamental conceptions,
where "privilege" is baldly stated to be the opposite of "duty".[34] For this reason, Glanville Williams suggests that the table should be amended to read
"privilege not" as the opposite for "duty", or "duty not" as the opposite of
"privilege"[35] – ie the opposite of being under a duty to do something is a privilege not to do that thing, or, of being under a duty not to do it is a privilege
to do it.

Williams considers that this amendment to the table reflects Hohfeld's
explanation of his conceptions, and is not worried by the ensuing asymmetry,
produced by the addition of a negative suffix to one of the first four conceptions:[36]

Even if the suffix is only a visual irritant, it prompts us to ask why the offending "privilege not" can not be replaced by a "no-duty", in order to restore the
symmetry. According to Hohfeld's text, a privilege of entering (ie *not* staying
off) the land is equivalent to no duty to stay off the land. And Williams reiterates that a "liberty not" is equivalent to "no duty".[37]

If it really is the case that "a given privilege [albeit a privilege not] is the
mere negation of a duty" a more fundamental point can be raised. There is
no need to adapt the offending eyesore on aesthetic grounds; it can be demol-
ished. If privilege is the negation of duty, then it cannot be retained as a fundamental conception. It may be argued that it is a matter of convenient
terminology to retain it,[38] but this is not sufficient to give it the status of a
fundamental conception: it can be reduced to the negation of another conception, and is therefore, strictly speaking, superfluous.

The enthusiasm for the use of a privilege as a term to describe "no duty"
serves to obscure this point. In Hohfeld's table, "no right" borrows some
respectability as a fundamental conception from being correlated to "privilege", a respectability it could hardly maintain on the ground of being merely
the negation of a right. But if "no duty" is substituted for privilege, we are
then presented with "no duty" and "no right" as the second pair of correlatives.

---

[34] FLC, 65.

[35] "The Concept of Legal Liberty" in Robert Summers (ed.), *Essays in Legal Philosophy*,
(Oxford, Basil Blackwell, 1968) (hereinafter, Williams), at 128ff.

[36] Williams, 131. It should be noted that no such suffix is required for the no-right.

[37] Williams, 130.

[38] cp Williams, 132.

RIGHT   N0-DUTY

DUTY   NO-RIGHT

Hohfeld could not then claim to have identified two further fundamental conceptions, simply by stating the negations of the first pair. It would be like a zoologist discovering a new animal by coining the term "no-cow".

However, to accuse Hohfeld of counterfeiting fundamental conceptions in this abstract way is to ignore the fact that his conceptions are circulated in practice. Privilege and no-right are used to analyse a number of concrete situations: a privilege to enter land, a privilege to publish defamatory materials, etc. It is as though the "no-cow", whose existence we have just ridiculed, is now to be found actually eating grass.

When speaking of a privilege to enter land, enjoyed by the landowner, Hohfeld is stating more than that the landowner is under no duty not to enter the land, he is speaking of a position positively protected by the law, in that, for example, the landowner cannot be lawfully ejected from the land, for trespass. Without such positive protection, the privilege of the landowner is meaningless. If X's privilege of entering the land, in relation to Y, consists only in X being under no duty to Y not to enter the land, this means solely that X is not in breach of a duty to Y if he enters the land; nothing is implied by this to prevent Y making it impossible for X to enter the land – by using threats, or violence, by building walls, constructing moats filled with piranha fish, etc; nor does X being under a duty to Y not to enter the land mean that Y cannot throw X off the land once he has managed to enter it. The privilege of a landowner, X, to enter his land in fact involves not only that Y may not lawfully prevent him from entering the land, but also that Y may not lawfully eject him once he has entered.

In this sense, privilege is a distinct conception, since apart from entailing the absence of a duty not to do the privileged act, it additionally involves recognition and protection by the law in doing the act: it is more than the mere negation of a duty.

There are, accordingly, three distinct terms:

(a) duty: X is under an obligation to Y to act in a certain way;
(b) no-duty: X is under no obligation to Y to act in a certain way;
(c) privilege: X is protected from Y preventing him acting in a certain way.

Privilege, (c), as used in Hohfeld's practical illustration of the landowner's privilege to enter his land, is not the same as the privilege that is equivalent to a no-duty, (b), which appears in Hohfeld's general definition.

The inconsistency is facilitated by the ambiguity of *opposite*, noted above. Both (b) and (c) are opposites of (a), but whereas (a) and (b) are opposites of negation, (a) and (c) involve opposites of extreme: being obliged to do something (duty) and being positively allowed to do something (privilege) represent the two extremes of bound and free under the law.

Hohfeld's use of *opposite* in the text quoted above is even more convoluted. This is due to the fact that he is engaged in constructing the opposite of a phrase with two terms, and he does so by tinkering with both terms. The phrase, "a duty to stay off the land", is composed of the concept, "a duty", and a content, "to stay off the land".

First, Hohfeld deals with the concept: "a privilege is the opposite of a duty". Given the illustration used by Hohfeld in this context of contrasting the privilege of a landowner to enter his land with the duty of staying off the land, we have seen that this appears to involve an opposite of *extreme*. Yet Hohfeld proceeds to assert that "the privilege of entering is the *negation* of a duty to stay off", and explains this on the basis that the duty has "a content or tenor precisely opposite to that of the privilege". But Hohfeld is dealing here with the content, not the concept. The content of the privilege to enter land, and the content of the duty to stay off land (not to enter land), are opposites of *negation*.

Moreover, an opposite of negation, here, would mean that privilege amounts to no-duty. But we have seen that this does not fit Hohfeld's analysis which requires a "privilege *not*" to amount to "no-duty", or a privilege to amount to "no-duty *not*".

Hohfeld's opposite is a hybrid, formed by taking the opposite of extreme for the concept and the opposite of negation for the content, in arriving at "a privilege of entering land". It is rather like saying that the opposite of "a black cat" is "a white dog".[39]

Such hybrid opposites can best be classified as an opposite of *alternative*, since the net effect is to produce something which is neither the negation nor the extreme of the complete original, but which is mutually exclusive with it. A privilege to enter land implies that there is no duty to stay off the land. This falls short of Hohfeld's assertion that it is the "equivalent" of no duty to stay off.

The asymmetry in Hohfeld's table of conceptions, revealed by Williams' amendment of "privilege" to "privilege not", can be regarded not merely as a visual irritant but as a manifestation of the underlying inconsistency in Hohfeld's use of opposite. "Right" and "no-right" are straightforward opposites of negation; but "duty" and "privilege not" are opposites of alternative. The awkward negative suffix appended to privilege is the result of it being constructed as a hybrid opposite of alternative, rather than as "the precise negation" it is represented as.

---

[39] A strict parallel would be "a white no-cat" (involving an opposite of extreme for the first term, and an opposite of negation for the second). Not every conceivable opposite is useful for making practical comparisons.

5 HOHFELD'S PRIVILEGE — AS PROTECTING RIGHTS

If a privilege is not simply the negation of a duty, this avoids the criticism that it is reducible to the negation of another conception. Yet if a privilege consists rather of the protection afforded by the law to permit X to do some act, this protection can be broken down into a set of rights with correlative duties: rights in X that Y does not do all those acts which would amount to interfering with X doing the permitted act. For example, if we take X's privilege to enter Y's land by using a right of way, the permitted act of entering Y's land is protected by duties owed by Y to X such as a duty not to physically eject him, a duty not to obstruct the right of way, a duty not to keep a fierce bull in the vicinity of the right of way, etc. Again privilege is denied the status of being a fundamental conception on the ground that it is reducible.

The idea that a legal privilege, or liberty, consists of a set of protecting rights has been widely held, both before and after Hohfeld's analysis. It is accordingly, a criticism of his analysis that both Hohfeld and his apologists have had to answer.[40]

The defence of Hohfeld's concept of a privilege consists of admitting that protecting rights often accompany the holding of a privilege whilst denying that the privilege can be identified with such protecting rights. The privilege to do the permitted act is considered to be quite distinct from the right not to be interfered with in doing the permitted act. The final proof of this contention is provided by identifying a case of a privilege with no protecting rights.

Hohfeld himself purports to give such an example in the case of the shrimp salad. He cites Gray's example of the owner of a shrimp salad, and analyses his legal position with regard to eating the salad as consisting of privileges and rights against other parties (who are under the correlative no-rights and duties): privileges[41] to eat the salad, and rights that the other parties do not interfere with his doing so.

Hohfeld then states that in another example the privilege of eating the salad could exist without the protecting rights. The example, together with his analysis, is as follows.

"A, B, C, and D, being owners of the salad, might say to X: 'Eat the salad if you can; you have our license to do so, but we don't agree not to interfere with you.'

---

[40] Frederick Pollock, writing before Hohfeld, *Jurisprudence*, 2ed., (London, Macmillan, 1904) at 62 states: "Sometimes it is thought that lawful power or liberty is different from the right not to be interfered with; but for the reason just given this opinion, though plausible, does not seem correct." A statement considered by Hohfeld at FLC 48, n59 – discussed below at n48. Subsequently, the same point has been raised as a criticism, or even misrepresentation, of Hohfeld's theory. As the former, it is dealt with by Williams, 137; as the latter, it is dealt with by Finnis, 379, n9.

[41] It should be remembered that a different privilege exists in relation to each party, albeit there is a common content: to eat the salad.

In such a case the privileges exist, so that if X succeeds in eating the salad, he has violated no rights of any of the parties. But it is equally clear that if A had succeeded in holding so fast to the dish that X couldn't eat the contents, no right of X would have been violated."[42]

All that is established by Hohfeld's analysis of this example is that X does not enjoy the same rights to protect his privilege of eating the salad as those rights enjoyed by the owner of the shrimp salad in Gray's example, in particular, a right that A, B, C, and D do not hold on to the plate in order to deter X from eating the salad. This is far from establishing that the privilege to eat the salad can exist without any protecting rights.

Perhaps X is taking part in some sort of trial of strength, or eating competition – he may only eat the salad if he can free the dish out of the hands of the others and consume the contents before the others do. In this case, he will certainly lack rights that A, B, C and D do not interfere with his eating of the salad in the ways allowed by the rules of the competition, or the conditions of the test. But to say that his privilege of eating the salad is not protected by any rights is to erode the privilege of all content.

Suppose that X manages to take the plate out of A's hands, take a forkful of the salad before anyone else can do so, and empty the contents of the fork into his mouth. Can A, B, C and D continue to interfere with X's eating, by holding his nose, dealing a blow to his solar plexus, etc? Or, should a morsel of shrimp enter A's stomach, can A, B, C and D then detain him until he pays for the salad?

There is a whole catalogue of activities that are open to A, B, C and D to discourage X from taking the salad, to impede X in the act of eating the salad, and to harass X should he eat any of the salad; and each is capable of being prohibited by forming the subject of a duty with a correlative right in X. If X is to have no protecting rights to prohibit any of these activities his licence to eat the salad is wholly nugatory, and the privilege that this is meant to constitute has no significance whatsoever.

In the assumed eating competition, X will have the right that A, B, C, and D do not interfere with his eating of the salad once he has got it to his mouth, and also that they do not prevent him from taking the food by methods not permitted by the rules of the competition.

Hohfeld claims that the significance of the privilege lies in X having no duty: "if X succeeds in eating the salad, he has violated no rights of any of the parties." But a "licence", although *implying* no duty not to do the permitted act, cannot be *constituted* by the no duty. However qualified the licence may be, inasmuch as a licence is given there must be some permission that is recognised and protected by the law – and this protection is constituted by a number of rights, which will vary with the extent of the permission granted by the licence.

[42] FLC, 41.

Hohfeld's confusion arises out of treating the privilege of the owner as the same as the privilege of X, and classifying both as "a privilege to eat the salad". This is inaccurate. The owner may eat the salad, on his own terms, as, when, and how he wishes; X may only eat the salad on the terms of the permission granted him. The owner of the salad has a privilege to eat it that is constituted by a whole plenum of rights protecting every aspect of his ownership. X's privilege is constituted by a lesser number of rights which protect his qualified permission to eat the salad. The privilege of X may exist without *all* of the protecting rights enjoyed by the owner, since it is a lesser privilege, but it cannot exist without *any* protecting rights.

Glanville Williams also purports to identify a privilege (or liberty) existing without protecting rights, in order to establish that Hohfeld's concept of a privilege is distinct from the right not to be interfered with in doing the permitted act. In all, he suggests six examples: (1) liberty of passage along the highway; (2) liberty to pick up an abandoned gold watch; (3) liberty to employ a good cook; (4) liberty of a licensee of land; (5) liberty to erect a house; (6) liberty of speech.[43]

In examples (1) and (6), Williams concedes that there is a right not to be physically interfered with in exercising the liberty, but dismisses this on the ground that it is part of the ordinary law of assault. This argument overlooks an important feature of Hohfeld's analysis – cardinal feature (4), above[44] – namely, that the analysis is concerned with stating the effect of all legal material on a particular situation. It is accordingly irrelevant whether a pertinent part of the legal material appears under the guise of the law of assault in the sources.

In examples (1), (4), (5) and (6), Williams argues that the right not to be interfered with does not exist by specifying a particular right that does not exist to protect the given privilege. For example, in (4) Williams mentions that the licensee does not have a right not to be interfered with by third parties. This is to repeat Hohfeld's error: identifying one right that the liberty holder does not enjoy is not to show that his liberty is unprotected by any rights. In (4), the licensee has rights not to be interfered with by the licensor, in accordance with the terms of the licence. Again, the error can be traced to a failure to define clearly the nature of the privilege. The privilege of a licensee is not the same as the privilege of an owner. The basic error is to state the privilege (liberty) in terms that are too loose, which do not properly reflect the legal position being analysed: a licensee does not have an unqualified privilege over land, but a privilege that is limited by the terms and nature of his licence.

---

[43] Williams, 137ff. A variation on example (2), picking up a five pound note lying on the pavement, has been used more recently to suggest the separation of liberties from protecting rights – N.E. Simmonds, "The Analytical Foundations of Justice" (1995) 54 *Cambridge Law Journal* 306 at 321.

[44] section 2.

Examples (2) and (3) betray an even looser use of language. Both examples deal with the situation where A and B have a lawful opportunity to do something, in which only one of them can actually succeed – picking up the abandoned watch, employing the good cook. Williams analyses A's position as having a privilege to do the act, picking up the watch, say, whilst having no right that B does not interfere with this by doing the act, picking up the watch, himself. He thus concludes that the privilege exists without the right not to be interfered with.

However, the privilege in such an example is not a privilege to do the act, but a privilege to endeavour to do the act. The law does not give A the privilege of taking the watch, to the extent that it will protect him from others taking the watch instead of him – this is the privilege given to the owner of the watch (or, *mutatis mutandis*, the person for whom the cook is already contractually bound to work). The law simply gives A the lawful opportunity to pick up the abandoned watch (to employ the unemployed cook) if he manages to do so before B, or anybody else.

This lesser privilege will be protected by A's rights not to be interfered with in his attempt to do the act – to the extent that the law protects his opportunity to do it. For example, in the race to pick up the watch, B may not trip A up; B may not threaten A's life in order to deter him from employing the cook. The dividing line between lawful competition (B running faster than A; B offering the cook a higher salary than A) and unlawful competition, which A is protected from by rights that B does not engage in it, will define the scope of the opportunity that the law gives A to do the act in question.

None of Williams' examples represents a privilege without protecting rights, any more than does Hohfeld's variation on the shrimp salad affair. For the sake of completeness, we should consider one other case. It is possible that instead of a privilege to do something, we may come across a privilege not to do something. This type of privilege features among Hohfeld's examples. Again, a distinction can be drawn between a privilege existing as the opposite of extreme of a duty and a privilege as a mere negation of a duty. To take the example of a privilege against self-incrimination in the law of evidence, Hohfeld says of this, "the privilege against self-crimination signifies the mere negation of a duty to testify."[45]

That this is not so can be shown by the same approach as adopted above:

(a) duty: X is under an obligation to Y to testify;
(b) no duty: X is under no obligation to Y to testify;
(c) privilege: X is protected from Y compelling him to testify.

There is a similar switch here from the law being unconcerned if X does not do an act, in (b), to the law positively permitting X not to do the act, in (c).

---

[45] FLC, 46.

It is evident that the privilege of not incriminating oneself is one that only exists as a significant legal position where it is actually protected by legal rights – that Y does not apply a truth drug to X, threaten X, assault X, or imprison X if he fails to give evidence, etc. Indeed, Wheeler Cook acknowledges the need for "a right *stricto sensu*"[46] here.

6 HOHFELD'S PRIVILEGE – CONCLUSION

We may conclude that Hohfeld's concept of a privilege, if it is to have any legal significance, represents the protection afforded by the law to permit A to do, or refrain from doing, some act. As such, a privilege may be further broken down into a set of protecting rights. And, on this ground, it can no longer be accepted as a fundamental conception.

This conclusion, in itself, does not present a novel criticism of Hohfeld's theory. As already mentioned, the idea that a legal privilege, or liberty, is constituted by a set of protecting rights has been widely held. Accordingly, it might reasonably be asked how Hohfeld's theory has managed to withstand the repetition of this criticism, if the criticism is valid.

In reply, it is perhaps worth summarising the main points of the argument used above, in order to demonstrate how the criticism has not been so much met as avoided.

We commenced by noting the ambiguity of the term "opposite", and pointing out that it is possible for a number of opposites to exist in relation to the same thing. For convenience, three particular types of opposite were identified: an opposite of extreme; an opposite of negation; and an opposite of alternative.

I argued that Hohfeld is inconsistent in his definition of the concept of a privilege as the opposite of a duty in his table of conceptions, and suggested that this inconsistency is facilitated by the ambiguity of *opposite*.

The inconsistency essentially concerns using two distinct conceptions of a privilege. The first, which appears in the general definition of a privilege, equates this concept with a no-duty – this is an opposite of negation. The second, which is derived from the practical illustrations given of a privilege, amounts to a positive protection given by the law to do a permitted act – this is an opposite of extreme.

If we examine the first definition, equating privilege with no-duty, then the concept of a privilege can be reduced to the negation of another concept, and on the ground of being reducible can be denied the status of a fundamental conception.

Against the adoption of the first definition are the points that it fails to account for the negative suffix identified by Glanville Williams as required by

---

[46] FLC, 7 n3.

Hohfeld's use of privilege, and also that privilege is used to describe actual legal positions.

If we examine the second definition, whereby a privilege amounts to a positive protection given by the law, then that protection can be broken down into a set of right-duty relations, and again the concept is reducible, and therefore not fundamental.

In considering the practical illustration of a privilege, from which the second definition is derived, we also examined the possibility of a counter-example, of a privilege existing in practice with no protecting rights. The suggested counter-examples of Hohfeld and Williams were dismissed as fallacious. In particular, the confusion between different types of privilege concerned with the same act was noted.

In order to avoid this confusion, it would be more appropriate to speak of the *rights* not to be interfered with in doing the privileged act, rather than the singular *right* not to be interfered with, which may misleadingly stand for a variety of different sets of rights, varying according to the extent of the privilege in question.

We concluded that the second definition of a privilege was to be accepted, if the concept was to have any legal significance, and that a privilege was constituted by the set of protecting rights. This lays the concept open to the charge of being reducible and therefore not fundamental.

Hohfeld avoids this conclusion, not simply by inconsistency in his use of opposite, reflected in the two definitions of privilege, but by what amounts to a strategic vacillation between the two definitions.

If we suspect that privilege is redundant, because it is simply the negation of a duty, we are presented with a practical illustration where the privilege is something more than that: being given positive permission by the law to do some act. If we then look at this idea of a privilege as a positive permission, and argue that this can be broken down into a set of protecting rights, we are faced with Hohfeld's claim that the privilege consists not in the protection given by the surrounding rights, but in the negation of a duty.[47] It is a sort of conceptual three card trick: we need to turn over both definitions at once to show that there is no fundamental conception there.

I have argued that the verbal sleight which Hohfeld uses to bring off his illusion of a fundamental conception is to combine the two definitions of a privilege, based on opposites of extreme and negation, in a hybrid opposite of alternative: using the extreme of the concept and the negation of the content. And I have suggested that this is betrayed by the asymmetrical "privilege not", which on closer examination, appears in Hohfeld's table of conceptions.

[47] This sidestep is cited by Hohfeld's apologists: Williams, 137; Finnis, 378–9. It is also interesting to compare the problems faced by Georg Henrik von Wright, *Norm and Action* (London, Routledge and Kegan Paul, 1963) at 85 in dealing with the question whether "permissive norms" are definable in terms of "obligation norms" and in his use of negation – at 140. Philip Mullock, "The Hohfeldian Jural Opposite" (1971) 13 *Ratio* 158 at 160 suggests that Hohfeld's theory can be regarded as an "informal and legal precursor of von Wright's deontic logic".

Finally, it is interesting to note that when Hohfeld himself does attempt to meet Pollock's assertion that a lawful liberty is no different from the right not to be interfered with,[48] he steps outside the framework of his own analysis. He states, "A rule of law that *permits* is just as real as a rule of law that *forbids*; and, similarly, saying that the law *permits* a given act to X as between himself and Y predicates just as genuine a legal relation as saying that the law *forbids* a certain act to X as between himself and Y." Hohfeld is not presenting here an analysis in terms of fundamental legal conceptions, but a description of legal material as it is found written in the sources. (See cardinal feature (4), above.)

The wording of a statute may predicate "a genuine legal relation", but that is not necessarily a relation of fundamental legal conceptions. If it were, then anything could be a fundamental legal conception, provided only that it were found expressed in the words of a statute – or other "rule of law". So, a property right would be a fundamental legal conception, if only we could find a statute speaking of the interest of an owner in his property. This is clearly not what Hohfeld intended. Hohfeld's difficulty in meeting Pollock's point is indicated by his transgression of the principles upon which his own system is founded.

7 HOHFELD'S OTHER CONCEPTIONS

The rejection of a privilege and its correlative, a no-right,[49] as fundamental legal conceptions, raises doubts about whether the remaining four conceptions can maintain their status.

The power-liability correlatives describe a relation where A is in a position to change B's legal situation.

This relation may be considered inadequate to explain all the facets of a legal power, but I am only concerned here to examine the concept proposed by Hohfeld. He himself considered his definition to be limited to the practical problem of analysing legal positions: "too close an analysis might seem metaphysical rather than useful; so that what is here presented is intended only as an approximate explanation, sufficient for all practical purposes."[50]

In Hohfeld's words, a power exists where "a given legal relation may result . . . from some superadded fact or group of facts which are under the

---

[48] FLC, 48 n59.

[49] A no-right is only properly a correlative of a privilege which is equivalent to a no-duty; as such it is reducible to the negation of another concept (in substance, as well as name). As remarked above, it borrows some status from being correlated to a privilege in the stronger sense of a positive permission to do an act. This privilege has been broken down into a number of protecting rights – whose correlatives are not a no-right but a corresponding number of duties.

[50] FLC, 50. Contrast H.L.A. Hart, *Essays on Bentham* (Oxford, Clarendon Press, 1982) at 195: "But much more than Hohfeld gives us is needed to display the notion fully and to analyse legal powers in their variant forms, and to exhibit the character of the laws which create or confer them." See further, ch III.

volitional control of one or more human beings."[51] That is to say, A has a power in relation to B (who is under a liability) where:

(i)   A may do (has "the volitional control" over) something ("some super-added fact or group of facts"), and,
(ii) a legal relation of B results.

The first constituent reflects the truism that the law deals with actions rather than mere states of the mind: if A wishes to execute a power to change B's legal position, it is not enough that he makes the decision to do so; he must express his decision by some act – even if it is only the act of speech.

For example, if B has already made an offer in contract to A, then A is said to have the power to impose a contractual obligation upon B, by posting a letter of acceptance.[52] The action of A (posting the letter of acceptance) brings about the legal relation of B (being under a contractual obligation).[53]

Yet if the first constituent of Hohfeld's power is the law permitting A to do some act, this will amount to A having a privilege, which, as we have seen, can be further broken down into a set of protecting rights. Hohfeld himself links a privilege of entering land with the power to divest an estate by entry,[54] but does not acknowledge that the privilege is a constituent of the power.

The second constituent is a potential legal relation,[55] contingent upon the exercise of the privilege. In the example above, the potential legal relation amounts to B having a duty, to fulfil his contractual obligation. Other examples of powers may involve the possibility of placing B under other legal relations. If A has the power to make B his agent,[56] this is a power in A to place B under a power.

In this latter example, the potential legal relation of B involves a power which itself will have two constituents: (i) a privilege in B to do some act, and (ii) a legal relation resulting from the exercise of the privilege. Although there may be a succession of powers created by powers, ultimately the potential legal relation forming the second constituent must involve permitting N to do something or obliging N to do something – since a power to give a power cannot mean anything in itself: there must finally be a power to do something either permitting of obliging some act(s) and/or omission(s), by some person(s). The second constituent of the final power will accordingly involve potential privilege(s) or duty(ies),[57] respectively. The succession of powers can accordingly be analysed in terms of a privilege, plus potential privileges in the successive possible power holders, culminating in potential privilege(s) and/or duty(/ies).

---

[51] FLC, 50-1.
[52] FLC, 55.
[53] It will also bring about a corresponding contractual obligation in A himself.
[54] FLC, 55.
[55] Potential legal relations are recognized by Hohfeld, in relation to sanctions – n23 above.
[56] FLC, 52.
[57] Together with a correlative right; or, a right with a correlative duty.

As a corollary, it should be pointed out that if a liability features in the analysis, this too may be analysed in terms of (privileges) rights and duties, such as are correlative to those forming the power – to the extent that liability is the correlative of a power.

Since privileges have been analysed as amounting to a set of protecting rights and correlative duties, a power can be broken down into right-duty relations: actual rights forming the privilege of the first constituent, and potential rights and duties forming the second constituent. This will be the case whether the potential legal relation involves rights, duties, privileges,[58] or powers and liabilities.

It may be argued that this analysis overlooks immunities, and disabilities, but if these are to be regarded as the negations of liabilities and powers,[59] it follows that these too may be expressed in the constituents which powers and liabilities have been broken down into.

A further criticism of Hohfeld's conception of a power must be made before the full picture can be given. Hohfeld's attempt to contain the power-liability relation in an analysis involving only the two parties to the relation is an over-simplification. This becomes apparent once we reduce the power-liability relation to its constituent right-duty relations. A clear demonstration of the point is furnished by the following example.

Suppose A has the power to vest a legal estate in land[60] in B. This involves a change in B's legal relation not only with A, but also with X, Y, Z, etc, since a legal estate in land gives B rights with correlative duties in these parties, as well as in A. If one were to set aside the relations with X, Y, Z, etc, A's power would be something less than a power to vest a legal estate in land in B: it would, at the best, be a power to give B a contractual right to the land, enforceable only in person against A himself.

The second constituent of a power, the potential legal relation, should accordingly be regarded as comprising potential right-duty relations in B and possibly other parties as well. The number of these potential legal relations will reflect the scope of A's power – for example, whether it is a power to give B a contractual right against himself, or title to land good against third parties.

Moreover, the first constituent of the power, A being permitted to do some act, cannot be regarded exclusively as a privilege in relation to B, the person whose legal position is to be changed. It is possible that a third party, X, may be able to prevent A doing the act, in which case, if A is to retain the power, he must have a privilege to do the act in relation to X, as well.

---

[58] No-rights are ignored, since these can no longer be regarded as the correlatives of privileges – n49 above.

[59] The assumption will be examined shortly, when fuller treatment will be given to immunity and disability.

[60] A power to vest or divest title to land is mentioned by Hohfeld – FLC, 52ff.

An example to illustrate this point is where A is the agent of X, and has a power to sell X's goods to B,[61] thus making B the owner of the goods. This power can only exist where A has the privilege, in relation to X, to hand over the goods. More generally, even where A is purporting to sell his own goods to B, this will only be a valid power where A has the privilege of handing the goods over, in relation to parties other than B – ie nobody else has a legal interest in the goods (X has a charge over the goods, Y is in fact the owner, etc) which can prevent A handing them over to B.

A full analysis of a power will accordingly be constituted by:

(i) a privilege of A to do an act, which will amount to protecting rights in A and correlative duties in B, X, Y, Z, etc;

(ii) potential legal relations of B, which will amount to rights and duties in B with correlative duties and rights in A, X, Y, Z, etc.

It follows from this analysis that the liability of B (consisting of duties, and potential rights and duties) is only a partial correlative to the power of A, since it does not account for the legal relations with X, Y, Z, etc, which are involved in A's power to change B's legal position.

The number of right-duty relations of the first constituent will determine the *strength*[62] of A's power, and the right-duty relations of the second constituent will determine the *scope* of A's power – ie the extent of its effect on B's legal position.

Since a power has been analysed to be an aggregate conception, covering legal relations extending beyond the power holder and the person under the liability, the concepts of immunity and disability cannot be simply represented as negations of liability and power.

If A has no power (a disability) to change B's legal position B is said to have an immunity in relation to A. The concept of an immunity must be capable of reflecting the complexity found in the concept of a power. In particular, an immunity must be able to cover both constituent elements of a power. So, for example, if B has an immunity against A divesting him of his title to land,[63] the immunity may consist of:

(i) B has rights that A does not do an act which purports to divest his title; and, if A does so act,

(ii) B has potential rights as against A, X, Y, Z, etc, that they do not act upon A's purported act of divesting as valid.

---

[61] An example of a power given by Hohfeld – FLC, 52.

[62] A feature of a legal power which should not be lost on land lawyers. For example, A, a squatter of 10 years, may have the power to vest title of land in B, as far as X and Y are concerned, but not so far as Z is concerned, where Z is the absent owner of the land. Z could prevent A transferring the land to B.

[63] An example given by Hohfeld – FLC, 60.

The exact nature of B's immunity will be determined by the number of such rights, or potential rights, that he possesses.[64] Without any such rights, no matter how loquaciously B may assert that A had no power to divest him of his title, the immunity is meaningless.[65] It should be noted that immunity, like power, will also extend beyond the simple bipartite relation to include relations with third parties. A's disability (consisting of duties, and potential duties) to change B's legal position will, accordingly, be only a partial correlative to B's immunity, which will involve legal relations with X, Y, Z, etc.

8 CONCLUSION

I have attempted to show here that six of Hohfeld's conceptions are reducible (privilege, no-right, power, liability, immunity, disability) in terms of the other two (right and duty), and accordingly must be denied the status of being fundamental conceptions.

It is interesting to ponder why the other six conceptions should be considered for the role of fundamental conceptions in the first place. The most compelling reason is that as a matter of practical convenience, it is often more useful to talk in terms of the aggregates which these conceptions represent, rather than the right-duty relations by which they are constituted. For example, sometimes we will want to know whether A is permitted by the law to do a certain activity, rather than to know of all the acts of interference which B, C, D, etc, may not do, which have the effect of leaving A free to act. So, a privilege becomes a basic concept of legal discourse. Likewise, a power, and an immunity, and their correlatives.[66]

If we recall that Hohfeld attaches his conceptions to a bipartite relation, we have a hint as to the particular context in which these conceptions have their usefulness. Two parties appear as the basic elements of litigation. The four correlative pairs of conceptions represent the four basic positions of litigants: A may claim that B should do something; A may claim that he is free to do something without B's interference;[67] A may claim to be able to alter B's legal position in some way; A may claim that B is unable to alter his legal position

---

[64] The nature of an immunity may be illustrated by considering an immunity from being divested of a right of way over land (a privilege, in Hohfeld's terms, to enter and cross the land). The strength and scope of the immunity will vary depending on whether the holder of the right of way is a contractual licensee, has an equitable easement, has a legal easement, or is the owner of the land.

[65] Wheeler Cook shows some hesitancy to disassociate an immunity from protecting rights (FLC, 8 n6a and 9 n9), but does not concede that the immunity is constituted by such rights.

[66] Whereas the analysis above shows that the correlatives liability and disability represent aggregate positions with a particular significance, we have seen that the same cannot be said for a no-right (n49, above). It is, therefore, not surprising that Hohfeld found it relatively easy to find terms for the former conceptions, but could not find an available term for the latter.

[67] This represents the relation of a privilege and a duty (correlative to a protecting right of which the privilege is composed), rather than the discarded no-right.

in some way. The aggregate conceptions are necessary in order to express the answers that the law will give to certain disputes that will arise in practice.[68]

However, representing the conceptions of privilege, power and immunity, and their correlatives, as *fundamental* legal conceptions results in a failure to analyse clearly the nature of the legal positions that they represent. The privilege of an owner to enjoy his property is confused with the privilege of a licensee; the power to give a contractual right to property is expressed with the same term as the power to give title to property. Such positions cannot be fully explained without referring to the right-duty relations by which they are constituted, and which may embrace others than the parties to a single bipartite relationship. These constituent right-duty relations will reveal the *extent* of the privilege; they will reveal the *strength* and *scope* of the power, or immunity.

A basic concept of legal discourse should not be confused with a fundamental conception of legal analysis. This is to run the risk that Hohfeld readily recognised: to impair the analysis of legal problems by "the commendable effort to treat as simple that which is really complex."[69]

---

[68] The full range of answers will be expressed in the four basic concepts of legal discourse and, of course, their negations. In this respect, no-duty may have a particular significance in representing the outcome of litigation (eg, D has no duty to pay £x to P under the contract because the contract has been frustrated) but this position, as the discredited variant of Hohfeld's privilege, should not be confused with the other where the law provides positive protection to A so as to permit his conduct. D does not require the law's protection in not paying the £x, simply the law's declaration that he need not pay it.

By contrast, A's privilege to walk on Whiteacre will be constituted precisely by a particular set of protecting rights with correlative duties not to interfere, which mark out the extent of the privilege. Similarly, the privilege against self-incrimination insofar as it exists as a significant legal position requires a specific set of protecting rights (text at nn45–46 above).

Of course, it may prove necessary to move from a position of no-duty to a position of privilege involving positive protection, should the frustrated claimant seek to obtain what the law has decided that there is no duty to give. So, in a case of disputed ownership of a picture if the court decides in favour of D, holding that D is under no duty to give up the picture to P, D may also want to enjoy the various privileges of ownership of the picture against P consisting of protecting rights with correlative duties on P not to interfere with D's enjoyment of those various aspects of ownership. Although the positions of no-duty and privilege here are compatible, and related inferentially, they are not equivalent: the no-duty may have arisen in other circumstances and not be linked to *those* privileges (protecting rights) – eg, D holds the painting on a lien until P pays him for the work he has done for P in restoring the picture.

The contrast between litigation rights and other notions of rights is developed in ch V.

[69] FLC, 26.

III

The Concept of a Legal Power

1 INTRODUCTION

If power has a tendency to corrupt its holders, it may also be regarded as tending to distort the perspective of those who behold it. H.L.A. Hart within the space of a single essay[1] observed that neither Hohfeld nor Bentham provided a clear picture of the concept. Upon Hohfeld's analysis Hart remarks:[2]

> "But much more than Hohfeld gives us is needed to display the notion fully and to analyse legal powers in their variant forms, and to exhibit the character of the laws which create or confer them."

And although Hart appears to favour Bentham's analysis, he recognises:[3]

> "Unfortunately Bentham nowhere clearly or exhaustively explains what it is that distinguishes a mere liberty of this sort, or a power which is not 'the work of the law', from a legal power. . ."

Hart himself offers not so much a definition of a legal power but a "wide characterization" which covers a "range of situations". The range is illustrated with a number of examples[4]:

(1) A policeman's power of arrest.
(2) Parliament's power to legislate.
(3) A minister's power to make regulations.[5]
(4) A Corporation's power to make by-laws.
(5) A judge's power to make an order.
(6) A judge's power to sentence.
(7) A judge's power to vary a settlement.
(8) The Lord Chancellor's power to appoint county court judges.
(9) An individual's power of appointment over trust property.
(10) A tenant for life's power of sale.
(11) A landowner's power of alienation.

---

[1] *Essays on Bentham* (Clarendon Press, Oxford, 1982), Essay VIII: "Legal Powers" – hereinafter, Hart.

[2] Hart, 195–6.

[3] Hart, 198.

[4] Hart, 194–5.

[5] I have amended Hart's examples in a number of minor respects for present purposes. Examples (3) and (9) are contracted instances of the fuller examples given by Hart at these points; in the original example (12), Hart describes the power holder as "an owner of a property"; in general, where Hart speaks of the powers of the holder I have given a singular instance.

(12)   A landowner's power to walk over his land.
(13)   A landowner's power to lease his land.
(14)   An individual's power to make a will.
(15)   An individual's power to make a contract to marry.

Of these fifteen examples Hart categorises (1)–(8) as powers held by officials or public bodies, (9)–(11) as powers held by individuals which are commonly referred to as powers, and (12)–(15) as powers held by individuals which are usually described in other terms (right/capacity/competence). The "wide characterization" which brings all these examples under the description of a legal power embraces a situation:[6]

> "Where persons are enabled by the law either to do actions physically affecting other persons or things, or to bring about changes in the legal positions of others or of themselves, or of both themselves and others."

From Hart's comments that have been quoted above, a number of issues concerning the concept of a legal power emerge: (i) How much (if any) more than Hohfeld gives us do we need in order to identify the concept of a legal power? (ii) How broad is the range of legal powers? (iii) On what basis(es) might we analyse the different forms of legal powers? (iv) How are legal powers to be distinguished from other legal and non-legal concepts? I shall focus here on the first and last of these issues, though some comments will be made in passing on the middle two.[7] My present concerns are to evaluate Hohfeld's conception of a legal power, to move beyond it to a fuller conception, which I believe will identify the key characteristic of a legal power, which will in turn assist to clarify the relationship between legal powers and legal rights. My broader concern is that if, as Hart has the tendency to suggest, legal rights are reducible to legal powers, then this should exert a primary influence on any analytical study of legal rights. My rejection of this suggestion is a prerequisite to taking this particular study in other directions.

   These concerns will be tackled within three separate sections of this chapter. I shall commence by considering the different approaches of Hohfeld and Bentham to a legal power and whether Hart's "wide characterization" can stand. I shall then suggest a key role for decision, rather than choice, in under-

---

[6] Hart, 194.

[7] For further discussion on issue (iii), see C.F.H. Tapper, "Powers and Secondary Rules of Change" in A.W.B. Simpson (ed.), *Oxford Essays in Jurisprudence (Second Series)* (Oxford, Clarendon Press, 1973) – hereinafter, Tapper; Torben Spaak, *The Concept of Legal Competence*, translated by Robert Carroll (Aldershot: Dartmouth, 1994) – hereinafter, Spaak: ch 6. One important aspect of powers which may be used in the analysis of different forms (recognised by Tapper at 273 (e)) is the nature of the procedure that must be employed in their exercise. This has been extensively investigated by D.J. Galligan, *Discretionary Powers* (Oxford, Clarendon Press, 1986) – see also his "Rights, Discretion and Procedures" in Charles Sampford and D.J. Galligan (eds.), *Law, Rights and the Welfare State* (London, Croom Helm, 1986) ch 8. For present purposes, it is sufficient to identify the common characteristic to be found in all examples of a legal power, rather than those characteristics by which different forms of legal powers can be identified.

standing the nature of legal powers. Finally, I shall consider the implications of this for the relationship between the concept of a legal power and the concept of a legal right.

2 THE APPROACHES OF HOHFELD AND BENTHAM

(1) Hart on Bentham

The most obvious comment to make about Hart's "wide characterization" is that it amounts to two broad characteristics in the alternative: (i) being legally enabled to do actions physically affecting other persons or things; or, (ii) being legally enabled to bring about changes in the legal positions of persons (others/self/both). This corresponds to two categories of legal power posited by Bentham: (i) powers of contrectation, which permit the physical handling of persons or inanimate things;[8] (ii) powers of imperation, which (as Hart explains) permit either the sovereign, or a lesser body taking a "share" in the sovereign's command by specifying the particular individual who will fall under the general command of the sovereign, to affect the legal positions of individuals by subjecting their behaviour to sanction or reward.[9]

Of Hart's fifteen examples given above all but two fall under characteristic (ii) – enabling change, with only (1) the policeman's power of arrest and (12) the landowner's power to walk over his land falling under characteristic (i) – enabling physical action.[10]

Under Hohfeld's scheme of analysis, a legal power is restricted to cases where one person has the legal ability to change the legal position of another[11], which corresponds to Hart's characteristic (ii).[12] For Hohfeld the legal ability to do (or refrain from) a physical act, whether affecting another

---

[8] Jeremy Bentham, *Of Laws in General* (ed. H.L.A. Hart) (London, Athlone Press, 1970) – hereinafter, OLG: 81, 137ff nh; Hart, 196ff.

[9] OLG, 18 nb, 137 nh, 259-60, 262; Hart, 200ff. Bentham distinguishes two types of powers of imperation – "power of legislation" and "power of aggregation or accensive power" (OLG, 81ff). The latter type which deals with the power of individuals to change legal relations in accordance with existing laws is of more interest to the present study, and where reference is made subsequently to Bentham's power of imperation it should generally be understood as dealing with accensive power. There is some controversy over the relationship between these two types of legal power (legislative and accensive), and on what basis they might be considered to fall within a single classification (see Tapper, and Spaak ch 6.3), which need not detain us here.

[10] The policeman's power of arrest loosely speaking may be taken technically to represent either a Hohfeldian privilege to physically deal with the person arrested or a Hohfeldian power to subject the person arrested to new legal relations which arise from his arrested state (or both). It is clear from the context that Hart is using the term only to cover the former.

[11] Walter Wheeler Cook (ed.), *Fundamental Legal Conceptions as Applied in Judicial Reasoning* by Wesley Newcombe Hohfeld (New Haven, CT, Yale University Press, 1919 – revised edition with new foreword 1964) – hereinafter, FLC – 50ff.

[12] Hart's variant involving a change in the legal position of oneself should more strictly in the Hohfeldian scheme specify the position of oneself in relation to another, and in this sense all legal powers must involve a change in the legal position of another.

person[13] or an inanimate thing, which amounts to Hart's characteristic (i), is a legal privilege.[14]

Indeed, in the introductory quotation from Hart we observed that he criticised Bentham for failing to distinguish a legal power from a "mere liberty" (which in Hohfeld's scheme is synonymous with privilege[15]). Nevertheless, Hart proceeds to defend Bentham's analysis on the basis that the required distinction can be made out from the illustrative material and "rather vague observations"[16] that Bentham provides:[17]

> "The distinction seems to be as follows: a legal permission only constitutes a *legal* power if it is in some way an exception to or contrasts with general duties imposed by law and so can be regarded as a kind of legal favour or advantage and not merely as an absence of duty."

Hart refers to two examples from Bentham to demonstrate the "legal favour or advantage" which marks out a legal power from a legal privilege and is itself marked out by exception or contrast. The landowner's legal ability to use his own land is a legal power because he holds this ability in contrast to others who are under a general duty not to use his land. The citizen's legal ability to make an arrest is a legal power because he holds it in contrast to his general duty not to meddle with the persons of others.

There are two faults in this device for distinguishing power from privilege. First, it can be regarded as insignificant that the privilege exists by contrast to a general duty. For all privileges involve the absence of duty.[18] What then is the legal significance of that duty which is absent in the holder of the privilege being generally present elsewhere? At the most it is surely only of sociological interest that one particular privilege is enjoyed exclusively whilst another is a matter of common enjoyment, and, at that, only the basis for classifying privileges as elite or popular rather than the basis for proclaiming a new concept. A Ferrari is an exceptional car but it is still a car.

Yet Hart's distinction would appear to make us call a landowner's legal ability to walk over his own land a legal *power*, whilst we must call the general public's legal ability to walk over the same land by way of a public footpath a legal *privilege* – since the former is exceptional whilst the latter is common. Hart argues that the factor of exception or contrast is significant

---

[13] Since all Hohfeld's conceptions are placed within a bipartite relationship, then whether the privilege physically affects a person or a thing it must be owed to a person – considered further in 2(3).

[14] FLC, 38ff.

[15] That is not to say that the term liberty may always be regarded as a synonym for Hohfeld's privilege, but it is frequently preferred as an alternative title for Hohfeld's concept, and the context (Hart 197–8) makes it clear that Hart is using the term in this sense. I use privilege, liberty and (what Hart also uses at this point) permission as synonyms for present purposes hereinafter.

[16] Hart, 198.

[17] *ibid.*

[18] Hart, 197; FLC, 38ff.

because it demonstrates that the law is bestowing an "advantage"[19] upon the person who is being exceptionally treated. But whether or not other people receive the same treatment by the law as I do, does not alter the fact that the law is giving me an advantage – although it might alter the extent (and the desirability) of the advantage. Each member of the general public possesses a legal advantage in the ability to walk over a public footpath, albeit that this advantage is less extensive than a landowner's ability to walk over his private footpath. I cannot deny that a Ford Cortina is a car, even if I would prefer a Ferrari.

More fundamentally, the second fault with Hart's device is that it is completely arbitrary. Any privilege may or may not be categorised as exceptional (and thus as or not as a power) at the whim of the taxonomist depending upon which general duty he chooses to chart the exception from. This point can be demonstrated by examining the two examples referred to by Hart that have been mentioned above. The landowner's power is contrasted with the general duty of *others* not to use his land, whereas the citizen's power to make an arrest is contrasted with *his* own general duty not to meddle with the persons of others.

The landowner's power would however be regarded as a mere privilege if compared with the ability common to all citizens in relation to any land that they own to use it;[20] the power of arrest a mere privilege if compared with the ability other citizens have to make an arrest. Likewise, the general public's legal ability to use a public footpath, which we have just categorised as a mere privilege by applying Hart's distinction, may as easily be rendered a power by not comparing it with the abilities of others to do the same thing but by contrasting it with the general duty of the holder (and others) not to do a similar thing in different circumstances: a right of way over a public footpath is an exception to the general duty not to walk over another's land, and so according to Hart is now a legal power.

The use of exception or contrast by Hart as the basis for distinguishing Bentham's concept of legal power from a legal permission/liberty/privilege may on these grounds be regarded as illusory, since the position of the second concept may at any time be occupied by the first – rather like those films involving identical twins where the one is always being mistaken for the other, which are brought off by the careful use of photography to hide the fact that one actress is playing both parts. The celluloid illusion is limited by the impossibility of filming both twins simultaneously. The limitations of Professor Hart's conceptual illusion may be judged by the fact that his distinction is drawn so as to always posit the second concept as distinct from the first which is being examined, without ever bringing an actual instance of the second into the picture. Hart gives no example of a mere legal privilege.

---

[19] Hart, 198 – corresponding to the "favour" of the law which is the characteristic of a legal right for Bentham: OLG, 84.

[20] A danger recognised but ignored by Hart – Hart, 198.

(2) Bentham Reinterpreted

Hart's defence of Bentham's concept of legal power, inasmuch as the concept needs to be distinguished from a legal privilege,[21] may be regarded as a failure. Moreover, it is questionable whether Hart's exegesis of Bentham's text is reasonable. Admittedly, Hart does point out the vagueness of Bentham's observations as a preliminary to his construction of Bentham's concept, but nevertheless does purport to give the "general character"[22] of the concept. This general character involves first the feature of exception or contrast, which in turn serves to distinguish the concept of a legal power from a legal pemission/liberty/privilege.

Hart's construction of Bentham's concept is based upon three key passages in Bentham's text.[23] The first passage deals with the relationship between the sovereign and a subordinate power-holder; the second with the position of a person who is not bound by the law; the third with the relations that the law may create over a piece of land.

The first point to note is that the feature of exception or contrast is not used by Bentham as it is by Hart. We have seen that Hart has characterised the landowner's legal ability to use his own land as a legal power because he holds this ability in contrast to others who are under a general duty not to use his land. Yet Bentham, in the third passage portrays three different scenarios in relation to the hypothetical piece of land: the first scenario leaves the land "the common property of us all" and Bentham speaks of "an inexclusive power over the land";[24] the second scenario leaves it as the property of a limited number of persons who are styled as having a power that is "once inexclusive and exclusive"[25] – inexclusive amongst themselves but exclusive in relation to others; the third scenario leaves it as the property of a single person, granting him a power that is "exclusive with respect to all".[26] Each scenario involves what Bentham describes as a power over the land, but the distinguishing characteristic which Hart proposes for a legal power over land is completely absent in the first scenario and only present in the second scenario in a qualified sense.

The second point to note is that Bentham does not make the distinction that Hart makes between a power and a permission/liberty/privilege. On the

[21] It is Bentham's power of contrection rather than his power of imperation which Hart considers needs to be distinguished – the remark quoted at n3 above appears in a section of Hart's essay entitled "Powers of Contrection". As will appear subsequently (below, 2(3)), the power of imperation is quite distinct from a legal privilege. However, Hart's discussion breaches the distinction between powers of contrection and powers of imperation – one of the key passages he cites (Hart, 198 n13), OLG 27, clearly deals with a power of imperation. The distinction is also blurred in Hart's own "wide characterization" – see text at n6 above.

[22] Hart, 198.

[23] Hart, 198 n13: OLG, 27, 56-7, 255-6.

[24] OLG, 255.

[25] *ibid.*

[26] OLG, 256m.

contrary, in the first passage Bentham states that the position of the subordinate power-holder in relation to the sovereign "consists in a *bare permission.
. .* the not being made the subject of a law commanding him not to issue the subordinate mandate".[27] In the third passage Bentham expresses the power of the landowners in terms of liberty ("of those whom it has left thus at liberty: it is spoken of as having given them or rather left them a *power over* the land"; "leaving you and certain others at liberty. . . it gives you a power"[28]). There is no requirement of exception or contrast in order to distinguish the power from a "mere liberty".

Moreover, Hart's claim that this distinction between liberty and power is sometimes expressed by Bentham in terms of "a power which is not 'the work of the(*sic*) law'" and "a legal power",[29] is contradicted by the second passage in which the phrase "not properly speaking. . . the work of law" is applied by Bentham to a *power* of contrectation ("*autocheiristic* power") which clearly is a legal power.[30]

The position that these three passages do support Bentham as taking is a position of some unease over labelling anything as legal which would have quite happily occurred without the existence of law, and to whose occurrence the law when it does come into existence makes no positive contribution. So, Bentham makes the point in the first passage that the part the sovereign plays in not forbidding the subordinate power-holder from issuing a mandate is a part played "by every the merest stranger" and so it is not "worthwhile, or indeed proper, to notice him as taking any part at all".[31] Similarly, in the second passage Bentham runs into his comment that a power of contrectation is not properly speaking the work of law from his observation upon a person who is not bound by the law that "his condition as far as depends upon this part of the law is just the same after the making the law as it was before; and as it would have been if there had been no law made about the matter."[32] And in the third passage, first scenario, Bentham exclaims that the law "does nothing at all in short in relation to the land: and of course, nothing in your favour. What is the result? On all sides liberty as before."[33]

Bentham is not thus far making the distinction between a legal power and a legal privilege, but doubting whether a legal power can be regarded as distinct from a *non-legal* permission/liberty/privilege. If in the state of nature men were free to eat apples, and upon the arrival of law they are left free to

---

[27] OLG, 27 (my emphasis).

[28] OLG, 255 (original emphasis) – cp OLG, 256: where Bentham speaks of "The power or liberty. . ."; and Jeremy Bentham, *An Introduction to the Principles of Morals and Legislation*, 1781 (eds. Burns and Hart) (London, Athlone Press, 1977) – hereinafter, PML – 206: where Bentham states, "Power. . . is constituted. . . by permission".

[29] Hart, 198.

[30] OLG, 57 ne. Bentham speaks here in general terms that cannot be taken to be referring to any distinction between different kinds of powers, or between powers and liberties.

[31] OLG, 27.

[32] OLG, 57.

[33] OLG, 255.

eat apples, in what sense is their legal power to eat apples any different from their pre-legal liberty?

Bentham allays his own unease in two ways. First, he notices that the negative part played by the law in failing to forbid something may be regarded as having a significance when placed alongside the fact that the law could have forbidden it – the sovereign, unlike "every the merest stranger", could have countermanded the subordinate power-holder's mandate;[34] or, which is making the same point more strongly, the law has actually forbidden it in other cases: others are under coercion not to act in this particular way; we may not use other pieces of land as we may use this piece of land.[35]

The factor of exception or contrast which Hart discerns in Bentham's text is being used by Bentham not in order to distinguish a legal power from a legal privilege but in order to distinguish a legal power from a non-legal privilege; and the significance of the exception or contrast consists not in the difference between one person's legal position and another's (or one person's legal position in different circumstances) but in the fact that it demonstrates that the law could have acted otherwise and forbidden what is being permitted. The position of a legal power holder is legally significant, even if he is only empowered to do what he could have done anyway without the law, because he is now empowered to do so when he could be legally disempowered from so doing. Eating apples could now be legally prohibited; an absence of legal prohibition is now a significant factor which could not have arisen in the state of nature; so my legal power to eat apples is distinct from my pre-legal liberty.

The second palliative that Bentham takes is to observe the existence of "ulterior corroborative laws"[36] which maintain the power holder's legal position by commanding or prohibiting others in such ways that support the enjoyment of the power:[37]

> "In this case the law not only permits you to exercise such power over the land as without its interference you were enabled to enjoy, but interferes itself in your favour, and takes an active part in your favour in securing to you the exercise of that power by taking measures for averting such obstacles as might be opposed to the exercise of it by the enterprizes of other men."

And Bentham appears to recognise that the *legal status* of the power that they protect is provided by such corroborative laws, when he contrasts the power of contrectation which is "not properly speaking. . . the work of law" with

---

[34] OLG, 27.
[35] Evidenced by a "superventitious law" which creates an exception to a general law at OLG 57, and by the general approach of the law to "the greatest part of the land under its dominion" at OLG 255.
[36] OLG, 27; cp OLG, 57 and 256.
[37] OLG, 256.

the "measures that are taken to secure. . . the possession of the power" which can properly be attributed to "the law indeed".[38]

(3) Bentham and Hohfeld

If Hart's attempt to defend Bentham's concept of a legal power by distinguishing it from a legal privilege is to be regarded not only as a failure but also as an exercise which is incompatible with a proper reading of Bentham's concept, then it might appear that Bentham's concept of a legal power can be assimilated under Hohfeld's concept of a legal privilege. However, this conclusion cannot be reached without qualification and without first clarifying a number of details.

It has already been mentioned that Bentham does not have just one concept of a legal power but two, the power of contrectation and the power of imperation. It is the former, which permits the physical handling of persons or inanimate things, which obviously falls within Hohfeld's concept of a legal privilege, which permits a person to do or refrain from some act without transgressing a legal duty to another person.[39] But Bentham himself regards his power of imperation as being reducible to a power of contrectation,[40] so it would appear that to allow the power of contrectation to be assimilated would be to swallow up every vestige of a legal power from Bentham's theory. This would then deflect the probe to the concept of a legal power which exists distinct from a legal privilege in Hohfeld's scheme of analysis.

Before returning to the difficulties associated with Bentham's two concepts of legal power, I shall proceed to use the general term legal power to cover a power of contrectation in Bentham's theory, and examine how this can be assimilated under Hohfeld's concept of a legal privilege.

Hohfeld's privilege to do an act amounts to the absence of a duty not to do that act.[41] Similarly, for Bentham, "Power, whether over a man's own person, or over other persons, or over things, is constituted in the first instance by permission. . ." and permission is the "negation" of "prohibition".[42] Without differences of detail, the two approaches may be presented as equivalent in the following diagram:

---

[38] OLG, 57 ne. Bentham does not appear to have a completed doctrine on the nature of corroborative laws; in other places, he speaks of the corroborative laws as being necessary for the "force and efficacy" of the laws that they support (OLG, 27), and as being partially inherent in an exclusive power (OLG, 257). (cp PML, 206.)

There is a striking parallel here to the idea of Hohfeld's privilege/liberty being constituted by the set of protecting rights, discussed in ch II.

[39] above, n14.

[40] Hart, 200f; OLG, 137 nh.

[41] above, n18 – but see the qualifications made upon this statement in ch II.

[42] PML, 206 ne2.

HOHFELD:	Privilege	=	No Duty not to
	=		=
BENTHAM:	Power	=	No Prohibition not to

The differences in detail emanate from the fact that the starting point of Bentham's analysis is "some manifestation or other of the legislator's will"[43] whereas the starting point for Hohfeld is the bipartite relationship of litigation.[44] So Hohfeld's duty (and thus his privilege) must be owed or held in relation to another litigant, whilst Bentham's prohibition (and thus power) must be held under the sovereign legislator. This in itself does not cause incompatibility between the two approaches: Bentham may be regarded as focusing upon the source of the legal position and Hohfeld upon its practical outworking in the courtroom. However, the different emphases do lead to divergence in that Hohfeld's privilege must involve two persons, whereas Bentham's power may be a power exercised by one person over an inanimate object.

This is not to say that Hohfeld's privilege cannot be exercised over an inanimate thing, say land, but such a privilege must be exercised with regard to another person who is a potential party to a dispute over the exercise of the privilege. Bentham may speak of a person having a power over land, but Hohfeld insists upon stating that a person has a privilege to do something upon the land in relation to another person.

Hohfeld's analysis may be regarded as more accurate at this point, inasmuch as the power over (or privilege to deal with) an inanimate thing is an alegal power. I have the physical ability to pick up an apple and eat it; my baby son does not. The emergence of law cannot alter the presence or absence of this physical power over the apple. The only difference the law can make is to prevent the exercise of the physical power that I possess over the apple by giving *some person* the legal authority to prevent me exercising that power: placing me under a duty to someone not to eat the apple;[45] or, to permit the exercise of the physical power over the apple by not giving *some person* the authority to prevent me: granting me a privilege in relation to that person to eat the apple.

The same holds for a physical power over a person. It too must be regulated in relation to a person (whether or not the same person) in order to attain a legal status. Jack may have the physical power to apprehend John, but whether to do so is legal or not will depend upon whether some person has the legal authority to prevent Jack exercising that power or not: whether

---

[43] PML, 206 ne2.

[44] See ch II.

[45] I do not deal here with the problem of self-regarding duties, or the common criticism of Hohfeld's scheme that in the criminal law in general we cannot really speak of a duty being owed to a particular person. These points may require a refinement of Hohfeld's theory, but the point remains that in order for a relationship to an object to have legal significance it must be enforceable in relation to a person.

Jack is under a duty to someone or enjoys a privilege in relation to that person, to apprehend John. A successful arrest will require that Jack has the physical power to apprehend John; a *lawful* arrest will require in addition that Jack owes no duty to someone not to arrest John.

Nevertheless, the insistence upon speaking of a legal ability to physically control a person or inanimate thing as being held in relation to another person need not mar the assimilation of Bentham's analysis under Hohfeld's. It is a minor adjustment for Bentham's analysis to make, which does not alter its fundamental character, and which is half foreseen by Bentham himself.[46]

The question remains whether Hohfeld's privilege (or liberty) or Bentham's power is a more appropriate name for the concept. Terminological tussles should be regarded as secondary to identifying the concept, but awkward terminology may prove as troublesome to a concept in its future development as an awkward name to a child arriving at school, and should be avoided.

On the basis that the concept we have identified is a *legal* concept, the name we choose for it should reflect its *legal* character. For this reason, Hohfeld's "privilege" or, as some prefer, "liberty" seems a more appropriate name for the concept of being free to perform some physical act upon another person or inanimate thing, since it is the freedom (absence of legal restraint) to perform the act which is bestowed by the law − rather than the power to perform the act which the law does not nor can bestow.

We may therefore assimilate Bentham's power of contrectation under Hohfeld's privilege and reject the first alternative of Hart's "wide characterization" of a legal power, together with examples (1) and (12) which illustrate it. By so doing we are not of course denying any legal interest to such positions,[47] but we are rejecting them as instances of a legal power.

On the other hand, Hohfeld's concept of a legal power, Bentham's power of imperation, and Hart's second alternative do display a feature which might maintain their status as a legal power. Each of these is concerned with the ability of one person to change the legal position of another person. Although it has been argued that the ability to affect the *physical* state of a person[48] (eg by apprehending him) should be regarded as an alegal *physical* power, there is no objection against regarding the ability to affect the *legal* state of a person as a *legal* power. We might then regard Hohfeld's concept of a legal power and the corresponding items in the theories of Bentham and Hart as being a fit subject for study in our investigation of the concept of a legal power. Before proceeding with this investigation in the following sections, there is one point that needs immediate attention, in order to justify any further investigation of such a legal power.

---

[46] The doubts expressed at OLG 57 ne.

[47] Such positions are considered in ch II.

[48] Or thing − but there will not be a corresponding legal power in relation to the thing, but in relation to a person concerned with the thing.

We have already noted that Bentham regarded his power of imperation as being reducible to a power of contrectation. The reason given by Bentham for this is that the power of imperation which is exercised over the "active faculty" of a person (ie his will) is dependent upon a power of contrectation over the "passive faculty" of that person (ie his body) for its efficacy.[49] So, the power (of imperation) to issue an injunction requiring a violent husband or cohabitee to exercise his will not to molest his partner will be ineffective unless accompanied by powers (of contrectation) of arrest and of imprisonment upon his body for breach of the injunction.

However, to say that the power to grant the injunction is *dependent* for efficacy upon the powers, or more accurately privileges of arrest and imprisonment is not to say that it is *reducible* to them. The existence of the privileges of arrest and imprisonment cannot itself determine the existence of the power to issue an injunction against molestation. Grant the privileges, but until you have also granted the power, the privileges are useless.

3 POWERS, DECISIONS AND CONDITIONS

(1) The Feature of Decision

This feature of a legal power may be related to the capacity, or authority, of the power holder. By the feature of decision I refer to the fact that the power holder has the capacity or authority to decide an issue where the decision will have legal repercussions upon the position of another.

The feature of decision can be regarded as the first feature of legal power in that it will be present in any instance of a legal power, since every legal power affords the power holder the opportunity to exercise the power and affect the legal position of the other subject to it by the expression of his decision upon the matter. The power of Parliament to legislate (2) finds expression in the passing of an Act of Parliament; the power of a minister to make regulations (3) in the making of a ministerial regulation; and so on, for each of the above remaining thirteen (or any other) examples.[50]

The extent of this feature of decision may vary in accordance with the number of occasions upon which the power holder may express his decision. So, to take the power of the Lord Chancellor to appoint county court judges (8), this power may vary in extent along the feature of decision depending upon how many judges the Lord Chancellor may appoint. Clearly, the power to appoint one county court judge differs from the power to appoint forty, or fifty, or a hundred – in that the lesser the number of occasions the sooner the

---

[49] Hart, 200-1; OLG, 137 nh.

[50] The manner of expression may be accompanied by greater or lesser degrees of formality: eg contrast the power to make a contract for the sale of land with the power to make an ordinary contract of sale.

power will be exhausted. As another illustration, we can distinguish the power of a man to make a contract to marry (15) under English law from the power under Islamic law also in terms of extent along the feature of decision: in that under English law the power holder may express his decision only once.[51]

(2) Making Decisions, Fulfilling Conditions

The elevation of decision to the paramount practical feature of a legal power has a number of repercussions upon our theoretical investigation of the concept. I shall suggest that it assists in the solution of a well known conundrum, sheds light on the reason for recognising legal power as a distinct concept, and paves the way for establishing the relationship between legal powers and legal rights. In each of these respects, a distinction between making a decision to bring about change and fulfilling a condition for change will be central.

The idea that legal change can be brought about through the fulfilment of a particular condition by the occurrence of some event is uncontroversial to the point of banality. Water escaping from a reservoir, a person coming of age, moving house, a slate on a roof becoming dislodged by a gale – each of these events amounts to the fulfilment of a condition for the emergence of new legal relations (as well as extinguishing old ones). If we wish to express this more formally, we may say that the existing law provides for a number of eventualities by attaching legal consequences to their occurrence in the form:

$$c \rightarrow r$$

– where c is the event required to satisfy the condition, and r is the resulting legal position. So, if (c_1) the water escapes from the reservoir, then (r_1) the owner of the land with the reservoir becomes liable to compensate his neighbour for damage caused to him; if (c_2) a person comes of age, then (r_2) he may drink alcohol in a public house; if (c_3) a person moves house, then (r_3) he is under a duty not to cause a nuisance to his new neighbour; if (c_4) the slate becomes dislodged, then (r_4) the occupier of the premises is under a duty to prevent it falling and injuring a visitor.

In cases such as these, r is not at the time before the occurrence of c an existing legal position, but is of course contingent upon the occurrence of c. Although r is a contingent legal position it is nevertheless a fixed legal position, in the sense that the law has already determined what is to happen should c occur: establish the occurrence of c and r is necessarily recognised.

It would seem that all this can be adequately expressed in whatever legal terms are considered apt to describe the position r together with the qualification that such a legal phenomenon remains contingent upon the

---

[51] Upon divorce, or death of the spouse, the power holder is of course reinvested with the power that was exhausted upon marriage.

occurrence of event c. There seems to be no need to find some further legal entity to fit c. If c happens, then the law will be provoked into recognising r, but c itself has no intrinsic legal status: it is an ordinary event which might or might not occur irrespective of the attention that the law pays to it. Indeed, for the four examples given above, nobody would wish to say any more than that.

However, there are some cases where some (though not all) commentators find it necessary to say that c amounts to the exercise of a legal power.[52] In Hohfeld's choice of words it is when "some superadded fact" [ie the occurrence of an event c] is "under the volitional control of. . . [a] human being".[53] So, in the case of (c_5) a person accepting a contractual offer bringing about (r_5) an obligation to perform the contractual undertaking, we are now to recognise that the event c_5 does have legal status in that it amounts to the exercise of a legal power by the person who makes the acceptance.

Two intriguing questions are posed at this juncture. First, what is it that makes it necessary to recognise a legal status for some events that result in legal consequences but not for others? Related to this, the second question is where do we draw the line between those events that do possess this legal status and those which do not?

The crucial feature in Hohfeld's way of looking at things is the volitional control of a human being. It is the presence or absence of this which distinguishes between the exercise of a legal power and a mere condition.[54] However, Raz has pointed out that this alone is not enough.[55] For we could say that c_3, moving house, is under the volitional control of a human being,[56] but we do not want to say that moving house amounts to the exercise of a legal power to bring about the duty not to commit a nuisance.

Raz considers the attempt to circumvent this problem in *Salmond on Jurisprudence*[57] by stipulating that an exercise of power must be directed at the change in legal position that it brings about. So, moving house does not amount to the exercise of a legal power because the person moving house does not do so in order to put himself under a duty not to cause a nuisance to his new neighbour. However, Raz remains dissatisfied because there are some cases where a person does do something in order to bring about a change in

---

[52] Kelsen is an extreme example of those who do not find it necessary – for which Hart upbraids him (Hart, 196). MacCormick reveals some tendency towards Kelsen's position in "Voluntary Obligations and Normative Powers", (an essay in two parts contributed by MacCormick and Raz – hereinafter, (VO&NP) (1972) 46 *Proceedings of the Aristotelian Society, Supplementary Volume 59* at 78.

[53] FLC, 50.

[54] *ibid*.

[55] VO&NP, 80ff.

[56] In a weaker sense, it could also be maintained that c_2, coming of age, is also under the volitional control of a human being – if we accept volitional control by omission.

[57] 12ed, PJ Fitzgerald ed. (London, Sweet & Maxwell, 1966), 229 – cited by Raz, VO&NP, 81.

legal position but we would still want to deny that he is exercising a legal power.[58]

Raz gives two such cases.[59] A person may in fact choose to move house in order to bring about a change in legal position – an example would be in order to fall within a school catchment area, another would be in order to lessen a tax burden. A person may commit an offence in order to be punished – the example from WH Davies' *Autobiography of a Super-Tramp* is furnished by MacCormick,[60] where the tramp ensures hospitality in a warm cell on a cold winter's night by committing a minor offence. In such cases, we would not say that the person is exercising a legal power in order to bring about the desired legal consequence, yet the consequence is brought about by an event under his volitional control (and it is directed at that end). This is a well known conundrum.[61] An extreme example well illustrates the reason for reservation against finding a legal power in this sort of case: the person who commits murder thus changes the legal position of the judge who is now in a position to sentence him. Why do we not say that the murderer has exercised a legal power over the judge?

Raz proposes a solution to the conundrum by focusing upon the reason why the law recognises an act [c] as bringing about a legal change:[62]

"An action is the exercise of a legal power only if one of the law's reasons for acknowledging that it effects a legal change is that it is of a type such that it is reasonable to expect that actions of that type will, if they are recognised to have certain legal consequences, standardly be performed only if the person concerned wants to secure these legal consequences."

Applied to the two examples above, we may then conclude that there is no exercise of a legal power because moving house is not normally done only in order to fall within a school catchment area (or to avoid paying taxes), and because committing a minor offence is not normally done only in order to obtain bed and breakfast in a police cell. By contrast, (c_5) accepting a

---

[58] Raz has a further objection. He considers that this stipulation is too restrictive in that he wishes to include within the exercise of legal power a case where a person inadvertently brings about a legal consequence – I shall discuss this below.

[59] VO&NP, 81.

[60] *HLA Hart* (Stanford, CA, Stanford University Press, 1981), 73ff.

[61] MacCormick attempts to deal with the conundrum by insisting that for a legal power to exist the power holder must "invoke the rule in some way" (*op. cit.* 73). This would appear to require the conscious reflection upon the law of contract by every consumer who buys a bar of chocolate – or else a denial that the consumer ignorant of the law of contract has the legal power to make a contract. MacCormick may claim to circumvent this difficulty by pointing to his watered down invocation based upon an "imputed. . . intention of invoking the rule" (74), but it is difficult see that it is a "reasonable and probable interpretation" (*ibid.*) of the behaviour of the average customer in the newsagent's shop that he intends to invoke the law of contract when purchasing his chocolate. In the case of W.H. Davies's "Super-Tramp", who deliberately broke the law in order to obtain a comfortable stay in prison for the Winter, MacCormick denies that the tramp is exercising a legal power without explaining why he cannot be said to be invoking the law. See further, Spaak ch 5.

[62] VO&NP, 81.

contractual offer does amount to the exercise of a legal power because it is normally done only in order to bring about (r_5) an obligation to perform the contractual undertaking.

This expanded qualification from Raz appears to draw the line between powers and mere conditions more satisfactorily than the rejected Salmond stipulation, but some awkward difficulties remain. If we return to our first question, which asks why we should bother to recognise legal powers at all, then Raz's formula taken from the perspective of the lawgiver does not provide a satisfactory answer. If the lawgiver's concern is only to recognise that a particular legal change has occurred when a person has indicated that he has wanted to secure that change, this may be clearly stipulated in whatever event, c, is required to bring about the change, but that is not to say that this c must then take on a legal status above that afforded to another c where this particular requirement is not made. The fact that the lawgiver is willing to make one legal consequence follow from an event involving a person's desire, and another legal consequence from the malevolence of the wind can be adequately expressed without attributing a legal power to the person, or indeed a legal power to the wind.

In fact, the interests of Raz's lawgiver appear to be more sophisticated. He wishes to discount the possibility of giving a legal power to the maverick who does want to bring about a particular legal consequence by doing some act which is not normally done in order to bring about that consequence: the tramp is not to be given a legal power to obtain bed and breakfast in a police cell by committing an offence. Yet the lawgiver is not going to deny the tramp his bed and breakfast! What then is the point in denying (or conceding) him the legal power? The issue appears to be completely superfluous to the practical viewpoint of the lawgiver, or of the tramp.

It appears that Raz is concerned with the perspective of the lawgiver, for he asserts that the answer to the conundrum is to be found "not in the intention with which power-exercising acts are performed but in the reasons for which they are recognised. . .".[63] However, even if we view his suggestion from the perspective of the person performing the action which has the legal consequence, it is still difficult to provide a satisfactory answer to the first question. If the basis of saying that the person has a legal power is that he is allowed to secure the legal consequence that he wants, then we should have to acknowledge that the legally facilitated maverick has a legal power. But the whole point of the exercise is to deny this.

A further difficulty with Raz's approach relates to the second question concerning where the line between powers and mere conditions is to be drawn. For Raz's formula only requires that the "standard" case of performing the action should be accompanied by a desire to secure the legal consequence, and he stresses the inclusion within the exercise of legal power a case where one

---

[63] VO&NP, 81.

"make[s] a contract or some other legal transaction with no intention to do so, [where]. . .one does not correctly appreciate the legal consequences of one's action."[64]

The location of a case where a person has "no intention" to bring about a legal consequence (the illustration Raz gives is the objective contract) in a category whose defining characteristic appears to require that a person "wants to secure these legal consequences"[65] is awkward indeed. There is of course nothing difficult in saying that a contract that is based upon an objective agreement (where one party did not intend to enter the agreement but the reasonable inference from his behaviour was that he did) falls into the same category as a contract based upon subjective agreement (where both parties did actually intend to enter the agreement), inasmuch as both are valid contracts. And, there are obvious policy reasons for holding this to be so. But the merits of certainty in commercial transactions require only that we hold the dealing which has all the appearances of an actual agreement to be an enforceable contract. And this desideratum is wholly satisfied by the stipulation that if (c_{5a}) the reasonable inference of a person's behaviour is that he is accepting a contractual offer, then (r_{5a}) there is an obligation to perform the apparent undertaking as a contractual undertaking. There is no policy requirement for the conceptual contortion of holding that the position of a person who does want something to happen is a position occupied by someone who does not intend that very thing.

Raz's difficulties may be regarded as clustering around the idea that a person wants a legal consequence – Hohfeld's volitional element. What is it that makes a condition, c, for a legal result, r, different from any other condition when it includes this volitional element? Why is it that the inclusion of this volitional element is material in some cases but not in others? Why should the absence of this volitional element be overlooked in some cases? Yet it is apparent that Raz's focus upon the volitional element is what makes it possible for him to make the advances that he does make upon earlier approaches to the problem. It is submitted that the proper role of the volitional element in the task of recognising and describing legal powers falls into place when we acknowledge the importance of decision in our analysis of legal powers, and that this acknowledgment will dispel the difficulties noted above.

(3) The Significance of Decisions

If decision is the paramount practical feature, the first feature, of every legal power, then whatever the effect of the exercise of a particular power that

---

[64] *ibid.*

[65] Raz is rather more elliptical in that the person wanting to secure the legal consequence is not a requirement of the lawgiver but a reasonable expectation of the standard case. Nevertheless, the prominence of this characteristic in the definition is established.

effect will be decided upon by the power holder. We may represent the decision as follows:

$$d(r)$$

– where r, as above, is the resulting legal position,[66] and d is the function of decision. And we may then indicate the existence of a legal power, p:

$$(c \rightarrow r) \ \& \ (c = d(r)) \leftrightarrow p$$

The case of the murderer or the maverick does not then amount to a legal power, because in the former we do not have $d(r)$ (I assume for the present that we do not have a maverick murderer, but if so, proceed to the next case); and in the latter although we have $d(r)$, it is not the case that $c = d(r)$. The maverick may decide to bring about a short spell in prison, but it is not this decision which is the condition for bringing it about.

Moreover, the distinction between $c = d(r)$ and $c \neq d(r)$ can readily be appreciated to be significant, once it is observed that to make a particular legal consequence dependent upon a condition which is constituted by a human decision places the person appointed to make the decision in a legally significant position *before the decision is made*.

Whereas there is no legal interest in asking after the event whether the condition that had to be satisfied in order to establish the legal position that is being maintained involved a human decision, the malevolence of the wind, or the force of water. There is legal interest which can attach before the event to a human decision, which cannot attach to the malevolence of wind or the force of water. The simple fact is that humans and their decisions are subject to the law, whereas the wind and water and whatever they may do are not – as Xerxes discovered at the Hellespont.

So, the position of the power holder can itself be legally regulated, rather than simply being an event which the law recognises in regulating other behaviour. Moreover, the position may be legally transferred by the holder –

---

[66] There is a compression of expression here which it is important to unpack at this point. By "the resulting legal position" I mean "the resulting position that is given legal recognition". This clarification becomes significant when discussing $d(r)$ because otherwise it could be thought that what is required is for the power holder to decide to bring about a change in position *on the understanding that the law recognises this new position*, rather than to decide to bring about a change in position – which the law recognises. The former interpretation would take us back to MacCormick's requirement that the power holder invokes the law (rejected at n61 above). The alternative view being advanced here is that although the power holder *may* be consciously invoking the law, this is not a necessary condition for identifying an exercise of legal power, which depends solely upon showing that the power holder decided to bring about the change in position, which the law recognises and gives effect to. Hence we need talk only of a decision to enter a binding agreement, rather than a decision to satisfy the doctrines of the law of contract, when depicting a legal power to contract. Of course, the more formal the requirements that the law imposes on the expression of that decision (see n50 above), the more likely it is that the power holder may be consciously invoking the law in conforming to those formalities. Even so, this remains incidental to the recognition of the legal power – the land owner ignorant of the law may have his own reasons for recording in writing an agreement to sell the land.

an option not available to the positions of wind or water. And, in addition, from the viewpoint of the power holder, the position provides an opportunity to participate in the legal determination of future events (not once the power has been exercised, since to exercise it is to extinguish it – at least in relation to that particular occasion), which we cannot provide to the wind and water unless we are willing to grant them rationality.

Even if that is accepted as a convincing demonstration of the significant difference between those conditions for legal consequences that rest upon human decisions and those that depend upon inanimate events, not all that has been said applies equally to make the difference significant between the power holder and the maverick. In particular, it can be argued that whether a person holds a legal power which can be exercised to bring about a legal consequence or whether he is capable of doing an act which is the condition for bringing about a legal power in another which will be exercised to bring about a legal consequence (and so we deny him the status of holding a legal power), is immaterial if he does want to bring about that consequence – in both cases he may participate in the legal determination of future events (albeit more indirectly in the latter case).

It has to be conceded that in those circumstances there is no material distinction between the position of the power holder and the position of the maverick. But this assimilation of the two is the chance product of the maverick ambition coinciding with an orthodox legal purpose: it is contingent upon the maverick's desire for warmth and food being satisfied by the penal solution to the offence he commits. The true distinction between the two may still be maintained in practical terms by pointing out that the consequence will befall the person who does what the maverick does whether he wishes it or not, but will only befall the power holder when he decides it.

There remains one difficulty mentioned above that has not been addressed, the difficulty it was suggested faced Raz when he wanted to include the making of an objective contract within an exercise of power. Clearly, upon the analysis proposed here, we would have to deny that this was an exercise of power, since the contracting party in this case has not decided to enter the agreement and we have $c \neq d(r)$. It is submitted that this is the better view for a number of reasons. First, it has already been pointed out above that the policy concern is only to recognise a valid contract, not to recognise a legal power. Secondly, the reasons given above for finding significance in the distinct position of a power holder do not apply to this case (and others are lacking) – in particular, the opportunity to participate in the legal determination of future events is as much impossible for the objective contractor as it is for the wind and water. Finally, it can be suggested that the attraction of including this case within an exercise of power stems from a false assessment of the volitional aspect, which can be traced to Hohfeld's terminology.

Hohfeld places under his "volitional control" not the change in legal position but the "superadded fact" which brings it about.[67] The erroneous conclusions which follow from a straightforward application of Hohfeld's terminology have been recognised by Raz. It is suggested that to include the objective contractor is another. For although it is the act of the objective contractor under his volitional control that is taken to bring about the contractual obligation, there is no volitional aspect in relation to the consequence of a binding agreement, and this, it is submitted, is fatal to the finding of an exercise of legal power.[68]

I have endeavoured to show in this part how the distinction between legal powers and other conditions for legal change can be understood and coherently maintained once we recognise the significance of decision in our analysis of a legal power. I shall pursue this key feature of legal powers further in the final part of this chapter which will deal with the relationship between legal powers and legal rights.

4 LEGAL POWERS AND LEGAL RIGHTS

(1) Decision or Choice?

The centrality of decision in the analysis of legal power contrasts with the significance that Hart gives to choice. In his "Definition and Theory in Jurisprudence"[69] Hart suggests that the legal recognition of an individual's choice is an idea that pervades each of the dominant positions in Hohfeld's schema – (claim)right, privilege/liberty, power and immunity.[70] And Hart's characterisation of rights in terms of "the obligation to perform the corresponding duty is made by law to depend on the choice of the individual who is said to have the right. . ."[71] leads naturally to a reduction of legal (claim) rights in terms of the power to enforce a duty:[72]

> "The case of a right correlative to obligation then emerges as only a special case of legal power in which the right-holder is at liberty to waive or extinguish or to enforce or to leave unenforced another's obligation."

[67] FLC, 50f.

[68] It so happens that there is an overlap here in the law between providing a power to the voluntary contractor, and imposing a condition on the involuntary contractor. The existence of two distinct legal provisions can be overlooked because the same conduct, viewed objectively, by the contractor satisfies them both. However, the two provisions are there to serve two different social objectives: enabling individuals to make binding agreements, and providing for certainty in transactions. In other cases, it might be thought appropriate to have the provision of a power but not the imposition of a condition – such as in the power to marry, where there is no overlapping condition.

[69] Hart's inaugural lecture, reproduced in (1954) 70 *Law Quarterly Review* 37 – hereinafter, D&T. (Also found in H.L.A. Hart, *Essays in Jurisprudence and Philosophy* (Oxford, Clarendon Press, 1983) ch 1).

[70] D&T, 49 n15.

[71] D&T, 49.

[72] *Essays on Bentham* (Oxford, Clarendon Press, 1982), Essay VII: "Legal Rights" – hereinafter, EonB – 188.

There remains a serious impediment to this line of argument, an impediment which is half adverted to by Hart himself when he points out at the end of his footnote: "If there are legal rights which cannot be waived these would need special treatment."[73] Clearly, if rights are seen in terms of having the choice to enforce a duty, and there exist duties which will be enforced whether the right holder chooses so or not, the only character left to these rights is that of invisibility. Yet the existence of such rights is far from the conditional state that Hart leaves them in, and they merit more than the "special treatment" that Hart would afford them.

(2) Choice or Interest?

Rights without the choice to enforce a duty are among the most ordinary rights that the law protects. Perhaps the most compelling example is the right of a citizen not to be unlawfully killed, where the right holder cannot choose to waive the protection of the law either before or after the event.[74] MacCormick in fact suggests a number of other counterexamples, in championing the "interest theory" of rights against Hart's "will theory" (or, choice theory).[75]

Hart may be regarded as confusing the position of having an interest protected with the position of being able to divest oneself of that protection – which may, or may not, be concomitant with the former position. The former position may be referred to as possessing the right(s) correlative to the duty(/ies) not to harm the interest in question[76] – the interest of having a contract performed, the interest of remaining alive, to cite but two examples. The latter position is granted the contracting party who may choose to discharge

[73] D&T, 49 n15. The significance of the remark is noted by Finnis in *Natural Law and Natural Rights* (Oxford, Clarendon Press, 1980), 227: "That 'special treatment' has not been forthcoming, and the existence of such rights does tell against the 'choice' theory."

[74] The only minor qualification to this proposition is that a person may waive the protection of the law of murder whilst retaining the protection of the law of manslaughter by taking part with his killer in a suicide pact which proves unfulfilled in the case of the killer – Homicide Act 1957, s 4. There are no exceptions after the event.

[75] In his two essays: "Children's Rights: a Test-Case for Theories of Right", (1976) LXII *Archiv für Rechts- und Sozialphilosophie* 305, reproduced in *Legal Right and Social Democracy* (Oxford, Clarendon Press, 1982), ch8 – hereinafter, CR; "Rights in Legislation" in PMS Hacker and J Raz (eds.), *Law, Morality, and Society* (Oxford, Clarendon Press, 1977) – hereinafter, RL. The other counter examples are: the right of a child to be cared for (CR, 156–8; RL, 198); the right not to be assaulted in a sexually perverted manner (RL, 197: *Donovan* [1934] 2 KB 498 – and, more recently, *Brown* [1993] 2 WLR 556); certain entrenched employees' rights (RL, 198). MacCormick points out the absurdity of the will theory holding that as the criminal law gets more serious in protecting some of the more serious assaults (culminating in fatal assaults) by making the protection inalienable so the rights evaporate (RL, 199): "if the will theory is correct, the more they are inalienable, the less they are rights."

[76] Whether the interest lies in what the right holder may have another do (Hohfeld's (claim)right), or in what he may do himself (Hohfeld's privilege/liberty) – that both of these positions are ultimately correlative with a duty or duties is maintained in ch II.

the other party from his contractual obligation, but is, as we have noted, denied both to Brutus and to his corpse.

Even where the power to divest is present as a concomitant of the right, it should not be equated with it. The contracting party who chooses to discharge the contractual obligation is not thus exercising his right but terminating it.[77] In changing the legal position of the other party (and himself), he is exercising a legal power; but it is in the possession and enjoyment of his anterior position that we can discern his legal right. The right to be paid £200 under a contract cannot be equated with the power to dissolve the obligation to pay, any more than living in a house can be equated with moving out of it.

Indeed, MacCormick suggests that the "ancillary" power of waiver can properly be understood "in the context of a liberal legal system",[78] where it is regarded as normal to permit the right holder himself to choose whether or not to enforce his right. And he argues not merely that the right is independent of the power to waive the duty but also that the right may be prior to the duty, in a justificatory or explanatory sense[79]: the right (interest) of the child justifies placing the parent under a duty to care for the child;[80] the right of a child of an intestate to the intestate estate accounts for the duty that is imposed *subsequently* upon the person appointed to administer the estate.[81]

However, Hart does possess some possible rejoinders to these arguments. Where it can be shown that duties exist without the possibility of waiver by the person whose interest is being protected, it is possible to simply deny that the person whose interest is being protected has a right correlative to the duty. Hart displays a willingness to deploy this argument in relation to duties owed to babies,[82] and to the duties of the criminal law.[83] So, the baby has no right to be cared for, Brutus has no right not to be killed – at least correlative to the respective duties. Hart is not unaware of the usage of ordinary language which does invoke rights to describe the positions of Brutus and the baby in just these situations, but he distinguishes this talk of rights as being a language

---

[77] Cp MacCormick's comments on the discharge of the parental duty by a care order – CR, 157.

[78] CR, 164.

[79] For the moment I ignore the important distinction between these two roles for the "prior right", which in fact relate to different notions of a right. MacCormick's first example may be regarded as dealing with a moral right, whereas his second example is more troublesome for Hart in that it deals with a case where there is a *legally* recognised right prior to the imposition of the duty. The different notions of a right are considered in ch V.

[80] CR, 158, 162.

[81] CR, 162; RL, 200, and at 203 MacCormick speaks of "duties. . . necessarily consequential upon conferment of the relevant rights."

[82] "Are There Any Natural Rights?" (1955) 64 *Philosophical Review* 175, reproduced in Jeremy Waldron (ed.), *Theories of Rights* (Oxford OUP, 1984) 77 at 82. But note the vacillation to use it for children in general (EonB, 184) by suggesting that children exercise their rights through their representatives. MacCormick has demonstrated that on such an interpretation it is still possible to find a duty that cannot be waived by the representative – CR, 156–7.

[83] EonB, 184, 185, 186.

deployed "by the constitutional lawyer and the individualistic critic of the law" whose concern is "basic or fundamental individual needs".[84]

This latter point could be developed a stage further in order to meet MacCormick's argument that a right may be regarded as prior to a duty. It could be asserted that not only the constitutional lawyer and the critic but also the legislator is capable of recognising "individual needs" which are to be afforded the protection of the law by the imposition of duties upon others: the need of the child for care, the need of the child of the intestate to gain the intestate estate, may then be regarded as rights prior to the duties that will be imposed to protect them, and may well appear explicitly in the language of the legislator.[85] Acknowledging the presence of these need-rights would not commit Hart to accept that correlative rights based upon choice exist in such situations. Hart would thus be free to concede to MacCormick the existence of children's need-rights, whilst insisting that the rights correlative to duty are "a special case of legal power" and denying that children possess such rights.

Two important points emerge from this hypothetical extension of the Hart-MacCormick debate. First, it suggests compatible locations for the will and interest perspectives upon legal rights. For Hart's "need" is difficult to distinguish from MacCormick's "interest", despite Hart's explicit disavowal.[86] Given that, the needs or interests protected by the law may then indeed be seen in some sense as rights prior to the duties imposed by the law for their protection, and as distinct from the correlative rights furnished by the law that may involve allowing a party to regulate the use of that protection as he may choose.[87]

Secondly, it emphasises that the will/choice theory is, as Hart reveals, based upon who controls the *exercise* of the position identified as the right:[88]

> ". . . it is hard to think of rights except as capable of exercise and this conception of rights correlative to obligations as containing legal powers accommodates this feature."

[84] EonB, 193.

[85] As the latter does in the Succession (Scotland) Act 1964, s 2(1)(a) – CR, 161–2; RL, 200–2. The fact that we are dealing with "need-rights" here rather than the "correlative rights" (see below) should be discerned by anyone familiar with Hohfeldian analysis when MacCormick refers to "the right of ownership" (RL, 201–2).

[86] EonB, 192–3. The disavowal is maintained by (a) ignoring the position of the legislator by sticking to the constitutional lawyer and critic only (189, 191, 192, 193), and by (b) treating the benefit theory solely in terms of Bentham's idea of general utility (193). In treating the law against murder Hart thus concedes "rights to life" but treats them as "redundant" for the task of "expounding the criminal law" (192) – such limited exposition clearly only makes sense (if at all – see the discussion of the right to life in *Airedale NHS Trust v Bland* [1993] 2 WLR 316) when we are considering the position of the judge or other aforementioned public official who is bound to carry out the criminal law, not when we are considering the position of the legislator who will necessarily have just such rights in mind when determining the proper shape of the law he is making.

[87] The suggestion requires far more amplification than can be provided here. Further discussion on "need" rights prior to enforceable legal rights, which could accommodate the suggestion, is to be found in ch V.

[88] EonB, 184.

We have already noted the danger of confusing the exercise of a right with the power to waive it,[89] but even if we regard the power to enforce or waive the right as obliquely amounting to controlling the exercise of the right, there are a couple of untoward consequences if we treat the right as being *constituted* by that legal power – consequences which Hart himself shows no sign of embracing.[90]

If we do consistently accept that control of the exercise of the position "is sufficient and necessary",[91] then we would have to talk about officials who have the control but no (personal) interest as nevertheless possessing rights. The Attorney-General, for example, through his *nolle prosequi* and exclusive powers of prosecution would then assume an extaordinarily large and clumsy collection of rights *correlative to the duties protecting the interests of other individuals and the state.*[92] We would normally, with less erratic vocabulary, speak of the Attorney-General's power (or even solecistic right) to initiate or stay proceedings in a prosecution for homicide rather than talk about the Attorney-General's right that Brutus should not be killed.

This points to the other consequence of regarding the right as constituted by the power. There really would be no need to continue to use the term right at all. Why should the power to extinguish/enforce a duty be described in any other terms than those? However, every example that Hart adduces of a right correlative to a duty possesses not only the power that Hart depicts as sufficient and necessary but also some interest in the right holder as well.

(3) The Significance of Decision

The idea of choice cannot be regarded as the "unifying element"[93] that Hart claims it to be. Nor even can choice be regarded as the basic element of legal power. Hart's suggestion that in the case of a power, "the law gives legal effect to the choice of an individual . . . that the legal position of some other person be altered",[94] overlooks the cases of power holders who have no choice in the exercise of their power. The power of the judge to pass a mandatory sentence discussed above is sufficient demonstration of the point that legal power may exist without choice. Other examples of commonly held legal powers with the absence of choice abound. The landowner who has entered a contract to sell his land retains the power to transfer title to his land but

---

[89] above, 4(2).

[90] Hart helps to distance himself from these consequences by speaking of the rights "containing" legal powers (EonB, 184) rather than being constituted by them. But elsewhere (EonB, 188) he clearly regards the rights as the powers.

[91] EonB, 188.

[92] For example, the Attorney-General's consent for a prosecution under the Official Secrets Act.

[93] D&T, 49 n15.

[94] *ibid.*

does not retain any choice over the matter.[95] The request of a beneficiary absolutely entitled to the trust property that the trustee transfer the property to him leaves the trustee with a power to transfer the property but with no choice in the matter. Yet the judge, the landowner, and the trustee, in these cases, are still required to express their decision – to sentence, to transfer the land, to transfer the property – in order to effect the change in legal position that is wrought by the legal power.

The double rejection of Hart's position – that choice characterises legal power, and that power characterises legal rights – has profound significance for the investigation of legal rights. By preferring decision to choice as the key characteristic of power, we remove an essential identification of the position of the power holder with his own choices, and permit the possibility of the decision of the power holder being exercised in accordance with social responsibilities, or even social obligations to further the interests of others – without losing that crucial concern of legal powers to facilitate social arrangements that Hart has been preeminent in bringing to our attention.[96] And by relegating such powers that may accompany legal rights in order to facilitate their exercise, to a role that is ancillary to the role of the right in protecting interests, we are more likely to focus on the primary issue of which interests the law might be called upon to promote. To employ a metaphor that Hart himself provides, we have deposed the right holder as sovereign,[97] but have perhaps thereby instated the right with far greater importance.

---

[95] Assuming that the other contracting party has registered his interest.

[96] *The Concept of Law* (Oxford, Clarendon Press, 1961) – see in particular 27, 32.

[97] EonB, 183–4. The dangers of this sort of metaphor are explored in detail in ch VII below, which considers Unger's use of similar metaphors to depict the traditional doctrine of rights in legal theory.

IV
Rights and Claims

1 INTRODUCTION

Although the idea of a claim features prominently in Hohfeld's analysis of rights, Hohfeld himself devoted little attention to it. The idea of a claim and its relationship to rights occupies a strategic significance within the literature. A prominent contribution to the debate over this relationship has been the discussion between Alan White and Neil MacCormick.[1] This discussion yields issues of wider importance for the theory of rights and the general methodology of analytical jurisprudence.[2] The key positions held by White in this discussion are maintaining that there is but one kind of right, and that a right to something does not imply (nor is implied by) a claim to that thing.[3] I hope within this chapter not simply to dislodge White from these positions by clarifying the relationship between rights and claims, but also in doing this to contribute some broader insights to our understanding of rights.

2 THE ANALYSIS OF CLAIMS

(1) White's Idea of a Claim

White in his analysis of claims seeks to rebut the common view that there is "a necessary connection between rights and claims."[4] This is part of White's wider thesis that the idea of a right cannot be reduced to or be made equivalent to any other normative concept (ought, obligation, duty, liberty, privi-

---

[1] Alan White, "Rights and Claims" (1982) 1 *Law and Philosophy* 315 (hereinafter, White 1982a); Neil MacCormick, "Rights, Claims and Remedies" (1982) 1 *Law and Philosophy* 337 (hereinafter, MacCormick 1982); White, "Reply to Professor MacCormick" (1982) 1 *Law and Philosophy* 359 (hereinafter, White 1982b); see also, Samuel Stoljar, "White on Rights and Claims" (1985) 4 *Law and Philosophy* 417. In addition, White's wider discussion of rights may be found in his book, *Rights* (Oxford, Clarendon Press, 1984) – hereinafter, White 1984 – and I follow the author's preference ("Do Claims Imply Rights?" (1986) 5 *Law and Philosophy* 417 (hereinafter, White 1986) at n1) in citing from that work rather than White 1982a, but do cite from White 1982b since the latter is not fully reproduced in the book. There is also an earlier article of White's which contains an argument that is central to the ideas that White advances in the above publications: "Meaning and Implication" (1971) 32 *Analysis* 26 (hereinafter, White 1971). For bibliographical material on the wider discussion of rights and claims, see White 1984: 115 nn1–5.

[2] A point recognised by MacCormick, 1982: 356.

[3] 1982b: 362–3; 1986: 417.

[4] 1984: 115.

lege, power, claim).[5] White's preferred technique is that of ordinary language philosophy: an examination of the ways in which the ideas are used.[6] His main argument accordingly proceeds along the lines: these are the ways in which we use the idea of a right – these are the ways in which we use the idea of a claim, which are distinct from and not necessarily connected to the ways in which we use the idea of a right – therefore, the idea of a right neither implies nor is implied by the idea of a claim and is accordingly not equivalent to it. The presentation of this argument is made more straightforward by White insisting that there is only one idea of a right, and one idea of a claim. For once we allow that either word, "right" or "claim", may be used to convey a plurality of ideas, we generate a number of permutations of equivalence: $right_1$ and $claim_1$, $right_2$ and $claim_1$ . . . $right_1$ and $claim_2$ . . . . And each possible equivalence must be shown to be false before the argument can be accepted. Moreover, given White's preferred technique, a further difficulty arises to complicate the argument, if we do allow a plurality of ideas. For before any equivalence can be tested, it is necessary to show which of the ordinary ways in which the word ("right", "claim") is used relates to which of the ideas ($right_1$, $right_2$ . . . $claim_1$, $claim_2$ . . .) that the word may be used to convey. Although White acknowledges "the diverse ways in which the notion of a claim is ordinarily used",[7] he argues that this diversity can be accommodated within a single idea of claim; ie it does not require more than one sense or meaning for "claim":[8]

> "This idea takes three different forms, which are, however, not due to, nor do they imply, different senses of the word 'claim', but syntactically different constructions which explain different implications and different characteristics."

White gives as the "basic idea" of a claim, "a call (Latin *clamare*) for the acceptability of something admittedly contestable",[9] which is then elucidated in its three forms, or syntactical constructions: the indicative use, a call for the acceptability of what is presented as being the case;[10] the subjunctive use, a call for the acceptability of what is presented as ought to be the case;[11] and, the possessive use, where "the [indicative or subjunctive] claim is, prima facie at least, either true or justified."[12]

White's interesting and illuminating distinctions between indicative, subjunctive and possessive uses of "claim" have not been directly challenged. MacCormick's argument that there is a fourth use to be found in the imperative[13] has met with a vigorous counterargument from White finding the

[5] 1984: 11, 173.
[6] 1984: 10–1, 115.
[7] 1984: 115.
[8] 1984: 116.
[9] 1984: 115.
[10] 1984: 116.
[11] 1984: 117.
[12] 1984: 121.
[13] 1982: 350–4.

imperative form to be merely an expression in direct speech of the subjunctive use of claim.[14] Even if White's triple syntactical distinction is regarded as helpful and unassailable, he is still vulnerable to attack regarding his point that there is only one meaning for "claim" itself.

In fact, White does not explicitly state that "claim" does possess only one meaning, but we may conjecture this to be his position from two points already noted: White's insistence upon a single meaning of "claim" within the three syntactical constructions, and the fact that he argues against the additional use of "claim" proposed by MacCormick. (If, on the other hand, White considers there to be a further, as yet undebated, meaning of "claim" – i.e. another idea of claim which the word is used to convey, then there exists a permutation of equivalence between right and claim against which White's argument has not been tested.)

However, it is difficult to find any substantial argument to support the contention that "claim" does possess only one meaning. The etymological link with the Latin *clamare* hardly suffices to ground a singular meaning for the word: the Latin *clamor* conveys a loud call or shout, with meanings ranging from applause to outcry. Indeed, *The Oxford English Dictionary* informs us that the English "claim" at the time of Spenser could be used to mean a call or shout. And even if the argument for a single meaning of "claim" were to be restricted to contemporary usage, it would be an argument that defied the learning of the lexicographers.[15]

Indeed such evidence as we do find in White's discussion of the three syntactical constructions tends to jeopardise his contention that there is only one meaning for "claim". For White himself observes a significant difference between the indicative and subjunctive uses of claim on the one hand and the possessive use on the other hand:[16]

> "The peculiarity is that, though indicative claims can be true or false, and subjunctive claims can be either justified or unjustified, the phrase 'to have a claim' . . . seems to imply that the claim is, prima facie at least, either true or justified. Though someone can *make* a false or unjustified claim, he cannot be said to *have* a false or unjustified claim."

And given that "a true/justified claim" conveys a very different idea to "a false/unjustified claim" (or even "a claim that may or may not be true/justified"), the possessive syntactical construction clearly conveys a different idea, which may be at variance with the idea conveyed by the indicative/subjunctive syntactical construction, and cannot be said to be merely explaining a different "implication" or "characteristic" of the same idea.

---

[14] 1982b: 360–2; 1984: 119–20.

[15] Even if found in a dictionary more concerned to provide accessible guidance on ordinary colloquial rather than obscure usage: *The Oxford Paperback Dictionary* (Oxford, OUP, 1979), provides three meanings for claim – a demand as right; the right to something; an assertion. What follows will not attempt to challenge this. (See subsequently n65 below.)

[16] 1984: 121.

A possible response here is one that is not made by White in relation to claims but is made by him in answer to MacCormick's allegation that White is failing to recognise a number of different kinds of rights.[17] Since the argument that White mounts in relation to rights could be mounted in relation to claims, and since moreover one may suspect that this argument unarticulated undergirds White's rather compressed assertion that the three syntactical constructions do not disclose more than one meaning for "claim",[18] it seems appropriate to consider this argument now.

The argument was originally put forward in a paper by White that was not concerned with rights and claims but sought to demonstrate what White perceived to be a common fallacy that dogged attempts in a variety of contexts to establish a distinction between different senses of a particular word.[19] The principle whose fallaciousness is usually "glaringly obvious" is as follows: "'If pr implies q, while ps does not imply q, then the sense of 'p' in the former is different from its sense in the latter.'"[20] Quite simply, you cannot argue that you have found two meanings for a word from the fact that the use of the word in one context or syntactical construction[21] produces different results from its use in another. The crudest illustration of this, which White himself uses,[22] is that otherwise we should have to find a different sense for a word whenever we used it with a negative. Clearly, the difference between having "some money" and having "no money" is not attributable to two different senses of "money" but to the presence or absence of the negative.

Applied to "claim" and the three syntactical constructions, the argument may then be mounted that although it is conceded that different results follow from the use of "claim" in one syntactical construction rather than another (eg the difference conceded by White for the possessive use, that we have noted), that is not to say that we have different senses of "claim". The difference is attributable not to different meanings of "claim" (ie different ideas of claim) but to different syntactical constructions.[23]

If we represent the argument by symbolic expression, as is used to represent the fallacious principle, and employ c to represent a claim, s_1 and s_2 to represent different syntactical constructions, then it may be argued: It is *false* to assert the following – "If cs_1 implies q, while cs_2 does not imply q, then the sense of 'c' in the former is different from its sense in the latter."

This argument is irrefutable. But it is also possible for the argument to be immaterial, in two particular cases. The first case is where the object of enquiry is not the constant primary idea c, but the compounds in which it is

[17] See text at n67 below.
[18] n8 above.
[19] White 1971.
[20] 1971: 26.
[21] The significance of the variation in syntactical construction is noted in White's original paper – 1971: 30.
[22] 1971: 26.
[23] As argued in 1971: 30, in relation to "belief-in".

found – cs_1 and cs_2. Obviously, cs_1 does differ from cs_2. The second case is where c is not a constant, where the same word is used with a different meaning in each of the two different contexts, ie where to be more accurate we should speak of c_1s_1 and c_2s_2.

The first case is almost noted in passing by White when he states in relation to his fallacious principle, "the statement expressed by the whole 'pr' is different from the statement expressed by the whole 'ps'",[24] but is ultimately neglected due to his treating 'pr'/'ps' as a statement rather than an idea. White's reference to statement sustains the view that we are interested in p in different contexts (or statements) where the variables are represented by r and s, but his illustrations cover the possibility of an interest in pr and ps themselves as compound ideas formed by taking p with some qualifier r or s: eg the distinction between "(causally) responsible" and "(legally) responsible".[25]

Once we do recognise that we are dealing with a case where pr and ps, or cs_1 and cs_2, represent compound ideas, then it is evident that there is a distinction between these compound ideas and also that it is immaterial to this distinction that there may be a constant element which has been used in the construction of each compound idea.

The point may be simply made by considering the variation in meaning produced by a mere change of epithet. A dog is a dog, but "a bad dog" is different from "a good dog". A car is a car, but "a new car" is different from "a scrapped car". A friend is a friend, but "a disloyal friend" is different from "a faithful friend". Now if we accept, which we must, that different syntactical constructions are employed to convey different meanings (eg the different meanings of: "She has loved him all the time", and "She had loved him all the time"), then the same point that applies to a change of epithet also applies to a change of syntax. The change in syntactical construction may produce a different compound idea with a new meaning.

I am not ignoring the fact that a change in syntactical construction will not necessarily involve a change in meaning; ie two different syntactical forms may express the same meaning (eg "He can run fast", and "He is a fast runner"). This may equally be true for a change in epithet (eg "a faithful friend", and "a loyal friend"). In either case the meaning will be constant for the same reason, because the epithets or syntactical constructions are synonymous. The point still holds: the meaning of the phrase in which the primary idea (friend, car, dog, love, fast) is found is a product of the meaning of that primary idea in conjunction with the meaning(s) of any other factor(s) present in the phrase.

Accordingly, the uncontroversial truism concerning the constancy of the primary idea is irrelevant to the task of distinguishing the meaning of different phrases (here, different syntactical constructions) in which the primary idea is found. And, contrary to what White asserts, the different syntactical

[24] 1971: 30.
[25] 1971: 28.

constructions do not "explain different implications and different characteristics" of the one idea,[26] but convey different (compound) ideas. "A good dog" conveys a different idea from "a bad dog", and not just a different characteristic of dog.

At the very least then, we have within White's syntactical constructions different compound ideas relating to the constant primary, or "basic",[27] idea of claim. This in itself is sufficient to require some qualification upon White's thesis that a right is not equivalent to a claim, indicating that the thesis excludes any compound idea of claim; or else, to require the further work necessitated to maintain the thesis through the additional permutations of equivalence generated by the compound ideas of claim.

In fact, it can be established that the divergence goes deeper: that we are not dealing merely with different compound ideas whose expression involves the word "claim", but with a word "claim" that itself possesses different meanings, conveys different ideas. In order to help us to see this, we should first consider generally the second case where White's irrefutable argument concerning the fallacy in inferring different meanings from different implications is immaterial.[28]

This second case is where "c" does possess two meanings, where we do not have a constant c within the two syntactical constructions, ie we actually have c_1s_1 and c_2s_2. White himself admits that in some cases a word does possess two meanings and that it is this difference in meaning that accounts for the different implications that follow from the use of the word in different contexts.[29] But if this is the case, it follows that alongside the fallacy that White has detected[30] we could place an equally fallacious converse: If pr implies q, while ps does not imply q, then the sense of "p" in the former is not different from its sense in the latter. For from the bald fact that pr implies something different from ps we cannot tell whether the difference is due to a difference between r and s alone, or to a variation in p between the two cases, or to a combination of the two; and it is fallacious to state that any one of these possibilities is necessarily so (though any one *may* be so).

In other words, until we have isolated p as a constant, it is insignificant to invoke the argument that the assumption that "p" varies in meaning is fallacious, for we could equally invoke the argument that the assumption that "p" does not differ in meaning is fallacious. It gets us nowhere in determining whether "p" does or does not differ in meaning. And if in fact we can demonstrate that p is not constant, that "p" does have different meanings, then it becomes immaterial to cite the argument, for although it remains technically

---

[26] n8 above.

[27] at n9 above.

[28] See text at n26 above.

[29] 1971: 30 – in his concluding paragraph.

[30] See text at n15 above – applied to claims within different syntactical constructions, see text at n26 above.

correct it warns against reaching a conclusion by invalid means when we have already reached that conclusion by other proper means.

The only significant use of this argument is when we have demonstrated that "p" does have only one meaning in order to counter the false conclusion that "p" has different meanings. And the very invocation of the argument as significant thus begs the question that "p" does possess only one meaning – if this has not already been demonstrated.

Returning to our particular interest in claims, it follows that the invocation of this argument cannot be significant (and could even be question begging if presented as significant), *until* we have established whether or not we have more than one meaning for "claim" in the different contexts that we are examining. For until then we could match this argument with the converse: It is *false* to assert the following – "If cs_1 implies q, while cs_2 does not imply q, then the sense of 'c' in the former is *not* different from its sense in the latter.

The preliminary need to establish that we do have a single meaning for "claim" is not satisfied in White's discussion. On the contrary, both White's initial analysis of claims and his subsequent stand in the debate with MacCormick provide evidence of more than one meaning for the word.

MacCormick, in discussing White's three different syntactical constructions does not treat these as phrases which in some way involve "claim" but describes them as "claims" – ie whatever idea (compound or primary) is conveyed by each of these constructions is an idea that the word "claim" may itself convey. Furthermore, MacCormick provides some synonyms for three claims he himself wishes to elucidate: demand, allegation, contention.[31] Let us for the moment ignore the differences in taxonomy between MacCormick and White in referring to the different syntactical constructions, the fundamental point to be made is that the word "claim" inasmuch as it is being used to stand for different syntactical constructions which have different meanings is itself being used with different meanings – a point that is clearly underlined when we note the different synonyms that are used for the different senses of the word: an allegation means something quite different to a demand, and may also be distinguished from a contention.[32]

White, in his thorough reply to MacCormick,[33] does not object to either of these features of MacCormick's discussion which manifest the difference in

---

[31] 1982: 350. The synonyms are expressed in the original in forms apposite for claiming rather than claim but this is immaterial.

[32] In general a contention conveys more substance than an allegation, the former bearing the connotation of having reasoned argument or evidence to support it, whereas the latter may be mere assertion with nothing to back it up. MacCormick at one point puts forward a distinction on the basis of general ground/particular facts (1982: 350-1), but since both are being represented as *existing* it is difficult to see how this can be simply related to the distinction between subjunctive and indicative uses which MacCormick is employing (see further the analysis of the bases of subjunctive claims, in sections 2(2) and 4 below, and in particular the discussion in n58). Nevertheless, MacCormick is clearly using the two synonyms to render different meanings of claim.

[33] 1982b, partially reproduced in 1984.

meaning for "claim". Indeed the former feature, referring to the syntactical constructions themselves as claims, is evident in White's own discussion both prior and subsequent to MacCormick's contribution,[34] though it is perhaps less prominent in the earlier work where the *different claims* (indicative, subjunctive, possessive[35]) are introduced by subtitles indicating *different uses of claim*. Moreover, in his reply to MacCormick, White goes some way to endorsing one of MacCormick's synonyms, demand, as suitable for an imperative/subjunctive claim.[36]

We conclude then that in the range of examples found in White's analysis of claims we are not dealing with "different implications" or "different characteristics" of one idea; nor are we dealing with different "uses" of one idea; we are not merely dealing with different (compound) ideas produced by placing one primary idea in different contexts (different syntactical constructions); we are dealing with a word which possesses a number of meanings – which is used to convey different ideas.

(2) The Validity and Strength of Claims

What then are these different ideas, and how, if at all, do they relate to each other? It is worth going back to the different syntactical constructions of White's analysis, and returning to the precise point at which the divergence of meaning was detected. This, it will be recalled, was where White observes the difference between the indicative/subjunctive use and the possessive use. In fact, White does not treat these as three uses in the same way. The possessive use "is not a kind of claim, or a kind of claiming, additional to the indicative and subjunctive."[37] And further down the same page, White indicates that the indicative/subjunctive distinction works alongside the possessive/non-possessive distinction so that an indicative claim may be a claim that we could or could not describe a person as having depending upon whether it is true or false, and a subjunctive claim may be a claim that we could or could not describe a person as having depending upon whether it is justified or unjustified.[38] We may then regard each of White's distinctions as fixing a

---

[34] For example, White 1982a reproduced in 1984: 117 – "A subjunctive claim . . . Such a claim . . ."

[35] White does not actually speak of a possessive claim (1984: 121–4) though MacCormick does (1982: 350). A possible explanation for White's reticence is provided below (n38).

[36] 1982b: 362, 1984: 120.

[37] 1984: 121.

[38] I ignore for the moment the prima facie qualification upon true/justified (quoted at nn12 & 16 above) as not impinging upon the relationship between White's two distinctions. I shall, however, consider its significance below (at n45).

Apart from the first two paragraphs of 1984: 121, further indications of the nature of White's scheme are provided by his labelling of MacCormick's imperative use not as a fourth but "a third type of claim" (1982b: 360, 1984: 119) and perhaps by his reticence to talk of a possessive claim (n35 above).

separate coordinate of a claim, and present the four types of claim that emerge from White's analysis in the following table.

	possessive:	non-possessive:
indicative:	true claim	false claim
subjunctive:	justified claim	unjustified claim

This representation of White's analysis permits some sense to be made of what otherwise appear as oddities in the exchange between MacCormick and White.

Whereas White talks of the three types of claims based upon the three syntactical constructions – indicative, subjunctive, possessive; MacCormick responds with a discussion of the trio – indicative (alleging), subjunctive (contending), imperative (demanding). But MacCormick discusses his trio without disputing "Professor White's ingenious elucidation of 'indicative', 'subjunctive' and 'possessive' claims."[39] Why then is there no reference to possessive claims in MacCormick's discussion? White, as we have noted, counters by regarding MacCormick's imperative claim as merely an expression of his subjunctive claim.[40] One of the arguments used by White is that MacCormick's imperative, like his own subjunctive, is a demand.[41] But White does not address MacCormick's identification of his (White's) subjunctive as a contention which MacCormick sees as distinct from a demand, nor does he note MacCormick's refinement of this "species of demand":[42] "presuppos[ing] legitimate entitlements",[43] which leads to MacCormick talking about "a justified claim".[44] Surely this should locate MacCormick's imperative with White's possessive claim (which we have observed is singularly absent from MacCormick's discussion)?

The apparent confusion in terminology can be resolved by reference to the table above, if we regard MacCormick as distinguishing his imperative from White's non-possessive subjunctive, and White as treating MacCormick's imperative as though it were a non-possessive subjunctive; whereas MacCormick's imperative should be regarded as being (or expressing) White's possessive subjunctive: a justified claim.

Although this may help us to clarify the dialogue between MacCormick and White, the tabular representation of the four types of claims cannot be regarded as furnishing a completely satisfactory analysis of claims. For there is some hesitation to be found in both authors when talking about justified claims. White, we have seen, qualifies his justified claim with the introductory

---

[39] 1982: 350.
[40] n14 above. White does concede (1984: 120) that the existence of imperative claims in direct speech does increase the variety of the vocabulary of claims.
[41] n36 above.
[42] White 1984: 120, quoting MacCormick 1982: 351.
[43] MacCormick 1982: 351.
[44] 1982: 353.

"prima facie at least",[45] and MacCormick talks about those claims "which purport to be founded on some entitlement".[46]

The basic problem, that is manifested in this hesitation, is that whether we are talking about indicative claims or subjunctive claims, to pronounce upon the validity (to use a term to encompass both the truth of what is claimed indicatively and the justification of what is claimed subjunctively) of a claim is something which will depend upon the extent of knowledge available to the person making the pronouncement,[47] and given that our knowledge may be restricted our ability to pronounce upon the validity of a claim may equally be so.

This aspect of claims cannot be accommodated within the above tabular representation of the four types of claims. Nevertheless, the aspect is present in White and MacCormick's deliberations: not only in the hesitation just noted, but also in the recognition that what is claimed may range from what is validly claimed to what is completely bogus.[48] It is not enough to say that bogus (or mistaken) claims can be fitted into the above table as false or unjustified claims, for this final conclusion as to the (in)validity of the claim cannot be made without the necessary evidence – which, clearly, is absent for the person suffering from the mistake and is intended to be absent for the person made the victim of the bogus claim. Even in the case of claims that are ultimately found to be valid, we may not have sufficient knowledge to make this pronouncement at the time the claim is initially made. Similarly, even a person making a claim in good faith may be ignorant of the fact that his claim is ultimately invalid.

This aspect of claims may be brought into the analysis by recognising different strengths of a claim, in terms of the extent to which the claim is perceived to be valid. White refers to strength as a characteristic of indicative claims, but ignores it for subjunctive claims.[49] For the moment let us put aside the distinction between indicative and subjunctive claims, and focus generally upon the strength of a claim – though subsequently we shall need to consider the relevance of this characteristic of claims to the distinction between indicative and subjunctive claims.

A claim may be made without any evidence to support it. It is impossible for a person without access to any evidence to say whether the claim is valid or invalid. In another case, a claim may be supported by some evidence, such

[45] 1984: 121, at nn12 & 16 above; cp Joel Feinberg, *Rights, Justice and the Bounds of Liberty* (Princeton, NJ, Princeton University Press, 1980) at 152 insisting on speaking not merely of having a claim but of having a *valid* claim.

[46] 1982: 352, emphasis added.

[47] Who may be the person making the claim or his audience.

[48] For example, the fraudulent claim of a reward (MacCormick 1982: 351); cp White's more abstract discussion (1984: 11/–8).

[49] 1984: 117 & 117–8. White does specifically deny that some characteristics of indicative claims apply to subjunctive claims but says nothing here about the strength of subjunctive claims. This is a characteristic of claims (without differentiation) recognised by Feinberg, above n45 at 152).

as to indicate that it at least merits attention being paid to it, though ultimately it may turn out to be invalid. In a third case, a claim may be supported by substantial evidence which indicates that it is prima facie valid, though ultimately it may still turn out to be invalid. Finally, a claim may be established from a consideration of all the evidence as valid. These four examples which have been taken to illustrate the variation in the strength of a claim may be depicted as ranging from the weakest, a claim that is merely vocalised, to the strongest, a claim that is established. As the strength increases, the probability of the claim being invalid diminishes, until the point of the established valid claim is reached. It should be noted that any of the weaker claims may turn out to be stronger (once further evidence is adduced). The range of strengths is then a measure of the validity of a claim as we perceive it to be, but it may also be a measure of the extent of our perception of the validity of a claim (where further evidence to which we do not have access is in fact available to increase the strength of the claim). The four strengths selected may be presented as follows, in a cumulative ascending order:

(1) vocalised claim: may be valid or invalid
(2) supported by
        some evidence: possibly valid
(3) supported by
        substantial evidence: prima facie valid
(4) established by
        all the evidence: known to be valid[50]

The particular point a claim occupies within this range of strengths may vary with the person perceiving it. For example, a speaker without the knowledge of all the circumstances may make a claim that he perceives to be only prima facie valid, whereas his audience who has access to all the relevant information may perceive it to be valid. Also variation in the strength of a claim may occur over a period of time, as the perception of the claim varies with the accumulation of more information about it. A notable example of this arises in the period between the making of a statement of claim by the plaintiff and its being upheld by the court.[51]

It is illuminating to consider the extremes of this range of strengths. Strength 1, it may be noted, is not an invalid claim, but a claim that may be valid or invalid, for it would be nonsensical to make a claim supported by evi-

---

[50] This may well be a contingent validity, depending either upon some limit set on what amounts to "all the evidence", or upon some artificial constraint on what will be counted as such. As an example of the latter, take the legal constraint imposed by accepting only the evidence that has been presented in court. Formal and informal examples of the former abound, as a matter of bureaucratic necessity or personal convenience.

[51] MacCormick's (1982: 352–3) characterisation of a statement of claim as an imperative claim is too simplistic in failing to account for its change in status as the trial progresses to judgment. At 353 he refers to it as "a justified claim", which is how *the plaintiff* represents it, even if he does not regard it so – consider a tactical action where a plaintiff expects to lose the case.

dence which indicated it to be invalid.[52] That is not to say that the perception of this cannot vary amongst persons. In the case of a bogus claim, the speaker knows it is invalid but is relying on his audience to be ignorant of the relevant information so as to treat his claim as having at least strength 1. Conversely, in the case of a mistaken claim, the speaker will perceive his claim as having at least strength 1, whereas an enlightened audience will know it to be invalid.

At the other extreme, strength 4 is a valid claim, and it is here that a significant difference occurs between indicative and subjunctive claims. Once an indicative claim reaches strength 4 it is no longer a claim. For example, John claims to have climbed Everest. You may regard this as a claim with strength somewhere between 1 and 3. Perhaps John brings forward some evidence of his exploit: a detailed account of his adventure with photographs – you advance to strength 3. Finally, reliable witnesses emerge, a television news reel – you reach strength 4: you regard his claim as valid. But you would no longer say that John claims to have climbed Everest; you would now say that it is a fact that John climbed Everest. The epithet valid actually refers to the claim that John *had* made (before you knew it was valid). Any statement that John makes after you are convinced of his exploit is not a claim but a statement of fact in your eyes.[53] Of course, John may advance his statement as a claim, being unsure of its reception; but once he were sure that his statement had been accepted as fact, nor would he describe it any longer as a claim. To talk of an indicative claim as valid (as true, substantiated, etc) necessarily posits a period of time between the advancing of the claim and its acceptance; and the conclusion reached at the end of that period (this claim is valid: true, substantiated, etc) marks out the status of the claim advanced at the beginning of that period, but also marks the end of the possibility of advancing (amongst the parties involved) the claim *qua* claim (though what was claimed may continue to be discussed among them as *accepted fact*).

The analysis of an indicative claim may accordingly be portrayed as extending from the point that known falsehood is left behind to the point where accepted fact is approached. But given the variation in perspectives of person that has been stressed, the analysis does not present itself as a simple linear gathering of strength until the point that accepted fact is reached. It is only when (i) the speaker himself knows and (ii) he is also aware that his audience knows that he is dealing in falsehood that we cannot commence our analysis of claims. Fraudulent claims become possible as soon as the second requirement is unsatisfied. At the other boundary, it is only when (i) the speaker

---

[52] Cp Feinberg above n45 at 152 – the highwayman has to *demand* his victim's money rather than *claim* it.

[53] Of course some people are convinced more easily than others of the fact. It is possible to come across a person who believes that to say man has reached the moon is a fantastic claim – most of us accept it as fact. Although the application of the distinction to a particular statement varies with the credulity/suspicion of the individual audience, the distinction still holds: what an individual regards as a claim is not regarded as a fact, and vice versa.

himself accepts and (ii) he is also aware that his audience has accepted that he is dealing in truth that our analysis of claims is superseded by accepted fact. In between these fixed boundaries our analysis of claims must deal with the nuances produced by the possible variation in perception between speaker and audience, and by the awareness or lack of awareness in the speaker of his audience's perception.

In contrast to indicative claims, when a subjunctive claim reaches strength 4, ie is regarded as valid, it is still described as a claim. For example, suppose that John's rich Uncle Edward had promised him £5,000 if he succeeded in climbing Everest. Uncle Edward is convinced by all the evidence that it is a fact that John has climbed Everest, and John knows this. Although neither of them would now talk about John claiming (indicatively) to have climbed Everest, they may still sensibly talk of John claiming (subjunctively) the £5,000. "So, you have come to claim your prize – well done!", Uncle Edward greets him. There is no doubt in either of their minds that the claim is valid, but the claim is still made. However, that is not to say that subjunctive claims never reach their termination. This obviously happens once the claim is complied with. Once Uncle Edward has paid John the £5,000, neither would say that John has a valid claim to the money; though they might report that John had had a valid claim. Whereas the indicative claim is terminated[54] at the moment the thing claimed is accepted as true, the subjunctive claim is terminated at the moment the thing claimed is done. Bearing in mind, as White suggests we should, the etymology of claim,[55] we might suggest as the central meaning[56] of "claim", a call for the acceptance of something that has not yet been accepted[57] – in the case of an indicative claim, something that has not yet been accepted as true; in the case of a subjunctive claim, something that has not yet been accepted to be done. In either case, there is no sense in clamouring for something that you have: the claim will not arise if you already have it; the claim will terminate once you have it (the statement accepted as true, the thing done).

Although "claim" may be used both indicatively and subjunctively in its central meaning, we must not ignore the significant distinction that we have noted between indicative claims and subjunctive claims at the extreme of strength 4 – at the point of validity. For this distinction points to a greater complexity for subjunctive claims, and also reveals the possibility of a relationship between the two.

---

[54] I use terminated here as of trains, meaning to complete its course. Claims may otherwise perish when found to be invalid.

[55] 1984: 115; see at n9 above.

[56] But not the only meaning: other meanings will be considered below.

[57] In this I follow but then diverge from White's "call . . . for the acceptability of something admittedly contestable" (1984: 115). There may be nothing contestable about what is claimed, never mind "admittedly contestable". It may be merely that the audience has yet to give the claim his consideration – he has not accepted it not because he wishes to dispute it but because he wishes to evaluate it (once evaluated the evidence may point ineluctably to the acceptance of the claim); or because the formal opportunity to accept the claim has not yet arisen.

It will be recalled that a subjunctive claim may reach strength 4, be found valid, and yet (unlike an indicative claim) not be terminated. This will occur where it is accepted that the claim that something ought to be done is valid in the sense that the audience accepts that the thing ought to be done, but nevertheless the thing as yet remains undone. We might then ask what it is that gives a subjunctive claim its validity short of actually doing the thing. The basis may be twofold: it may be accepted that there is a certain justification for requiring the thing to be done, and secondly, that the claim as made factually falls within that justification.[58] For convenience, I shall label these the justificatory basis and the factual basis. Consider as an example a young man upbraiding one of the palace guard for failing to bow to him. The young man declares to the guard that he is a prince, and so the guard ought to bow to him. The guard as yet remains unbowed.

We may describe the young man's remonstration with the guard as follows: He claimed to be a prince, and that the guard ought to bow to him. Now before the guard is going to accept this claim as valid, he will want to be satisfied of two things: (1) that it is the proper thing to bow to princes, (2) that this young man is a prince. The former is the justificatory basis, the latter the factual basis, for the guard accepting the young man's claim that he ought to bow to him as valid. Note that the guard may be dissatisfied with the claim on either basis. Perhaps, being a good royalist, he accepts the justificatory basis in (1), but is utterly unconvinced by the young man's demeanour that he is in fact a prince. On the other hand, the guard may accept the factual basis in (2), but being a staunch republican find no justification for bowing to princes. In either case, the guard will not find the young man's claim valid.

A similar analysis may be made of our earlier example. Uncle Edward accepts John's claim as valid on the basis that: (1) it is the proper thing to give John the promised £5,000 if he has satisfied the condition of climbing Everest, (2) that John has climbed Everest.

Usually the justificatory basis will be taken for granted between the parties. There would be little point in the young prince entering a republican stronghold and making his claim. Equally there would be little point in John

---

[58] It is sufficient for present purposes to demonstrate that in *some* cases this dual basis may be made out. In some circumstances the justificatory basis may be taken for granted (see text at n59 below), and in other circumstances the factual basis may be taken for granted or even be redundant (see text at n88 below).

This dual basis may be compared with MacCormick's discussion of the conditions required for a justified imperative claim (1982: 350–1 – above n32). Apart from his preferred focus upon the imperative mood, I depart from MacCormick's approach in disagreeing with his characterisation of the justificatory basis ("general ground") as itself a subjunctive claim ("contending"). Although the justificatory basis may itself be claimed subjunctively (see n59 below), it is not necessary (nor, I would argue, usual) for this to be the case. Moreover, in MacCormick's particular example it will not be the case unless the creditor has foolishly lent money to a debtor who does not accept the propriety of repaying loans (see also the example of John and Uncle Edward, see text at n59 below).

making his claim if he knew that his Uncle Edward reneged upon his promises with notorious consistency or regarded every undertaking he made as a flippant quip.[59] In practice then, the factual basis is likely to be paramount, and the strength of the subjunctive claim will depend upon the extent to which this factual basis is accepted by the other party. Where the factual basis has not been accepted by the other party,[60] then the party advancing the subjunctive claim will be put in the position of having to claim the factual basis as true as a necessary part of advancing his subjunctive claim. In short, an indicative claim will be bound up with, and will determine the strength of the subjunctive claim.[61]

In those cases where the justificatory basis for a subjunctive claim is accepted by the parties, and the strength of the claim is determined by the strength of the factual basis, we may indicate the range of strengths of that subjunctive claim and its relationship to any relevant indicative claim there might be as follows:

	strength of subjunctive claim:	*factual basis:*
(1)	may be valid or invalid	indicative claim strength 1
(2)	possibly valid	indicative claim strength 2
(3)	prima facie valid	indicative claim strength 3
(4)	valid	accepted fact

The exposition of indicative and subjunctive claims up to this point has suggested a number of things. First, the strength of a claim has been regarded as an essential feature to recognise in order to determine the status of a claim. Secondly, the status of a claim has been observed to vary as between persons, and also over time. Thirdly, the distinction between indicative and subjunctive claims has been explored to reveal that subjunctive claims are more complex, and also that they may be related to indicative claims which form their factual basis. But so far nothing has been said to suggest that the central meaning of

---

[59] I avoid making the argument unnecessarily cumbersome here through considering in the main text the more complex case where A claims the justificatory basis for his ulterior subjunctive claim (eg the young prince attempts to inculcate the staunch republicans with the values of royalism as a prelude to claiming a bow from them). In such a case, however, the analysis advanced so far may be employed by regarding the claim that the royalist cause is of value either as an indicative claim (which will be accepted as fact or not), or as a further subjunctive claim that the republicans ought to adopt the royalist cause which is itself to be analysed as having some basis . . . and so on. No matter how tiresome and prolonged the debate becomes, it will only be ultimately resolved by the other side accepting something as *fact* – even if it is the fact that he accepts a particular value for which he can provide no justification. (See further, text at n88 below.)

[60] Note that even where there is every confidence that it will be accepted there may nevertheless be a requirement that the acceptance be made formally – as with the case of an out of court settlement laid before the court.

[61] MacCormick (1982: 350–1) recognises the possibility of such a connection, but is at pains to divide the two, regarding (in my terms – MacCormick employs different terms which are linked to his argument for recognising imperative claims) the indicative claim as a "condition" of the subjunctive claim rather than as a part of it.

claim (a call for the acceptance of something that has not yet been accepted)[62] cannot accommodate the variety of status, perspective, and complexity, that has been noted. Where then are we to find the different meanings for the word claim, whose elucidation was the primary purpose of this discussion?

The answer to our quest lies not in denying the generality of the central meaning of claim, but rather in stressing it. For much like its Latin predecessor whose generality sufficed to cover the extremes of approval and disapproval, the very generality of the word is sufficiently vague to encompass what on a more precise level may be quite distinct.

(3) Two Kinds of Claims

Without wishing here to attempt a complete catalogue of meanings of the word claim, I do want to point to two meanings which are quite distinct and which are of fundamental importance to the wider discussion on rights and claims which is our present concern. Moreover, the latency of this distinction in White's own discussion lurks as a powerful counterargument to the theses which he advances. There is also a further distinction in usage which relates to MacCormick's concern with imperative claims that is important to mention.

The key distinction is to be found between a claim (indicative or subjunctive) of strength 1–3 and a claim (subjunctive) of strength 4. For the former, which may or may not be valid differs significantly from the latter which is valid. And if in particular we take the former to cover an indicative claim, or a subjunctive claim whose justificatory basis has been accepted and whose factual basis alone is at issue, then the former amounts to, or involves, an assertion of fact. And in any case amounts to nothing more than an assertion – of what is the case or of what ought to be done. Whereas the latter valid claim involves an acceptance of any relevant fact (factual basis), together with any justificatory basis for the claim, and amounts to a justified requirement that something be done. These two meanings to the word claim, **assertion** and **justified requirement**, are sufficient to rebut White's denial of a number of meanings for the word, and demonstrate that the word may be used to convey quite distinct ideas.

The further distinction in usage relates to the meaning of claim as justified requirement. For this claim (unlike the claim as assertion) may be spoken of either as being used by its holder to require the thing to be done of another party, or as describing the position of the holder who is capable of making the requirement: the claim may be made or it may be held. In the former usage we may find it in MacCormick's imperative claim as justified demand, in the latter as White's possessive subjunctive claim. However, the different usage is not merely a distinction between direct and indirect speech, as White

---

[62] at n57 above.

suggests,[63] for the holder could well state in direct speech, "I have a valid claim to Whiteacre", without making the claim upon the present occupier to hand over possession. Rather the different usage points to the feature of a valid claim as justified requirement in affording its holder[64] not only the possibility of **making a justified requirement** upon another but also **enjoyment of the advantage which that possibility brings** to him.[65]

This key distinction between claim as assertion and claim as justified requirement, and the accompanying distinction in usage between making a claim as justified requirement and holding a claim as justified requirement, are crucial to the investigation of the relationship between rights and claims. I shall argue that White's failure to admit this distinction is fatal to his argument that a right to something does not imply (nor is implied by) a claim to that thing, and moreover, ironically, that the very distinction is what sustains the credibility of White's argument.

3 DIFFERENT KINDS OF RIGHTS

Before proceeding to the investigation of the relationship between rights and claims, we need to pause briefly to consider White's view that there is only one kind of right.[66] Our assessment of this view can be conducted more sum-

---

[63] nn14 & 40 above.

[64] It should be apparent by now that indicative claims cannot be held in this sense, and indeed that White's characterisation of a valid indicative claim as possessive is inexact. We have already seen that the simple tabular representation of claims in terms of White's two coordinates is incomplete, and that White himself concedes that to have a claim does not necessarily mean that the claim is valid but may only indicate a prima facie case (at n45 above). The point to be made in relation to an indicative claim is that "having a claim" can *only* indicate a prima facie case. And the use of this expression to indicate for a factual assertion "that there is at least some substance in his claim even if it is not conclusive" (White 1984: 121) should not be confused with holding a *valid* claim (ie justified requirement).

[65] These two usages of claim as justified requirement may be seen in the first two of the dictionary meanings of claim noted in n8 above.

[66] n3 above. One kind of right is but one formulation that White employs. He speaks also of rejecting a plurality of notions, or senses, of right (1984: 19). I take notion as a synonym of idea, and sense as a synonym of meaning – as the latter terms were employed in the previous discussion of claims. Whereas a kind of right seems to me to be sufficiently loose to cover either different ideas of right of different meanings of "right", it might also convey an even looser basis of distinction: in the way that we can speak of Darjeeling being a different kind of tea to Assam without employing a different idea of tea or meaning of "tea" – effectively, drawing a distinction between different kinds of a thing on the basis of a characteristic which is not essential to the definition of that thing. Since I consider the denial of distinction as to kinds to be a weaker version of White's thesis (as I think does White – "or even different kinds of rights", 1984: 19), I shall be content to attack the stronger thesis in terms of notions (ideas) or senses (meanings). Certainly for Hohfeld, whom White explicitly denounces (1982b: 363), to talk of different kinds of rights was to talk of different ideas or meanings – see, Walter Wheeler Cook (ed.), *Fundamental Legal Conceptions as Applied in Judicial Reasoning* by Wesley Newcombe Hohfeld (New Haven, CT, Yale University Press, 1964) – hereinafter, FLC – at 38–40 & 65–6.

Stoljar, above n1 at 113 n21, observes that White does in one place allow for different kinds of rights, but this concession is excised in White's subsequent book – contrast White 1982a: 332 last paragraph with the corresponding paragraph in 1984: 64.

marily due to the reappearance here of certain points that were treated more laboriously when we considered White's assertion that there is only one meaning for claim.

The most concentrated expression of White's argument against different kinds of rights is to be found in a passage of his reply to MacCormick.[67] There are three strands intertwined in the argument here. Once unravelled, and examined in the light of the points emerging in our previous discussion of claims, they are insufficient to support White's contention that there is only one kind of right.

The first strand is what amounts to a question begging assumption that there is only one kind of right. White uses here explicitly the argument that I have suggested undergirds his treatment of claims.[68] He attacks MacCormick for falling into "the fallacy of supposing that because '*ab*' implies something different from that which '*ac*' implies, therefore the difference must be due to different kinds of *a* or even different senses of '*a*'."[69] I have demonstrated[70] that for this argument to be material, we must be assuming (or already have shown) that there is only one *a*, rather than different kinds of *a* which conjoin with *b*, *c*, etc. White assumes *ab*, *ac*, etc, whereas we might in fact have a_1b, a_2c, etc.

Even though all of the a_1, a_2, etc may be regarded in the one general sense to be *a*, we have seen that the existence of one general meaning for a word does not preclude the possibility of a number of more specific distinct meanings for that word.[71] It seems significant that elsewhere White contents himself with proposing a general sense of right.[72] Without decrying the value of establishing the general sense of a word,[73] and without denying the possibility of the general sense of a word being capable of covering all of the more specific meanings, it is nevertheless erroneous to take the general sense as excluding all other meanings.

The second strand is the assumption that we are dealing only with a primary idea rather than a compound idea, when examining the concept of a right.[74] So, White talks analogously of the concept of a penalty, rather than

---

[67] 1982b: 362–3; see also 1984: 11, 19 & 172, in particular; and for the original run of much of this argument see 1971.

[68] See text at n17 above.

[69] 1982b: 362.

[70] See text at nn23–32 above.

[71] See text at n62 above.

[72] "Whoever has a right has a title, something which entitles him, which gives him a sort of ticket of justification . . ." (1984: 174).

[73] White gives as his motivating force for denying different kinds of rights the belief that refuge is taken in the assertion of different kinds of rights in order to avoid "facing up to the difficulties of discovering an analysis of *right* which will account for these differences" (1982b: 363). A sharp contrast in approach is provided by Hohfeld (FLC, 36), who may be regarded as the obvious target of White's remark. But neither can the discovery of several particular meanings avoid the need to consider the possibility of a general meaning, nor can the discovery of a general meaning avoid the need to consider the possibility of different particular meanings.

[74] I employ the term "primary idea" and "compound idea" as used above, see text at nn23–30 above.

the concept of a legal penalty; or, of the idea of being in charge, rather than the idea of being in charge of Scotland.[75] But we have seen that the constancy of the primary idea is irrelevent to the task of ennumerating the variety of meanings that may occur in the compound ideas in which that primary idea plays a part.[76] And given that "right", like "claim",[77] is a word which may be used not just for the abstract or general idea but also in apposition to the particular instances where that idea is found expressed (ie in compound ideas), then the assertion that we have only one kind of right must be proven not simply in relation to any primary idea of right but also in relation to any compound idea of right.

The third strand is the denial that the different consequences or implications that follow from rights to different kinds of things are sufficient to demonstrate that we have different kinds of rights.[78] But as we have seen in relation to claims,[79] neither is the observation of different consequences sufficient to show that we do not have different kinds of rights. The detection of a difference in the consequences produced by placing two things in the same circumstances is one of the most basic techniques of analysis for establishing that the two things are different: a drop of acid placed upon a piece of litmus paper will produce a different consequence from a drop of an alkaline substance placed upon a piece of litmus paper, for example. But this is obviously quite different from the different consequences produced by placing the same thing in different circumstances: a burning torch placed in oxygen will produce a different consequence from a burning torch placed in water, for example. In either case the different consequence points to *some difference* in the factors present on the two occasions, the real question is where the difference was to be found and where (if at all) the constant. If White's denial of different kinds of rights is to be accepted, it must follow that every difference in consequence detected in examining two rights is due to the different circumstances in which those rights are found whilst the meaning of "right" itself remains constant. But if this is the case, then it must be possible to demonstrate that constancy. White does not attempt to do this, nor would he be successful if he tried to do so.[80]

---

[75] 1982b: 362. The persistence of White's assumption is demonstrated when he plays his analogy through to the conclusion – "This is akin to arguing . . . that since being immune from taxation *is being immune from a different kind of thing* from being immune from criticism . . .". What White fails to address is the point that being immune from taxation *is a different kind of thing* from being immune from criticism. (My emphasis.)

[76] See text at nn23–30 above.

[77] See text at n31 above.

[78] 1982b: 362 & 363. It is here that White explicitly attacks not only MacCormick but also Hohfeld.

[79] See text at n26 above.

[80] Take as one example the pair of rights: A's right that B delivers a car that he has bought from B to A's house; and, A's right to collect the car that he has bought from B from B's garage and drive it to his house. Place the two rights in the same circumstances: A wants B to bring the car to his house and B refuses. Consider the consequences in each case.

Of course, there are trivial examples of where the difference in consequence is not due to a

The most White can demonstrate is that the different consequences that follow from rights to different kinds of things do not jeopardise the constancy of the general abstract sense of right. But this we have seen is beside the point. White's argument proceeds along the same lines as a person declaring that from the facts that a different consequence follows from a person eating a quantity of sodium chloride with his meals than that which follows from a person eating the same quantity of sodium cyanide with his meals, it would be erroneous to conclude that we do not have the same element of sodium present in each case. The problem is that we are not dealing with the pure element of sodium in these cases, but with two quite different sodium compounds, and the failure to recognise the difference between them is fatal.

In fact White himself has to concede some difficulty in denying any distinction between different rights that may be exercised in practice. Adopting his own preferred approach of elucidating the concept of a right by "turn[ing] for understanding it to the circumstances in which it is used . . .",[81] White concludes his separation of rights and claims with a list of how rights can be used and a different list of how claims can be used.[82] However, elsewhere White provides us with a fuller account of the different ways in which rights can be used – of their "characteristics", and acknowledges that, "Rights to particular kinds of things . . . may lack various of these qualities . . .".[83] But given that these are the qualities that are the characteristics of rights, their presence and absence in some rights in some combinations and in other rights in other combinations cannot be explained away, as White attempts to do so, by the mere attribution of them to "the differences in what they are rights to".[84] If one thing qualifies as a right by displaying one combination of characteristics, and another thing qualifies as a right by displaying another combination of characteristics, then we have two kinds of rights.

And as much as it is of importance not only to the theory of the chemist but also to the practice of the diner who sprinkles the sodium salt upon his food that there should be recognition of the different kinds of sodium salts, so too it is of importance not only to the legal theorist but also to the person whose position the law in practice prescribes to recognise the different kinds of legal rights. For else the ambiguity of some vague general sense of a right, albeit capable of spreading comprehensively over every instance of a legal right, will confuse one legal position with another, and will promote dispute at law at the very point where the law should curtail dispute: "the . . .

different meaning of "right". Substitute as the second member of the above pair: A's right that B delivers a bicycle that he has bought from B to A's house – and consider the different consequences of A making the same request as above in each case. It is the existence of such examples that gives the initial force to White's point.

[81] 1984: 10–1.
[82] 1984: 13?
[83] 1984: 17–8 at 17.
[84] *ibid.*

inadequacy and ambiguity of terms unfortunately reflect, all too often, corresponding paucity and confusion as regards actual legal conceptions."[85]

4 RIGHTS AND CLAIMS

A preliminary obstacle to discussing the relationship between rights and claims is the confusing variety of claims that can be made in relation to a right. In addressing some deficiencies in the argument of his antagonists, White has done much to reveal this obstacle and to help us over it.[86] In an effort to prevent the subsequent discussion becoming stuck upon this obstacle, it will be useful to specify some of the main claims that may relate to a particular right. It may also be helpful to arrange these claims in what might be a chronological order, if we were to imagine some of these claims preceding the establishing of the right and others following on from possible events after the right had been established.

Let us take for the purpose of our illustration a right of A that B pay him £x. Prior to the establishing of this right, A may want to claim that he ought to have the right to the money. For example, A may be campaigning for a change in the law to bring it about that elderly parents have a right to be paid maintenance by their wealthy children, and that as such he, A, ought to have a right to be paid £x as maintenance by his son, B. In such a case as this, A is acknowledging that the law[87] does not as yet provide him with this right. In another type of case, again prior to the establishing of the right, A may claim that he does have the right to the money, but there may be some dispute over this, or, at least, he may need a formal declaration that the right has been accepted as valid. For example, A may claim that he has a right to be paid a legacy by B who is the executor of a will, but the will has been challenged, or has not yet received probate.

Once the right has been established, then a third claim may be made by A: he may simply claim that B pay him the money. And finally, where B refuses to comply with the request to pay A the money to which A has a right, then A may claim a remedy against B. These four claims together with the right to which they relate may be listed as follows:

---

[85] Hohfeld FLC, 35–6. Both of the first pair of rights considered in n80 above might loosely be described as A having a right to the car – indeed the contract between A and B may specify that A has this right at a particular date and time. But the dispute that ensues requires us to consider whether, in Hohfeld's terms, A has the *privilege* to bring the car to his house or the *claim-right* that B bring it to him. The particular terminology employed is of secondary importance. But the recognition that some rights allow the holder to do something whereas other rights allow the holder to get somebody else to do something alerts us to the unsatisfactory state of the ambiguous contractual formula that A has a right to the car.

[86] 1982b: 359; 1986: 417 *et passim*.

[87] A legal right is selected as perhaps furnishing the clearest illustration of the points at issue, but the discussion may equally be applied to moral, customary, conventional, etc rights.

ClaimA : A claims he ought to have the right that B pay him £x

ClaimB : A claims he has the right that B pay him £x

Right : A has the right that B pay him £x

ClaimC : A claims that B pay him £x

ClaimD : A claims a remedy for B failing to pay him £x

A number of comments may be made about these different claims and their relationship to the right.

The basic difference between claimA and claimB, is that the former is made by a speaker who acknowledges that the law does not recognise the right but he considers that it should, whereas the latter is made by a speaker who argues that the law does recognise the right but he acknowledges that this has not as yet been accepted (even if it is only a formal acceptance that is lacking). The obvious point to make is that claimA is a subjunctive claim whereas claimB is an indicative claim. A more interesting point to note is that the strength of the indicative claimB will be tested by examining legal material, to see whether the existing body of law recognises the right, ie will involve argument within the law – as well as a testing of the purely factual material, to see whether the facts alleged to give A the alleged legal right can be made out. But the strength of the subjunctive claimA will be tested by examining material outside the law, to see whether the existing body of law should be altered to recognise the right, ie will involve non-legal argument.

It is here that the justificatory basis, rather than the factual basis, of a subjunctive claim comes to the fore. A person claiming that the law ought to recognise a right will be preoccupied with demonstrating the worth of the principle or policy that justifies recognition of the right by the law, rather than being concerned to demonstrate that he himself (or some other particular person) factually satisfies the criteria of the general principle or policy. Indeed, claims for law reform are usually found in a general form ("The law ought to recognise the rights of parents to maintenance from their children" rather than "The law ought to recognise my right to maintenance from my child") which avoids any need for a factual basis for the claim. Whatever the strength of this claim its justificatory basis must be found outside the law, for if we argue that the justificatory basis is to be found within the law then we are merely disputing whether as a matter of fact the law does accept the justificatory basis for the claim – and, if so, the law necessarily recognises the right – which takes us to the indicative claimB. This itself may then range between strengths 1–3 (at strength 4, the right is accepted and the claim to the right becomes redundant).[88]

When there is a dispute about the existence of a legal right in a hard case, the argument raised may take the form of claimA or claimB, or may blur the two, but the distinction remains of jurisprudential interest.[89] However,

---

[88] See text at nn51–61 above.

[89] Ronald Dworkin, *Taking Rights Seriously* (London, Duckworth, 1977) ch 4 would argue that the appropriate claim is always claimB.

neither claimA nor claimB can be regarded as entering the debate as to
whether the right is implied by the claim, given that both are made in order
to establish the right and may occur without the right existing; or the debate
as to whether the right implies the claim, for both become redundant once the
right is accepted.[90]

As for claimD, as expressed it could be an indicative or a subjunctive claim,
but for it to be of any interest to us it needs to be treated as a valid subjunctive claim, for indicative or lesser subjunctive claims to a remedy could obviously be made without implying or being implied by the right, since such
claims could anyway turn out to be invalid. Even as a valid subjunctive claim,
claimD is clearly contingent upon a number of factors apart from the existence of the right: that the right has not been satisfied, that the person who
holds the right also has recourse to claiming the remedy,[91] that as a matter of
policy the remedy claimed is available in the particular circumstances.[92] We
cannot then say that the right implies claimD. However, it would be possible
to say that claimD implies the right. But this is a trivial truth: given that the
claim to the remedy factually asserts the existence of the right which has not
been satisfied, the validity of the claim necessarily involves the existence of
the right. And it tells us no more about the relationship between rights and
claims than the observation that A's valid claim to be paid child benefit
implies that she has a child tells us about the relationship between children
and claims.

[90] *A fortiori* so does any right to make the claim, *pace* Feinberg above n45 at 141. It is possible to see in Feinberg's apparently redundant right to claim a right a clumsy expression of the
possibility of exercising a right/making a claim in addition to holding it – see text at n63 above
and n110 below.
   The suggestion that the existence of the right necessarily implies the *historical* existence of the
claim, as put forward by Vinogradoff's requirement that for rights to exist they must be claimed
(Sir Paul Vinogradoff, "The Foundation of a Theory of Rights" (1924) 34 *Yale Law Journal* 60)
is given short shrift by White (1984: 125), as it has been by others previously: W.J. Brown, "Re-
Analysis of a Theory of Rights" (1925) 34 *Yale Law Journal* 765 and Glanville Williams,
"Language and the Law" (1946) 62 *Law Quarterly Review* 387 at 398.
[91] This may be analytically contentious in cases such as third parties benefitting under contracts, where there may be a dispute over whether to regard the third party as a right holder.
Even in cases where the analysis is less contentious there may still be practical problems – eg,
consider A's right not to be killed. Both cases are discussed in David Lyons, "Rights, Claimants,
and Beneficiaries" (1969) 6 *American Philosophical Quarterly* 173.
[92] There are two important points here. First, the determination of the availability of a particular remedy is not dependent upon the existence of the right, or even the characteristics of that
right, alone, but may be based on broader issues of policy – consider, eg, the availability of public law remedies. Secondly, even where the remedy is generally available, it may still be subject
to the discretion of the court whether to grant it at all – eg equitable remedies – or the extent to
which it is granted – eg the quantum of damages. MacCormick's assertion that, "What remedy
it is relevant and appropriate to claim depends on the kind of right . . ." (1982: 353) cannot be
regarded as the whole truth; and his treatment of the discretionary element of remedies overlooks
the point that "a number of factors [that] have to be weighed" (1982: 355) are not factors that
relate to the "kind of right" alone.
   In general, these three extrinsic factors must be overcome by any theory which purports to link
rights to remedies – eg, Jules Coleman and Jody Kraus, "Rethinking the Theory of Legal Rights"
(1986) 95 *Yale Law Journal* 1335.

We are left with claimC, and it is here that the possibility of mutual implication between the right and the claim – even to the point of finding the two equivalent[93] – becomes most plausible.[94] This is the moment for a thorough examination of White's arguments for denying any implication between the two. Moreover, we shall test White's arguments at their strongest point, by attempting to demonstrate the equivalence of the two. White's rejection of this is delivered in the shape of three fundamental arguments: (1) rights in general exhibit different characteristics to claims; (2) there are some things to which there can be rights to which there cannot be claims; (3) there are some things to which there are claims without there being rights to them.

In order to rebut these arguments, I shall argue respectively: (1) in order to distinguish the characteristics of rights and claims, White is forced to choose the characteristics of one kind of claim rather than another, and that his argument does not hold for the other kind of claim; (2) although there are things to which there can be rights to which there cannot be claims, these are things to which the right is of a particular kind, and in cases where another kind of right applies there will also be a claim to the thing; (3) in arguing that there are claims to things without there being rights to them, White is either again turning his argument on a particular kind of claim, or is providing a false account of the relationship between a claim and a right where the equivalence does hold. In general then, it is being argued that it is White's failure to see the different kinds of claims and rights[95] that is to blame for his error in denying the equivalence between a right and a claim which holds for a particular kind of right with a particular kind of claim: A's right that B do something, and A's claim in the sense of justified requirement that B do something.

The distinction that White draws between the characteristics of rights and claims[96] depends upon his taking characteristics of a claim as assertion rather than claim as justified requirement. This comes out most strongly when White points out that "one can claim almost anything", and points to things that can be claimed but to which one cannot have a right, such as a claim to be a particular size.[97] Both the width of the general statement and the particular examples given indicate that White has assertions rather than justified requirements in mind. And when White concludes his discussion with a summary of the differing characteristics of rights and claims, the distinction only holds if we assume that we are dealing with claims as assertions, for whereas assertions

---

[93] White considers, and rejects, the three possibilities: that the right implies the claim, that the claim implies the right, that the right and the claim are equivalent – 1984: 128, 132.

[94] Hohfeld, FLC, 38; Lyons, above n91 at 174; Feinberg, above n45 at 139, 148–9. However, both Lyons and Feinberg stray to some extent: Lyons between claimC and claimD (*loc. cit.*); Feinberg, between claimC and claimB (at 141, 150-1). For an example of vacillation between claimA and claimC, see Sir Paul Vinogradoff *Common Sense in Law*, 3ed. revised by H.G. Hanbury (London, Oxford University Press, 1959) at 46–8.

[95] See text at n62 and n81 above.

[96] 1984: 132.

[97] 1984: 129.

clearly do not possess the characteristics attributed to rights of being able to "be given, conferred, taken away, earned, enjoyed, or exercised",[98] these characteristics may be attributed to claims as justified requirements, for the position of holding this kind of claim (which is a usage for claim as justified requirement that we have noted[99]) may "be given, conferred, taken away, earned, enjoyed, or exercised" (although it is a bit strained to employ all of these actual terms directly with claims of this kind[100]).

In indicating the things to which there can be rights to which there cannot be claims, White provides examples of A's right to do something, say something, think something, or feel something, but does not give an example of A's right that B do something.[101] In fact, White does concede that where it is a case of "rights to have something done to one" then the "idea of a claim to something, like the idea of a request or demand for it, is appropriate".[102] But White does not go far enough, for the idea of a claim *as a justified requirement* is more than appropriate in this case, it sounds very much as though it falls under what White elsewhere gives as the general sense of a right: "a title, something which entitles him, which gives him a sort of ticket of justification to . . . be given so and so . . .".[103] But White veers from reaching this conclusion not only by failing to clarify the kind of claim he is dealing with but also by repeating his refusal to recognise different kinds of rights.[104]

When White argues that there are some things to which there are claims without there being rights to them,[105] he employs two arguments. The first is the straightforward citing of examples of claims without rights. Here again his argument depends upon citing particular kinds of claims other than a claim as justified requirement. So, he cites indicative assertions, for example the claim to be surprised at something, or (more subtly) to be the long-lost heir, or to ache all over, or to be the inventor of a process;[106] and he cites subjunctive assertions, for example a claim to be given some protection, or to be allowed entry as an immigrant to this country, which are of lesser strength than a valid subjunctive claim, ie justified requirement.[107] White's second

---

[98] 1984: 132.
[99] See text at n63 above.
[100] This point is discussed more fully below – see text at n110 below.
[101] 1984: 131–2.
[102] 1984: 131.
[103] 1984: 174.
[104] 1984: 132.
[105] 1984: 128–9, 130.
[106] 1984: 128, 128, 129, 130. The claim to be the long-lost heir is more subtle because it easily runs into the subjunctive claim to be given the inheritance. The indicative claim should not however be confused with the subjunctive claim that it may be the factual basis for – see text at nn58-61 above.
[107] 1984: 128, 130. White does not provide sufficient detail in these examples for us to be able to say exactly what he has in mind, but it is clear that he must have something less than a valid subjunctive claim, justified requirement, in mind for otherwise we could readily reach the conclusion (as at n104 above) that the maker of the claim has a right to protection or entry, which White denies. There is the possibility of a more complex analysis being required in these sorts of

argument is less straightforward. He argues that having a subjunctive claim "does not imply having a right . . . for one's possession of a claim may be based on other considerations, such as the justice of such treatment."[108] But this argument assumes that the right must be regarded as the *basis* for the claim, and proceeds by establishing another basis for the claim to deny the implication of the right. But if the claim and right are treated as equivalent, whatever is the basis for the claim may also be the basis for the right. It is quite feasible to take the "justice of such treatment" to be the basis of a right as much as a claim.

A possible explanation for the readiness to treat a right as the basis·of a claim[109] is the failure to acknowledge the twin usage of a claim as justified requirement noted above:[110] the claim may be held or it may be made (as the right may be held or exercised). Focusing solely upon the making of the claim leaves open the issue of describing the position enjoyed by the person making the claim before he made it, and his holding of the right naturally rushes in to fill the void, from which it is but a small step to regard the right that was held as the basis of the claim that was made. But equally we could come up with the claim that was held as being the basis of the claim that was made, or the right that was held as the basis of the right that was exercised, or the orange that was bought as the basis of the orange that was eaten . . .

If we then conclude that the particular kind of claim and the particular kind of right mentioned are indeed equivalent, what follows? First, something that does not follow. We have not decided that the two are the same, only that they are equivalent.[111] By which I mean that everywhere you see the word right (and it is a right of this sort) you cannot substitute the word claim (meaning a claim of this sort), but you could express the position described by the right in an equivalent way by expressing it in terms of a claim. In the same way, but perhaps more obviously, to describe the relationship between A and B in terms of A being the parent of B is equivalent to but not the same as describing it in terms of B being the child of A. This important point explains why some of the terms used by White to describe the characteristics of a right are not directly transferable to claims. For example, we freely talk about conferring rights but it sounds awkward to talk about conferring claims – nevertheless we could as an equivalent to talking about conferring a right (of the appropriate sort) talk about putting a person in a position where he

---

cases. Perhaps the claim to protection is asserting a moral right (the audience is bigger than and capable of looking after the speaker), where there is no legal right. Perhaps the claim to entry is an indicative claim to satisfy the criteria upon which the quota of immigrants will be selected. Cp Stoljar above n1 at 106, 110.

[108] 1984: 130.

[109] MacCormick 1982: 353, 354; Lyons above n91 at 182; Feinberg above n45 at 151. Stoljar does suggest that the basis for the claim may also be the basis for the right, above n1 at 108–9 – *pace* White (1986: 420) who represents Stoljar as stating "one's moral claim . . . *must* rest on one's moral rights" whereas Stoljar states, "having a claim . . . must amount to a right" (at 109).

[110] See text at n63 above.

[111] White distinguishes the two – 1984: 132.

has a claim (of the appropriate sort). Similarly, we may talk about exercising rights or making claims. This point also indicates the danger of collecting terms that are associated with a particular idea as a means of making a hard and fast distinction between that idea and another idea.

Secondly, inasmuch as the two ideas are equivalent but are not the same, they must be relating to some common notion but from different perspectives. The common notion is the justified requirement of behaviour from another. The etymology of the words perhaps helps us to discern the difference in perspective. Whereas a right springs from the justified element of the compound idea, a claim springs from the requirement element (a call for . . .). The former takes on a particular meaning by moving to deal with what it is justified for one person to ask of another; the latter takes on a particular meaning by moving to a position where the call upon another to act is accepted as legitimate; and these two particular meanings of these words become equivalent. That is not to say that they become the same, for even within these two particular meanings the words may bear some legacy from their derivation that makes the usage of the one differ from the usage of the other without precluding the possibility of covering the usage of one with a different usage of the other – this has already been remarked upon. In particular here, it is easier to adapt a right to directly describe the position of the person who can make that requirement when the position is created or transferred, since a right by derivation relates more to the propriety of the position; whereas a claim by derivation is more comfortably expressed at the point when that position is used to call for the required behaviour. Hence, as noted, the conferring of rights but the putting a person in a position where he has a claim. Conversely, the making of a claim but the rather more oblique exercising of the right. However, the distinct ancestral features should not distract us from recognising the equivalent standing of particular offspring from the two strains. Nor is it impossible for the two strains to find closer union: the direct conferring and transfer of claims has evolved in one particularly rugged context, the gold rush.[112]

Thirdly, it follows from the equivalence of this particular kind of claim and this particular kind of right that (for this kind of right) we do not actually need to speak of rights at all, for everything could be spoken of in terms of claims. This immediately lessens the rhetorical force of these rights as somehow possessing a quality which sets them apart from other considerations in a normative debate and diminishes the analytical eminence that rights characteristically receive.[113] And if A's rights to do (say, think, feel) something

---

[112] The claim that is staked may be regarded as a title (Feinberg above n45 at 150), and thus qualify as a right (White 1984: 174 – n72 above), and may be conferred, transferred, etc without any awkwardness of expression.

[113] White talks of rights being "differentiated" from other normative concepts (1984: 16). MacCormick comments on "legal and political philosophy . . . concentrating heavily on rights" (1982: 356). For a challenge to the orthodox concentration on rights, see Joseph Raz, "Liberating Duties" (1989) 8 *Law and Philosophy* 3.

himself are regarded as consisting of rights that others do not interfere, as it may be argued,[114] the challenge to the rhetorical and analytical supremacy of rights might be taken further. Yet White himself should be capable of contemplating even the complete elimination of rights from our normative discourse, for he readily recognises "The late birth of the idea of a right . . ."[115] – and it is inconceivable that what we find to express through the language of rights was a matter for complete indifference to the Greeks and the Romans. As is the suggestion that our "emphasis on the individual"[116] can provide the explanation for the absence of rights in the sort of culture which could exalt an individual to excesses beyond our common experience. Is the concept of *patria potestas* not readily expressed in our tongue in the language of rights?[117] And if so, must we not acknowledge that the Romans also knew what we speak of as rights without needing to speak of them as such?

Finally, and more generally, given that they do occupy such prominence in our normative discourse, how are we to approach the analysis of rights? Some of the lessons learned in this limited study, which has focused upon a particular kind of right, may provide pointers for a broader enterprise. First, we need to recognise that the word we employ for one idea of a right may be a word with a number of meanings, capable of conveying other ideas of rights. Hohfeld himself has drawn our attention to the diversity of rights, but there are two further lessons that go beyond Hohfeld's concerns. Secondly, we need to recognise that the meanings of right may be contingent upon the different perspectives of person and time. And thirdly, we need to recognise that what we think of and express in terms of a right might be thought of and expressed in terms of other ideas – ideas which can assist in our understanding of rights. And if we recognise these things then we must recognise that for any fruitful discussion of rights we need a framework which is capable of accommodating a full diversity of rights, but equally within which the different perspectives and associated ideas can be orderly approached. Without this our discussion of rights is likely to resemble the noise of a flock of starlings, who have the capacity equally to sound as though they are saying the same thing but disagreeing, or to sound as though they are saying different things but agreeing. In either case a din.

---

[114] See ch II. See also the endorsement of Bentham's views in Lyons above n91 at 174. Feinberg goes further, for whilst announcing his intention to deal with "only one of the four concepts of a right distinguished by Wesley Hohfeld" (above n45 at xi), he in fact subsumes Hohfeld's concept of a privilege under a claim-right (at 148–9).

[115] 1984: 175; cp John Finnis, *Natural Law and Natural Rights* (Oxford, Clarendon Press, 1980) at 206-10, 228; Richard Tuck *Natural Rights Theories* (Cambridge, Cambridge University Press, 1979) at 9–10.

[116] White 1984: 175.

[117] See, eg, W.W. Buckland, *A Text-Book of Roman Law*, 3ed. revised by Peter Stein (Cambridge, Cambridge University Press, 1975) at 103.

Part 3
Discussing Rights

V

A Framework for
Discussing Rights

1 INTRODUCTION

For the platitudes and truisms that follow I make no apology. The purpose of this chapter is to assemble that which is generally accepted, has been frequently stated, or would be taken to be trivially true if anybody bothered to express it – in relation to man, the societies in which he dwells and the rights which are attributed to him. My ultimate objective in collecting these simple truths is to demonstrate their selective neglect in some of the apparently complex debates that have raged over rights. More immediately, I hope to achieve two things: a recognition of the different uses to which the term "right" is put, and a clarification of those issues that can intelligibly be related to these different uses. A successful outcome to these two objectives will provide a framework for discussing rights,[1] within which differences of perspective can be identified and upon which clashes of opinion can be argued, but from which spurious arguments can be rejected.

It would be naive to assume that every discussion of rights can be accommodated within a framework constructed from a common stock of simple truths alone. At some points of the discussion different participants may accept very different premises. The simple truths of the framework must accordingly be supplemented by these variations in premises, in order for a wide range of discussion on rights to be covered.

Faced with such a bewildering disarray of issues and opinions that exist in relation to rights, there is an obvious danger that any attempt to construct a framework for discussing rights will simply add yet another opinionated perspective upon the subject with a correspondingly selective arrangement of issues. Hence the adoption of a strategy for constructing the framework which is sensitive to this danger by utilising as much common ground as is possible and by providing as comprehensive an opportunity as can be managed for the voicing of disparate opinions. Ideally, every argument admitted into the framework would be one whose intelligibility (albeit not acceptability) could

---

[1] The need for "an argumentative framework" is recognised by L.W. Sumner in *The Moral Foundation of Rights* (Oxford, Clarendon Press, 1987) at 0. "The need for some such framework is now acute. It is the agility of rights, their talent for turning up on both sides of an issue, which is simultaneously their most impressive and their most troubling feature."

be demonstrated from some common ground and the arguments that would be shut out of the framework would be those that were demonstrably incompatible with some common ground. However, as has already been intimated, we cannot expect the framework to be founded entirely upon common ground, and there will accordingly be some arguments whose intelligibility or otherwise will be contingent on the selection from different premises built into the framework.

Nevertheless, the importance of the common ground exerts a dominating influence upon the strategy to be followed. It accounts for the attachment to platitudes and truisms admitted in the introductory sentence. It also explains why the construction of the framework is undertaken as an enterprise in itself, prior to detailed examination of any actual theories of rights.[2]

The construction of the framework proceeds by considering separately three contexts in which rights can be invoked. It should be pointed out that these contexts are considered for present purposes independently of the consideration of any possibly significant distinctions between legal, moral and other normative orders. The three contexts are: the nature of man; the nature of society; and, the regulation of disputes. Within each context, an attempt will be made to establish both the common ground and obvious variations in premises which could affect the discussion of rights. And then drawing upon these observations, the aim will be to arrange the materials they yield in a framework so as to clarify the different issues that can intelligibly be discussed for any notion of right that we have found.

2 MATERIALS FOR A FRAMEWORK

(1) The Nature of Man

I am not concerned here with what is the nature of man but merely with the question of how we can derive rights from the nature of man, whatever we regard his nature to be. Take any conception of human nature, however individualistic, however social, we do not reach the beginning of rights-talk until two further things are present: (i) an assessment that our conception of human nature ought to be realised; (ii) the possibility of some obstacle to the realisation of that human nature.

It is more likely that when we talk of human nature as being worthy of realisation that we are talking not of human nature in the raw but of some conception of the good man that can be realised from the potential provided by human nature as channelled through the pathway of some practical wisdom, cultural image, or ideological norm. But whether we believe that natural man is inherently good, or we believe that natural man needs some whittling before

---

[2] This is undertaken in chs VI–IX below.

he assumes a desirable shape, the point is that we cannot establish a ground for rights in the nature of man until we have assessed that our conception of human nature is good, commendable, or desirable in some sense.

The obstacle that we have referred to in requirement (ii) must concern the exercise of human will, rather than arising through some natural or impersonal occurrence. So for example, we could talk of the right of a child to receive drink from its parent, but it would be nonsensical to talk of the right of a child in some drought afflicted country to receive rain. To invoke a right is to call upon the possibility of some human response which will satisfy or maintain the right – the absence of that response being precisely the obstacle to the realisation of what the right promotes.[3] In the case of the child dying in the drought, we could of course speak of its right to receive water if by that we meant that some human response from the international community was being called for. But Robinson Crusoe on his deserted island could have no rights[4] because there was no human response he could call upon.

We may state these requirements as two general principles –

I. For rights to be based upon the nature of man we require an assessment that our conception of human nature ought to be realised as being good, commendable, or desirable, and so provides an entitlement to what promotes its realisation.

II. We also require the possibility of some human response (act or omission) forming an obstacle (whether unwittingly or deliberately) to the realisation of that human nature.

And we have noted the possibility of divergent premises being attached to I –

I(a): human nature is good, commendable, or desirable completely and inherently.
or,
I(b): human nature is good, commendable or desirable in part, to the extent that it satisfies some criterion of the good man.

(2) The Nature of Society

This section follows the approach taken in the preceding one, and builds upon the conclusions reached in it. It introduces a number of complications. Much

---

[3] This point that a right requires a human response is commonly found expressed in the converse, that the demand for the human response is justified by the right – eg by H.L.A. Hart in "Are There Any Natural Rights?" (1955) 64 *Philosophical Review* 175, reprinted in Jeremy Waldron (ed.), *Theories of Rights* (Oxford, OUP, 1984); and by Joseph Raz, *The Morality of Freedom* (Oxford, Clarendon Press, 1986) at 166 hereinafter, MofF.

[4] Although interestingly it could be argued that he was subjected to duties: eg, from certain moral perspectives, the duty not to take his own life.

of this complexity can be traced to the possibility that we may be dealing with an ideal society or an actual society which is less than ideal.

If we take an ideal society, is it possible for our conception of the ideal society to be in conflict with our conception of the nature of man (or our conception of the good man) when it comes to the discussion of rights? The answer to this would seem to be a startlingly simple, No. For given what has already been accepted: that the nature of man only serves as the basis for rights once either it has been shown to be inherently good (premise I(a)) or it has been whittled down to satisfy a criterion of the good man (premise I(b)); and, that for rights to arise we must place Robinson Crusoe in the company of his fellow men (principle II) – it follows that any rights that can be derived from the nature of man must be practised in the company of other men, and promote the good of each man (since the nature of man is common to all, so that each could invoke the rights thus obtained). And what would our conception of an ideal society be if it did not promote the good of each of its members in the company of each other? We might then happily conclude that the rights derived from our conception of the nature of man and the rights derived from our conception of the ideal society are nothing more than two ways of talking about the same thing.[5]

However attractive this position is, it seems to have been reached by overlooking two fundamental factors, one being the possibility of conflict between different members of a society and the other being the possibility of conflict between the individual and society.

(1) Conflict between Members of a Society.

In this case, our conclusion appears to ignore the differentiation of roles, or division of labour, of the members of a society. How can we talk about a common set of rights derived from our conception of the nature of man for every member of society, when different members of society are performing different functions? For example, the rights of an employer differ from the rights of an employee; the rights of a parent differ from the rights of a child. The response to this point may be either that the differentiated rights relating to different functions are themselves derived from an exercise of the common rights derived from our conception of the nature of man (eg the different rights of employer and employee are both derived from their common right to enter binding agreements); or, that the common rights derived from our conception of the nature of man in fact present a stock of rights that relate to the different functions that a man may perform, and each may draw the

---

[5] The argument here proceeds on the premise that all men share in the same nature, a premise that is not universally adopted. Where a society is based on the assumption that some men partake of a superior nature to others, and that society is constructed to promote the interests of the "superior race", then the ensuing society is only ideal for the members of that race. Nevertheless, the same basic point holds, that rights derived from the conception of the ideal society and from the nature of man, *for that race*, coincide.

appropriate rights from this stock when performing a particular function (eg the parent will draw those rights which relate to the nature of man as expressed in parenthood, which will obviously differ from the rights drawn by the child).

There still remains the problem of the possibility of conflict between these different roles. Conflicts between employers and employees, parents and children, etc are all too familiar in actual societies – and at least in the rhetoric of the conflict the opposing positions are often couched in rights. Is there any danger that the rights derived from our conception of man, once worked through to their exercise by different parties or in different functions, yield conflict?

In order to answer this we must first dispel a common misconception of conflict. It is often thought that conflict arises between the rights of two parties where the two parties are in competition for one prize. For example, both A and B want to employ a gifted cook, C, in their households. We might say that both A and B have the right to employ C, but clearly where the one succeeds the other must fail. Hence the appearance of conflict between their respective rights. It is only an appearance, however, which arises from the loose expression which bestows upon each party the right to employ C. This in fact is a right which neither possesses in the scenario envisaged. Each has the right to endeavour to employ C, but neither A nor B has the right to employ C, short of some prior arrangement which gives them some sort of first refusal over employing C.[6] So, rights that may be exercised in competition between the holders do not imply a conflict between the rights; and where competition is both a natural and a good or proper[7] practice for man we can expect the rights derived from our conception of the nature of man to permit just that: a right to compete for x.

A true conflict would occur where both A and B have the right to x, and where for one of the parties to have x it necessarily follows that the other party cannot have x; or where A has the right to x and B has the right to y, and x and y are incompatible. Is it possible for this type of situation to arise among the rights that are derived from our conception of the nature of man? Of course, it is possible to envisage conflict naturally arising between A and B, as it does between two birds fighting over a prospective mate or between a fox and a rabbit, but where this conflict naturally arose we should have to channel man's natural potential into some notion of the good man (as envisaged by premise I(b)) before we could derive rights from it. It is impossible for this conflict to involve rights, given principle I.[8]

---

[6] I have discussed this example in relation to the analysis of Hohfeldian privileges in ch II:5.

[7] It is possible for cases of competition arising naturally to be regarded as improper – premise I(b).

[8] We should remind ourselves of the point raised in n6 above: that we are dealing with a conflict between two members of a society. For example, in the case of the conflict between fox and rabbit, we must be dealing with a society for both animals before the need arises to modify the natural tendencies of its members in order to reach rights. If we construct a society merely

For we cannot say that both something and the negation of that thing are good, commendable, or desirable and so ought to be realised: we cannot prescribe both x and $\sim x$. So we cannot say that A has a right to x and that B has a right to x or to y, if B having x or y necessarily means that A cannot have x. For this would be to prescribe both x and $\sim x$ in relation to A.

It may be helpful to give concrete examples of what we have decided is possible or not in relation to conflict and rights. We can say, for example, that both A and B have the right to be considered for king (to compete to be king) of their society. We cannot say that both A and B have the right to be king of their society, or that A has the right to be king whilst B has the right to have no king over him – since in both of these cases to prescribe the fulfilment of B's right is necessarily to prescribe the negation of the right of A.

There are two situations that are not covered by the above discussion. One is where the conflict is between different conceptions of man or different ideologies,[9] rather than a conflict between the rights exercised by different parties derived from the same conception of man. So it would be possible for A to have the right to be king under a royalist ideology whilst B has the right to have no king over him under a republican ideology. This clearly is not a conflict of rights, for the rights do not come into conflict since they do not exist within the same system; if I speak of A's right within the system based upon a royalist ideology then B's right does not exist; if I speak of B's right existing within the system based upon a republican ideology then A's right does not exist. It is a conflict of ideologies, a conflict between the systems of rights derived from different ideologies, but not a conflict between the right of A and the right of B.

The other situation is where the conflict is not a necessary conflict between the right of A and the right of B, but a contingent conflict activated by insufficient resources to fulfil in practice both the rights of A and B. Whereas the right of A to be king and the right of B to be king are necessarily in conflict, since it is impossible from the nature of the subject matter of the right for both rights to be fulfilled; the right of A to be fed and the right of B to be fed are not necessarily in conflict, since it is possible to fulfil both rights. However, in practice, there may be insufficient food to feed both A and B, and the conflict arises. But strictly speaking this is a conflict between the choice of fulfilling one right or the other,[10] and not a conflict between the right of A and the right of B.

We may then conclude that a true conflict between the right of A and the right of B – as opposed to the rights of A and B to compete, or a conflict between systems of rights based on different ideologies, or a conflict between

---

for foxes, then there is nothing to stop the natural conflict between fox and rabbit remaining unabated and for the fox to have a right to eat the rabbit.

[9] The disputants may agree on accepting premise I(a) or I(b) but still differ on their conception of the nature of man or on their criterion of the good man.

[10] This conflict may nevertheless be significant. It is dealt with below.

the choice of fulfilling one right or another – cannot arise in the rights derived from our conception of the nature of man. However, our matching of the rights derived from our conception of the nature of man and the rights derived from our conception of the ideal society still faces the accusation of having overlooked a second fundamental factor.

(2) Conflict between the Individual and Society.

The match of rights appears to dispense rather too easily with the debate which sets the interests of the individual against the interests of society, which occupies not only political theory but also the deliberations of the courts. But this very real clash of interests can simply be explained on the basis that we are dealing with the interests of human nature in the raw rather than human nature as found expressed in the good man (premise I(b)), and/or that we are dealing with the interests of a society that is less than ideal. We can in these ways preserve the match between the rights derived from our conception of the nature of man and the rights derived from our conception of the ideal society, but in so doing we open up the question of how these rights relate to the rights in an actual less than ideal society.

Why might a society be less than ideal? There are two obvious possibilities. It could be because of the state of its members (they are ignorant of the good to pursue, they prefer to pursue short-term selfish aims rather than the good) or because of the state of its resources (the fields do not provide enough grain, there are insufficient funds to provide school places for every child). The structure of a society, although capable of preserving its less than ideal state, cannot be regarded as a primary reason for it, since the structure of a society must have historically arisen through the actions of its members in response to the resources available to them.

If we accept that the state of its members is at least in part to blame, then we are endorsing the view that human nature requires some refinement (premise I(b)). On the other hand, to the extent we lay the blame at the poor resources of a society, then subject to that poverty being removed, we must recognise that the rights derived from our conception of the ideal society (nature of man) cannot be simply transported into the actual society that we are dealing with.

Let us take a concrete example. Suppose that in the realisation of the ideal society (nature of man) each person is given the opportunity to pursue a full education and each person is provided with adequate housing, but in our actual society there are insufficient resources to build the schools, colleges, universities and homes that would be required to fully implement both of these aspects of the ideal society. What use then are the rights to education and housing derived from our ideal society in constructing our actual society with its limited resources? Clearly these rights in themselves cannot determine the policy to be implemented, for any practical policy will involve a part that cannot be justified by our conception of the ideal society (nature of man) for it will necessarily deny it. The reason for distributing the resources so as to favour one right as against the other, or so as to adjust the distribution in some way between the two rights, must be found outside of that which justifies the implementation of the full rights.

It is clear that the rights derived from our conception of the ideal society (nature of man) cannot of themselves determine the rights to be enjoyed in an actual less than ideal society, but do they have any part to play in determining the rights of such an actual society? One suggestion might be that they offer a pool of acceptable opportunities for pursuing the good from which the architect of the actual society may choose as a matter of policy and expediency. So, it does not matter if he chooses education as opposed to housing, or housing as opposed to education, but he could not choose providing all of his ministers with Volvos to the neglect of either.

Another suggestion might be that the rights derived from our conception of the ideal society are attainable in a linear progression as the resources available increase (first basic food supply, then basic shelter, then basic education . . . and so on), so that for any point on the scale of impoverished resources it is possible to determine a corresponding point on the progression of attaining rights which will fix which rights the limited resources should be expended on.

Opposed to both of these suggestions is the view that our conception of the ideal society has no part to play in the administration of the less than ideal society: that all rights derived from the former must be suspended whilst we go through the process of attaining it – they are regarded as the prize at the end of our attainment rather than imprinting themselves upon the means of attainment (in the way that the early Romans would suspend their regular constitutional practices and appoint a dictator in times of national emergency in order to safeguard their subsequent enjoyment of those practices).

Another view which also challenges the first two suggestions arises from a recognition that the less than ideal state of society is to be attributed not merely to the shortage of resources but also to the less than ideal state of its members (premise I(b)), in which case certain unidealistic pragmatic factors may have to be given a weighting even if our objective is to attain the ideal. For example, it may be thought necessary to give the Minister of Housing his ministerial Volvo in order to induce him to use his time and energy towards the optimal promotion of the housing stock.

A final view, which ameliorates the absence or reduction of the ideal rights in the last two views, is that however austere or pragmatic our policies have to be in the less than ideal circumstances we find ourselves in, there is a certain minimum of rights derived from the nature of man (which we would find in our ideal society amongst the other fuller rights that resources there would permit us to realise) which cannot ever be neglected – the strongest example being the right to life.

It is important to point out that on this last view the rights are not being derived from our conception of the nature of man merely as offering the fulfilment of some potential, but as possessing some status irrespective of the fulfilment of that potential (but which will also be found within the fulfilment of that potential) – which effectively gives us a subset of basic status rights from the set of all rights derived from our conception of the nature of man. In accepting these status rights within our viewpoint and taking a position that transcends the view of man's worth only in the fulfilment of his capacity, we are acknowledging some value for man himself such as found in the Judaeo-Christian perspective on the sanctity of life, or the Kantian rejection of using man merely as a means to an end.[11]

In summary, from our discussion of the relationship between the rights derived from our conception of the nature of man (which we have seen we can equate with the rights derived from our conception of the ideal society) and the rights to be found in an actual less than ideal society, we can add to the two requirements for rights to be based upon the nature of man, one further principle and a variety of premises which may (singly or in some cases in combination) be attached to it –

III. The rights derived from our conception of human nature (which are equivalent to the rights derived from our conception of the ideal society) cannot of themselves determine the rights in a less than ideal actual society.

And the relationship between the rights derived from our conception of the ideal society (human nature) and the rights found in a less than ideal actual society may be viewed in a number of ways (some of which are exclusive and some of which can be combined) –

III(a) **a pool of possible goods**: The rights in our actual society are selected as a matter of policy from the rights of our ideal society, which must be given priority over other considerations.

III(b) **a fixed progression of goods**: The rights in our actual society are determined by calculating the amount of resources available to our society which will indicate what can be presently realised from the rights of our ideal society which are arranged in a fixed order based upon resources.

---

[11] This point needs amplifying in order to avoid confusing it with what would amount to a rejection of what has been asserted above. I am not suggesting that a status right can be enjoyed by an individual in isolation from his potential for membership of and acquiescence in human society. So, his right to life is dependent upon the response of his fellow citizens (principle II) *and* also upon his respecting the right to life of his fellow citizens – else his right to life may cease to exist in the face of their legitimate acts of self-defence. The point is rather that a status right cannot be overridden by an individual's failure to achieve what is regarded as the potential for man within that society or within some ideal society. So, his status right cannot be curtailed because he is, for example, illiterate, unemployed, handicapped, or insufficiently educated to appreciate the value of government policy. The *moral* aspects of this point are considered further in ch VIII.

III(c) **goods as ends but not means**: The administration of our actual society need not feature any of the rights of our ideal society, which can be suspended whilst we strive to reach them.

III(d) **goods mixed with pragmatism**: In deciding which of the rights of our ideal society can be realised within our actual society we must take account of other pragmatic considerations.

III(e) **goods securing status**: No matter how less than ideal the condition of our actual society it must contain a minimum number of the rights of our ideal society, those basic rights which protect the status of an individual irrespective of the fulfilment of his potential in accordance with the ideal scheme of things.

This much can be said about the rights found in our actual less than ideal society in relation to the rights derived from our conception of the ideal society (nature of man). But there is more to be said about the rights in such a society.

(3) Ideal Rights and Policy Rights

In most, if not all, societies some ideal is being pursued. Even the most despotic or partisan administrations manage to suffuse their cruelties with idealism, and perhaps the need for idealism becomes stronger as the cruelties increase: few seek from history or their contemporaries the accolade of being judged a cruel evil man who inflicted unnecessary suffering on others.[12] But even where our less than ideal actual society is being administered with the objective of achieving what is possible of a conception of the ideal society, in one of the ways indicated above, there remains the possibility of the entitlements of the members of that society being derived not merely from the conception of the ideal society but also from the policies which are formulated to settle matters apart from the realisation of those ideal rights. These may be matters that are treated as pure coordination problems[13] (eg who gives way when two drivers approach a roundabout from different roads), or dealt with in an entirely executive or pragmatic manner (eg what the rate of duty on alcoholic drinks will be), or where a pragmatic compromise is reached in the face of competing conceptions of the ideal society (nature of man) which fre-

---

[12] The idealism that masks the cruelty frequently employs the device of finding one race of man superior to another (n6 above). An equally popular instrument in the intellectual armoury of tyrants is the idealism that sets the goals but leaves the means unrestrained (premise III(c) above).

[13] John Finnis notes the stricter sense of "coordination problems", although employing a looser sense of the term himself in *Natural Law and Natural Rights* (Oxford, Clarendon Press, 1980) at 255 – hereinafter, NL&NR. Yasuo Hasebe has suggested that the Japanese indifference to individual rights springs from a perspective which regards potential social conflict as a coordination problem in the narrow sense: "Why the Japanese don't take rights seriously", unpublished seminar paper presented at Reading University, March 1990.

quently arise in pluralist societies (eg the time limits placed on lawful abortion). Once these entitlements have been determined by policy they may also be regarded as rights within the society in which they are established.

It will be convenient to employ the term **ideal rights** for those rights derived from our conception of the ideal society (nature of man), and to contrast these with what we might term **policy rights** signifying those rights that are not derived from any conception of the ideal society (nature of man) but come about as a result of the decision to implement a particular policy. Policy is being used here to denote precisely a way of dealing with things that can be chosen by a person who is not under some predetermined constraint as to how things are to be done. (If such societies exist that are totally divorced from any ideal, then *all* of the rights brought about in these societies may be regarded as policy rights.)

In this respect the idea of policy may vary in strength. For the policy element of a given decision may be weaker or stronger depending on how tightly or loosely drawn are the parameters around the choices available to the person who will determine how things are to be dealt with. In the extreme case the policy element may be nothing more than the determination of a choice restricted to equally weighted varying forms of the ideal.[14]

Nevertheless, the crucial difference between the ideal rights that can be derived from our conception of the ideal society (nature of man) and policy rights is that the former can be traced back to some conception that precedes their establishing within our actual society, and can accordingly be discussed and campaigned for as *rights* grounded within that conception irrespective of their implementation in our actual society, whereas the latter only obtain the ground of entitlement (and thus only attain the status of rights[15]) once they have been determined through the implementation of policy within that society.

However, the practical importance of this distinction between ideal rights and policy rights may soften as we approach the less than ideal condition of our actual society. For we have seen that the ideal rights cannot of themselves determine the rights in a less than ideal actual society (principle III). And depending upon which of the premises III(a)–(e) we adopt, there is the possibility of the questions whether, and the extent to which, any ideal right beyond a secured minimum (III(e)) is realised in an actual society, being determined by policy. Indeed, unless we adopt premise III(b) the response to these questions will necessarily involve the formulation of policy, and even for III(b) there is the possibility of formulating policy to determine the order of ideal rights, unless this is regarded as self-evident.

---

[14] See Finnis on "implementation" or "specification" – NL&NR, 284–6; "On 'The Critical Legal Studies Movement'" in John Eekelaar and John Bell (eds.), *Oxford Essays in Jurisprudence, Third Series* (Oxford, Clarendon Press, 1987) at 146–7, 160–1.

[15] This is not to say that policy rights acquire the same status as ideal rights. Clearly, a policy right established within a particular society may be at variance with an ideal right derived from a particular conception of the ideal society (nature of man).

For the purposes of analysing the rights in an actual less than ideal society, we shall accordingly need to speak not merely about ideal rights and policy rights but also about **established rights**. By their nature all policy rights will be established rights for their being established in a particular society is what brings them into being. But in the case of ideal rights we may distinguish between those that are not established and those that are established in the particular circumstances prevailing in a given society.[16]

Nothing so far has been said about constitutional rights. How do they fit into the discussion of ideal rights and policy rights? The simplest way of dealing with constitutional rights would be to regard them as a formalised type of ideal rights, specifying the rights derived from some conception of the ideal society (nature of man) which is articulated within the constitution when a society is founded. But although this may well account for some constitutional rights, others are clearly policy determined, such as a constitutional right providing a particular mechanism to change the constitution subject to certain safeguards. Where constitutional rights can be regarded as a formalised type of ideal rights, their treatment can vary in accordance with the different perspectives found in premises III(a)–(e), and this variation may well occur even among the rights found within the one constitution – eg some constitutional rights may be regarded as forming a pool of priority goods (III(a)) such that their enforcement is not universal, whilst others may be regarded as securing the minimum status acceptable for citizens (III(e)) which must accordingly be respected at all times.

Enough has already been said to enable us to appreciate some of the multiple ambiguities which may arise when rights are discussed, but before attempting to present a framework that is alert to these ambiguities there is one further source of confusion that we must investigate. Our deliberations have as yet treated rights only in a very general way without descending from our abstractions to the level where the precise extremities of rights are reached and our delineation of the features of rights is sharpened.

(4) The Regulation of Disputes

It is perfectly possible for two people to agree upon the existence of a whole host of rights in the abstract and yet for each of them to have very different ideas of what is conveyed by each of those rights (eg, Does the right to freedom of expression include the facility for public demonstration outside Parliament?); or, having agreed on each of these rights in the abstract for them to have genuine problems in resolving the conflict that arises between two of these rights in a particular concrete situation (eg, Does the right to free speech or the right to religious practice hold sway where one party wishes to publish

---

[16] cp Raz, MofF, 172.

something that another party considers blasphemous?). It should be stressed that these difficulties are not sufficient to deny the existence of the rights. It is possible for an agreement to be reached upon the existence of a right in general terms where the legitimate point to be made is to rebut the assertion that the right does not exist at all,[17] and then, without departing from that general abstract agreement, for one party to deny the right in relation to a particular concrete situation. And having appreciated this point, it is possible to see how the conflict between rights in a particular concrete situation does not suffice to make it impossible for these rights to coexist in the abstract. For unlike our earlier illustration of conflict, where the alleged right of one party conflicted with the alleged right of the other party so as to totally exclude it,[18] the exclusion in this case is local and does not operate so as to totally exclude the other right *in the abstract*.

Having said that, a right whose existence in the abstract could not be instantiated in *any* concrete situation would be entirely vacuous. And it is precisely at the point of these concrete situations that we can discover the true extent of a right, and also the extent of the coexistence or conflict between different rights.[19] We may also thereby find how far in practice the agreement between the two persons over the existence of the right in the abstract actually extends.

The location for marking out these concrete situations is a dispute. The dispute may be actual or hypothetical. It may be entered with great animosity between the parties or as a calm enquiry undertaken by them in order to resolve some uncertainty.

By characterising the location as a dispute I intend to indicate two things. First, there will be posited a concrete situation which can be decided one way or another, to the advantage or disadvantage of somebody – usually one of the parties (and possibly, though not necessarily, to the disadvantage or advantage of another). The regulation of this dispute will determine whether or not an entitlement exists for the person who may be advantaged, and an entitlement so established will amount to a right for that party.

Secondly, by characterising the location of the concrete situations which provide us with the boundaries of our rights as disputes, there is no limit set upon the precision with which these boundaries can be drawn. For as much

---

[17] This was the purpose of the French and American declarations, in the face of the denial of rights by the French Monarchy and the British. The French Declaration has the stated intention of countering "ignorance, forgetfulness or contempt of the rights of man" – found in Jeremy Waldron, *Nonsense upon Stilts* (London, Methuen, 1987) at 26. Cp Eugene Kamenka: "The demand for rights in the seventeenth and eighteenth centuries was a demand *against* the existing state and authorities, against despotism, arbitrariness and the political disfranchisement of those who held different opinions. . . . They were claiming 'liberty' and not 'liberties', and beginning to assert general [ie abstract] and not specific rights." – "The anatomy of an idea" in Eugene Kamenka and Alice Tay (eds.), *Human Rights* (London, Edward Arnold, 1978) at 5, 9.

[18] 2(2)(1) above.

[19] There would be complete conflict and no coexistence only if every concrete instantiation of R_1 conflicted with an instantiation of R_2.

as it is possible to argue for finer detail in marking out the boundary of a right by insisting on some distinction between one possible instantiation and another, then it is possible to incorporate that finer detail by treating the point of distinction as a dispute, whose resolution will fix the boundary of the right.

We may accordingly add to ideal rights and policy rights, those rights which come about through the regulation of disputes, which we may conveniently term **dispute rights**. Like policy rights, all dispute rights will be established rights, for it will be at the point that the dispute is regulated that the right is established and comes into existence.

As has already been indicated, the basis for regulating the dispute may actually be a right whose existence has already been recognised in the abstract (this right may either be an ideal right or a policy right) but this is by no means the only way that disputes can be settled. The dispute can be settled by having an authorised person determining *de novo* the outcome without recourse to any preexisting right. The resolution of the dispute in this manner may nevertheless still generate a dispute right. Maine has pointed out that a distinction can be recognised between a preexisting principle that is used to determine disputes found in later Greek, and the judgment *de novo* that determined the matter which alone is to be found in Homeric Greek – in the use of the two terms $\nu o\mu o\varsigma$ (nomos) and $\theta\epsilon\mu\iota\varsigma$ (themis).[20] The distinction that is evident from the practices of the Homeric kings is sometimes more reluctantly admitted in relation to modern legal practice.

Nevertheless, this distinction suggests the recognition of a similar relationship to that noted between the rights of an ideal society and the rights of an actual society, occurring between the rights of an actual society established in the abstract and the dispute rights of that society. For as the ideal rights may but need not necessarily determine the rights of an actual society, so too the established abstract rights may but need not necessarily determine the dispute rights.

The pressing question to ask is when, if at all, can we say that an established abstract right will necessarily establish a dispute right. In order to assist in answering this question, I shall introduce a form of notation which we can employ to signify the different concrete situations which may form the instantiations of a particular abstract right –

s : a concrete situation instantiating an abstract right

s_n : one of a number of such concrete situations

s_0 : the null element, where none such situation exists

Σ_1^n: the sum of such situations, s_1 to s_n

Using this notation we can state more precisely what is constituted by an agreement between two people that a particular right exists.

---

[20] Sir Henry Maine, *Ancient Law*, 10ed. with Introduction by Sir Frederick Pollock (London, John Murray, 1920) ch I.

The weakest form of agreement over the existence of a right is:

$$\sim s_0$$

This is to say that all parties agree that there is at least one s for the right. But this is not to say that they agree upon which s. It would in fact be possible for the agreement to be wholly negative in character, ie every party denies that there is no instantiation of the right but no parties agree over one particular instantiation. It is worth dwelling on this point, for it indicates a significant ambiguity in the expression of agreement over the existence of a right. Such solidarity of expression may reflect a solid support for one or a number of concrete situations or may turn out to be a feeble illusion in practice where no alliance can be mustered over any practical outworking of the right.[21]

Stronger agreements over the existence of a right will take the form:

$$\Sigma_1^n \text{ where } n \geq 1$$

The stronger the agreement, the greater the value of n will be.

We can now deal with the issue of whether an established abstract right necessarily determines a particular dispute right. We are concerned here with a situation where the abstract right has been established, and the dispute right could be regarded as a concrete instantiation of it. That is to say we are not dealing with a pure judgment *de novo*, where no relevant abstract right has been previously established. But there is also another point to overcome before we can properly address this situation. For it might be argued that whether the dispute right can be deduced from the abstract right is merely a matter of interpretation: ie if we have an abstract right to ϕ, R, the question whether s is an instantiation of R is answered by interpreting ϕ to see whether it covers s.

However, to see the issue in terms of interpretation like this[22] is to confound it with another issue. For we are now dealing not with the issue of whether we can employ a process of deduction to derive s from R, but the issue of what R means, in fact what ϕ (the subject matter of R) means. To see the question of whether the abstract right necessarily determines the dispute right wholly in terms of interpretation is to assume that the issue of

---

[21] It can still be argued that there is a residuary agreement, albeit extremely weak, on the basis that the different instantiations of the parties all reflect some underlying value. The disagreement is essentially over when this value overrides other values or considerations.

[22] The view that a process of interpretation can be viewed as providing a *necessary* answer as to whether a particular instantiation of a right should be recognised by the law has been advanced by Dworkin (the complexities of Dworkin's view are discussed in Stephen Guest, *Ronald Dworkin* (Edinburgh, Edinburgh University Press, 1992) ch 2). Minow's approach to interpretation, "Interpreting Rights" (1987) 96 *Yale Law Journal* 1860 (discussed in ch I), may be contrasted, as may the views of Andrei Marmor, *Interpretation and Legal Theory* (Oxford, Clarendon Press, 1992), and Stanley Fish, *Doing What Comes Naturally* (Oxford, Clarendon Press, 1989) – both of which are critical of Dworkin. See further, Andrei Marmor (ed.), *Law and Interpretation: Essays in Legal Philosophy* (Oxford, Clarendon Press, 1995).

meaning has been resolved affirmatively (or mistakenly to assume it is a non-issue). We can only use the process of deduction to derive s from R once we *have shown* that ϕ can be interpreted to cover s.

For us to be able to say that R *necessarily* determines s, we must accept that every possible instantiation of R holds. This would give us:

$$R \leftrightarrow \Sigma_1^n \text{ where there are n possible instantiations of R}$$

This would obviously be the case where $n = 1$ (and our issue could be disregarded); ie where R is an established concrete right with only one possible instantiation.[23] With equal necessity it would also be the case where it could be shown:

$$s_p \leftrightarrow s_{p-1} \text{ where p is a positive integer} \geq 2$$

This would be the case where R is a general *concrete* right: ie where every s is generated by a variable whose different values can have no bearing upon the normative significance of s, where the variable is normatively constant so as to essentially repeat the same concrete situation in each case.[24] However, neither of these situations represents the case where R is a general *abstract* right.

Indeed, to see the abstract right R as necessarily determining all of its possible instantiations is to fundamentally confuse an abstract right with a general concrete right.

We may conclude that a dispute right may in fact not be determined by an established right, either because it is determined *de novo* with no relevant abstract right previously having been established, or because although there is a relevant abstract right of which the dispute right is a possible instantiation it does not necessarily follow from the established abstract right that this instantiation will be accepted.

(5) The Instantiation of Abstract Rights

On what basis, if any, can we say that a particular instantiation of an abstract right will be accepted? There may be a number of answers to this question, rather like we saw the numerous possibilities of answering the question as to how the rights derived from our conception of an ideal society might be implemented in a less than ideal society. There is an important difference in that whereas the rights derived from our conception of an ideal society may form

---

[23] For example, R is found in a private Act of Parliament such as a marriage enabling Act.

[24] Note such normative constancy across the different concrete instantiations generated has an internal aspect and an external aspect. So, for example, criticising the government and uttering defamatory remarks may differ as instantiations of free speech in respect to their internal characteristics. Whereas, criticising the government during peace time and during war time may differ in respect to external features.

an integrated set of rights capable of coexisting in a practical concrete way (if our conception of the ideal society has been drawn in sufficient detail), and the reason why they cannot be wholly transplanted into our less than ideal society is that the ideal conditions necessary for this set of rights to thrive together are absent in the less than ideal society, in the case of a set of abstract rights it is not the conditions for their existence that act as an obstacle to their realisation in every concrete instantiation but the abstract nature of the rights themselves which precludes their stock transfer into every possible instantiation.

To talk of a right in the abstract is essentially to divorce the interest that the right protects from the detailed factors that may threaten that interest,[25] but nevertheless to insist that this interest is of sufficient value to counter some threat to its realisation: another person cannot simply disregard this interest at will. For this abstract notion to be sustained it must be the case that there is at least one concrete instantiation of the right. For if in *every* possible instantiation the interest allegedly protected by the right were defeated, then it would become false to maintain that the interest is of any value sufficient to defeat a threat to its realisation. Hence:

$$\mathbf{R} \leftrightarrow \sim s_0$$

But, as has already been remarked upon, this does not necessitate the acceptance of any particular possible s.

However, a weaker proposition can be advanced for any particular possible s. For given that the value of the interest that has been upheld by protecting the interest in s_1, consistency of treatment will demand that we explain why that interest is not being valued, or not being valued sufficiently to protect it in the possible s_2, s_3, etc.

This may be because the value of the interest in s_1 is of instrumental value and depends upon circumstances that are to be found in s_1 but not to be found in s_2 (eg free speech is of value in promoting the fulfilment of the potential of every member of society – this value is to be found in s_1 where A is allowed

---

[25] Talking of a right in the abstract here differs from talking of *rights* in the abstract. Two distinct senses of "abstract" are being employed. The first deals with the subject matter without testing it within the practical realities of concrete experience, and hence the abstract proposition may not hold for all possible concrete instantiations. The second deals with the subject matter by distilling a quality found in all concrete instantiations and giving it a pure non-concrete form. In this case, although differing from the concrete instantiations, the abstract proposition does hold in relation to each of them. This distinction can be found in the OED, between entries A.4 and B.3 for "abstract". The contrast between the historical sources cited provides further illumination: eg respectively, GLADSTONE – "What I understand by an abstract resolution is a resolution which does not carry with it an operative principle likely to produce within a reasonable time particular consequences."; TUCKER – "Our abstracts derive all originally from the concrete." The point is laboured here because of a common tendency to confuse the two, and erroneously regard an abstract right in the first sense as derived from all concrete instantiations of it, and then to falsely infer that all concrete instantiations must hold. This error is considered further in ch VI.

to criticize government policy, but is absent in s_2 where A is forbidden to incite the killing of B).

It may be because the value of the interest (whether intrinsic or instrumental) although found in s_2 is there outweighed by a greater value that was not to be found in s_1 (eg although the value of free speech is regarded as being of value in permitting an individual to express himself, this value is outweighed by the value attached to securing the safety of B's life in s_2 above).

Thirdly, it may simply be the case that a competing value is found in s_2 which was not present in s_1, and although insufficient to outweigh the value of the interest protected in s_1, a policy decision has to be reached on which value to favour and this goes against the value of the interest protected by R (eg the value of permitting an individual to express himself in s_1 is brought into conflict with the value of confidentiality in s_2, and although it is not regarded that the one value is sufficient to outweigh the other, as a matter of policy the value of confidentiality in s_2 is preferred).

We may present these findings in the form of a further principle together with possible premises that may be attached to it as a means of accounting for whether a particular instantiation of an abstract right will be accepted –

IV The acceptance of a possible instantiation of an abstract right cannot be determined by the existence of the abstract right alone, although that does give a reason to ask why the instantiation is not accepted.

IV(a) instrumental value absent: The interest found in all accepted instantiations of the abstract right is of some instrumental value which is not made out on this occasion.

IV(b) value outweighed: The value (whether intrinsic or instrumental) of the interest to be found in this possible instantiation of the abstract right is outweighed by a conflicting value that is present on this occasion.

IV(c) conflicting value selected: A conflicting value that is present on this occasion is not sufficient to outweigh the value of the interest to be found in this possible instantiation of the abstract right but is nevertheless preferred as a matter of policy.

IV(d) value prevails: The value of the interest to be found in other accepted instantiations of the abstract right is present in this possible instantiation of the abstract right and is not defeated by any conflicting value or other consideration, and so the instantiation is accepted. (This amounts to a rejection of IV(a)–(c).)

And it will also be helpful to add a principle to express the distinction we have noted between an abstract right and a general concrete right –

V A general right may be regarded as a general concrete right (as opposed to an abstract right) where all possible instantiations of the right are accepted, if the different instantiations are generated by one or more variables that are all accepted to be normatively constant.

Of course, it would be quite possible for one person to regard a general right as an abstract right and another to regard it as a general concrete right due to a disagreement over whether a particular variable was normatively constant or not. An absolutist approach to free speech effectively turns an abstract right into a concrete one. This point should not be confused with the difficulties that may be encountered in clarifying the terms of a general concrete right, due to imprecision in language. The crucial distinction remains once any linguistic ambiguity has been tidied up: does the general right as now understood generate instantiations that are all to be treated in the same manner (general concrete), or that fall to be treated possibly in different ways in accordance with further considerations (abstract).

A related point may be made in the case of imprecision that is not linguistic in origin but due to the historical process by which the law is evolved, particularly in the Common Law tradition, whereby legal principles are stated with only sufficient clarity that may be needed to dispose of the case at hand. Legal doctrine enunciated in one case may accordingly undergo a process of clarification in subsequent cases, but the crucial distinction noted in the preceding paragraph still applies to the right encompassed by that doctrine, once the further clarification has been completed.

3 CONSTRUCTING THE FRAMEWORK

We are now in a position to arrange the materials collected in the previous section so as to construct a framework which is capable of indicating the intelligible issues that may arise within a discussion of rights. The raw materials of the framework are the different notions[26] of a right that we have identified and the relationships that may exist between them. The purpose of the framework is also to reveal specious issues and spurious arguments that may obscure the discussion of rights.

Perhaps the simplest and most fundamental issue in the discussion of rights is what right is being discussed. For A to assert that a right, R, exists and for B to deny it, may seem the simplest of controversies, but in fact the parties may be referring to quite different notions of R, and the disagreement may be more or less extensive accordingly. Far murkier does the discussion become when A and B are apparently in agreement over the existence of R, but due to their employing different notions of R they are in fact taking antagonistic positions in the discussion. At the outset then, it is important to set out these different notions of a right that have been identified. For A to be asserting (or

---

[26] I deliberately employ as a loose term here "notion" in preference to "concept", with a view to indicating that the identification of these differences does not necessarily rest upon an analytical distinction between different concepts of a right but may be attributed wholly to the different environments or contexts in which a single concept is placed. This is not to deny the significant implications of these differences.

denying) the existence of R, he may be employing any of the notions of a right found in Table 1.[27]

Without clarifying which of the notions in Table 1 is being employed by each party to a dispute, or agreement, over the existence of R, it is not possible to say precisely what it is that the parties are disagreeing or agreeing about. And even after we have clarified the notion(s) being employed, if we are dealing with abstract rights (R1/4/5) we may still want to press the parties to consider their positions more fully in order to reach a precise idea of how far the agreement or disagreement goes. This is not to say that every discrepancy between notions will be so significant,[28] though some may be remarkable.[29] However, each of these nineteen notions of a right needs to be recognised, and the implications of their differences become more significant as the subjects involving them become more complex.

A second issue that naturally arises in a discussion of rights is what relationship may exist between different rights. Typically we shall want to know, if A and B agree on the existence of R_1 whether we can infer that they agree on the existence of R_2. To address this issue, it will be helpful to arrange the nineteen notions of a right identified, in Table 2, which displays some[30] of the possible connections between them.

Given that we have established that there is not a necessary derivation either from the rights derived from our conception of the ideal society (nature of man) to the rights established in a less than ideal society, or from an abstract right to a dispute regulating right which is a concrete instantiation of it, the connections in these cases do not amount to the one right establishing the other though the existence of the one is part of the reason for the existence of the other. This connection is depicted by a broken arrow in Table 2. The only case where one right does establish another right is where an established concrete right (whether general or particular) is used to derive a dispute right, for we have seen that in this case all the instantiations of the former right are necessarily derived from it.[31] This connection is depicted by an unbroken arrow.

In those cases where the dispute right is not preceded by an established right, the determination of the dispute right will itself establish a right. The connection between the dispute right and the established right in such a case will accordingly flow in the opposite direction to the connections found in the table above. This sort of connection is shown in Table 3, with a necessary derivation again being depicted by an unbroken arrow and a possible derivation by a broken arrow.

---

[27] For ease of reference the various tables are collected together at the end of this chapter.

[28] eg R8/R17, or R17/R18.

[29] eg R1/R18, or even R1/R4.

[30] I ignore for the moment the horizontal relationships. Their significance is commented on shortly.

[31] The precise nature of the relationship in the case of one right establishing another in this way is considered in detail in ch VIII:5.

It is particularly interesting to note the implications of R19, a dispute right determined *de novo*. This will necessarily establish a particular or a general concrete right – the latter where other instances can be extrapolated from the dispute right by the operation of a normatively neutral variable which can be regarded as generating this particular dispute right among other instances. Of wider repercussions, however, is the possibility of additionally establishing an abstract right, of which the dispute right is regarded as but one instantiation. Since this is obviously not a necessary derivation, the intriguing question to ask is when it is appropriate to consider the dispute right as an instantiation of an abstract right. The simple answer to this must be found in the basis for determining the dispute right. Where the basis of the right is restricted to the merits of a concrete situation then the furthest we can go is a general concrete right, R7, but where the basis is found in the merits of some abstract value then we are justified in extrapolating as far as an abstract right, R5. Although the latter is potentially far wider in its scope, we should refer back to Table 2 to remind ourselves that, unlike the general concrete right, it does not necessarily establish further dispute rights.

A third issue that is closely related to the previous two is how we know that the right exists, for this will obviously depend on what notion of right we have in mind but, as we have seen, this may also depend (at least to some extent) on the connection it has with another right whose existence has already been accepted. Reference to Tables 2 and 3 may be made in order to see when it is possible to establish one right on the basis of the existence of another right (the unbroken arrows), and where one right may be established in part on the basis of another right but cannot be determined by that other right alone without the play of other factors (the broken arrows).

The tables also give some indication of where a right is established without any reference to another preexisting right. In the case of the rights R1/2/3, derived from our conception of the ideal society (nature of man), the right exists purely as a mental construction which is employed to express some facet of the image or vision of the ideal society. However, in the case of the rights R5/7/9/19, established in an actual society either prior to or in the last case within the regulation of a dispute, although the right may still be regarded as existing as a mental construction,[32] it is more than that in that it is being used to express what has come about through an actual event (the emergence of custom, the decision of a court, the enactment of Parliament, the promulgation of a constitution). The existence of the right in this case may accordingly be tied to the occurrence of an event, whereas in the former case it floats free of such a restriction depending only upon the facility of the mind to conceive of the ideal society (nature of man) from whatever inspiration or introspection that appeals.

In the case of a right that may be established in part on the basis of another

---

[32] *Pace* Alan White, *Rights* (Oxford, Clarendon Press, 1984), ch 1.

right but which cannot be determined by that other right alone, the short answer to the question of how we know the right exists is that we do not know it until it has been established (as in the case of the unconnected rights just considered). However, the potential influence of the rights which may be partly responsible for establishing the rights in this category prompts a more careful consideration of the following issue in these cases.

The fourth issue is what rights we should have. In the cases of unconnected rights (R1/2/3/5/7/9/19), this is an issue that is resolved by finding the answers to other questions. Decide what ideal society you want, or let those who have the position to do so determine what sort of actual society they want, and this will necessarily establish the rights which reflect the relevant facets of those societies. In the case where rights are connected to other rights which are sufficient to establish them (the unbroken arrows in Tables 1 and 2), it is not an issue. It is in the case of the connected rights where the other rights are not sufficient alone to establish them (the broken arrows) that the issue of what rights we should have is of particular interest.

The appropriate argument for advancing a potential right of this sort (R_2) will depend on the nature of the connected right (R_1) that may be partly responsible for establishing it. Where R_1 is an ideal right, then the question that arises is how the parties to the discussion view the relationship between the rights derived from our conception of the ideal society (nature of man) and the rights established in an actual less than ideal society. Views on this may vary, being composed of one or more of a number of premises that we have identified above (III(a)–(e)). Where the parties share a common view, then intelligible discussion may proceed on whether R_2 should be established, and depending upon the premise adopted the discussion may venture upon the determination of policy in some respect or another. On the other hand, where R_1 is an abstract right, then the issue will turn on what value the parties to the discussion place upon those instantiations of the abstract right that are accepted, and how they relate this to the value(s) they detect in that instantiation which amounts to the potential R_2. These possibilities are covered by the premises IV(a)-(d) which have been identified above.

The preceding two issues, of whether we do have a particular right, and whether we should have a particular right, are summarised together in Table 4, for the range of different notions of a right found in Table 1.

So far we have concentrated on the vertical relationships between the different notions of a right; it is now time to consider the horizontal relationships. In doing this we shall gain another important perspective on the framework. For although focusing on the vertical columns of rights in Table 2 onwards helps us to understand how rights are established, and how we may go about the process of arguing in favour of a particular right, it does so at the expense of suggesting that these columns of rights stand as exclusive groupings into which particular types of rights are separated. It is now time to correct this impression.

In fact, two points of counter evidence have already surfaced. We have noted the possibility of a connection between R19 and rights in other columns, in Table 3. Also, Table 4 indicates that the abstract right which is used in the regulation of a dispute, R10/11/12, has to satisfy the premises required for establishing a concrete instantiation of an abstract right (IV(a)–(d)); ie, in establishing an abstract right at the level of a dispute we are also establishing a concrete right. This is evident on a moment's reflection, for since the process of establishing the abstract right here is the settling of the dispute between the parties, it necessarily involves the determination of the concrete right which is being contested in the dispute between them.[33]

This might suggest that the columns of the framework are inclusive, as we move from left to right: establishing abstract rights, includes establishing general concrete rights, includes establishing particular concrete rights. However, the picture is more complex than this. For one thing, the apparently inclusive effect we have noted is restricted to the bottom level of the columns, in the regulation of disputes. More fundamentally, to rush into a hypothesis of straightforward inclusion ignores the lack of a necessary derivation between concrete and abstract rights.

In fact, all that our observations so far point to is that the establishing of an abstract right at the level of dispute regulation means that *some* concrete right is simultaneously established. It does not follow that *all* concrete instantiations of that abstract right now hold. It does not even follow that a general concrete right (R13/14/15) is established, for it is conceivable, though highly unlikely, that the circumstances of the dispute are so peculiar to the parties involved that the only concrete right established is a particular concrete right (R16/17/18).

We may follow these horizontal relationships through in Table 5, commencing with the establishing of R10. This involves establishing an R13, or alternatively only an R16 – a possibility we shall ignore for general illustrative purposes. We can now go further. From Table 3, R13 necessarily involves establishing R6. And since the source of R10 is an ideal right, R1, we are dealing with an aspect of our conception of the ideal society (nature of man), and thus also recognising R2. From Table 2, R6 also necessarily involves recognising R14. Furthermore, again from Table 3, R10 necessarily involves establishing R4, which gives rise to the possibility of establishing further dispute rights of the type R11, in accordance with premises IV(a)-(e) (see Tables 2 and 4). Returning to the horizontal plane, it also follows that if a general concrete dispute right, R13, is recognised, then all those particular instantiations of it, of the type R16, must necessarily be recognised (including the particular

---

[33] This may be so even if the plaintiff does not succeed in obtaining the concrete right in the circumstances of that particular occasion. For example, in *Hedley Byrne* v *Heller* P lost his right that the bank exercise care in preparing the reference due to the bank's waiver of liability, nevertheless the instantiation of the abstract right and a general concrete right were established for such situations on occasions where there is no waiver. For further discussion, see ch VI:2.

instantiation in the dispute before us[34]). And finally, from R16 we can move in similar directions as we did from R13, to take in R8, R3 and R17. The final picture portrayed in Table 5 shatters the idea of exclusive columns of rights within the framework, but it also indicates that the pattern of interrelationships between the different notions of rights is more complex than might at first be thought.

The same sort of exercise could be done, if instead of starting with R10, we had a case of R11 or R12.[35] Whether or not our starting point is a right that is itself linked to a conception of the ideal society (nature of man), the movement from the abstract to the concrete through the process of settling a dispute does more than merely settle the outcome for the parties to the dispute. We can see depicted in Table 5 how the further ramifications of that process include an elaboration of the conception of society, which prior to the recognition of R10, existed merely in the form of an abstract ideal R1. We move through R10 to R2 and R3, fleshing out our abstract conception of an ideal society with concrete particulars, by settling the dispute over whether a particular instantiation of that abstract right should be accepted.

It is not only our conception of an ideal society (nature of man) that is elaborated in the process. For our conception of an actual society is similarly developed, as we take in R4, R6 and R8. And this latter development of a non-ideal conception of society will accompany any of the processes, commencing with the recognition of R10/11/12. Even in the case of R12 with no link to the ideal, our conception of an actual society would be broadened in a similar way by moving to include R7 and R9 with the original R5.

This observation may at first sight seem to endorse the prominent role Ronald Dworkin has given to rights in his view of judicial reasoning,[36] and also his subsequent related development of the idea of integrity in the law.[37] However, quite the contrary is the case. For although we have noted that *within the process of recognising rights* in a particular dispute we are simultaneously developing our conception of society, we have not noted that *rights themselves* determine how the dispute is to be settled (or our developing conception of society).

Indeed, the nature of the process of recognising a particular concrete instantiation of an abstract right, as has been described here,[38] refutes both of Dworkin's ideas: the prominence of rights is deflated by the recognition of

---

[34] Unless we have a situation as discussed in n33 above, in which case we can still recognise a number of rights of the type R16, though they will remain hypothetical until other relevant concrete situations arise.

[35] With R11, we would lose the connections in the first left hand line of Table 5; with R12 there would be further restrictions, omitting the first two left hand lines and all connections with the first level involving an ideal conception of society. Partial tables for R11 and R12 are to be found in Tables 7 and 8 below.

[36] *Taking Rights Seriously* (London, Duckworth, 1977).

[37] *Law's Empire* (London, Collins, 1986). The link between rights and integrity is made at 223. There is discussion of "integrity" in relation to constitutional rights in ch VI at n146.

[38] See Table 4, and for detailed discussion of premises IV(a)–(d), section 2(5) of this chapter.

other factors in the relevant premises; and the idea of law's integrity is dismissed by the fact that selection from the range of factors that are relevant is not predetermined, so that different judges may advance different conceptions of society (and hence different integrities) *even if starting from the same abstract right.* The same points apply doubly if in addition to the process of recognising a particular concrete instantiation of an abstract right, we are also involved in the process of establishing an actual right from an ideal right.[39]

One further observation may be of general importance. It is possible to distil a basic case of the legal development of rights from the elaborately detailed depiction in Table 5 of the process of recognising the concrete instantiation of an abstract right. Let us accept for the moment[40] that at times, in the Common Law world at least, we are dealing with an R10 type of right.[41] That is to say that the abstract right in question is linked to some conception of an ideal society (nature of man) rather than being merely linked to pragmatic or policy considerations (which would have given us R12 as an instantiation of R5); and that the abstract right in question has not as yet been established (which would have given us R11 as an instantiation of R4).[42] I take this to be the basic case because other cases which are less elaborate can readily be related to it,[43] and also because in the *development* of the law it is likely to have greater significance than other cases which proceed from already established rights.[44]

The key points in Table 5 relating to the development of the law, rather than to the elaboration of our conceptions of society, are the establishing of R4, as an abstract right which *may* give rise to other rights of the type R11, and the establishing of R6 as a general concrete right, which *will* give rise to other rights of the type R14. This is represented in Table 6, as a partial form of Table 5. Given that we have seen that if R11 is recognised as an instantiation of R4, this necessarily involves the recognition of concrete rights,[45] and also that R14 involves the recognition of particular rights, Table 6 provides us with an interesting depiction of the processes of developing rights in our basic case, which combines a full interplay between the abstract, concrete, general and particular.[46]

---

[39] Or singularly, in similar fashion, if we are dealing only with the establishing of a concrete actual right. Dworkin's view of rights is considered in ch IX.

[40] An example is provided in ch VI:2.

[41] The Common Law qualification serves to take us to R10 rather than R11. In Civil Law systems we would be more likely to be deriving our particular concrete instantiation from an established abstract right found in the Code, R4. However, the switch to R11 that this would necessitate does not make that much of a difference – see n35 above.

[42] See n41 above.

[43] Compare Tables 7 and 8 with Table 6 below.

[44] In other words, it provides a model for the seminal developments of the law.

[45] Or, at the very least, a concrete right.

[46] One may speculate on particular cases of R19 giving rise to the inverse image of this process. We have noted in Table 3 the possibility of a link between R19 and R5. Now suppose that in fact the abstract value that can be discerned in R19 relates to a particular conception of an ideal society (nature of man), the link would then be with R4 and R1, rather than R5. If, as is likely,

We can perform a similar exercise for cases involving R11 or R12, instead of R10. The partial tables for these rights are to be found as Table 7 and Table 8.

Finally, it may be helpful to provide a set of illustrations of the different notions of a right identified in the framework, as a way of recalling the differences between them. This is undertaken in Table 9. It should be borne in mind that although the variety of subject matter for the different illustrations in Table 9 occasionally relates to the particular characteristics of the notion of a right that is being illustrated, a great number of different notions of a right can be illustrated using the same subject matter, causing there to be different notions of "the same right", as Table 5 demonstrates. Detailed illustrations of the operation of the framework are provided in the following chapter.

Table 1

---

  (1) **Ideal Abstract Right**
  (2) **Ideal General Concrete Right**
  (3) **Ideal Particular Concrete Right**
  (4) **Established Ideal Abstract Right**
  (5) **Established Policy Abstract Right**
  (6) **Established Ideal General Concrete Right**
  (7) **Established Policy General Concrete Right**
  (8) **Established Ideal Particular Concrete Right**
  (9) **Established Policy Particular Concrete Right**
 (10) **Dispute Right determined from (1)**
 (11) **Dispute Right determined from (4)**
 (12) **Dispute Right determined from (5)**
 (13) **Dispute Right determined from (2)**
 (14) **Dispute Right determined from (6)**
 (15) **Dispute Right determined from (7)**
 (16) **Dispute Right determined from (3)**
 (17) **Dispute Right determined from (8)**
 (18) **Dispute Right determined from (9)**
 (19) **Dispute Right determined *de novo***

---

the other link from R19 in Table 3 is with a general concrete right rather than a particular one, we would then need to adjust to R6 rather than R7 to take into account the switch to a link with a conception of the ideal society (nature of man). We then end up with R4 and R6, as in our basic case, approached from the other side. Such cases of R19 that may exist should then be regarded as covert instances of our basic case, where the determination of the dispute right is in fact linked to a conception of the ideal society (nature of man) which remains unarticulated by the judge. All this assumes that one can in fact discern the unarticulated judicial conceptions of society, an assumption that John Griffith explores in *The Politics of the Judiciary*, 4ed. (London, Fontana Press, 1991). (A similar point about inverse images can be made in relation to other cases of R19, where the link is with R7 or R9.)

Table 2

	ABSTRACT:	GENERAL CONCRETE:	PARTICULAR CONCRETE:
conception of IDEAL society : (nature of man)	1	2	3
ESTABLISHED in less than : ideal society	4 5	6 7	8 9
used in regulation of : DISPUTE	10 11 12	13 14 15	16 17 18 19

Table 3

	ABSTRACT:	GENERAL CONCRETE:	PARTICULAR CONCRETE:
conception of IDEAL society : (nature of man)	1	2	3
ESTABLISHED in less than : ideal society	4 5	6 7	8 9
used in regulation of : DISPUTE	10 11 12	13 14 15	16 17 18 19

or

Table 4

Notion of Right:	Relevant Premise:	Means of Advancing Acceptance as Right:	Basis for Accepting Existence as Right:
1 2 3 }		argue for conception of ideal society (with appropriate detail)	accept conception of ideal society
4 6 8 }		argue for 1/2/3, AND as appropriate from:	established by appropriate event
	III(a) –	argue for policy of preferring over other possible rights	
	III(b) –	demonstrate or argue for policy of giving priority in order of rights	
	III(c) –	deny only appropriate as unattained end	
	III(d) –	argue for policy of accepting as matter of pragmatics	
	III(e) –	argue for recognition of status	
		OR derive necessarily from 10/13/16	
5 7 9 }		argue for appropriate policy	established by appropriate event
		OR derive from 19 – 9: necessarily 7: by demonstrating normatively constant generator 5: by demonstrating basis in abstract value	
10		argue for 1, AND as appropriate from:	established by authorised judgment
	III(a) –	argue for policy of preferring over other possible rights	
	III(b) –	demonstrate or argue for policy of giving priority in order of rights	
	III(c) –	deny only appropriate as unattained end	

Notion of Right:	Relevant Premise:	Means of Advancing Acceptance as Right:	Basis for Accepting Existence as Right:
	III(d) –	argue for policy of accepting as matter of pragmatics	
	III(e) –	argue for recognition of status AND ALSO as appropriate from:	
	IV(a) –	argue instrumental value present	
	IV(b) –	argue value greater	
	IV(c) –	argue for policy of selecting value	
	IV(d) –	argue value prevails	
13 } 16 }		argue for 2/3, AND as appropriate from:	established by authorised judgment
	III(a) –	argue for policy of preferring over other possible rights	
	III(b) –	demonstrate or argue for policy of giving priority in order of rights	
	III(c) –	deny only appropriate as unattained end	
	III(d) –	argue for policy of accepting as matter of pragmatics	
	III(e) –	argue for recognition of status	
11 } 12 }		show[47] 4/5, AND argue as appropriate from:	established by authorised judgment
	IV(a) –	argue instrumental value present	
	IV(b) –	argue value greater	
	IV(c) –	argue for policy of selecting value	
	IV(d) –	argue value prevails	
14 } 15 } 17 } 18 }		show 6/7/8/9, AND derive necessarily	established by authorised judgment
19		argue for appropriate policy	established by authorised judgment

[47] ie, show 4/5 has been established – there is no need to argue for rights that have already been established.

Table 5

	ABSTRACT:	GENERAL CONCRETE:	PARTICULAR CONCRETE:
conception of IDEAL society : (nature of man)	1	2	3
ESTABLISHED in less than : ideal society	4 5	6 7	8 9
used in regulation of : DISPUTE	⑩ 11 12	13 14 15	16 17 18 19

Table 6

	ABSTRACT:	GENERAL CONCRETE:	PARTICULAR CONCRETE:
conception of IDEAL society : (nature of man)	1	2	3
ESTABLISHED in less than : ideal society	4 5	6 7	8 9
used in regulation of : DISPUTE	⑩ 11 12	13 14 15	16 17 18 19

Table 7

	ABSTRACT:	GENERAL CONCRETE:		PARTICULAR CONCRETE:

conception of
IDEAL society :
(nature of man)

| | 1 | 2 | | 3 |

ESTABLISHED
in less than :
ideal society

| | 4 5 | 6 7 | | 8 9 |

used in
regulation of :
DISPUTE

| 10 ⑪ 12 | 13 14 15 | | 16 17 18 19 |

Table 8

	ABSTRACT:	GENERAL CONCRETE:		PARTICULAR CONCRETE:

conception of
IDEAL society :
(nature of man)

| | 1 | 2 | | 3 |

ESTABLISHED
in less than :
ideal society

| | 4 5 | 6 7 | | 8 9 |

used in
regulation of :
DISPUTE

| 10 11 ⑫ | 13 14 15 | | 16 17 18 19 |

Table 9

---

(1) **Ideal Abstract Right** – right to free speech.

(2) **Ideal General Concrete Right** – on the death of intestate parents, all surviving children have a right to inherit equal shares of the estate.

(3) **Ideal Particular Concrete Right** – (taking a royalist ideal conception of society) the King has the right to grant a patent giving an exclusive licence to print materials.

(4) **Established Ideal Abstract Right** – constitutional right to free speech.

(5) **Established Policy Abstract Right** – statutory right of natural parent to have access to child where it is in the best interests of the child.

(6) **Established Ideal General Concrete Right** – statutory right providing as (2).

(7) **Established Policy General Concrete Right** – statutory right for all victims of car accidents to recover compensation from state insurance fund.

(8) **Established Ideal Particular Concrete Right** – constitutional provision providing as (3).

(9) **Established Policy Particular Concrete Right** – right of specified individual to marry in a marriage enabling Act.

(10) **Dispute Right determined from** (1)

(11) **Dispute Right determined from** (4)

(12) **Dispute Right determined from** (5)

(13) **Dispute Right determined from** (2) granting a right

(14) **Dispute Right determined from** (6) providing as related right

(15) **Dispute Right determined from** (7) in circumstances of dispute

(16) **Dispute Right determined from** (3)

(17) **Dispute Right determined from** (8)

(18) **Dispute Right determined from** (9)

(19) **Dispute Right determined *de novo***

(a) **where further link with** (5)/(4)[48] – P granted a right to be protected from unnatural dangerous activities on neighbouring land.

(b) **where further link with** (7)/(6) – P granted a right where he has been defrauded by a rogue claiming to be someone else known to P, to recover his goods from an innocent purchaser of the goods from the rogue.

(c) **where further link with** (9) – Agamemnon granted a right to Achilles' prize of war.[49]

---

[48] See Table 3, and n46 above.

[49] The right was granted to Agamemnon by himself as Commander-in-Chief of the Achaean forces at Troy (though upheld by Athene's intervention with Achilles) – see Book I of *The Iliad*. It is difficult to see how such a notion of a right could arise outside the primitive context of a regal judgment. The modern understanding of law places any judgment in a context where it is capable of being generalised, as with cases (a) and (b) above – cp Finnis, NL&NR, 269.

VI

Applying the Framework

1 INTRODUCTION

The previous chapter commenced with the absence of an apology for drawing upon observations concerning rights that in themselves lacked any great originality or profundity. This chapter should start with an apology for leaving the reader at the end of the previous chapter trapped in a framework which is undoubtedly complex in its structure, based on nineteen notions of a right, five general principles, and eleven related premises.

The defence of the approach taken in the previous chapter was based on the assertion that much of the heated debate over rights has been fuelled by the neglect of some fairly simple truths about rights, which has had the effect of making rights discourse more complex and more bellicose. In particular, it was suggested that much of the difficulty in resolving arguments over rights can be traced to the combatants exploiting different uses of the term "right". The way in which this enterprise which commenced with lauding simplicity has ended in such complexity, clearly calls for amends. The purpose of this chapter is to show how the complex structure of the framework is in fact necessary if we are to distinguish the different statements about rights, and render them intelligible. I shall attempt to do this by means of a number of illustrations from different arenas in which rights are contested: private law rights, constitutional rights, and rights under international law.

It is worth reiterating that the success of the framework is to be measured in identifying differences of perspective, permitting clashes of opinion to be intelligibly argued, and rejecting spurious arguments.[1] The enterprise is to construct a framework for discussing rights, not a machine for producing rights. Indeed, one obvious corollary of a successful outcome would be a greater awareness of the limitations of invoking rights to settle an argument, and the extent to which other factors need to be addressed if intelligent discussion is to continue.

One feature of rights that has been given prominence in the construction of the framework is their capacity for taking on an abstract nature. This quality more than any other is responsible for the possibility of rival positions in legal or moral argument masquerading as champions under the same banner. We have already noted scepticism over the looseness of rights talk,[2] yet this abstract quality is occasionally praised.

[1] ch V:1.
[2] ch V, n1.

Steven Lukes has advocated keeping a list of human rights "reasonably short and reasonably abstract" in order to be able to command a broad consensus for it.[3] But Lukes goes on to acknowledge that this very abstract quality which has been employed to muster a consensus will itself be the cause of disagreement once the issue of a particular concrete right is faced.[4]

Of course, for some individuals the abstract quality of established rights may be worked to their advantage, in that the very looseness of the language of the established abstract right can be exploited to argue for the particular instantiation that favours the individual's position, even where the right was originally established by those who would not have looked favourably on that position.[5]

Whatever the benefits in terms of political expediency or rhetorical advantage that abstract rights may bestow, the movement from abstract to concrete (or concrete to abstract), and the distinction between abstract and concrete forms of rights must be studied more carefully than the concerns of the politician or advocate would allow for, if we are to discuss rights in an intelligible manner. We shall frequently focus upon issues related to the nature of abstract rights in the illustrations that follow.

2 RIGHTS IN THE TORT OF NEGLIGENCE

(1) *Donoghue* v *Stevenson*

The conventional way of discussing the tort of negligence is to explore the duty of care owed by the potential defendant. However, this discussion is simply another way of addressing the possibility of the potential plaintiff enjoying the correlative right that the defendant exercise care so as not to injure the plaintiff's interests. The development of the tort of negligence in the Common Law then furnishes a rich array of illustrative material for studying how different rights emerge and relate to each other.

In *Donoghue* v *Stevenson*[6] the disagreement in the House of Lords over whether to recognise a general principle of liability for negligence was settled

---

[3] "Five Fables about Human Rights" in Stephen Shute and Susan Hurley (eds.), *On Human Rights: The Oxford Amnesty Lectures 1993* (New York, NY, Basic Books, 1993) at 38.

[4] *ibid.*

[5] David Feldman has pointed out in the context of human rights treaties, that once the treaty has become effective, "the content of the guaranteed rights will become largely a matter for dynamic interpretation over which the drafters and the contracting states can exercise only limited control." – "Human Rights Treaties, Nation States, and Conflicting Moralities" (1995) 1 *Contemporary Issues in Law* 61 at 66. The same point is made in relation to the USA's constitutional rights at 69. Cp Francis Jacobs, *The European Convention on Human Rights*, 1ed. (Oxford, Clarendon Press, 1975) at 18: "the Convention . . . must be interpreted in the light of developments in social and political attitudes. Its effects cannot be confined to the conceptions of the period when it was drafted . . .".

[6] [1932] AC 562. The correlativity between right and duty is made explicit by Lord Macmillan at 619.

by a bare majority led by Lord Atkin. The differences between this view of the law and the minority viewpoint forcefully argued by Lord Buckmaster can be illuminated by tracing their Lordships' reasoning through the framework developed in the previous chapter.

It was common ground between the two viewpoints that the Common Law (and Scots law) prior to that case had recognised a number of general principles of liability for negligence operating within specified categories: (1) involving an article that was inherently dangerous; (2) involving an article that was not inherently dangerous but had to the knowledge of the defendant become dangerous; (3) involving the defendant being in control of dangerous premises to which the plaintiff had been invited.[7]

In terms of the framework, this provides us with at the very least three established general concrete rights, which with reference to Table 1 and Table 2[8] we may designate $R7_1$, $R7_2$, and $R7_3$. Each of these rights will in turn necessarily lead to the recognition of rights in particular disputes where the plaintiff's position can be brought under one of the established categories: giving us any number of rights in the form $R15_1$, $R15_2$, and $R15_3$.

It may be the case that these established general concrete rights in fact are derived from more than the pragmatism of policy, and can be related to some conception of the ideal society (nature of man), in which case we would need to designate them $R6_1$, $R6_2$, and $R6_3$; and, correspondingly, the related dispute rights, $R14_1$, $R14_2$, and $R14_3$. This difference is not for the moment a material one.

The crucial distinction between the viewpoints of Lord Atkin and Lord Buckmaster was that whereas Lord Buckmaster was adamant that the Common Law stopped at the recognition of those categories, represented by the R6/R7 rights,[9] Lord Atkin was equally adamant that more could be said, so as to bring in the injury caused to Mrs Donoghue by the negligent process of manufacture by Stevenson which had permitted the introduction of a snail into the ginger beer that she had drunk.

The key to Lord Atkin's process of reasoning is to be found in the proposition contained in the second of the two following sentences:[10]

"In this way it can be ascertained at any time whether the law recognises a duty, but only where the case can be referred to some particular species which has been examined and classified. And yet the duty which is common to all the cases where liability is established must logically be based upon some element common to the cases where it is found to exist."

---

[7] *ibid.* at 569, 573 (Buckmaster); 594–595 (Atkin). These three categories figure prominently in the speeches in *Donoghue v Stevenson*, but are not exhaustive. There is, for example, a category relating to bailees, which was given greater emphasis in the discussion in *Hedley Byrne v Heller* (considered below).

[8] The Tables referred to in this chapter are all to be found at the end of ch V.

[9] [1932] AC 562 at 569, 573–574, 576.

[10] *ibid.* at 580.

The proposition is then reiterated by Lord Atkin[11] –

> ". . .in English law there must be and is some general conception of relations giving rise to a duty of care, of which the particular cases found in the books are but instances."

– before enunciating his famous neighbour principle:[12]

> "You must take reasonable care to avoid acts or omissions which you can reasonably foresee would be likely to injure your neighbour. Who then, in law, is my neighbour? The answer seems to be persons who are so closely and directly affected by my act that I ought reasonably to have them in contemplation as being so affected when I am directing my mind to the acts or omissions which are called in question."

We may paraphrase Lord Atkin's neighbour principle in terms of an abstract right enjoyed by the plaintiff: that the defendant exercise reasonable care in his conduct so as to avoid injury to the plaintiff where the defendant should reasonably contemplate the plaintiff as likely to be affected by his conduct. The question is where this right comes from. Lord Atkin speaks of it being an established right in English law – "there . . . is some general conception of relations". But its existence in English law is based upon the logical necessity of deriving it from the particular categories which have previously been recognised by the law.

What this then amounts to is deriving an established abstract right, R4/R5,[13] from the established R6/7 concrete rights, as a matter of logical necessity. The framework clearly shows this to be spurious. Logic cannot support this proposition.

The flaw in Lord Atkin's logic can be demonstrated by taking the three established categories of liability as instances of a general moral prohibition against harming others, as Lord Atkin recognises they are, and from this deduce that the law upholds the general moral prohibition, which Lord Atkin recognises it does not.[14] Put more formally, Lord Atkin is guilty of a false syllogism, such as is commonly given an illustration along the lines: all cats are

---

[11] [1932] AC 562 at 580.

[12] *ibid.*

[13] The distinction is again not for the moment material.

[14] [1932] AC 562 at 580. The logical flaw is nonetheless easily overlooked, particularly after the event, once the general principle purportedly derived from the law *has been given* legal status through the authority of precedent by the case in which the spurious reasoning has been embraced. For the previously existing legal general concrete rights can then be said to fall under the now established legal abstract right. It seems a simple matter then also to make the connection the other way round, and speak of the abstract right being reflected in the general concrete rights which preceded it. So, for example, H.L.A. Hart in the posthumously published Postscript to his *The Concept of Law*, 2ed (Oxford, Clarendon Press, 1994), edited by Penelope A Bulloch and Joseph Raz, at 268, described *Donoghue v Stevenson* as "[a] modest exercise of constructive interpretation . . . identify[ing a] latent legal principle". But the general (abstract) principle established in *Donoghue* was not a *legal* principle prior to that case which established it, and cannot accordingly be identified (however latent) as a legal principle among the general concrete rights established in the cases that preceded *Donoghue*.

animals, my dog is an animal, therefore my dog is a cat. Here: all these categories of liability involve negligence, this situation involves negligence, therefore there is liability in this situation. The logical flaw is to take an "element common to the cases" and assume that all other cases having this element can be treated in the same way as the given cases.

The clash between Lord Atkin and Lord Buckmaster is not then a matter of logic. The true source of Lord Atkin's right is rather his conception of society:[15]

> "I do not think so ill of our jurisprudence as to suppose that its principles are so remote from the needs of civilised society and the ordinary claims which it makes upon its members as to deny a legal remedy where there is so obviously a social wrong."

And it is here that the clash occurs with Lord Buckmaster. For whereas Lord Atkin's conception of society is willing to embrace an approach that upholds the interests of consumers in being protected against the negligence of manufacturers, Lord Buckmaster emphatically endorses a different conception of society in which manufacturers should be unencumbered by the burden of taking care not to injure their consumers.[16]

The right established through Lord Atkin's neighbour principle may accordingly be regarded as an abstract right derived from Lord Atkin's conception of society, used in the regulation of a dispute – R10, rather than the established right, R4/5, as it is purported to be. See Figure 1 below.

However, two further rights can be linked to the outcome of *Donoghue v Stevenson*. From the establishing of R10, we may infer (see Table 6) an established abstract right, R4, which will now through the operation of precedent be in place for future cases.

The other right is an established general concrete right, R6, since the instantiation of the abstract right upheld in the case is regarded as being an instance of a general category. This is clear from Lord Atkin's formulation of the legal question at issue in the case as involving the general point of liability of "the manufacturer of an article of drink",[17] and by the general proposition of law formulated at the conclusion of his speech:[18]

> "a manufacturer of products which he sells in such a form as to show that he intends them to reach the ultimate consumer in the form in which they left him, with no reasonable possibility of intermediate examination, and with the knowledge that the absence of reasonable care in the preparation or putting up of the products will

---

[15] For a general view of Lord Atkin's conception of society, see Geoffrey Lewis, *Lord Atkin* (London, Butterworths, 1983).

[16] Lord Buckmaster endorses the sentiment of Lord Anderson in an earlier case that "it would seem little short of outrageous to make them responsible to members of the public for the condition of the contents of every bottle which issues from their works." – [1932] AC 562 at 578.

[17] *ibid*. at 578.

[18] *ibid*. at 599.

result in injury to the consumer's life or property, owes a duty to the consumer to take that reasonable care."

This then provides an established general concrete right, R_{64}, for consumers against manufacturers, which may be applied in future cases, to provide rights of the form R14.

We are now in a position to clearly see that there are two distinct rights established by the case of *Donoghue* v *Stevenson*: R4(the neighbour principle) and R_{64}(the liability of manufacturers to consumers). By appreciating the existence of both rights, and their different characters, we can understand more about how the Common Law has developed subsequently.

Figure 1

	ABSTRACT:	GENERAL CONCRETE:	PARTICULAR CONCRETE:
conception of IDEAL society : (nature of man)	1	2	3
ESTABLISHED in less than : ideal society	4 5	6_4 7	8 9
used in regulation of : DISPUTE	⑩ 11 12	13 14_4 15	16 17 18 19

(2) Subsequent Development in *Hedley Byrne* v *Heller*

Of all the cases following *Donoghue* v *Stevenson* arguably the most intriguing is *Hedley Byrne* v *Heller*.[19] This is so for two reasons: not simply because it developed the existing liability for negligence in a way which was highly significant and yet not uncontroversial,[20] but also because the principles of liability established by the case itself have given rise to enduring controversy.

The two particular features of the facts in *Hedley Byrne* that caused controversy were that there was a negligent statement, rather than conduct having a physical impact, and that the loss occasioned was purely financial, or as it is usually described, economic. The plaintiff advertising agency sought to recover for their loss caused by relying on a credit reference supplied by the

---

[19] [1964] AC 465.
[20] It overruled the earlier Court of Appeal majority decision in *Candler* v *Crane, Christmas & Co* [1951] 2 KB 164.

defendant bank on one of their clients, which they had relied on in allowing the client to run up credit with them, when the client went bankrupt.

I want to consider in some detail how the Law Lords in *Hedley Byrne* regarded the law as established in *Donoghue* relating to the issues facing them, before commenting on how the law that they themselves established has proved to be so controversial in its own application. At both stages, I shall suggest that much confusion has been caused by a failure to fully appreciate the two notions of rights established in *Donoghue*, as identified above.

It is quite extraordinary that the five Law Lords in *Hedley Byrne* do not even agree as to whether *Donoghue* is relevant to the case before them. Lord Reid is the most outspoken on the one extreme. He regards it as inapplicable.[21] Lord Devlin represents the other extreme, and we shall commence with an examination of his reasoning.

Lord Devlin, in applying *Donoghue*, makes a clear distinction between the abstract right and the general concrete right established in that case, which we have referred to above as R4 and R6$_4$ respectively. Unfortunately, in doing so he does not clearly identify the characteristics of these rights, or the manner in which they are related to other rights. Lord Devlin's clear distinction is put in the following terms:[22]

> "Lord Atkin did two things. He stated what he described as a general conception and from that conception he formulated a specific proposition of law."

The "general conception" (which in the lines following Lord Devlin also refers to as "a 'general conception of relations giving rise to a duty of care'",[23] "the principle of proximity",[24] and "the general conception of proximity"[25]) is specifically filled out by citing Lord Atkin's neighbour principle.[26] This general conception then encompasses R4.

The "specific proposition of law" is then indicated to be the statement about the liability of a manufacturer of products, cited above,[27] which accordingly encompasses R6$_4$. Moreover, Lord Devlin speaks of, "The specific proposition arising out of [the general] conception . . .".[28]

The same distinction is employed by Lord Devlin when he comes to stating the effect of the law established in *Hedley Byrne*. For he speaks of a specific proposition involving "a relationship equivalent to contract" where "there is an express or implied undertaking of responsibility",[29] and states, "I regard this proposition as an application of the general conception of proximity."[30]

---

[21] [1964] AC 465 at 482.
[22] *ibid*. at 524.
[23] *ibid*.
[24] *ibid*.
[25] *ibid*. at 531.
[26] *ibid*. at 524.
[27] n18 above.
[28] [1964] AC 465 at 574
[29] *ibid*. at 530.
[30] *ibid*.

From the way that Lord Devlin discusses the "general conception" and the "specific propositions", it is clear that they and the rights which they encompass are abstract and general concrete in nature respectively, in the way that we have depicted these properties in R4 and R64. For he states of the general conception that although it is applicable, it cannot of itself determine whether there is a right in the particular case:[31]

> "[The appellants] asked whether the principle of proximity should not apply as well to words as to deeds. I think that it should, but as it is only a general conception it does not get them very far."

On the other hand, having established the specific proposition resting on equivalence to contract plus undertaking of responsibility, Lord Devlin indicates:[32]

> "Where there is a general relationship of this sort it is unnecessary to do more than prove its existence and the duty [/right] follows."

He then raises the possibility of a different specific proposition arising in the future to deal with a case where there is reliance but no equivalence to contract, since "the statement is not supplied for the use of any particular person".[33] If so,[34]

> "it will then be necessary to return to the general conception of proximity and to see whether there can be evolved from it, as was done in *Donoghue* v *Stevenson*, a specific proposition to fit the case."

Lord Devlin does not commit himself to a formulation of such a proposition,[35] so the existence of it remains hypothetical. Nevertheless, Lord Devlin has said enough to indicate that if the proposition were to be established it would involve a different proposition from the one established in *Hedley Byrne*.

We may then represent the general conception, the different specific propositions, and their resolution of the disputes that may be brought under them, in terms of the rights that they encompass, in two variations on Table 7, which appear as Figures 2 and 3.

---

[31] [1964] AC 465 at 525. Earlier (at 524) Lord Devlin speaks of seeking to use "proximity" as the test of liability as "a misuse of a general conception". Similarly, Lord Diplock in *Home Office* v *Dorset Yacht Co* [1970] AC 1004 at 1060 speaks of the misuse of the neighbour principle "as a universal" being "manifestly false". Cp Holmes J in *Lochner* v *New York* (1905) 198 US 45 at 76: "General propositions do not decide concrete cases. The decision will depend on a judgment or intuition more subtle than any articulate major premise." See further, George Christie, "The Uneasy Place of Principle in Tort Law" in David Owen (ed.), *Philosophical Foundations of Tort Law* (Oxford, Clarendon Press, 1995).
[32] [1964] AC 465 at 530. Cp Lord Diplock, *loc. cit.* n31 above, allowing, by contrast to the neighbour principle, that the "specific proposition" relating to a manufacturer's liability could be treated "as a universal".
[33] [1964] AC 465 at 531.
[34] *ibid.*
[35] *ibid.*

Figure 2

ABSTRACT:	GENERAL CONCRETE:	PARTICULAR CONCRETE:

conception of
IDEAL society :
(nature of man)

1   2   3

ESTABLISHED
in less than :
ideal society

4   5 6_5 7   8   9

used in
regulation of :
DISPUTE

10 (11_5) 12   13 14_5 15   16 17 18 19

Figure 3

ABSTRACT:	GENERAL CONCRETE:	PARTICULAR CONCRETE:

conception of
IDEAL society :
(nature of man)

1   2   3

ESTABLISHED
in less than :
ideal society

4   5 6_h 7   8   9

used in
regulation of :
DISPUTE

10 (11_h) 12   13 14_h 15   16 17 18 19

In Figure 2: R4 is the abstract right established in the neighbour principle in *Donoghue*; R11$_5$ is the instantiation of that abstract right accepted in *Hedley Byrne* depending on equivalence to contract plus assumption of responsibility; R14$_5$ is P's general concrete right which necessarily accompanies the establishing of R11$_5$ in the settling of the dispute between the parties, or may be derived in any other particular case where "the duty follows";[36]

---

[36] As it would have done in *Hedley Byrne* itself had it not been for the bank's waiver of liability. In other subsequent cases the link between R6 and R14 would be in the opposite direction, since by now we would be proceeding from an already established general concrete right, R6, and the whole process of development necessary could be captured by this link alone.

and, $R6_5$ is the general concrete right encompassed in the specific proposition resting on equivalence to contract plus assumption of responsibility, which is established together with the recognition of $R14_5$.

Figure 3 can be understood similarly, with the substitution of: $R11_h$ as the hypothetical instantiation of the abstract right established in *Donoghue* depending on the criteria (as yet undecided) in a case where the statement is not supplied for the use of a particular person; $R14_h$ as P's general concrete right that would follow if the "relevant criteria" were to be recognised and satisfied in the facts of P's case;[37] and, $R6_h$ as the hypothetical general concrete right encompassed in the other specific proposition for such a case.

So far the application of the framework to Lord Devlin's reasoning appears relatively straightforward. Yet I prefaced our examination of his reasoning with a caution, which now needs to be amplified. There are two objections to raise. The first point to challenge is principally a matter of terminology, though combined with the second it creates confusion over the characteristics of the rights established in *Donoghue* and *Hedley Byrne*, and the manner in which they relate to each other.

We have seen that although Lord Devlin has clearly identified the abstract nature of his general conception,[38] the term "general conception" does not clearly mark it out as such. Equally, the term "specific proposition" does not clearly indicate the general nature of the principle from which a number of specific concrete rights may be derived.[39]

If the failing were nothing more than this it could be corrected by a simple modification to the terms Lord Devlin employs. However, the second point is evidence of a deeper confusion in Lord Devlin's reasoning.

Although Lord Devlin twice clearly indicates that the general conception can only be used as an abstract conception, from which concrete rights do not necessarily follow,[40] he still speaks of the relationship between the two in terms of the general concrete right (encompassed in the specific proposition) as "arising out of" the general conception,[41] as though it were simply a matter of deriving the one from the other.

This false suggestion is strengthened by Lord Devlin's further exposition of the process of reasoning employed in deriving the specific proposition (general concrete right) from the general conception (abstract right) which he then provides:[42]

"What Lord Atkin did was to use his general conception to open up a category of cases giving rise to a special duty. It was already clear that the law recognised the existence of such duty in the category of articles that were dangerous in themselves.

---

[37] [1964] AC 465 at 532.
[38] n31 above.
[39] It covers "the present case" and "others of the same type" – [1964] AC 465 at 531.
[40] n31 above.
[41] n28 above.
[42] [1964] AC 465 at 524-525.

What *Donoghue* v *Stevenson* did may be described either as the widening of an old category or as the creation of a new and similar one. The general conception can be used to produce other categories in the same way."

This passage is beset with confusion, sufficient to lose completely the clarity of Lord Devlin's earlier observations in distinguishing the abstract nature of the general conception.

The first source of confusion is the repetition within the first three sentences of this passage of Lord Atkin's fallacy that the abstract right (conception) can be derived from the established general concrete right (existing category), which was commented on in the previous section.[43] Some further comment is, however, called for. For Lord Devlin refers to this process not, as Lord Atkin did,[44] as deriving the general conception from the common element found in all the particular categories, but "as the widening of an old category or as the creation of a new and similar one."

Nevertheless, this awkward locution must ultimately be only another way of describing the flawed process engaged in by Lord Atkin. Consider the first limb – widening an old category. The category so widened must now contain all the old members with some new members. They must all (old and new) share a common element, otherwise they could not be contained in the one category. Yet this common element must differ from that common element shared by the old members which made them members of the old category. For if that were the element common to old and new members, there would never have been the need to widen the category in order to welcome the new members, since they would already have been members of it.

So, this new common element that is required to widen the category is found among the old members, but is not in fact the element common to them that made them members of the category. This is incorporating precisely the same logical flaw as Lord Atkin in finding "some element common to the cases" on which he can then found his general conception, so as to treat other cases possessing this element in the same way.

Consider the second limb of Lord Devlin's formulation – creating a new and similar category. This simply amounts to a more refined version of the first limb. Insofar as the new category is similar to the old category, the members of the new category must share an element common with the members of the old category. Let us call it the "similar element". But insofar as the new category is new, the members of the new category must share a distinctive element which is not shared by the members of the old category. Let us call this the "new element". But equally, the members of the old category must also share a distinctive element, which must be different from the new element (since they do not possess it) and must also be different from the similar element, for if this were the element that defined their membership of the old

---

[43] Text at nn 13 and 14, above.
[44] See text at nn 10 and 11, above.

category, then the new members (which also have the similar element) would also from the start have been members of the old category and there would never have arisen the need to create a new one.

We are now in a position to see how the second limb is engaging in the same exercise as the first limb in order to bring the new members inside a recognised legal category, for this is being done on the basis of finding "some element common to the cases", the similar element, on which can then be founded a recognised legal category for the new members. The only difference is that an additional step is taken. Instead of welcoming the new members into the same category as the old members, they are given a recognised category of their own with its own distinctive element. But the first step in recognising the members of this new category at all is on the basis of the similar element,[45] which is a mere repetition of the fallacy disclosed in the first limb.

An analogy illustrating Lord Devlin's logical flaw in its two variant forms, that more closely resembles the language of categories he employs, would be along the following lines. Variant 1: eating crisp apples is good for your teeth; crisp apples are fruit; oranges are fruit; therefore eating fruit (which includes oranges) is good for your teeth. Variant 2: eating crisp apples is good for your teeth; crisp apples are fruit; oranges are fruit; therefore eating crisp apples, and eating oranges, is good for your teeth.

The second source of Lord Devlin's confusion is found in the play he makes of categories in this passage, which blurs the distinction between abstract rights and concrete rights. In the first sentence, the general conception is spoken of as being used to open up a category of cases. In the third sentence, the general conception is itself explained as the process of widening an established category, or creating a similar category to an established category. (And we have just been given an example of an established category in the second sentence to demonstrate that there was a category in existence ready to be widened.) Finally, in the fourth sentence, we are told that the general conception can be used to create new categories in the same way as an established category was used (widened) to bring about the general conception.

We are left with a forceful image of the prolific asexual reproduction of categories. An established category widens to give off a general category, which is itself capable of widening to give off further categories.[46] Within this fecund imagery Lord Devlin's confusion is now completed by suggesting that the derivation of the abstract right from the general concrete right arises "in the same way" as a general concrete right is derived from an abstract right. The distinction between abstract rights and general concrete rights, that was evident in the other passages from Lord Devlin's speech examined above, is completely lost.

---

[45] As Lord Devlin himself puts it in the sentence immediately following the passage cited: "An existing category grows as instances of *its application* multiply, until the time comes when the cell divides." (emphasis added) – [1964] AC 465 at 525.

[46] The reproductive image is Devlin's – see n45 above.

One may suspect that the judicial tendency to represent the processes of dealing with abstract rights[47] as somehow equivalent to the comfortable logical process of dealing with general concrete rights by locating an instance within a defined category,[48] has a lot to do with their feeling uncomfortable in providing an alternative explanation for what is actually going on.[49] And this may in turn explain why it is that the distinction between abstract rights and general concrete rights is so easily lost. Yet to confuse the nature of this distinction is the source of greater confusion.

This is evident if we turn to the other Law Lords in *Hedley Byrne* and ask why it was that they could not agree on the applicability of *Donoghue*. Lord Reid in holding *Donoghue* inapplicable does so because "the law must treat negligent words differently from negligent acts."[50] But this is an objection[51] that can only survive if we do not recognise *Donoghue* as establishing both the general concrete right, R_{64}, which deals with the acts of the manufacturer,[52] and the abstract right, R4, based on the neighbour principle.[53] It is obvious that R_{64} cannot help in *Hedley Byrne*. But if R4 is applicable, due to *the abstract nature* of R4 it will not be determinative of the case in the way that an established general concrete right would be. Moreover, if R4 is used in *Hedley Byrne*, the result will be establishing another general concrete right, R_{65}, in the further instantiation of the abstract right, which calls for a fresh examination of the appropriate premises (Table 4) and a distinct approach being taken to the case before the court, such that it is possible to "treat negligent words differently from negligent acts".

A fuller understanding of the nature of the abstract and general concrete rights established in *Donoghue* is accordingly capable of accommodating both Lord Reid's objection and Lord Devlin's enthusiasm. Of the other Law Lords, Lord Morris cites *Donoghue* only in relation to R4 and relies on other authorities to develop his argument;[54] Lord Hodson believes that *Donoghue* has a

---

[47] Both the process of deriving them in the first place, and the process of applying them to establish concrete rights.

[48] Of course, one could speak loosely of the category of all cases falling under the neighbour principle. But this is to employ an open category whose membership cannot be determined until we decide *how we are going to apply* the neighbour principle. In the neighbour principle category, we cannot use the category in order to determine how to deal with the case, but must first determine how to deal with the case before deciding whether it fits in the category. As Julius Stone puts it, in his criticism of the circularity or meaninglessness of the neighbour test: "it must be obvious . . . that there is some determinant of the actual decision other than what can be drawn by deductive logic from the category ostensibly used." – *Legal System and Lawyers' Reasonings* (Stanford, CA, Stanford University Press, 1964) at 260.

[49] John Bell in ch X of *Policy Arguments in Judicial Decisions* (Oxford, Clarendon Press, 1983) suggests that recognition of a "creatively political aspect" of the judicial function has a number of implications, particularly for the manner of selection of judges.

[50] [1964] AC 465 at 482.

[51] If objection at all – other members of the House disagreed on this point.

[52] n18 above.

[53] n12 above.

[54] *ibid.* at 496.

broader impact, but does not develop it;[55] and Lord Pearce speaks of *Donoghue* offering a "broad outlook" which may assist by analogy.[56]

There are then within the speeches in the House of Lords in *Hedley Byrne* varying degrees of recognition of the two rights, R4 and R64, established in *Donoghue*, but at the best incomplete and at the worst wholly confused. I want to now suggest that the failure to clearly recognise the two[57] has caused further confusion in working out the law established in *Hedley Byrne* itself.

(3) Further Developments

Hedley Byrne is accepted as establishing in the modern law of negligence the possibility of liability for economic loss, but the subsequent development of this area of the law must rate as one of the most incoherent areas of the Common Law. Commentators speak of the courts dealing with liability for economic loss in negligence in terms of a general principle of *not* allowing recovery for the negligent infliction of economic loss, to which *Hedley Byrne* is an awkward exception.[58] This clumsy formulation of the law is perhaps the best that can be done for the development of a principle that has gone through such inconsistencies of judicial attitude that one House of Lords case has been overruled by another on the way,[59] and another has suffered the fate of being distinguished on its facts.[60]

Even so, treating *Hedley Byrne* as an exception to the negative principle does not really do credit to the full range of judicial inconsistency which has been exhibited in the more recent decisions: to disallow liability for economic loss in a case involving negligent misstatement by the auditors of a company's accounts;[61] but to allow it in cases involving negligence by a solicitor in failing to draw up a will,[62] the negligent preparation of a reference,[63] and the negligent management of Lloyd's insurance syndicates.[64]

[55] n12 at 505–506.

[56] *ibid.* at 536.

[57] The point would hold for their recognition in the law of negligence generally, even if R4 is not seen as being established by *Donoghue*.

[58] See David Howarth, *Textbook on Tort* (London, Butterworths, 1995) ch 6. Cp B.S. Markesinis & S.F. Deakin, *Tort Law*, 3ed. (Oxford, Clarendon Press, 1994) at 84–7; W.V.H. Rogers, *Winfield & Jolowicz on Tort*, 14ed. (London, Sweet & Maxwell, 1994) at 93, 100-1.

[59] *Anns v Merton LBC* [1978] 1 AC 728 overruled in *Murphy v Brentwood DC* [1991] 1 AC 398. For criticism of the doctrinal arguments in *Murphy*, see J.W. Harris, "Murphy makes it Eight – Overruling comes to Negligence" (1991) 11 *Oxford Journal of Legal Studies* 416. See further, n71 below. For rejection of *Murphy* in the Commonwealth, see Ian Duncan Wallace, "Murphy Rejected: The Bryan v Maloney Landmark" (1995) 3 *Tort Law Review* 231. See further, n106 below.

[60] *Junior Books v Veitchi* [1983] 1 AC 520. For an overview of these developments, see Howarth, n58 above at pp 269–73.

[61] *Caparo v Dickman* [1990] 2 AC 605.

[62] *White v Jones* [1993] 3 All ER 481.

[63] *Spring v Guardian Assurance* [1994] 3 All ER 129.

[64] *Henderson v Merrett* [1994] 3 All ER 506. For comment see Howarth, above n58 at 280–93.

This incoherence and inconsistency can be explained to a great extent by the failure to fully appreciate the nature of the two rights involved in the development of the law of negligence, both in *Hedley Byrne* and the cases that have followed it. For the recognition of both an abstract right, and a general concrete right which may differ from case to case, allows the underlying thread to be maintained in the abstract right in providing the possibility of liability for economic loss, whilst acknowledging that its instantiation is a matter for fresh consideration in each potential general concrete right encountered in the different cases.

So, for example, *Caparo*[65] which denied liability for the negligent statement of the auditor, should not be regarded as inconsistent with *Hedley Byrne* in any respect. The denial of liability for this particular instantiation cannot be regarded as inconsistent with the abstract right in *Hedley Byrne*, R4, since it is in the nature of abstract rights that not every instantiation will be accepted in practice. But nor can it be regarded as inconsistent with the general concrete right established in *Hedley Byrne*, $R6_5$, for this is quite a separate matter from the concrete right that was under consideration in *Caparo*, as was made clear in Lord Devlin's speech,[66] represented in Figures 2 and 3 above. In effect, *Caparo* simply decides that $R6_h$ in Figure 3 is not to be established, which has no bearing at all on the rights established in Figure 2.

Yet this is not to say that the whole doctrine of tort law relating to liability in negligence for economic loss may suddenly be reduced to a coherent whole. The analysis offered does, however, account more precisely for how and where the incoherence arises, by indicating two particular phenomena.

The first is the relationship that we have noted between the development of rights, where an abstract right is involved, and the filling out of a conception of society.[67] This permits different judges to draw on their own peculiar conceptions of society, whilst developing the law, and for clashes to occur between different conceptions, such as we noted between Lord Atkin and Lord Buckmaster,[68] which may affect whether or not a particular instantiation of an abstract right is established. Even where there is not direct inconsistency between different cases, due to the fact that they involve quite separate general concrete rights (eg $R6_5$ and $R6_h$), we may still be able to detect a jarring between them, which can be traced to how different judicial conceptions of society influence how the premises are approached (see Table 6) in determining whether a particular instantiation is accepted or not.[69] So, David Howarth singles out Lord Keith for favouring a conception of society

---

[65] n61 above.

[66] Text at nn 33–7 above.

[67] ch V:4.

[68] nn 15 and 16 above.

[69] Significantly, Lord Pearce in *Hedley Byrne*, having referred to the "broad outlook" in *Donoghue*, states: "How wide the sphere of the duty of care in negligence is to be laid depends ultimately on the courts' assessment of the demands of society for protection from the carelessness of others." – [1964] AC 465 at 536.

that is particularly mean to those injured by the negligence of others, in contrast to other Law Lords whose conception is more generous.[70]

The second phenomenon arises out of the confusion between the two different kinds of rights. The failure to clearly identify them means that judges or commentators may play fast and loose with the established decisions, moving back to an abstract conception which allows them to consider afresh the instantiation at issue in the case before them even where a relevant general concrete right is established.[71] It also makes it easier to shrug off the argument seeking to establish a particular instantiation, as though the acceptance of the general concrete right in that case would bind them to accept it in other cases in which it is clearly unacceptable. This ignores the point that it would only be the abstract right that would be carried into the other cases, leaving open the question of whether a later instantiation should be accepted or not.[72] And the blurring of abstract and concrete means anyway that judges do not feel obliged to clearly indicate precisely what is the general concrete right that they are establishing when liability for negligence is accepted, since to do so would seem to shut off the possibility of further development in the law.[73]

[70] n58 above at pp 164, 206.

[71] A notable illustration of this confusion from economic loss liability is provided by *Murphy*, n59 above, in which the argument is adopted against allowing liability by builders for economic loss arising out of a negligently constructed building, that this would be contrary to the principles established in *Donoghue v Stevenson*. But the reference to *Donoghue* is to the principle encompassing the general concrete right relating to the liability of manufacturers (n18 above) – see J.W. Harris, n59 above at 422. So, Lord Keith refers to the *Donoghue v Stevenson* principle as one dealing with "defective chattels", [1991] 1 AC 398 at 462, 465, as does Lord Bridge at 475. Lord Oliver takes a similar line at 486H but then see-saws between the general concrete right and the abstract right at 487A-B, employing the uncertainties of the abstract right to justify not upholding the concrete right in the present case (instead of addressing whether a new instantiation of the abstract right should be recognised). The final full speech given by Lord Jauncey also refers to the general concrete right, and its correlative duty, established in *Donoghue* – at 493, 495, 497 – as a reason for denying liability. By contrast, in *Anns* (n59 above) which *Murphy* overrules, liability is established by reference to the principle encompassing the abstract right established in *Donoghue* (n12 above) – see Lord Wilberforce [1978] AC 728 at 751, 757; Lord Salmon at 763.

[72] The frequent use of the floodgates argument as a reason for denying liability for economic loss is an example of this phenomenon.

[73] This is seen strikingly in Lord Macmillan's celebrated phrase, "The categories of negligence are never closed." – [1932] AC 562 at 619. The phrase richly illustrates the confusion between abstract and general concrete rights. If Lord Macmillan meant the categories to refer to general concrete rights, then he should have said that the *number of categories* is not limited (since the recognition of a number of general concrete rights under an abstract right cannot close consideration of further general concrete rights as their potential instantiations arise). However, each category is itself closed in the sense noted above (n48 and text thereat), and hence the first point cannot be used as an excuse for not clearly stating what is the recognised category of a general concrete right on each occasion. If, on the other hand, Lord Macmillan meant to refer to the abstract right, there would only have been the need to refer to the one category, and it would be an unhelpful tautology to say that a category of instantiations of an abstract right never closed (n48 above). The problem is that Lord Macmillan never really addressed his statement in either of these two forms, because the distinction between the two kinds of rights was not faced, and we are left with a confused sentiment which only engenders further confusion in the law. An example is provided by Lord Devlin in *Hedley Byrne*. He cites Lord Macmillan's phrase, not only as a justification for not elaborating on a further hypothetical general concrete right (R6$_h$ in Figure

The analysis in terms of the framework also sadly sheds a degree of pessimism on those bold attempts by commentators to produce coherent principles of liability for economic loss in negligence, or to specify the categories where liability will be acknowledged.[74] For the recognition of the abstract nature of R4 as present alongside any specific general concrete rights of the kind $R6_n$ in the cases where liability for economic loss is established, means two things. First, that there does not exist a single coherent principle but an abstract principle encompassing R4, which offers up the possibility of applications that cannot be determined from that principle itself (see Table 4). And secondly, the range of categories already established in the law, even if they were all individually clearly defined, cannot settle the application of the law to all future cases for the same reason, since these categories consist of rights of the kind $R6_n$, which can determine the disposition of further instances of those general concrete rights of the form R14, but can not determine how further instantiations of the abstract principle, of the form R11, will be considered (see Table 6). Such pessimism may, however, be a small price to pay for greater realism in the law, which may yet yield greater clarity *within the limits of what is possible.*

(4) Some General Observations

The points made about the development of rights in the tort of negligence in relation to economic loss apply elsewhere in the same tort. The attempt to find coherence for the law through classifying the factors that will give rise to the recognition of a duty of care and the correlative right in the plaintiff is as much a frustrating exercise generally, as it is for economic loss.[75] Again the inconsistencies in judicial pronouncements can be related to the confusion that surrounds the failure to recognise the distinction between the abstract right R4 and the general concrete right $R6_n$.[76]

3 above and accompanying text), but also for not providing a full definition of the general concrete right ($R6_5$ in Figure 2) applied in *Hedley Byrne* – [1964] AC 465 at 531. This left unclear the significance of whether or not the person who had assumed responsibility for the statement had to be acting in a professional capacity (a matter that accordingly had to be considered in subsequent litigation – *Mutual Life v Evatt* [1971] AC 793, PC; *Esso Petroleum v Mardon* [1975] QB 819, CA).

[74] Jane Stapleton, "Duty of Care and Economic Loss: A Wider Agenda" (1991) 107 *Law Quarterly Review* 249, reacting against "[t]he outcome of three decades of litigation . . . a complex, uncertain and anomalous pattern of decisions" (at 258), proposes "the more coherent approach of analysing the duty issue according to the policies which the courts have decided should govern the recognition of a duty of care" (at 285). Basil Markesinis and Simon Deakin, above n58 at 86–118, following Feldthusen, suggest that the recognition of distinct types of economic loss will help to clarify the appropriate boundaries of liability for economic loss.

[75] Significantly, Howarth, above n58 at 331, concludes, after an extensive discussion of the factors affecting the recognition of liability for economic loss, that "the arguments for and against liability for pure economic loss are largely simply applications of arguments that apply in negligence generally".

[76] See n71 above.

This is particularly so in the area of liability for nervous shock, which was widened in one House of Lords case[77] only to be restricted in another[78] less than ten years later, with speeches by Law Lords on both occasions indicating that the different results were *determined* by the application of the general abstract conception established in *Donoghue*.[79]

The confusion can be seen initially in the diverging approaches within *McLoughlin* itself. There is a rather heated debate between Lord Wilberforce and Lord Edmund-Davies on the one hand and Lord Scarman and Lord Bridge on the other hand over the appropriate application of Lord Atkin's neighbour principle to the issue of liability for nervous shock. Lord Wilberforce, supported by Lord Edmund-Davies, applies the two stage test he had devised in *Anns*: foreseeability raises a presumption of liability, rebuttable by policy.[80] However, Lord Bridge, supported by Lord Scarman appears to differ here in accepting that the test of reasonable foreseeability is itself sufficient.[81]

The apparent difference is heightened by the sharp exchange between the two viewpoints, in which Lord Edmund-Davies criticizes Lord Scarman's assertion that "the policy issue . . . is not justiciable"[82] as being "as novel as it is startling",[83] with return fire from Lord Bridge in his expression of regret that Lord Edmund-Davies "stops short of indicating his view . . . as to the nature of the policy considerations . . . which he would invoke".[84]

But on closer examination it is clear that both Lord Bridge and Lord Scarman do leave room for policy in applying the neighbour principle;[85] it is simply a matter of rejecting any policy issues as being capable of rebutting the outcome of the foreseeability test in these circumstances, notably the floodgates policy factor that the Court of Appeal had adopted in this case.[86] *The* policy issue not justiciable for Lord Scarman was drawing a rigid line between different victims of nervous shock, as the Court of Appeal had done on the basis of whether or not they were present at or near the scene of the accident.

The disagreement within *McLoughlin* would have been more focused had their Lordships distinguished between the process of considering the abstract right encompassed in the neighbour principle so as to recognise an instantia-

---

[77] *McLoughlin v O'Brian* [1983] 1 AC 410.
[78] *Alcock v Chief Constable of South Yorkshire* [1992] 1 AC 310.
[79] n12 above.
[80] [1983] 1 AC 410 at 420-1.
[81] *ibid.* at 431 (Scarman), 441 (Bridge).
[82] *ibid.* at 431.
[83] *ibid.* at 427.
[84] *ibid.* at 443.
[85] Lord Scarman (*ibid.* at 431) speaks of applying it "in circumstances where it is appropriate" and identifies "factors to be weighed . . . when the test of reasonable foreseeability is to be applied". And Lord Bridge *considers* policy issues before rejecting them (at 441). Cp the discussion by Christie, above n32 at 128–9.
[86] [1983] 1 AC 410 at 430–1, 441–3.

tion of it in a case of nervous shock, and the process of applying one or more established general concrete rights to cases of nervous shock falling under it/them.[87] This would have made it clear that policy factors had to be addressed in determining whether to accept an instantiation of the abstract right, R4, and on what basis. This would in turn have provided the scope for the related general concrete right, R6, so established (see Table 7). If, in fact, there remained a disagreement between their Lordships as to the proper basis for establishing the right to recover for nervous shock, this would then be reflected in the extent of the related general concrete right and its applicability to subsequent cases. Instead the debate becomes bogged down in confusion over the process that their Lordships are engaged in with no clarification of what that process has actually led to.[88]

The confusion continues when the House of Lords reconsiders its position in *Alcock*. Although this case is taken to narrow the scope of liability for nervous shock in relation to *McLoughlin*,[89] it is done so by drawing on the mysterious element of proximity[90] as an aspect of the neighbour principle in *Donoghue* to complement foreseeability,[91] without any attempt to fix on general concrete rights that the law might have established. With Law Lords in both *McLoughlin* and *Alcock* treating the abstract right R4 as though it could determine the outcome of the case before them without a consideration of what general concrete rights had been established in the law, it is no wonder that the law sank into inconsistency. And this was helped along by another standard symptom of the confusion,[92] in that Law Lords in both cases saw no need for clarifying the concrete right that they were establishing due to the

---

[87] There may still be disagreement over whether a single general concrete right, R6, or a number of them might be appropriate for dealing with nervous shock. Cp the different forms of R6 for dealing with economic loss – Figures 2 and 3 above.

[88] The analysis of Lord Wilberforce's speech with the aid of the distinction between R4 and R6 is instructive. In the earlier part ([1983] AC 410 at 418-9) he moves towards defining one or more established general concrete rights recognised by the existing law, covering nervous shock suffered by P being in fear of or aware of injury to a spouse or child occurring in an incident experienced by P (points 1–3), or where P comes upon the immediate aftermath of the incident (add point 4), or where P is a rescuer (point 5). Lord Wilberforce then returns to the abstract right (at 420) before considering the various issues of policy in some detail (at 421–3). He then concludes "that the appellant's case falls within the boundaries of the law so drawn" (at 423), when in fact no such boundaries have been established! Lord Edmund-Davies similarly expresses a preference for "indicating with clarity where the limits of liability should be drawn" but dismisses this as "unfortunately unattainable" (at 426) – which can also be traced to confusing the inherent uncertainty over R4 with the possibility of establishing a particular R6 with a degree of clarity. Because of the confusion, the latter is never attempted – neither on the other side: see Lord Scarman at 431 and Lord Bridge at 442–3.

[89] For general discussion see Nicholas Mullany and Peter Handford, *Tort Liability for Psychiatric Damage* (Sydney, The Law Book Company Limited, 1993) at 83–5 *et passim*.

[90] For general criticism, see Jenny Steele, "Scepticism and the Law of Negligence" (1993) 52 *Cambridge Law Journal* 437 at 450–2.

[91] eg by Lord Keith, [1992] 1 AC 310 at 397, allegedly following Lord Wilberforce in *McLoughlin*.

[92] See above, n73.

fact that they had lost it in the confusion with the abstract right.[93] As a result, the law is left to idiosyncratic development by judges who fill out their own favoured conceptions of society with little regard for the established law that preceded them.[94]

Three further observations can be made, which take us beyond the law of negligence itself but have been illustrated in our examination of this tort. The first two relate to the way in which judicial reasoning is described. For the reasoning with rights that we have been examining is but one way of examining judicial reasoning in general.

One common description for certain cases of judicial reasoning that has been encountered in our examination of negligence is reasoning by analogy.[95] The recognition of the distinction between R4 and R6 reveals that this could amount to two quite different processes of reasoning, depending on whether we were reasoning by analogy with a recognised instantiation of the abstract right, or by analogy with a recognised instantiation of the general concrete right. The latter is more appropriately referred to as reasoning, because having identified the common characteristic(s) between the established instance and the case at issue as being what gives rise to the general concrete right, it then follows as a matter of deduction that the right is established in the case at issue.[96] Whereas identifying the common characteristic in both cases which makes them both potential instantiations of the abstract right, is not sufficient for the deduction that the right is established in the case at issue. It merely provides the possibility of considering the issue, in accordance with the appropriate premises, which we may respond to as we see fit.[97]

---

[93] Lord Wilberforce in *McLoughlin*: ". . . these indications, imperfectly sketched, and certainly to be applied with common sense to individual situations . . ." – [1983] AC 410 at 423. Lord Keith in Alcock: ". . . the proximity factors mentioned by Lord Wilberforce in McLoughlin . . . must, however, be taken into account in judging whether a duty of care exists." – [1992] 1 AC 310 at 397. See further, n88 above.

[94] The impact of this at the personal level is noted by Howarth, above n58 at 256, in relation to one of the plaintiffs in *Alcock* whose claim is dismissed "because he had offered no proof that he had a close relationship with his brother who was a victim of the disaster, which was not surprising since until the Lords' judgment in *Alcock* no one had ever suspected that such proof was necessary."

[95] The image is used, eg, by Lord Pearce in *Hedley Byrne* – [1964] AC 465 at 536; and by Lord Wilberforce in *McLoughlin* – [1983] AC 410 at 419. For general discussion, see Neil MacCormick, *Legal Reasoning and Legal Theory* (Oxford, Clarendon Press, 1978) ch VII; Edward Levi, *An Introduction to Legal Reasoning* (Chicago, IL, University of Chicago Press, 1949).

[96] The process of identifying the common characteristic(s) may involve some clarification of the general concrete right, in the sense remarked upon at the end of ch V:2 above. So, the general concrete right established in *Donoghue* relating to the liability of manufacturers itself underwent further clarification in *Grant v Australian Knitting Mills* [1936] AC 85, which indicated that there was no need for impossibility of intermediate inspection of the goods so long as there was no expectation of intermediate inspection. As remarked on in ch V:2, this is a characteristic of the Common Law case law development of legal doctrine, but the distinctive nature of a general concrete right is retained in that the category so clarified applies necessarily, and in the same way, to all of its instantiations.

[97] The possibility of the confusion between these two processes has been amply illustrated by the logical errors committed by Lord Atkin and Lord Devlin, in the search for the "common element" – text at n10 and following n44 above. It is also evident in the model of judicial

The other way in which the process of judicial reasoning employed in *Donoghue* is often portrayed is by the metaphor of moving between different "levels of generality".[98] There is, however, a danger here of losing sight of the distinction between abstract right and general concrete right by placing the abstract right at the highest level and assuming that as we descend we move from the abstract to the very general concrete, in the same way as we move from the very general concrete to the less general concrete, and so on; and worse, that moving in the opposite direction is pretty much the same thing too.[99] The image suggests a linear progression between concrete and abstract, which completely distorts the more complex picture indicating the relationship between the two (see Tables 2–3 and 5–8).

Finally, a general observation which is more positive, about the value of abstract rights. The criticism of how Lord Atkin in *Donoghue* depicted the derivation of his abstract right as coming logically out of the general concrete rights already in existence,[100] is not a criticism of Lord Atkin for establishing the abstract right encompassed by the neighbour principle. The impact that this principle has had on the Common Law, unequalled by any other judicial development in the Common Law world this century, shows that this abstract right was long overdue.

The brunt of the criticism has been to show that confusing the origin and nature of an abstract right does nothing to help in the coherent development of the law, nor does it even assist our understanding of the law that has already been established.

Although it may be tempting to conceal the origin of the abstract right in Lord Atkin's broader conception of society and the needs of its members, and

---

reasoning provided by Lord Diplock in *Dorset Yacht Co* – [1970] AC 1004 at 1058–9. Part of Lord Diplock's model, in specifying the particular characteristics (A, B, C, D, etc) required for a duty of care, relates to the clarification of a general concrete right, but he then equates this with the statement "in wide general terms" of the abstract right in *Donoghue* (at 1059). MacCormick, above n95, speaks of the use of analogy in developing the tort of negligence in terms of "extending the concrete application of a principle from case to analogous case" (at 192–193). He does not differentiate between the process as applied to abstract rights and concrete rights, but does stress "the interaction of arguments from principle and consequentialist arguments . . . in hard cases" (at 194) – a remark which is particularly appropriate for the process of reasoning by analogy with abstract rights. Levi, above n95, in discussing "reasoning by example" as a "key to many things" (at 4), does differentiate between different forms of such reasoning, but turns the distinction on the different roles he perceives for constitutional provisions, statute law and case law, and hence his depiction of reasoning by analogy with constitutional material gets closest to describing the process in relation to abstract rights – "conflicting ideals of the community in certain ambiguous categories" (at 5), "enormously ambiguous in its general provisions" (at 42). Though there is an acknowledgment that, "Case-law concepts deal with some of the same problems but less obviously." (at 43).

[98] See William Twining and David Miers, *How To Do Things With Rules*, 3ed. (London, Weidenfeld and Nicolson, 1991) 181 2 *et passim* the metaphor is applied to *Donoghue* at 51 7.

[99] As Lord Atkin did in *Donoghue* – text at nn 10 and 11 above.

[100] Section 2(1) above.

accept the ruse that it is necessarily derived from established law,[101] to do so does not grace the judicial role with legitimacy but rather opens it up to ridicule, over the muddle that then arises from the confusion of abstract and general concrete rights and the appropriate manner of dealing with each.

More fundamentally, it loses sight of the value that such an abstract right possesses, both at its inception and in its subsequent development, in extending the scope of the law's protection of individuals' interests in accordance with the respect that they merit as members of society.[102] To suggest that this role of the law cannot be contained in established concrete categories is only to confess that the law may be confronted by issues where the value claimed for one individual's interests as against another's needs to be examined,[103] and to admit that the past failure to examine it is a failure by the law to uphold the interests of all members of society.

By creating the abstract right in *Donoghue*, Lord Atkin made it possible to consider the value of the interests of the consumer as against the interests of the manufacturer. We can then see that at its inception the abstract right encompassed by the neighbour principle, although not being derived from established legal categories is not altogether removed from them, for it responds to a question posed by the established categories, but not answered by them. If the law respects the interests of those negligently injured by dangerous goods, or those who have been invited on to premises and suffered injury through the negligence of others, why should those who have suffered injury due to the negligence of others in different ways not also have their interests respected?

---

[101] See n49 above and text thereat. It is almost certainly the case that Lord Atkin was not taken in by his own ruse. Anecdotal evidence indicates that his decision to establish the neighbour principle was not taken merely by consulting the law reports, but also by discussing its merits with his children and grandchildren at family mealtimes – see Lewis above n15 at 57, confirmed by further anecdotal evidence given to the author by Richard Youard (a grandson of Lord Atkin) who recalls his mother relating these discussions to him. Moreover, at the very point where Lord Atkin "logically" derives the principle from existing law (cited at n10 above), he adds in the following sentence: "To seek a complete logical definition of the general principle is probably to go beyond the function of the judge . . .". This qualification of the role of logic is particularly forceful for immediately following Lord Atkin's invocation of logic as the basis for deriving the neighbour principle from existing law. Further illumination on the judicial resort to logic is provided by Lord Wilberforce in *McLoughlin*, where he speaks of the courts proceeding "in the traditional manner of the common law from case to case, upon a basis of logical necessity", and of a "process of logical progression" – [1983] AC 410 at 419. But the illustrations that Lord Wilberforce provides at this point indicate that the logic of the process is *secondary* to the conclusion that the two cases involved in the progression *merit* being treated alike. As Lord Wilberforce himself acknowledges (at 420): "a conclusion into the forming of which considerations of policy have entered".

[102] For detailed consideration of this point, see Peter Birks, *Harrassment and Hubris: The Right to an Equality of Respect*, the Second John Maurice Kelly Memorial Lecture (Dublin, Faculty of Law, University College Dublin, 1996). For an illustration in the context of environmental law, see Jenny Steele, "Assessing the Past" in Tim Jewell and Jenny Steele (eds.), *Law in Environmental Decision-Making* (forthcoming Oxford University Press). And for the same point in relation to constitutional rights, see Joseph Raz, "Rights and Politics" (1995) 71 *Indiana Law Journal* 27.

[103] Along the lines of the premises indicated in Table 4.

To suggest that the question posed by the limitations of the concrete categories of the established law is also answered by established law is a fiction, though a fiction that has its own precedents in the history of the law.[104] What it takes to provide an answer is not greater knowledge of the law but a broader vision of how the interests of members of society could be more properly respected, and hence a greater vision *for* the law.

To regard the development of abstract rights as being a legitimate role for a judge, is only to regard the judge as having a part to play[105] in ensuring that "community standards and expectations"[106] are rendered to all the members of the community.[107]

3 THE RIGHT TO FREE SPEECH

The right to free speech is an obvious choice for illustrating the framework. It combines the advantages of drawing on both constitutional and international law arenas, with a readily recognised abstract character which is acknowledged as potentially clashing with other rights. From the vast literature on this important right I want to select just one particular exchange which reveals how discussion of the right is approached, in order to suggest how the use of the framework could help to make discussion of the right more intelligible. I shall then comment in the following section on how some of the broader implications drawn from the application of the framework to the private law context also relate to the constitutional and international law arenas.

The exchange on the right to free speech considers its relationship to racial discrimination and the potential clash between the value of free speech and

---

[104] For a comparative perspective on the development of the Roman delict *iniuria* from a specific provision on assault to an abstract provision dealing with a wide variety of wrongs, see Birks, above n102. For a similar development in Jewish law, see David Daube, "Matthew v. 38f." (1944) 45 *Journal of Theological Studies* 177.

[105] Like any role it can be played well or badly. But we do not rid ourselves of bad actors by pretending that they are not acting.

[106] The phrase is taken from the Privy Council judgment in *Invercargill City Council v Hamlin* [1996] 2 WLR 367 at 378. The case upheld a divergent approach to *Murphy* in New Zealand law on the basis of different community standards applying in New Zealand than in the UK, and is by implication strong judicial recognition for the distinctive manner of reasoning with abstract rights, in involving (a) the possibility of more than one view as to whether an instantiation should be accepted, and there being "no single correct answer" (at 378B–C); and (b) the application of the abstract right being related to the conception of society taken – "'the court's assessment of community standards and demands'" (at 378E-F, citing with approval the Australian case of *Bryan v Maloney* (1995) 69 ALJR 375 at 377). The implication is needed because the remarks are made in the context of contrasting determinations of the application of an abstract right in two different societies, but if we recognise these points in relation to the possibility of different conceptions of society in different societies, it is a small step to doing so in relation to different conceptions of the same society. For general discussion, see J.W. Harris, "The Privy Council and the Common Law" (1990) 106 *Law Quarterly Review* 574.

[107] Captured in Lord Atkin's sentiment cited at n15 above.

the protection of another person's interests. Despite the recognition of the abstract character of this right, there is found within its discussion a failure to maintain the distinction between abstract and general concrete rights, and a failure to follow through the implications of dealing with these two different kinds of rights.

The exchange occurs in an essay by Christopher McCrudden[108] commenting on a view in David Feldman's book on Civil Liberties and Human Rights.[109] McCrudden argues that the reservations expressed by Feldman over the UK legislation on incitement to racial hatred[110] in its potential for clashing with the right to free speech are misplaced, and himself advocates a reconsideration of traditional views on free speech in the light of the demands of equality.

The key element in Feldman's position which provoked McCrudden's disagreement is the suggestion that a racial hatred provision can be justified as an encroachment on the right to free speech only because it satisfies one of the doctrines holding sway in the United States Supreme Court in considering exceptions to the First Amendment, of not discriminating against any viewpoint more than any other.[111] The UK legislative provision is regarded as not doing so because it deals with all threatening, abusive, and offensive speech, not merely racist speech. Feldman then endorses such a rationale for permitting exceptions to the right to free speech because it upholds "the importance to civil liberties of political neutrality".[112]

McCrudden argues to the contrary, that the fact that the speech is racist is enough to constitute a compelling social reason for making an exception to the right to free speech, and broadening his attack to take in the prevailing US Supreme Court "neutral, universalist approach", he advocates an approach that is "committed, contextualized and historically sensitive" so as to advance the demands of equality.[113]

Now the reason why Feldman as a proponent of civil liberties seeks a neutral justification for the racial hatred exception is because of the fear that if we take a position that specifically prohibits one viewpoint then that means that no viewpoint is guaranteed protection under the right to free speech, and therefore the viewpoint that we freely choose may be prohibited, so we have

---

[108] "Freedom of Speech and Racial Equality" in Peter Birks (ed.), *Pressing Problems in the Law, Volume 1: Criminal Justice and Human Rights* (Oxford, Oxford University Press, 1995) – hereinafter, McCrudden.

[109] *Civil Liberties and Human Rights in England and Wales* (Oxford, Clarendon Press, 1993) – hereinafter, Feldman.

[110] Public Order Act 1986, Part III, as amended by the Broadcasting Act 1990, s 164.

[111] Feldman, 553–4; McCrudden, 129.

[112] Feldman, 814. Although McCrudden uses this passage of Feldman's book to ground his discussion on, it should not be regarded as indicating unequivocal support by Feldman for viewpoint neutrality – contrast, eg, 864. For subsequent development of Feldman's ideas towards a more critical position on viewpoint neutrality, see his "Content-Neutrality" forthcoming in Ian Loveland (ed.), *Importing the First Amendment* (Oxford, Hart Publishing).

[113] McCrudden, 148.

lost our civil liberty of free speech. The natural consequence of such a process of thought is that the free speech of the racist could only be curtailed if the free speech of the non-racist were similarly dealt with.[114]

McCrudden attacks Feldman's approach for its consequences: it fails to uphold the just claims of the oppressed to equality.[115] But there is an additional objection to Feldman's approach, which is revealed by applying the framework to the right to free speech.

As an abstract right, the right to free speech cannot be guaranteed instantiation in every possible case. Some of the barriers may be found in considering the premises relating to translating an ideal right to a less than ideal society,[116] but let us put such possibilities to one side, and consider the right in the form R4 (eg as an established constitutional right). There must still be some barriers remaining from the very fact that it is an abstract right.[117]

Suppose, however, that we do recognise a case, (a), where the right is upheld, which gives rise to a general concrete right for every case which falls within those recognised circumstances, say $R6_a$ (see Table 7). We are then faced with another case, (b), which falls to be determined as a possible instantiation of R4. The determination of this case and with it the potential $R6_b$ is not dependent on the previous treatment of $R6_a$ – the position is exactly the same as for the two rights, $R6_5$ and $R6_h$, considered by Lord Devlin in *Hedley Byrne*.[118] Equally, nor can our determination of the potential $R6_b$ affect our already established right, $R6_a$.

Imagine now that case (a) involves fair comment[119] by a political journalist on the recent policies of the government in their attitude to a neighbouring country, accusing the government of being racist; and that case (b) involves the distribution of leaflets by a supremacist nationalist group accusing the immigrants from that neighbouring country of being responsible for various economic ills, and seeking to rouse support for a policy of repatriation by encouraging those who read the leaflet to make life as miserable as possible for these immigrants. However case (b) is decided, it cannot alter the right to free speech established as $R6_a$. More specifically, denying $R6_b$ as a right to free speech does not undermine $R6_a$.

This demonstrates the general point that to deny a right to free speech for promoting racial hatred as one concrete instantiation of the abstract right to free speech, $R6_b$, does not threaten the civil liberty composed by another instantiation of that abstract right in fair comment on government policy, $R6_a$. To link the fates of the two concrete rights, $R6_a$ and $R6_b$ together is to falsely maintain a common abstract form for them, R4, which they no longer

---

[114] McCrudden traces the American position through to this point – 138.
[115] McCrudden, 148.
[116] See Table 4.
[117] Premises IV(a)–(d) in Table 4.
[118] Figures 2 and 3, in section 2(2) above.
[119] Taking it out of the scope of any possible restriction based on defamation.

possess, and manifests yet another way in which the distinction between abstract rights and concrete rights is confused.

However, it could be argued that this fails to take into account two features of the right to free speech as a right protected by the constitution or by international convention. For, first, what is at stake is allowing the government to make a choice between different instantiations of the abstract right, not the point that denying one instantiation does not affect the fate of the other. If we allow the government to deny $R6_b$ and not $R6_a$, what is to stop them doing it the other way round and denying $R6_a$ and not $R6_b$? This would seriously threaten our civil liberty of free speech.

But this argument could be applied to any exception to the right to free speech that is recognised: if we allow the government to deny $R6_p$, what is to stop them denying $R6_a$? And everybody acknowledges that there are some cases of $R6_p$, even under the American Constitution.[120] So this cannot be the correct form of argument to allay that particular anxiety.

The proper location for dealing with the anxiety is found in the process by which the abstract right is given (or not given) a concrete instantiation, captured by premises IV(a)-(d) in Table 4. In particular, if we want to safeguard the civil liberty of criticising government policy in the process of recognising concrete instantiations of the abstract right to free speech, then we have to give some indication of the weight of different factors in applying these premises when we establish the abstract right, so as to ensure the appropriate civil liberty remains protected at the level of concrete instantiation. This is what is done in Article 10(2) of the European Convention on Human Rights, which provides not only an exhaustive list of competing interests that may be given a higher value,[121] but also indicates that these competing interests are to be evaluated by the test as to whether favouring them is "necessary in a democratic society".

The second feature of the right to free speech as a right protected by the constitution or by international convention that could be put forward as a counter argument is that this special status gives it a strong presumptive force that is not captured by the way the framework deals with it. The answer to this point is similar to the previous one. Any such presumptive force will be taken into account in the way that premises IV(a)–(d) are applied, since that process must consider particular indications of relative value as in the example of Article 10, or general indications of relative value such as might be found in the general presumptive force accorded to constitutional rights or rights protected by international convention.

In dealing with Feldman's position, the idea of neutral justification of an exception to the right to free speech should now be regarded as a misconceived effort to deal with the civil libertarian anxiety over allowing exceptions to abstract rights. The framework reveals that this anxiety can be met not by

---

[120] The American position is helpfully described by McCrudden at 131–8, 139–42, and n30.
[121] As in applying premises IV(b)/(c) in Table 4.

neutral justification but by the particular justification of different concrete rights. Moreover, the idea of neutral justification is nonsensical, for the admission of any particular exception must favour some values as against the values of free speech in that concrete situation,[122] since the viewpoint of those whose speech is being curtailed is being judged differently from the viewpoint of those who wish to see such speech prohibited. No matter how many viewpoints are placed within the prohibited category, this must always be the case.[123] Even if we add a prohibition against non-racist speech to the prohibition against racist speech in the "neutral" public order category, we are still judging the viewpoints of those who favour public order differently from the viewpoint of those who enjoy a bit of disturbance on the streets – whether as pure self-expression or as a means of promoting political convictions. And if this is nevertheless considered to be a securer bastion for civil liberties as against government tyranny, what if the government then decides that demonstrations against government policy (or their incitement, or speech which is likely to inflame them. . .) should also be added to this "neutral" public order category?

I now want to comment on the suggestions made by McCrudden on an alternative approach to free speech based on equality, so as to demonstrate that there may still be work for the framework to do in this area. It is only fair to say that McCrudden himself sees the approach as providing "the *beginning* of an answer".[124]

The approach favoured by McCrudden is that taken by the Canadian Supreme Court.[125] He considers this to be an "equality sensitive" approach because the Court has demonstrated in recent decisions that it is prepared to allow exceptions to the freedom of expression protected under the Canadian Charter of Rights and Freedoms for cases of racial hatred, in accordance with the Charter's formula of being demonstrably justified in a free and democratic country.

The first case, *Keegstra*, involved upholding a conviction on a teacher for wilfully promoting hatred against an ethnic group under the Canadian Criminal Code, where he had taught anti-semitism to his pupils and required them to reproduce lies about the Holocaust in their written work.[126] The

---

[122] See premises IV(a)–(d) of Table 4. Even in IV(a), if free speech is regarded as having an instrumental value that is not made out on this occasion, this favours the viewpoint of those who attribute that instrumental value to free speech, as against the viewpoint of those who are being prohibited from putting their speech to the service of a competing value.

[123] Cass Sunstein's distinctions between different forms of regulating free speech used by the Supreme Court (*Democracy and the Problem of Free Speech* (Riverside, N J, Free Press, 1993), at 11), cited by McCrudden at n30: content-neutral, viewpoint-based, and content-based, must accordingly all be viewpoint based in this sense, at a deeper level. For the "content-neutral" or "content-based" restrictions will still draw a line between speech that is restricted and is not, and therefore favour the viewpoints of those who wish to see such a restriction against those viewpoints which would find expression in the restricted speech.

[124] McCrudden, 146.

[125] McCrudden, 142–6.

[126] *R v Keegstra* [1990] 3 SCR 697.

words of Dickson J,[127] cited by McCrudden, are worth repeating as demonstrating how the instrumentality of the value of the abstract right[128] can be found absent on a particular occasion, so justifying a failure to recognise a concrete instantiation:

> "hate propaganda contributes little to the aspirations of Canadians or Canada in either the quest for truth, the promotion of individual self-development or the protection and fostering of a vibrant democracy where the participation of all individuals is accepted and encouraged."

In the second case, *Taylor*,[129] the Court upheld a provision of the Canadian Human Rights Act which made it unlawful discrimination to communicate racial hatred material on the telephone. But in both cases the decision was carried by the same bare majority of Justices. The dissenting judgment in *Keegstra* argued that to uphold the exception to free speech was wrong because of the dangers inherent in state censorship and the chilling effect of such censorship on legitimate speech, with similar sentiments being expressed in *Taylor*.[130]

In a third case, *Zundel*,[131] McLachlin J, who had led the dissent in *Keegstra*, found herself commanding a different bare majority that was prepared to strike out an exception to freedom of expression contained in another provision of the Canadian Criminal Code dealing with wilfully publishing a false statement likely to cause injury or mischief to a public interest, which had been applied to the publication of pamphlets denying the fact of the Holocaust. Part of the majority's reasoning again invoked the chill factor on legitimate speech.

McCrudden commends the approach of the Canadian Supreme Court revealed in these cases in a eulogy marking out nine or ten different virtues, among them being: "It has real bite when necessary in protecting appropriate freedom of speech." and "It adopts a view of the role of equality in freedom of speech which is consistent with developments in anti-discrimination law."[132] Now it is undeniable that the Canadian approach in these three cases does strike a balance in the sense that it is capable of accommodating the interests of the right not to suffer racial discrimination, whilst at other times it favours the right to free speech. But the balance remains precarious, and, on the evidence of these three cases, seems likely to fall down on the side mustering a majority in the Supreme Court, rather than being firmly established in the Charter itself.

More particularly, the "chill factor" played a dominant part in the minority's thinking in the first two cases,[133] and a significant part in the third case

---

[127] *ibid.* at 766.
[128] See premise IV(a) in Table 4.
[129] *Taylor v Canadian Human Rights Commission* (1991) 75 DLR (4th) 577.
[130] There is a full analysis of the judgments in McCrudden, 142–5.
[131] *R v Zundel* [1992] 2 SCR 731.
[132] McCrudden, 146.
[133] And could thus have been the determining factor in rejecting the exception if the numbers had fallen the other way.

which went the other way.[134] This indicates that the Canadian approach has not rid itself of the confusion between abstract and concrete rights which we saw in the American approach favoured by Feldman, thus preventing one potential concrete general right $R6_a$ being examined on its own merits. Whether it is instantiated as an established right to free speech, or rejected in favour of a conflicting interest, the matter should be determined without being affected by (or affecting) issues that pertain to a separate potential right $R6_b$.

The danger is that by simply making our approach to free speech "equality sensitive", we go no further than introducing equality as another abstract value,[135] leading to yet more confusion from the failure to work through the distinction between abstract and concrete rights.

4 BROADER ISSUES

Having illustrated how the confusion between concrete rights and abstract rights also dogs the discussion of the right to free speech, I want to now consider some of the other observations made in our examination of rights in the tort of negligence to see if they also apply to the rights found in the constitutional and international law arenas.

One of the most obvious points is that as we engage in the process of making concrete instantiations of abstract rights, we also undertake a filling out of our conception of society that is supported by those particular concrete instantiations and reflected in the manner we apply the relevant premises in Table 4. Thus as we saw in the law of tort, the process of accepting a

---

[134] In *Zundel* the majority decision in favour of free speech contained another ground apart from the chill factor, namely that the provision relied on to penalise the racial hatred speech was too wide and would therefore capture legitimate expressions of free speech even if the particular instance was regarded as illegitimate. ([1992] 2 SCR 731 at 770: "Any deliberate lie . . . which causes or is likely to cause 'injury' or 'mischief' to any 'public interest' is within the potential reach of the section".) This is not a failure to distinguish between two separate rights, but a failure of drafting in wording the provision so widely as to encompass *within it* instantiations that would be unconstitutional as well as those that would be constitutional, and the court has no choice but to strike out the whole provision as unconstitutional. The minority took the view that "public interest" could be interpreted judicially so as to narrow it down to an acceptable scope – at 805–6.

[135] McCrudden acknowledges that, "The powerful nature of the concept [of equality] is one which we have yet fully to realise." – at 147. Although the remark looks forward to greater significance for the concept, it also reveals that the idea has not yet been fully worked out. In the context of s 15(1) of the Canadian Charter of Rights and Freedoms which is an anti-discrimination provision explicitly resting on an individual being "equal before and under the law" and having the right to "equal protection and equal benefit of the law", it is interesting to note that the interpretation of equality has been both praised and criticised by feminists – see, respectively, Kathleen Mahoney, "The Constitutional Law of Equality in Canada" (1992) 24 *New York University Journal of International Law and Politics* 759; Diana Majury, "Equality and Discrimination According to the Supreme Court of Canada" (1990–91) 4 *Canadian Journal of Women and Law* 407 (both discussed in Didi Herman, "The Good, the Bad, and the Smugly: Perspectives on the Canadian Charter of Rights and Freedoms" (1994) 14 *Oxford Journal of Legal Studies* 589).

particular instantiation has far reaching implications (see Table 5). But given that in the case of constitutional rights and rights under international law we have entrenched within the constitution or the covenant an ideal aspect of society which is binding upon a particular actual society, does this make matters different?

In effect, the constitution through its founding, or the covenant through the ratification of a treaty, establish an abstract right, R4, in accordance with the conception of an ideal society that appealed to the founding fathers or the signatories to the treaty. But inasmuch as there is only the establishing of an abstract right,[136] the process of deciding potential instantiations of that right will necessarily fill out the ideal conception of a society (or at the very least that much of it that was deemed appropriate for the actual societies in which we dwell) with increasing detail that was absent in the original formulation.

There is then the possibility that different determinations of potential instantiations of the abstract right will do this drawing on conflicting conceptions of society, by giving different values to different conflicting interests, in much the same way that we saw Lord Atkin was prepared to value the interests of the consumer over the interests of the manufacturer. This phenomenon may be represented in Figures 4 and 5, where the two different determinations of separate instantiations of the abstract right are indicated by the subscripts x and y respectively. Of course, a refusal to accept an instantiation can be equally as significant in these respects, and it is possible to work through the framework with a negated instantiation in the same way, but for illustrative convenience we will take both our instantiations to be positive.

Figures 4 and 5 then show the ramifications of these two different instantiations of the abstract right R4. I have assumed that the conceptions of soci-

Figure 4

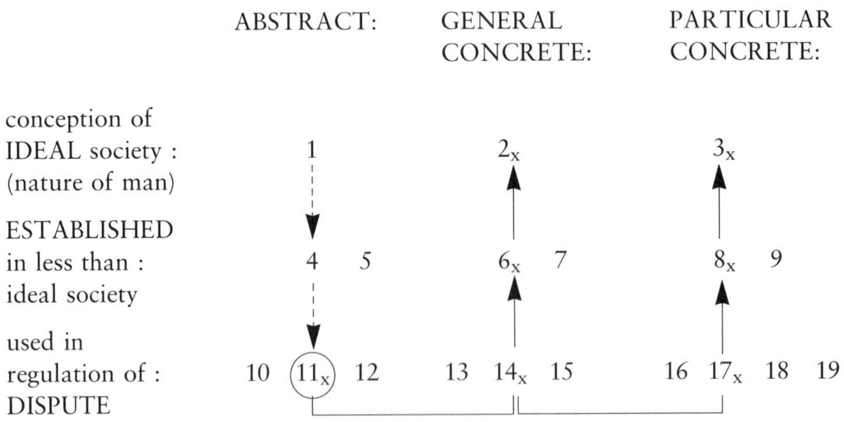

---

[136] There is no reason why constitutions or treaties should not contain general (or particular) concrete rights, as indeed they do.

Figure 5

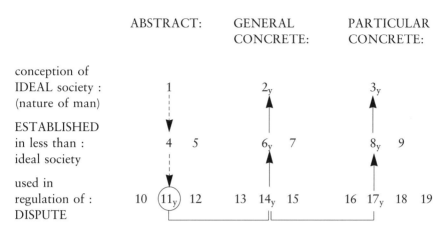

ety that lie behind them are idealistic, and hence the analysis reaches the top level of the framework. But even if not (omitting the links with R2 and R3), we would still be filling out our conceptions of actual societies in reaching R7 and R9.

Now it may be that the conception of society used in determining $R11_x$ is wholly compatible with the conception of society used in determining $R11_y$ in respect to the abstract right R4, in which case there would be no noticeable differences to Figures 4 and 5 if the first case had been decided by those determining the second, and vice versa. On the other hand things might be very different.

This is evident from the Canadian cases considered in the previous section. If the majority in the first two had held sway in the third we would have got a consistent conception of society being filled out, by rejecting all three instantiations of the right to free speech in favour of the protection of the victims of racial hatred.[137] This would still provide us with a conception of society in which the *abstract* right to free speech, R4, played a part, it would simply fill out our conception to show boundaries in concrete instantiations of R4 consistent with the protection of victims of racial hatred.

Similarly, if the majority in the third had held sway in the first two, accepting all three instantiations by giving priority to free speech over the interests of the victims of racial hatred, we would now have a different consistent conception of society being worked out, equally compatible with the *abstract* right to free speech, R4, but filled out with wider concrete boundaries for acceptable free speech.

[137] I ignore for present purposes the important point about drafting technique, which might be a different reason for rejecting an instantiation which does not relate to the conception of society linked to that instantiation – see n134 above.

We can generalise the possible outcomes for the determination of any two possible instantiations of an abstract right, $R11_x$ and $R11_y$, where these determinations may be made by two tribunals, A and B,[138] in Figure 6.

Figure 6

	A judges	**B judges**	**Result**
A & B	x	y	x,y
favour	y	x	x,y
both	x,y		x,y
instantiations		x,y	x,y
A	x	$\sim y$	$x,\sim y$
favours both	y	x	x,y
B	x,y		x,y
favours only x		$x,\sim y$	$x,\sim y$
A	x	y	x,y
favours both	y	$\sim x$	$\sim x,y$
B	x,y		x,y
favours only y		$\sim x,y$	$\sim x,y$
A & B	x	$\sim y$	$x,\sim y$
both	$\sim y$	x	$x,\sim y$
favour x	$x,\sim y$		$x,\sim y$
but not y		$x,\sim y$	$x,\sim y$
A & B	$\sim x$	y	$\sim x,y$
both	y	$\sim x$	$\sim x,y$
favour y	$\sim x,y$		$\sim x,y$
but not x		$\sim x,y$	$\sim x,y$
A	x	$\sim y$	$x,\sim y$
favours both	y	$\sim x$	$\sim x,y$
B	x,y		x,y
favours neither		$\sim x,\sim y$	$\sim x,\sim y$
A & B	$\sim x$	$\sim y$	$\sim x,\sim y$
both	$\sim y$	$\sim x$	$\sim x,\sim y$
favour	$\sim x,\sim y$		$\sim x,\sim y$
neither		$\sim x,\sim y$	$\sim x,\sim y$

[138] I use tribunals loosely to include: different panels of the same tribunal, and even the same panel on different occasions.

Keeping it relatively simple and assuming that in each of $R11_x$ and $R11_y$ we have to choose in a conflict between free speech and prohibiting racial hatred speech, we may get a coherent right of free speech being developed through the filling out of one conception of society that consistently favours free speech (x,y), that consistently favours prohibiting racial hatred speech $(\sim x, \sim y)$, or that consistently favours allowing free speech in the one set of circumstances but not in the other $(x, \sim y/\sim x, y)$. But we may get the appearance of coherence, depending on who is deciding the case, where there is in fact not a single conception of society at work; and the appearance will crumble as soon as a third case arises in which the conception favoured by the other tribunal will gain dominance in the sort of case where previously it was suppressed.

The picture can be far more complicated than this. In an extensive survey of the different rationales for the right to free speech, Tom Campbell observes:[139]

"The specific implications of the rationales vary with the particular epistemologies, theories of human nature and models of democracy that are adopted."

and he concludes:[140]

"the determination of what rights of free communication ought to be secured is a complex and open-ended matter which cannot be reduced to easy arguments from simple and straightforward premises."

There are three fairly obvious points to be made on the way that abstract rights in the constitutional and international law arenas can give rise to the sort of confusion that we identified in the private law development of rights in the law of tort.

First, apart from downright inconsistency in the established instantiations of such abstract rights, we can also get the jarring between different instantiations that we noted in tort law, where although each instantiation has a consistency of origin in being capable of being linked to an abstract right, there is in fact a conflict in the particular way that the premises (see Table 4) were applied in each case. Illustrations of this involving a variety of the rationales identified by Campbell for the right to free speech are given in Figure 7 at the end of this chapter. The jarring, if not conflict, is also manifested in the broad characterisations given to the dominant composition of the US Supreme Court at different times as being liberal or conservative. And it is a feature which there is some effort to minimise in the discretionary margin of appreciation given by the European Court of Human Rights to different member states.[141]

---

[139] "Rationales for Freedom of Communication" in Tom Campbell and Wojciech Sadurski (eds.), *Freedom of Communication* (Aldershot, Dartmouth, 1994). For further illustrations, see Figure 7 below.

[140] *ibid.* at 43.

[141] See J.G. Merrills, *The development of international law by the European Court of Human Rights* (Manchester, Manchester University Press, 1993) ch 7. The width of the margin can still

The line between outright conflict and accommodation of differences is one of the pricklier problems of abstract rights in international law.[142]

Secondly, the fact that the abstract right R4 can be filled out with different conceptions of society provides an opportunity for interested parties to promote particular conceptions of society, even with precise concrete detail, that can be argued for in the name of the abstract right in question – though more accurately, are arguments over what use the abstract right can be put to. A topical illustration of this phenomenon is the way that abstract provisions of International Law were employed to ensure that rape victims were given recognised rights as the victims of war crimes in the setting up of the International Criminal Tribunal for the Former Yugoslavia.[143] The success here was regarded as vindicating a conception of international society where women civilians in occupied countries were to be given proper respect, as opposed to the conception found in some traditional military practices of treating women civilians as inanimate prizes of war.[144]

excite controversy. Calls for reforms to effectively broaden the margin have been made by the Lord Chancellor, Lord Mackay. A Foreign Office statement issued in support of the proposed reforms succinctly captures the potential for concealing the inconsistency of different instantiations by tracing them to a consistency of origin in the abstract rights of the European Convention on Human Rights – "There is widespread agreement that the common standards of the convention have to be maintained. But equally it is widely recognised that differing circumstances and traditions in the way these standards are implemented in different countries have to be respected." (*The Times*, 12 November 1996).

[142] See Feldman, above n5. The standard illustration is cultural differences over female circumcision.

[143] The possibility of treating the rape of an individual woman as a war crime (as distinct from a crime against humanity, which requires systematic activity directed by the government; or as distinct from being an element of genocide) depended on showing that rape was so recognised under customary international law or amounted to a "grave breach" of the Fourth Geneva Convention Relative to the Protection of Civilian Persons in Time of War, 1949. Rape had not been recognised as a war crime under customary international law in the Nuremberg Charter but was present on the expanded list found in Control Council Law No 10 used by the occupying powers in Germany. Despite Article 27 requiring that, "Women shall be protected against any attack on their honour, in particular against rape . . .", Article 147 of the Fourth Geneva Convention does not list rape itself as a "grave breach", and the case, accordingly, had to be made out that rape fell under the category of "wilfully causing great suffering or serious injury to body or health" (see Article 2 of the Statute of the International Tribunal). It is this interpretation that has now prevailed, but not without a campaign to promote a conception of international society that provided women civilians with this degree of respect. See, Theodor Meron, "Rape as a Crime under International Humanitarian Law" (1993) 87 *American Journal of International Law* 424, and "The Case for War Crimes Trials in Yugoslavia" (1993) 72 *Foreign Affairs* 122; Christine Chinkin, "Rape and Sexual Abuse of Women in International Law" (1994) 5 *European Journal of International Law* 326. This may be regarded as one aspect of a broader campaign to instate a conception of society within international law that is more sensitive to the interests of women – see eg, Charlotte Bunch, "Women's Rights as Human Rights: Toward a Re-Vision of Human Rights" (1990) 12 *Human Rights Quarterly* 486; Joanna Kerr (ed.), *Ours by Right: Women's Rights as Human Rights* (London, Zed Books, 1993); Christine Chinkin, "Women's Rights as Human Rights under International Law" in Conor Gearty and Adam Tomkins (eds.), *Understanding Human Rights* (London, Mansell, 1996). And cp Elizabeth Kingdom, "Transforming Rights: Feminist Political Heuristics" (1996) 2 *Res Publica* 63.

[144] An illuminating historical summary of attitudes to the rape of women under the law of war, which reaches contemporary conflict, is provided by Theodor Meron, *Henry's Wars and Shakespeare's Laws* (Oxford, Clarendon Press, 1993) at 111–3.

This second point has a relevant corollary for the debate over whether the US Constitution should be interpreted in accordance with the intentions of the founding fathers, or in accordance with contemporary standards.[145] To the extent that the founding fathers only established an abstract right, their intentions cannot be relied on for how that right should be instantiated, since the link between the abstract right and its instantiation is not a necessary one (Table 4). Moreover, inasmuch as the link between an abstract right and its instantiation is capable of being filled out with various conceptions of society (depending on how the premises relating to it are approached), there is nothing to say that there was one conception of society (even if it had been worked out in sufficient concrete detail) in the various minds of the founding fathers. But nor is there anything to say that there is one conception of society in accordance with the various abstract values of today.[146]

Thirdly, the capacity to play fast and loose with the potential for confusion over abstract and concrete rights is as available in these arenas as it was found to be in the law of tort. International accords on rights are notorious for remaining in the realm of the abstract, for which signatories take credit that is not in fact due until the rights have been instantiated at a concrete level.

There is also the possibility of returning to the abstract in order to sidestep an unwanted concrete instantiation. *Brown* v *Education Board of Control*[147] is a famous illustration of seizing that opportunity.[148]

---

[145] See, respectively, Robert Bork, "Neutral Principles and Some First Amendment Problems" (1971) 47 *Indiana Law Journal* 1; Ronald Dworkin, *Freedom's Law: The Moral Reading of the American Constitution* (Cambridge, MA, Harvard University Press, 1996).

[146] Bork, n145 above, founds his argument (at 5) on the assertion that the rights have been "specified by the Constitution", but subsequently concedes "history does not reveal detailed choices" (at 13), and acknowledges a lack of detailed agreement among the founding fathers necessarily led to their resorting to an abstract right, or "majestic and ambiguous formula" (at 14). Dworkin, n145 above, whilst seeking to stress "the requirement of constitutional *integrity*" (at 10) as preventing judges using their own moral convictions in applying abstract constitutional rights, nevertheless admits "different, even contrary, conceptions" may satisfy this requirement (at 11), and allows a role for "political conviction . . . so long as it is openly recognised, and so long as the convictions are identified and defended honestly . . ." (at 37). For a critical account of Dworkin's idea of integrity, see Joseph Raz, *Ethics in the Public Domain* (Oxford, Clarendon Press, 1994), ch 12 and Appendix thereto. Raz's favouring of "local coherence: coherence of doctrine in specific fields" as opposed to "global coherence" (at 298) can be related to the distinction between general concrete rights and abstract rights. In relation to the Canadian Charter of Rights and Freedoms, Didi Herman, n135 above, observes (at 590) that "left-wing critics" see the Charter as "an instrument of *class* rule" whilst "right-wing critics" see it as "an instrument of '*interest group*' rule" – and concludes (at 603) that "the effects of rights documents are complex, contradictory, and, in many respects, unpredictable."

[147] (1953) 347 US 483.

[148] The abstract right to equal protection of the laws under the Fourteenth Amendment was returned to in *Brown*, so avoiding the "separate but equal" interpretation in *Plessy* v *Ferguson* (1895) 163 US 537 which would uphold the racial segregation of schools that *Brown* held unlawful. The reinterpretation of the abstract right in *Brown* lacked a technical legal basis. Indeed, Learned Hand, who was on the Supreme Court that decided *Brown*, subsequently in his Holmes Lecture in 1958 concluded that the decision was indefensible (discussed in Dworkin above n145 at 339–40). However, as Robert Bork observes, "The end of state-mandated segregation was the greatest moral triumph constitutional law had ever produced. It is not surprising that academic

And again, there is the possibility of avoiding an argument relating to one right, R6$_x$, by diverting attention to considerations relating to another right, R6$_y$. This was seen in the previous section in relation to racial hatred speech and freedom of political criticism. It is a phenomenon that has also entered the debate over pornography and free speech.[149]

These three points – the jarring and inconsistency, the competing conceptions of society, and playing fast and loose with the abstract/concrete confusion – are different facets of the relationship between abstract and concrete rights and the processes by which they are established, which the framework

lawyers were unwilling to give it up; it *had* to be right." – *The Tempting of America: The Political Seduction of the Law* (New York, NY, Macmillan, 1990) at 77. The discrepancy between the two decisions has been remarked upon by Sir Stephen Sedley, an English High Court judge, as an instance of how accepted rights are subject to "the localisation of ideas in time and place" – "Human Rights: a Twenty-First Century Agenda" [1995] *Public Law* 386 at 387 – this leaves open the issues of which ideas are localised at what time. Whether these issues are best left to judges has been subjected to critical enquiry – see, Cass Sunstein, *The Partial Constitution* (Cambridge, MA, Harvard University Press, 1993); Jeremy Waldron, "A Right-Based Critique of Constitutional Rights" (1993) 13 *Oxford Journal of Legal Studies* 18; James Allan, "Bills of Rights and Judicial Power – A Liberal's Quandary" (1996) 16 *Oxford Journal of Legal Studies* 337.

[149] Despite the endeavours of Catharine MacKinnon to mark off and reject a pornographic instantiation of free speech from other instantiations of the abstract right, notably in *Only Words* (London, Harper Collins, 1994), the debate has often sunk into a morass of confusion over the abstract right and general concrete rights, so that intelligible argument over the merits of particular general concrete rights is never reached. This is strikingly illustrated by Lynn Chancer, "Feminist Offensives: *Defending Pornography* and the Splitting of Sex from Sexism" [a review essay of Nadine Strossen's book] (1996) 48 *Stanford Law Review* 739. Chancer (at 747) adopts Strossen's view of MacKinnon's position, that it "would necessarily threaten other forms of political expression", and then avoids the possibility of addressing the debate between Strossen and MacKinnon by claiming (at n51) that MacKinnon "concurs" because she emphasises the political nature of a feminist critique of pornography, "specifically politics from women's point of view". In this way, Chancer totally confuses the political viewpoint by which a particular instantiation of an abstract right (leading to the general concrete right to express pornographic speech) is considered and rejected, with the content of one or more other general concrete rights dealing with political expression, by an unreflective equation of two uses of the term "political" which is sustained by a failure to distinguish between abstract and general concrete rights. The rejection of the possibility of a particular pornographic instantiation of free speech inevitably leads to the failure to consider rigorously the issue of what harm or value *that* particular instantiation of free speech might possess. Despite giving some space in ch 12 of *Defending Pornography: Free Speech, Sex, and the Fight for Women's Rights* (New York, NY, Scribner, 1995) to considering the possibility of harm being caused by pornography (though regarding censorship as ineffective in combatting any harm that might be caused), Nadine Strossen's main theme in her book is that any provision on pornography will inevitably spill over to other valuable forms of free speech, eg at 62: "all laws restricting free speech – including traditional obscenity laws . . . have consistently been used to suppress speech by members of unpopular or disempowered groups". Similarly, Dworkin, above n145 at 238, meets MacKinnon by making a general issue of "protecting equality in the processes through which the moral as well as the political environment is formed". This follows Dworkin taking the particular question of pornography out of those cases where restrictions on free speech may be legitimate so as to "protect the security and interests of others", so as to prevent "intimidating women with sexual demands" or "making their working conditions so humiliating as to be intolerable"; and submerging the pornography issue in "a right not to be insulted or damaged just by the fact that others have hostile or uncongenial tastes . . .". For a dossier on the harmful effects of pornography, see Catherine Itzin (ed.), *Pornography: Women, Violence and Civil Liberties* (Oxford, OUP, 1992).

seeks to reveal. In the case of constitutional and international law rights, these three points can take on a darker significance when the full impact of ideal rights is taken into account.

The overt significance of ideal notions of rights is often stressed in these arenas, which can cause greater potential for confusion. The premises that relate to the transference of rights from some ideal conception of a society to the conditions of an actual society are frequently ignored through the zeal of their promoter. The effect is that arguments are maintained for the establishing of an ideal abstract right in concrete form on the basis of considerations that might have held in the conception of an ideal society but are absurdly inapplicable to working through the realities of the actual society encountered, in which the right is to be established.

The right to free speech also furnishes us with an example to illustrate this phenomenon. The right is sometimes argued for in an absolutist manner, say for ensuring that truth will flourish, which assumes an ideal capacity in speakers and hearers for communicating and appreciating the truth, and then without noticing the transition to our actual less than ideal society the argument is mounted for allowing an instantiation of the ideal abstract right to free speech in circumstances far removed from the legitimate and fruitful mode of converse in the ideal society as conceived: a racist whose capacities for thought and comprehension are ravaged by hate communicates an incitement to terrorise the life of a member of a different race, to an audience whose own capacities have been displaced by an overwhelming need to find somebody to blame for their desperate misery.[150]

In all this caution against the dangers of abstract rights, there may seem something of a paradox when we remember the virtue that was being found for abstract rights at the end of section 4, in extending the scope of the law's protection of individuals' interests in accordance with the respect that they merit as members of society. However, this virtue was not attributed to abstract rights but the use that could be made of them.

Where no abstract right is recognised, then no opportunity occurs to consider whether the interests of an individual should be respected as an instantiation of that right. In that respect, the arenas of constitutional rights and international law may hold an advantage over underdeveloped areas of private law: the rights are already there to be able to argue a case upon. But to keep the right abstract and never to recognise a concrete instantiation can not advance the cause of anything.

A more subtle variant, but equally damaging, is to keep the abstract right locked into one concrete instantiation so as to prevent the proper consideration of the interests of those affected by a separate instantiation, and so deny them the respect they merit as members of the community. This is not to say that once heard their voices would prevail, but to deny the opportunity in this

---

[150] See McCrudden, and Campbell, above n139.

way ensures that competing interests (probably vested interests[151]) will prevail by default.

The advantage that the framework offers is to be able to identify where it is that issues can be intelligently discussed. This is not to guarantee their resolution. Far from it: the framework in stressing the need to select from the premises it identifies offers greater scope for disagreement. It may be that the point of disagreement is swiftly reached, but at least we should be clear what it is we are disagreeing about. Certainly, if that cannot be agreed, then any further talk is nothing more than combative rhetoric over a fence dividing positions taken up on different grounds, with the combatants not even aware of what it is they are standing on.

Figure 7

THE RIGHT TO FREE SPEECH

Premise	Illustration (Rationale at issue)
III(a)	The provision of broadcasting facilities for minority political parties should be secured by government funding. (Importance of free speech to ensure open debate in a democracy.)
III(b)	Government funding of the provision of broadcasting facilities for minority political parties should be withdrawn in the current round of budget cuts, so as to ensure sufficient funding of the education budget. (Importance of free speech to ensure discovery of the truth.)
III(c)	Censorship of criticism of government policy and other statements demeaning of the state should continue until citizens are sufficiently well educated to make rational judgments on competing claims to the truth. (as for III(a) or III(b) above)
III(d)	Guaranteeing the airing of different viewpoints through ensuring diversity in ownership of media interests has to accommodate the importance of ensuring large media groups so as to make it feasible for them to compete on an international scale. (Importance of free speech to ensure that competing viewpoints are heard, as a means to political liberty, or the advancement of knowledge, or permitting self-expression.)
III(e)	There should be no censorship of any statements critical of government policy, or of statements regarding the purported underlying facts on which government policy is based. (Essential for citizens to be able to comment freely on the activities of government, in order to participate as citizens of a democracy.)
IV(a)	Statements known to be false, made maliciously with the intention of harming another, should be prohibited. (Importance of free speech to ensure discovery of the truth.)
IV(b)	Statements about the private life of politicians should be publishable, even where they might otherwise amount to an invasion of privacy, if they are regarded as having any bearing upon the conduct by politicians of their role in public life. (Importance of free speech to ensure that an electorate makes an informed choice about politicians.)
IV(c)	Confidential information received in the course of a former employment should not be disclosed to a subsequent employer for a period of one year after the earlier period of employment has ended. (Importance of free speech to ensure discovery of the truth.)
IV(d)	Citizens should be permitted to air their views on any matter that they feel strongly about at Speakers' Corner. (any of above)

[151] McCrudden, 147–8; Campbell, above 139 at 36, 38.

VII

New Rights for Old?

1 INTRODUCTION

The framework constructed and illustrated in the previous two chapters attempts to render the discussion of rights more coherent by suggesting that different notions of a right found within legal and other materials need to be clearly distinguished, and the relationships between these different rights more fully understood. The framework does not, however, challenge the basic nature of rights as conventionally depicted in these materials. In this chapter I want to examine a challenge to the conventional representation of rights in Roberto Unger's approach to rights. I shall not be concerned with considering Unger's general approach to law,[1] or with other aspects of his legal theory.[2] Nor shall I question the assumptions that Unger may be making about the human condition or the nature of the world in which we live.[3] Ignoring these wider concerns, my objective is to demonstrate that the new rights of Unger's deviationist doctrine in fact embody the old rights of legal formalism that their author has purported to abandon.

The implications are twofold. First, for Unger's general enterprise: if it turns out that there is nothing new in his radical showpiece of rights,[4] then some aspersions must be cast on the claims of novelty and radical efficacy made for "the program of empowered democracy" in which this showpiece is set.[5] Secondly, of greater interest for our present concerns there are

---

[1] Considered in John Finnis, "On 'The Critical Legal Studies Movement'" in John Eekelaar and John Bell (eds.), *Oxford Essays in Jurisprudence, Third Series* (Oxford, Clarendon Press, 1987): 145 (also found in (1985) 30 *American Journal of Jurisprudence* 21); and in Neil MacCormick, "Reconstruction after Deconstruction: A Response to CLS" (1990) 10 *Oxford Journal of Legal Studies* 539.

Roberto Unger's ideas are to be found in "The Critical Legal Studies Movement" (1983) 96 *Harvard Law Review* 561, subsequently published as *The Critical Legal Studies Movement* (Cambridge MA, Harvard University Press, 1986) – hereinafter, CLSM with page references to the book version; and in *False Necessity, Part 1 of Politics* (Cambridge, Cambridge University Press, 1987) – hereinafter, FN.

[2] Such as the role of the judge – considered in J.W. Harris, "Unger's Critique of Formalism in Legal Reasoning: Hero, Hercules, and Humdrum" (1989) 52 *Modern Law Review* 42.

[3] Considered in Stanley Fish, "Unger and Milton" [1988] *Duke Law Journal* 975 – and for a view on Unger's assumptions about Economics, see Linda Schwartzstein, "Austrian Economics and the Current Debate Between Critical Legal Studies and Law and Economics" (1992) 20 *Hofstra Law Review* 1105 at 1122.

[4] Disbelief in the novelty of Unger's ideas has been aired before: Finnis, above n1 at 156–7; MacCormick, above n1 at 555.

[5] CLSM, 36 – the programme is described in the preceding pages 25ff; FN, ch 5.

implications for rights theory, if what is widely regarded as one of the most extreme challenges to conventional thinking on rights turns out to be capable of assimilation within the very thinking that it opposes. There is a strong suggestion that a conceptual core within rights theory remains constant, and unaffected by the fluctuations of conservative or radical political perspectives that might endeavour to fill out their visions of society by moulding conceptions of rights into conveniently supportive forms.

In pursuing this objective, I shall first examine Unger's depiction of the traditional rights of legal formalism, and elucidate the characteristics that these rights possess, placing emphasis on what Unger himself sees as the objectionable aspect of these rights. I shall then examine the new rights of Unger's deviationist doctrine in some detail, and endeavour to reveal that the same characteristics are to be found here as were identified for the traditional rights. Moreover, I shall argue that inasmuch as the traditional rights are to be regarded as displaying an objectionable aspect, so too Unger's new rights display this same aspect. In a concluding section, I shall offer the suggestion that the objectionable aspect is not properly associated with the right, in either its traditional representation or in its new guise, and shall allow myself the indulgence of commenting beyond the limit of this chapter in linking this suggestion to the wider concerns of Unger's theoretical approach.

2 UNGER ON TRADITIONAL RIGHTS

The essential contrast made by Unger between the old traditional rights and the new rights of deviationist doctrine draws upon his central concern to liberate society from debilitating and alienating social structures which entrench the control of one party over another. The old rights form part of these social structures which the new rights will stand against. The same point is made in two different ways: one is a sociohistorical account of the development of rights; the other is an analysis of the position of the right holder.

(1) The Sociohistorical Account of Traditional Rights

The alternative "forms" or "definition[s]" of rights[6] that appear in Unger's sociohistorical account are embedded in particular constitutional frameworks. On the one hand, we have a system of privileges,[7] where the "basic form of right" is "participation in a status that links public office and economic privilege".[8] On the other hand, we have a system of powers and immunities,[9]

---

[6] FN, 128, 133.
[7] FN, 128–30.
[8] FN, 128.
[9] FN, 130–3.

where the characteristic form of rights is property, which provides the property owner with both "an immunity against the state" and "a power to set terms to other people's activity".[10]

Both forms of the old rights share a common characteristic in combining the protection the right holder enjoys against state oppression with a capacity to oppress others, and it is this capacity for "private oppression" which is absent in the new rights, whilst the protection against "governmental oppression" remains.[11]

What is interesting about this sociohistorical account of rights is that Unger's concepts of rights are drawn wholly in terms of the constitutional or social structure of the societies in which they are found. Despite the use of the terms privilege and immunity/power which possess a resonance with more technical approaches to the definition of rights, Unger's employment of these terms is filled out purely with the matter of sociopolitical relationships. So, right as privilege depicts the position in society of one who through his participation in the structure of government enjoys a position of dominance over others, whereas right as immunity/power depicts the position of one who through his protection against the structure of government enjoys a position of dominance over others. And as we shall see when we come to consider the new rights, it is the relationship between the members of society and the structure of the society to come that Unger sees as giving the new rights their distinctive attributes.

But this identification of the right with its sociopolitical setting is misleading for a number of reasons, and largely because the right is used to represent far more than can be signified by noting this particular feature of it. There are three crucial features in either case of Unger's privilege or immunity/power. The first is the position of dominance over other members of society; the second is the extent of protection from government interference with that position; and the third is the width of access to that position.

In both cases the first two features may be present in an identical manner. Whether we have the "privilege" of a feudal lord in relation to a parcel of land, or the "immunity/power" of a capitalist landowner, the right holder can expect a measure of security in his holding of the land from the government of the day and can exploit that security of enjoyment in ways which bring him a position of dominance over others. It is only in the third feature that a material distinction arises. For here we note that access to the position of dominance enjoyed by the feudal lord is far narrower than the access to the position of the capitalist landowner, being restricted to those whose lineage provides them with a position in the feudal structure of government. As significant as this distinction on the third feature may be, it is erroneous to conclude that it necessarily imposes any distinction on the other two features of the rights.

[10] FN, 132.
[11] FN, 133.

Put simply, the "privilege" of Unger's feudal lord may be expressed in terms of an immunity against other feudal lords or the king within the feudal structure of government and a power over his serfs, as much as the "immunity/power" of Unger's capitalist landowner could be expressed as a "privilege" in contrasting his position with those who lack his capital resources. And although we have very different kinds of "privilege" in these two cases, that is not to say that the ensuing immunity or power differs in any respect.

There are two further observations to make about Unger's two forms of rights here. The one is to point out that any difference in the kind of "privilege", in the sense of a difference in the sociopolitical structure of a society that produces it, has no essential bearing upon the extent of opportunity that the privileged party is afforded to oppress others. The extent of the opportunity to do this is rather measured by the immunity/power that the privilege gives rise to – and the same immunity/power may arise from different "privileges". The exclusive enjoyment of a walled orchard may be as much a means of oppression of the starving villagers outside, whether the immunity/power of that exclusive enjoyment is derived from the "privilege" of noble birth or the "privilege" of industrial wealth.

The other observation is that Unger's concern to highlight a distinction based upon the sociopolitical setting of a right is connected to his thesis that the more rigid the form of the sociopolitical structure of a society, the greater the opportunity for oppression within that society.[12] Our deliberations so far would suggest that this is a distortion of a plainer truth. The more rigid the society, the greater the opportunity for oppression by those whose dominant positions are entrenched in that rigidity. But within a less rigid society there may be as great an opportunity for oppression, albeit afforded to a greater number of potential oppressors by wider access to the positions of dominance within that society.

(2) The Analysis of the Right Holder's Position

The other way in which Unger depicts traditional rights is by an analysis of the position of the right holder. This is brought out by his forceful metaphor: "The right is a loaded gun that the rightholder may shoot at will in his corner of town."[13]

It is clear that in his analysis of the position of the right holder Unger is making the same point about traditional rights that he makes in his sociohistorical account of the development of rights: in holding the right there is the opportunity for oppression of others. The point is implicit in Unger's choice of metaphor, and is made explicit when he states that the "zone of discretion"

[12] eg CLSM, 30; FN, 164–5.
[13] CLSM, 36.

given to the right holder which permits him to do what he wants is contrary to "the give-and-take of communal life" and the concern for others that we find in communal life.[14]

Interestingly, we also find here Unger making a link between oppression and rigidity of form. It is because the right holder can always get his way within the zone of discretion that the traditional right cannot yield to the interests of the other party that might on occasion be paramount from the perspective of communality that recognises "mutual responsibility" rather than the "absolute discretion" of the one party.[15] Again, it is pertinent to consider whether greater flexibility in the determination of whose interests prevail in social relationships reduces the opportunity for oppression or merely spreads the opportunity across a wider base.

However, we may at this stage conclude our examination of the way Unger depicts traditional rights by noting what is for Unger the essential characteristic of individual discretion that is found in traditional rights, which for Unger gives them the objectionable aspect of providing the opportunity to oppress others.

3 UNGER'S NEW RIGHTS

(1) Introduction

Unger does not in fact completely abandon the idea of a right based upon individual discretion when he unveils his new rights, but rather insists that this is only one of a number of species of rights, arguing that the impact of even a right based upon individual discretion cannot be ascertained without taking into account the broader sociopolitical setting in which it is found.[16] The claim to a radical departure from traditional thinking on rights is accordingly based on two assertions. First, "The concept of right is subsidiary to that of a system of rights."[17] Secondly, within a society benefiting from Unger's programme of empowered democracy, a system of rights is composed of a number of types of right where, "Each establishes a distinctive style of human connection that contributes to a scheme of collective self-government and resists the influence of social division and hierarchy."[18]

---

[14] *ibid.* – cp FN, 512–3.

[15] CLSM, 36, 38 – Note that although the "consolidated property right" is regarded by Unger as the paradigm, even "the very model" of the traditional right, there are other instances of traditional rights which share this form, notably contract rights (eg text at n29 below).

[16] CLSM, 38–9. I use the term "sociopolitical" here and throughout this article to convey something broader than a narrowly conventional understanding of "political" which fits with Unger's own broader deployment of the latter term (see *Social Theory: Its Situation and Its Task, A Critical Introduction to Politics* (Cambridge, Cambridge University Press, 1987) at 10 n).

[17] CLSM, 38–9. A critique of Unger's system of rights is provided by Horst Eidenmüller, "Rights, Systems of Rights, and Unger's System of Rights" (1991) 10 *Law & Philosophy* 1 and 119.

[18] CLSM, 39.

The drift of Unger's argument seems to be this. The old rights based upon individual discretion provided the opportunity for the right holder to oppress others because they permitted him to do what he wanted irrespective of the interests of other parties involved. A system composed of such rights alone inevitably produces social division and hierarchy. On the other hand, the new rights only permit the exercise of individual discretion within a system of rights that is not composed of rights based upon individual discretion alone, and so the existence of other types of rights which are not based upon individual discretion acts as a check to prevent those rights in the system that are based upon individual discretion from being exercised in a way that oppresses others, to the end of preventing social division and hierarchy.

However, Unger does not himself provide us with a sufficiently detailed model of the workings of a system of new rights to show precisely how the different kinds of rights are to combine together so as to effectively prevent social division and hierarchy. It is not even clear how Unger's categorisation of rights works in respect of rights based upon individual discretion. For having made the point that these form one species of rights, Unger proceeds to unwrap the "four types of right" that combine to produce the system of new rights without counting the species as one of the four types,[19] although rights based upon individual discretion feature occasionally within the subsequent exposition of these four types. There is then a possibility that Unger's classification of rights is worked out with a more complex set of divisions and perhaps subdivisions than what is explicitly presented.

What Unger does give us is exposition and some illustration of the four types of new rights, and it is this that we shall consider in detail in order to test whether Unger has in fact produced rights that differ from the traditional rights that he purports to have abandoned. We shall look at the four types of rights in turn.

(2) Immunity Rights

The first type of new right is labelled immunity rights. Immunity rights are designed to provide the citizen with a basic level of security in terms of bodily security, material welfare, and political involvement, which will be sufficient to persuade him that participation in the empowered democracy will not threaten what is most important for him.[20] In seeking to establish the dis-

---

[19] CLSM, 38–9.

[20] CLSM, 39, 54; FN, 513–4, 524–5, 528–30.
There are a number of points of interest concerning these rights which cannot be fully dealt with here. The protection afforded by immunity rights concerns what is regarded as important for the citizen from the ideological viewpoint of the empowered democracy rather than what he himself may regard as important (FN, 514, 524). The level of protection may be measured in both absolute and relative terms (FN, 524), but immunity rights afford only a minimum level of protection (CLSM, 54). It is not easy to reconcile these points with the stated objective for the rights to produce a contented citizenry.

tinctiveness of immunity rights as against traditional rights Unger initially employs two arguments, but subsequently gives up his use of the first.

The first argument is to indicate the non-absolute nature of immunity rights. Although approximating to the traditional right - the consolidated property right – which assures the holder of security by bestowing upon him absolute discretion over his property, immunity rights bestow only a "nearly absolute claim" and are characterised by a "scrupulous avoidance of the guarantees of security" that are afforded by the consolidated property right.[21]

However, elsewhere Unger hardens his immunity rights and treats them as being modelled upon the consolidated property right. Initially, this is done in the context of discussing exceptional cases,[22] and the reference to immunity rights is oblique, but in his later work Unger drops the first argument entirely. The guarantee of security that was previously scrupulously avoided is now extended: other rights in the system are not allowed to encroach upon the "safeguards" constituted by immunity rights, "which secure each individual in a proud and jealous independence".[23] This is brought about by giving immunity rights the "bright line" definition[24] characteristic of consolidated property rights, and indeed Unger acknowledges that the "structural characteristics" of immunity rights "in all but minor respects . . . coincide with the formal traits of consolidated property."[25] The "minor respects" appear to be limited to the difference in source which "does not make the other operational features of immunity rights any different . . .".[26]

This leaves Unger having recourse to the second argument. Although in structure immunity rights are the same as consolidated property rights, they differ in impact due to a difference in sociopolitical setting: "the social significance of the structural features changes radically with the shift in their institutional setting."[27]

Unger's retreat to the second argument may be regarded as indicating his eventual acknowledgment that if immunity rights are to have any substance and provide any sense of security to their holders, they must at some point be capable of firm exercise in order to draw a line against the intrusion of other interests – in precisely the way that traditional rights can be exercised. "Any solution to the problem of immunity requires that some rules remain stable and some resources be set aside."[28]

What precisely is left in the distinctiveness of Unger's immunity rights as against traditional rights? We may remind ourselves that the broad objective in maintaining their distinctiveness is to demonstrate that unlike traditional

[21] CLSM, 39.
[22] CLSM, 84–5.
[23] FN, 530.
[24] *ibid.*
[25] FN, 529.
[26] FN, 530.
[27] FN, 529 – cp 527.
[28] FN, 526.

rights they do not provide the opportunity to oppress others. The detailed differences are found in three points: their source, their flexibility, and their relation to other rights in the system.

The difference in source is, as we have seen, treated by Unger as a "structural feature" of the right, but might better be regarded as an aspect of its sociopolitical setting. For this difference as seen by Unger amounts to a derivation of the right in a manner different from the "traditional rights of contract or property, whose sources are articulated agreements or state-imposed duties."[29] However this is supposed to work in practice,[30] since the different source does not affect the "other structural features"[31] of the rights we may conclude that at most it affects the feature of width of access to the right.[32] This does seem to be the point that Unger is trying to make when he describes the source of an immunity right as "a situation" as opposed to the articulated agreement of contract or the state-imposed duties connected with property:[33] access to the immunity right is not restricted to those who have managed to bring it about through contract, or to those who have in some way acquired property which the state will protect by imposing duties on others, but is made universal by bringing about a common situation for all. This interpretation of Unger's point about source in terms of width of access gains an echo in his allusive comment that, "The immunity rights of an empowered democracy have the same relation to consolidated property that property has to caste."[34]

We have already noted that Unger's virtue of flexibility may arise in two ways:[35] in one case it opposes rigidity in the sociopolitical structure of a society; in the other it opposes the rigidity of opportunity provided to the holder of the right which permits him to get his own way. In relation to immunity rights, the latter type of flexibility (expressed as a withdrawal of guaranteed security from the right holder) we saw was first advanced but then abandoned by Unger. We shall consider it fully below in relation to others of Unger's new rights. Flexibility of sociopolitical structure is, however, maintained by Unger for immunity rights.[36] But given that the immunity rights within this sociopolitical structure have been granted a bright line definition, the impact of a flexible sociopolitical structure upon them must be limited to the feature of width of access to those securely defined rights. And it appears that the point of flexibility is merely another way of expressing the point made by Unger in declaring a difference in source for his immunity rights.

---

[29] FN, 530.
[30] The most elementary details are lacking in Unger's account.
[31] FN, 530.
[32] 2(1) above.
[33] FN, 530.
[34] FN, 526 – cp CLSM, 39.
[35] 2(1), 2(2) above.
[36] FN, 526.

Finally, we need to consider the distinctiveness of immunity rights that may arise from their relationship to other rights in the system. This possible difference also relates to the sociopolitical setting of the rights, since the system of rights as a whole provides the legal aspect of the sociopolitical structure of society.[37]

However, once Unger has conceded that immunity rights have a bright line defence against the encroachment of other rights, there can be nothing in the relationship between immunity rights and other rights of the system which detracts from the ability of the holder to exercise his individual discretion over the domain, or "zone", afforded to him by the immunity right – in the same way as the holder of a traditional right.

Nevertheless, there is the possibility of finding some bulwark against oppression for immunity rights in the relationship between different rights of the system, if we consider the relationship between the contents of different immunity rights. This can be done both intrinsically and extrinsically.

Intrinsically, if the immunity rights of a system of rights provide everyone with the same level of material welfare,[38] irrespective of whether that level is sufficient, there is not within that provision the opportunity for one person to oppress another. If additionally we relate the common provision of welfare to some extrinsic requirement of sufficiency, then there is a stronger safeguard effected by the immunity rights against the possibility of oppression coming from beyond the resources covered by the immunity rights. But this sort of protection against oppression has nothing to do with a different kind of right, and could equally be afforded by utilising traditional rights. If every villager owns an orchard, then there is no opportunity for those who own orchards to oppress those who do not.

There is accordingly nothing in what Unger proposes for his immunity rights to indicate that we are dealing with a different kind of right, "differing, in form as well as content . . . from the consolidated property right".[39] The most that we get from those points that Unger puts forward to establish the distinctiveness of his immunity right is a particular scheme of distributive justice, where the rights are combined in a sociopolitical setting to ensure equality of access to a common minimum level of resources.

(3) Destabilization Rights

We turn then to Unger's destabilization rights, heralded as being "the most novel and puzzling", "the most obscure and original part of the proposed system of rights and the one that best reveals the ruling intentions of the entire

---

[37] CLSM, 38.
[38] I choose material welfare for ease of illustration, but the same point could be made in relation to the other concerns of immunity rights.
[39] FN, 510.

program."[40] My purpose here will be to dispel the obscurity in order to reveal that what it conceals is lacking in the originality that Unger claims for it.

There are essentially two layers of obscurity covering Unger's presentation of destabilization rights. The first relates to the way in which Unger draws this category. Destabilization rights are categorised together through a common feature of bringing remedies to bear against an entrenched position of dominance with a view to breaking it up, and thus preventing social division and hierarchy and the opportunity to oppress others.[41] But this category is so loosely drawn that it contains quite disparate elements, and the disparities are often more significant than the common feature but lie concealed under the sweeping generalisations that Unger makes about all destabilization rights.

Within destabilization rights we find three distinct types of rights:

(i)   rights used to directly protect individual interests, which in fact overlap with immunity rights.[42]

(ii) rights used to determine the behaviour of public bodies.[43]

(iii) rights used to bring about a change in the law.[44]

Put in traditional terms we have, swept into the single category, private law rights enforced through civil litigation, public law rights enforced through judicial review, and constitutional rights exercised through electoral practices. Admittedly, each of these three types of rights may be used to "destabilize" what would otherwise become an entrenched position of dominance leading to oppression, but the differences between them are remarkable. In particular, the link between the perception of oppression and the effective obtaining of relief from it may be weaker or stronger depending upon which type of right is involved.

To categorise a private law right against some form of oppression as a right to "destabilize" the threatened oppression is one thing, for the effective remedy flows directly from the right. But to suggest that the right to vote[45] can be so categorised is quite another thing, for the prospect of obtaining relief from the oppression is far removed from the exercise of a single vote.

Yet despite Unger's recognition of the differences between some destabilization rights and others, this does not stop him making broad statements about the category when it comes to asserting the distinctiveness of destabilization rights as against traditional rights in familiar terms: no bright line definition, no zone of individual discretion.[46]

[40] CLSM, 39, 43.

[41] CLSM, 39; FN, 530.

[42] CLSM, 54, 55.

[43] FN, 532–3.

[44] FN, 533.

[45] It does not matter whether the vote is in an election for a government who will decide the matter or in a referendum that will directly decide the matter, which seems to be Unger's preference on some occasions (FN, 533).

[46] FN, 535. Unger also repeats here the argument of distinctiveness based on source, which was dealt with above in relation to immunity rights.

This assertion is obviously unfounded in the case of type (i) destabilization rights covering immunity rights, where the bright line definition has been conceded.[47] With respect to the other two types, the assertion has some semblance of credibility but on closer analysis this breaks down. For the lack of bright line, which is expressed in terms of the uncertainty of the right holder in obtaining relief,[48] relates in types (ii) and (iii) not to the definition of the right but to the strength of the link between having the right and the prospect of success in obtaining relief from the oppression. This says nothing about the bright line, and associated zone of individual discretion, that may inhere in the right itself, whether it be the right to bring an action for judicial review (*locus standi*), or the right to vote.[49]

In considering these three types of destabilization rights, I have been assuming that the right holder in Unger's destabilization rights actually enjoys some position from which he can seek to activate the relief required to prevent entrenched dominance and its attendant ills. However, Unger does not provide us with all the details necessary to establish the precise operation of destabilization rights, and it may well be that the right holder is not intended by Unger to be the one who is in a position to activate the relief himself. But in either case the second and more fundamental layer of obscurity conceals the true nature of the right.

The second layer of obscurity descends from a confusion between rights and claims.[50] Unger introduces destabilization rights by stating that, "They represent claims to disrupt established institutions . . .".[51] And in concluding that they lack the bright line definition of traditional rights, he comments "no bright line surrounds the area of the protected legal claim".[52] This description of the rights as claims obscures the difference between two quite different things.

A person may make a claim to relief which is not deemed justified and so relief is not granted; or he may make a justified claim to relief and the recognition of the claim as justified will lead to the granting of relief. It is only the latter justified claim that can be treated as equivalent to the right to relief. The former claim is at best a claim to have the right which fails.[53]

Unger exploits the ambiguity of claim to lump together both the justified claim to relief and the unfounded claim to relief as representing the destabilization right, from which position he may readily conclude that the right lacks the bright line definition and denies its holder the absolute discretion to determine whether relief will be granted, since some of the holder's claims to

---

[47] above at n24.

[48] FN, 535.

[49] I use traditional terminology. Unger indicates that in some cases novel institutions will be used to provide the relief (CLSM, 55; FN, 532) but this does not affect the point at issue.

[50] For the relationship between rights and claims, see ch III.

[51] CLSM, 39.

[52] FN, 535.

[53] It may of course be accompanied by the ancillary right (justified claim) to make the claim (as in *locus standi*) but this should not be confused with it – see further, ch III.

relief will succeed but others will fail. But if the destabilization right is, as Unger elsewhere informs us, "a right to have an organization or an area of social practice destabilized" or "the citizen's right to prevent any faction of the society from gaining a privileged hold",[54] then it is only the justified claims to relief that represent the destabilization right, and in these cases the bright line can be drawn and the individual discretion characteristic of traditional rights can be exercised.

Admittedly, we will not always know until after a process of adjudication or the like whether a justified claim has been established,[55] but in this case we equally do not yet know whether the claimant does in fact possess a specific right in such circumstances. Moreover this suspension of certainty also applies in the processes of establishing traditional rights. In short, the uncertainty relates to the process of establishing the right not to the right itself: it may be unclear whether a right to relief, for say negligent damage, in particular circumstances exists until after a process of adjudication; but once the right has been established by this process the right to relief in those circumstances will be clearly defined.

The problem of uncertainty associated with the process by which a right is established will figure largely in relation to solidarity rights, and there will be further opportunity to consider it below when this type of right is examined. However, there is a further strand to Unger's argument in relation to destabilization rights, which contributes to the second layer of obscurity and which needs to be considered here.

The idea that the unfounded claim to relief is somehow tied up together with the justified claim in the destabilization right is given further support by Unger's presentation of the destabilization right in both an abstract and a concrete form. Unger portrays the false claim as being discarded within the process of "specification" that takes us from the "abstract ideal" towards "the concreteness that enables . . . practical consequences".[56] This suggests that the unfounded claim is somehow part of the right at the abstract level and it is at this level that the claim is made, without as yet knowing if it will be established or not and thus with consequent uncertainty as to the precise definition of the right. Hence Unger speaks of a process of "redefinition" of the right[57] in moving from the abstract to the concrete, as though the unfounded claim is part of the earlier abstract definition of the right, in reaching his conclusion that the right lacks a bright line definition. But this line of argument is faulty, resting upon a confusion between abstract and concrete rights.

An abstract right may be established, and accordingly a justified claim to what that right affords may be made. But this justified claim, like its equiva-

---

[54] FN, 530, 531.
[55] FN, 533–5. It is immaterial to this point whether the claim to relief is made to a legislative, judicial, or administrative type of body.
[56] FN, 534–5.
[57] FN, 535.

lent right, can only be made in the abstract. A concrete claim, whether justified or unfounded, cannot be treated as part of the abstract right, for it is the nature of abstract rights that they are divorced from the detailed factors that may threaten their exercise in a concrete situation – those very factors that will go to determine whether a concrete right exists, and thus whether the equivalent justified concrete claim can be made.[58] So it is wrong to suggest that the unfounded claim, which is concrete in nature, can enter the definition of the abstract destabilization right.

The truth of the matter is that the unfounded claim never enters the definition of the destabilization right, either in the abstract or the concrete form. And the uncertainty surrounding whether a particular claim will prove to be justified or unfounded is merely the uncertainty inherent in any move from an abstract right to a concrete instantiation of it[59] – such as is found with the abstract right to free speech, for example – and introduces no uncertainty into the definition of the right itself.

There is a key deployment of this second layer of obscurity when Unger reaches his conclusion that destabilization rights are distinct from traditional rights. Unger picks up the unfounded claims to assert that destabilization rights cannot be regarded as sharing the objective of traditional rights "to demarcate a fixed zone of discretionary action, within which an individual rightholder may do whatever he pleases" and hence reaches the conclusion that "the controlling image" of destabilization rights "is the mandated, context-specific disruption of complex collective arrangements".[60]

But those unfounded claims that failed do nothing to inform us about a failure of the right holder to get his way, for there are no rights to correspond to the unfounded claims, so no right holders, and so nothing to be said about the individual discretion of right holders, on the basis of what might not have happened in these cases.

The fallacy in Unger's argument can be brought out by turning it onto the controlling image that he wants to establish for his rights. If those cases where the claims are unfounded are yet regarded as constituents of the destabilization right, then in those cases there will not only be a thwarting of the right holder's discretion but equally there will not be any destabilization occurring and so we can equally reach the conclusion that "context specific disruption" is not the controlling image for destabilization rights.

Moreover, the same faulty reasoning could be employed to upturn the characteristic of individual discretion that Unger has identified for traditional rights. For once we allow that an unfounded claim to what the right purveys may be counted for the purpose of analysing the right, then we must conclude that in such cases where the claim will fail the exercise of individual discretion is not provided for and so cannot be the characteristic of the right.

[58] For the relationship between abstract rights and concrete rights, see ch V.
[59] Considered further in ch V:2(5).
[60] FN, 535.

Put more formally, the fallacy is to take a right to φ and then to analyse the position of the right holder in the right to φ by examining whether the right permits him to θ. The process however becomes more subtle, and the fallacy more easily concealed, when we move from a right to (φ in x) to the activity of (φ in y) – or, from a right to φ in the abstract to the activity of (φ in y). A fallacy it nevertheless remains.

This error reveals much about the underlying confusion besetting Unger's treatment of traditional rights, and we shall return to it subsequently. For the moment we may merely observe that Unger has failed to demonstrate that destabilization rights lack the characteristic of individual discretion associated with traditional rights, and that far from providing a feature or "controlling image" that can be opposed to the characteristic of individual discretion, destabilization at the best affords a description of a common aspect of the contents of a group of rights. And where it is correct to state that these rights may be used by the holder to effect destabilization, it would equally be correct to state that the rights provide the holder with the opportunity to exercise his discretion to do just that.

(4) Market Rights

Unger's third type of new right is market rights. These represent "the rights employed for economic exchange in the trading sector of the society."[61] They may be dealt with summarily. For although Unger takes pains to point out the distinctiveness of "the practical effects and the imaginative message of the rights",[62] which emerge from the sociopolitical setting in which the rights are found,[63] he is ready to acknowledge that they share "the basic operational features" of traditional rights.[64] In particular, he concedes the bright line definition and the exercise of individual discretion that goes with it.[65] And any hesitation that Unger displays over matching market rights with traditional rights lacks articulation and in any case raises only points that have been dealt with in relation to the two types of rights already considered.[66]

---

[61] FN, 520 – cp CLSM, 39.

[62] FN, 523.

[63] There are two particular factors that go to compose this: the fact that the market right holders already have their basic security guaranteed by their immunity rights; the structure of the market based on the idea of "the rotating capital fund" which ensures wider access to the possession of capital and thus wider involvement in the market than would a traditionally structured market, and is reflected in the market rights assuming a character that has more in common with contract than consolidated property – FN, 522–3.

[64] FN, 522.

[65] *ibid.*

[66] As with immunity rights, the hesitation is found in the earlier CLSM, at 39. It touches upon the points of treating the rights as claims and their non-absolute nature, and as a backstop position Unger argues that even if market rights are found to have a degree of fixity there remain other types of rights which differ from them.

(5) Solidarity Rights

The final type of new right is solidarity rights, and this does require fuller attention, for it is with solidarity rights that Unger argues most forcefully for a distinctiveness from traditional rights based upon a lack of bright line definition and an accompanying absence of a zone of individual discretion.[67] The argument that was first advanced but then abandoned in the case of immunity rights and was more falteringly advanced in the case of market rights, which was wrapped in obscurity in the case of destabilization rights, is advanced and maintained with the greatest clarity in the case of solidarity rights.

Solidarity rights deal with "the legal entitlements of communal life", with "social relations of reliance and trust".[68] There are two reasons why Unger's argument against the bright line enjoys its clearest presentation here. First, the situations in which we find these rights illustrated are readily recognizable in traditional terms (eg a contractual relationship) so that it is easy to see in concrete terms where the differences lie between the old and the new. Secondly, Unger provides us with a relatively straightforward analysis of these rights in terms of "a two-stage career".[69]

The argument for the distinctiveness of solidarity rights as against traditional rights runs like this.[70] Take a traditional contractual relationship. The rights of the parties are set at the point of agreement, and subsequently should one of the parties wish to act in a way covered by the contract reference will be made solely to the terms of the agreement in order to establish whether he has a right to do so. No reference will be made to the wider issues involving the actual position at the time of performance of the other party, or of the effect that performance might have on the continuing relationship of interdependence between the parties. By contrast to this model of traditional contractual rights we can find a more flexible model of human relationships of interdependence in family life, in continuing business relationships, and even in certain areas of the law where fiduciary principles are allowed to upset the strict terms of agreements. This more flexible model is used as the basis for solidarity rights, which retain the ability to reflect all the nuanced considerations that would enter into the promotion of a continuing relationship of trust between the parties by insisting that the complete definition of their rights must await a detailed consideration of the factors present at each possible point of performance. Instead of a rigid bright line definition of the parties' rights emerging at the stage of agreement, with the consequent ability of a party to exercise his individual discretion within the zone covered by the agreement even where that may cause injustice or oppression of the other

[67] FN, 538.
[68] CLSM, 39–40, FN, 535.
[69] CLSM, 40.
[70] CLSM, 39–40, 57–86; FN, 536–8.

party, the agreement acts only as the first stage of the definition of solidarity
rights, and it will not be until the second stage – the point of performance –
when we can have a broader grasp of the issues involved that the definition
of the rights will be completed. Hence solidarity rights lack the bright line
definition of traditional rights, the characteristic of individual discretion is
absent, and the opportunity to oppress others is excluded.

Unger does not in fact regard the flexible two-stage model of solidarity
rights as always appropriate. He allows the recognition of "the classical form
of contract rights as a special case."[71] So in these limited examples of solidarity rights where everything is settled at the first stage there will be a bright
line definition with all that that entails. But what of the others, which Unger
sees as forming the majority? The recognition of the exception reveals more
than the width of Unger's classification of rights, for it tells us something
about how Unger perceives we look upon relationships of interdependence
that are the subject matter of solidarity rights. In some cases (for Unger the
exceptional ones) the relationship can accommodate what Unger characterises
as a "gamble".[72] The deal is struck, the rights of the parties are set, and subsequently at the time of performance those rights may work out to the advantage or disadvantage of the parties. In other cases (for Unger the majority) the
relationship cannot accommodate such a gamble but depends upon a determination of the entitlements of the parties in the light of the known circumstances prevailing at the time of performance.

But a relationship of interdependence in the latter cases would not be
thought of at the first stage as creating entitlements between the parties (that
would be one of the former cases) but at the most a tentative arrangement
which might or might not be ratified at the second stage. Once we get to the
second stage, there are two possibilities recognised by Unger.[73] One is that the
parties themselves will work out the entitlements, the other is that the entitlements will be worked out by judges or some sort of arbitrating body. In
either case, it is at this stage that the entitlement arises and if it is enforceable
it gives to the right holder a bright line zone of individual discretion, in the
same way as traditional rights.

However, Unger also puts forward the possibility of some solidarity rights
being unenforceable.[74] Where does this unenforceable right come from? If, as
Unger informs us, it proceeds from "a public declaration of a public vision,
extending, qualifying, and clarifying the ideals embodied in other, enforceable
parts of the system of rights",[75] it would appear that we have merely institu-
tionalized the value system or morality of the enforceable rights for situations
falling outside their scope, so that an individual in such a situation would know

[71] CLSM, 84–5.
[72] CLSM, 85.
[73] CLSM, 40, FN, 538–9.
[74] FN, 539.
[75] *ibid.*

his moral rights even if he could not enforce them as legal rights. To claim that this gives rise to a different kind of right is unfounded. It does nothing more than fix a different realm in which the right may be asserted. The right holder now has a bright line zone of individual discretion in which he can assert his moral entitlement rather than an entitlement that will be legally enforced. Moreover, such a practice can be found running alongside traditional legal rights, where the values embodied in enforceable legal rights arise in situations where it is thought better that the enforcement machinery of the law should not intrude, such as in the case of agreements "binding in honour only".

We may then conclude that with his solidarity rights Unger has again failed to provide us with a kind of right that is distinct from traditional rights with their essential characteristic of individual discretion. What solidarity rights may set out to achieve within "the program of empowered democracy" is greater flexibility and sensitivity in the way in which the entitlements of inter-dependent relationships are determined, thus drawing the line in a different place around those relationships whose consequences we are prepared to "gamble" on,[76] but once those entitlements have been established they may be expressed in precisely the same way as traditional rights.

In a less abstruse manner Unger repeats with solidarity rights the error we have detected in the earlier cases, of confusing the uncertainties that may be present in the process by which the right is established (seen as the uncertainty whether the relevant judicial or legislative body will establish the right, or the uncertainty whether a claim will be recognised as justified, or the uncertainty whether an abstract right will be instantiated in a particular concrete situation) with uncertainty in the definition of the right. In the case of solidarity rights which do not give rise to entitlements until the second stage, there simply are no rights at the first stage – or, at least, no rights to what the holder will be entitled to at the second stage. And the mere fact that we can say of the person at the first stage that we are uncertain whether he will acquire the rights at the second stage is no ground for saying that he therefore possesses those rights at the first stage but without a bright line definition. We might as validly conclude that traditional rights lack a bright line definition, by demonstrating, for example, that a person who has made an invitation to treat does not know at that stage whether it will be recognised that he has contractual

---

[76] CLSM, 85. In considering the practicalities of Unger's proposals, two points need to be borne in mind. (1) An alternative "gamble" may arise if interdependent relationships are left unfixed at the first stage yet deal in matters that are also the subject of further interdependent relationships – hence the virtue of certainty in commercial transactions. (2) The specification of fixed legal relationships should not be regarded as antipathetic to the promotion of interdependent relationships based on trust. For the relationship of trust may flourish by both parties choosing to ignore the strict legal position (see, eg, Hugh Beale and Anthony Dugdale, "Contracts between Businessmen" (1975) 2 *British Journal of Law and Society* 45 on the law of contract and continuing business relationships); and given that there is always the possibility that one of the parties may choose to abuse the relationship of trust the legal position may be regarded as a sensible fallback position (see further, Jeremy Waldron, "When Justice Replaces Affection: The Need for Rights" (1988) 11 *Harvard Journal of Law and Public Policy* 625).

rights, so that he possesses contractual rights without a bright line definition; or, that a person with capacity to marry who is engaged to be married to another does not know at that stage whether it will be recognised that he has the rights of a married party, so that he possesses the rights of a married party without a bright line definition.

It may well be that the programme of empowered democracy turns up a society where traditional firm offers are regarded as invitations to treat, and traditional marriage is regarded as "trial marriage". Such a society may seem strange to our eyes, and it may at first be difficult for us to work out exactly how and where the interpersonal entitlements, or solidarity rights, occur. But nothing Unger tells us about such a society can lead us to believe that the solidarity rights of the empowered democracy will be different in form from traditional rights.

Since our survey of the four types of Unger's new rights has led us to the conclusion that each of them shares the essential characteristic of individual discretion, which for Unger gives traditional rights the objectionable aspect of providing the opportunity to oppress others, we must conclude that inasmuch as Unger is correct in attributing this feature to traditional rights then so too Unger's new rights must be found to provide the opportunity to oppress others. The final section of this chapter will largely be taken up with the avoidance of this conclusion.

4 CONCLUDING REMARKS

The obvious starting point for any attempt to avoid the conclusion that it is the character of rights, whether new or old, to provide the opportunity to oppress others is a return to Unger's depiction of the traditional right in terms of a zone of individual discretion. Until now I have been content to accept this depiction without any real scrutiny, but now that we have reached the point where Unger's depiction of traditional rights is not only damaging to any esteem in which they might have been held but is also self-destructive in rendering his new rights incapable of performing their objectives, it is timely to reexamine with some care the elements in Unger's analysis of traditional rights.

We have seen[77] that Unger's analysis is built upon a bright line definition of a zone of conduct where the right holder has the discretion to do what he wants without taking into account any concern for the interests of any other party who might be affected. Perhaps the most crucial point to make in reexamining this analysis is that there is a connection between the defined zone of conduct and the discretion of the right holder, for Unger seems capable of overlooking this simple point with disastrous results.

---

[77] 2 above.

In the discussion of destabilization rights I indicated a fallacy in Unger's argument consisting of considering conduct that the right in question did not cover in order to reach a conclusion as to the right holder's position in relation to the conduct that the right did cover.[78] Then the fallacious reasoning was employed to falsely assert a lack of individual discretion for Unger's destabilization rights in order to keep them from that characteristic that Unger had associated with the opportunity for oppression. Now I want to suggest that the latent deployment of the same fallacy undergirds Unger's false attribution of the opportunity for oppression to the characteristic of individual discretion.

The opportunity for oppression is seen quite simply in terms of the granting of discretion to the right holder to behave as he wants with disregard for the interests of others. There is nothing to object to in presenting this as an opportunity for oppression. But a right does not convey to its holder a discretion to behave as he wants with disregard for the interests of others. It does not do this *a fortiori* because it does not convey to its holder a discretion to behave as he wants. What a right conveys is a discretion to behave or not to behave within the terms of the conduct limited by the definition of the right. Unger's depiction of the position of the right holder as enjoying the discretion to "act as he pleases",[79] and thus including the possibility of oppressing others, ignores the restriction imposed on the conduct of the right holder by the bright line definition of the conduct over which his discretion may be exercised. Unger thus falsely draws an analysis of the right holder's position from a broader investigation of positions conjured up by "doing what he wants" that may not actually be included in what the right covers.

We need to make it clear that it may well be that a right has been granted which does give its holder the opportunity to oppress others, but if this is so it is not because any right which conveys to its holder the discretion to behave in a specified area of conduct necessarily conveys the opportunity to oppress others but because in relation to the area of conduct specified in that particular right there is the opportunity to oppress others. It is not, as Unger would have us believe, the form of the right which provides the opportunity to oppress but its content.[80]

The role of the bright line in limiting that content, and potentially limiting the content of a right so that the holder does not possess the opportunity to oppress others, is completely overlooked by Unger because he is set upon looking over the line to the possible exercise of discretion within the boundary of the right rather than looking at the line to see the limitations that the

---

[78] 3(3) above.

[79] FN, 512 – cp FN, 535 ("untrammeled individual discretion"); CLSM, 36 ("shoot at will").

[80] Whether intrinsically (eg a right to hold a person for questioning for an unlimited period of time), or in relation to extrinsic factors, as with the example of the orchard above, 2(1) & 3(2).

The recognition of whether it is the content of rights that makes them oppressive as being a crucial question is found in Mark Kelman, *A Guide to Critical Legal Studies* (Cambridge, MA, Harvard University Press, 1987) at 274. But the question is not pursued.

boundary imposes on what the right holder can do. Seen from the perspective of this partial vision, Unger constructs the bright line definition of rights into an argument hostile to the form of traditional rights, but his argument is as distorted as his vision is obstructed.

The proper role of the bright line definition of rights becomes apparent as we subject Unger's new rights to more careful analysis and discover that they too must share in the form of the traditional rights that their author has sought to abandon. This conclusion is reached as we force Unger's argument along from uncertain speculation as to the prospect of particular rights, reject the spurious identification of that stage of uncertain speculation with the existence of the right,[81] and reach a point where that speculation is resolved to fix the entitlement of the party one way or another – and here we recognise that in the same way as the old rights Unger's new rights have a bright line zone of individual discretion. Seen like this the bright line zone is clearly not to be taken as the identifying characteristic of the opportunity for one party to oppress another, but rather the fixing of the relations between parties to ensure a fair resolution of any conflicting interests (or simply a convenient determination of uncertain mutual interests). But this may as easily be seen in the processes in which traditional rights are fixed.[82]

All that Unger offers are some vague suggestions as to how the processes in which rights are fixed could be handled so as to create greater sensitivity to the issues involved in drawing those bright lines that must be drawn eventually in any society. Such suggestions are neither particularly radical nor particularly novel.[83] And yet the appearance of an enterprise of heroic proportions is maintained by the illusion that all that has gone before is in some way defective in relation to all that is promised to come, an illusion that gains its momentum from purporting to attack the very form of the old rights and offering a form for the new rights which can guard against the defects of the old. We are offered no substance in Unger's new rights with which to halt the flow of his rhetoric as we demand a pause to compare the substance of the new with the old.[84]

---

[81] This may be regarded as deploying the converse of the fallacy which regards the bright line boundary of traditional rights as permitting unlimited or "absolute" discretion, and thus as being identified with the opportunity for oppression, for the dwelling upon the uncertainties attending the processes by which the rights are established permits us to ignore the boundaries that are found around those rights which are eventually established, from which we (fallaciously) infer that the rights cannot provide the opportunity for oppression.

[82] Finnis, above n1 at 149, significantly points out that Unger fails to mention how the "critical" processes are to differ from traditional ones. And for an argument on how traditional legal scholarship can be regarded as possessing the capacity to "reconstruct" legal materials in a vibrant way, see MacCormick, above n1.

[83] Compare the setting up of tribunals to administer the entitlements of the welfare state after World War II in the United Kingdom.

[84] Kelman, above n80 at 275, correctly observes that "the spirit of the antirights . . . approach is to abandon known distorting categories, to leap ahead, not fully aware how one will reconstruct the world . . .". The possibility of sinister implications for this approach in the works of Unger are picked up by William Ewald, "Unger's Philosophy: A Critical Legal Study" and

The same illusion can be discerned as attending the wider concerns of Unger's theory, for the central idea that holds together his broader political theory is that any dominant position must be subject to being overthrown in order to retain a political environment in which no person or institution can acquire the entrenched position from which others can be oppressed and their participation in effective democracy rendered nugatory. By elevating the mere form of critical challenge to what has been established into the basis for a "programme of empowered democracy", Unger is similarly dispensing with any substance in what his programme offers. We are constantly being invited to look upon the challenge to whatever has already been established in the security that whatever might ensue from the challenge need not trouble us since it will also be possible to challenge that in turn . . .[85] But this is not to offer a programme of political action at all.[86] For no matter how difficult it might be to draw the lines of the positions of different members of society in relation to each other, it is in those lines that the members of society have to live, not in the promise that the lines can be moved.[87]

Unger's call to accept new for old not only fails to deliver anything truly new, but, as often with such promotional literature, what we gain once we have traded in the substance of the old for the promise of the new turns out to have more sparkle than substance.

"Reply" (1988) 97 *Yale Law Journal* 665 and 773 at 741–748, 748–753, 755, 774; and also in David Price, "Taking Rights Cynically: A Review of Critical Legal Studies" (1989) 48 *Cambridge Law Journal* 271 at 297 n93.

[85] eg CLSM, 30–1.

[86] cp Fish, above n3 at 1008–12.

[87] It is significant that although much of the debate that has ensued over the CLS position on rights has been couched in terms of hostility towards or approval of rights, it is possible to find in both camps a recognition that certain lines need to be drawn – eg in Richard Delgado, "The Ethereal Scholar: Does Critical Legal Studies Have What Minorities Want?" (1987) 22 *Harvard Civil Rights – Civil Liberties Law Review* 301 (approving of rights) an insistence on drawing lines against racism (particularly at 321); and in Frances Olsen, "Statutory Rape: A Feminist Critique of Rights Analysis" (1984) 63 *Texas Law Review* 387 (hostile to rights) an insistence on drawing lines from a feminist perspective (particularly at 431) despite the earlier remonstrations against drawing lines (at 427, 429). From this observation follows an obvious suggestion, that much of the disagreement on whether or not to have rights can be resolved into the issue of what rights to have.

Part 4
Arguing with Rights

.

VIII

Rights, Utilitarianism and Morality 1 Some Preliminary Observations

1 INTRODUCTION

The discussion of rights and utilitarianism in ethical theory[1] has frequently been staged as a contest between the two, fought over the years by some extremely distinguished pugilists, championing the one cause or the other. After such a series of displays of fighting prowess there might seem little incentive to step into the ring, but nevertheless the fighting goes on.

The combative nature of the discussion can be traced to the emergence of utilitarianism into the modern arena in Bentham's polemical prose. Natural rights were one of Bentham's targets,[2] but by no means his sole target. His utilitarianism was declared the victor over all rivals in the moral arena.[3] More recently, utilitarianism has been assailed by three notable champions of rights, Rawls, Nozick, and Dworkin,[4] though the rights appearing on their banners no longer bear the title natural.

Contemporary discussion has included the voices of those who are prepared to discuss reconciliation.[5] Others are still concerned to emphasise the differ-

---

[1] I use the term loosely here to cover moral, political, and legal philosophy – though will focus subsequently on the moral context for reasons to be given.

[2] "Anarchical Fallacies" II.I contains the famous slur "nonsense upon stilts" – extracted in Jeremy Waldron (ed.), *Nonsense upon Stilts* (London, Methuen, 1987) at 53; also in John Bowring (ed.), *The Works of Jeremy Bentham*, 11 vols (Edinburgh, William Tait, 1838-43) vol II, 489.

[3] *An Introduction to the Principles of Morals and Legislation*, 1781 (New York, NY, Prometheus Books, 1988) (hereinafter, PML), ch II.I.

[4] John Rawls, *A Theory of Justice* (Oxford, OUP, 1971) – hereinafter, TofJ; Robert Nozick, *Anarchy, State, and Utopia* (Oxford, Blackwell, 1974) – hereinafter, ASU; Ronald Dworkin, *Taking Rights Seriously* (London, Duckworth, 1977) – hereinafter, TRS, and *A Matter of Principle* (Oxford, Clarendon Press, 1985) – hereinafter, MofP.

[5] Joseph Raz, *The Morality of Freedom* (Oxford, Clarendon Press, 1986) – hereinafter, MofF: 187, and "Hart on Moral Rights and Legal Duties" (1984) 4 *Oxford Journal of Legal Studies* 123 at 128; Michael Freeden, *Rights* (Buckingham, Open University Press, 1991) ch 6; Jonathan Glover, "Persons, Justice, and Rights" in Jonathan Glover (ed.), *Utilitarianism and its Critics* (New York, NY, Macmillan, 1990) at 88; Amartya Sen, "Rights and Agency" (1982) 11 *Philosophy and Public Affairs* 3; Randy Barnett, "Of Chickens and Eggs – The Compatibility of Moral Rights and Consequentialist Analyses" (1989) 12 *Harvard Journal of Law and Public Policy* 611 – and see further n7 below.

ences between rights and utilitarianism.[6] Perhaps the fighting currently remains its keenest where a growing movement of utilitarians has sought to capture the citadel of rights and re-establish it on a secure utilitarian base.[7] This daring strategy of the utilitarians has met with fierce resistance.[8]

With such classic contests of ideas one begins to suspect after several rematches that it is not simply a case of the one side being right and the other wrong, and one may doubt that the contest will ever yield an outright winner. It is not, however, necessarily a waste of time to continue watching the fight. For although we may be deprived of a conclusive outcome in that particular contest, the fact that the contest is still being fiercely fought may teach us something about the contesting views and the nature of what it is they are fighting about.

A good example of this phenomenon is the natural law positivism debate in jurisprudence, likened by Honoré to an interminable series of football tournaments. From the fact that the teams carried on playing, and their respective supporters did not grow tired of cheering them on, Honoré himself drew inferences about the nature of the contestants and the sort of contest they

[6] For a contextual deployment of the distinction see Stephen Parker, "Rights and Utility in Anglo-Australian Family Law" (1992) 55 *Modern Law Review* 311 – though for a different perspective on this subject see John Eekelaar, "Families and Children: From Welfarism to Rights" in Christopher McCrudden and Gerald Chambers (eds.), *Individual Rights and the Law in Britain* (Oxford, Clarendon Press, 1994) ch 10 at 302 n3. For an argument that the distinctive concept of rights brings "discipline and structure" to constitutional jurisprudence, see Gerald Postema, "In Defence of French Nonsense" in Neil MacCormick and Zenon Bankowski (eds.), *Enlightenment, Rights and Revolution* (Aberdeen, Aberdeen University Press, 1989) ch 5. For more general comments, see J.L. Mackie, "Can there be a Right-Based Moral Theory?" from Peter French *et al* (eds.), *Studies in Ethical Theory* (Minnesota, MN, University of Minnesota Press, 1978) in Jeremy Waldron (ed.) *Theories of Rights* (Oxford, OUP, 1984) ch VIII; David Lyons, "Utility and Rights" (1982) *Nomos XXIV* 107 – in Jeremy Waldron (ed.), *op. cit.* ch V; H.L.A. Hart, "Between Utility and Rights" (1979) 79 Columbia Law Review 828, and "Utilitarianism and Natural Rights" (1979) 53 Tulane Law Review 663, both in his *Essays in Jurisprudence and Philosophy* (Oxford, Clarendon Press, 1983) (hereinafter, EJP) chs 9 & 8, and "Natural Rights: Bentham and John Stuart Mill" in his *Essays on Bentham* (Oxford, Clarendon Press, 1982) (hereinafter, EonB) ch IV; John Finnis, *Fundamentals of Ethics* (Oxford, Clarendon Press, 1983) – hereinafter, FofE, at 103, 136; Jeremy Waldron, "Nonsense upon Stilts? – a reply" in above n2, and *The Right to Private Property* (Oxford, Clarendon Press, 1988) at 77-9; Joel Feinberg, "In Defence of Moral Rights" (1992) 12 Journal of Legal Studies 149; Joseph Chan, "Raz on Liberal Rights and Common Goods" (1995) 15 *Oxford Journal of Legal Studies* 15 – and see further n8 below.

[7] R.M. Hare, *Moral Thinking: Its Levels, Method, and Point* (Oxford, Clarendon Press, 1981), "Utility and Rights" (1981) *Nomos XXIV* 148, and "Rights, Utility, and Universalization: Reply to J.L. Mackie" in R.G. Frey (ed.), *Utility and Rights* (Oxford, Blackwell, 1985) ch 5; Allan Gibbard, "Utilitarianism and Human Rights" (1984) 1 *Social Philosophy and Policy* 92; L.W. Sumner, *The Moral Foundation of Rights* (Oxford, Clarendon Press, 1987); Richard Epstein, "The Utilitarian Foundations of Natural Law" (1989) 12 *Harvard Journal of Law and Public Policy* 713, and "Subjective Utilitarianism" *ibid.* 769; David Crossley, "Utilitarianism, Rights and Equality" (1990) 2 *Utilitas* 40; Richard Brandt, *Morality, Utilitarianism, and Rights* (Cambridge, Cambridge University Press, 1992).

[8] David Lyons, above n6; James Fishkin, "Utilitarianism Versus Human Rights" (1984) 1 *Social Philosophy and Policy* 103; J.L. Mackie, "Rights, Utility, and Universalization" in R.G. Frey (ed.) above n7, ch 4; Jules Coleman, "Tort Law and the Demands of Corrective Justice" (1992) 67 *Indiana Law Journal* 349 at 376; Eric Mack, "A Costly Road to Natural Law" (1989) 12 *Harvard Journal of Law and Public Policy* 753.

were involved in: "legal theory is in the end an elaborate form of exhortation or an elaborate display of commitment"[9] – legal theorists are prepared to back their favourite theories in the next competition even if they lost dismally in the last argument, just like loyal football supporters backing a team at the bottom of the division. Dias, in observing the lack of a result in the debate between the two, inferred a difference of perspectives that cannot meet but can for this very reason provide us with a fuller picture of the nature of law.[10] Perhaps the most stimulating observation on the debate is the suggestion by Finnis that the two approaches do not merely contribute to our understanding of law but do so by making sense of the contributions that each other gives.[11]

With no ambition to enter the ring where the champions of rights and utilitarianism are still battling it out, but with a keen interest in the fight from the comfort of the commentator's chair, I want to suggest that we may learn important things both about the contestants and the nature of what they are fighting about. I shall argue that neither is capable of being the victor – hence the battle continues; that the fundamental reason for this is common to both – which makes it all the more easier to enter the other's territory; but that we can nevertheless learn much from the failings of these contestants.

However, even if our purpose is only commentary it is difficult to select a contest of ideas that can be regarded as representative of rights and utilitarianism. The relationship between rights and utilitarianism has been the subject of so much discussion without either side of the relationship occupying a stable position. Utilitarianism over the years has developed a protean adaptibility to enable it to wrestle with whatever opponent might assail it,[12] and the capacity of rights to express such disparate positions has been stretched to the extent that it is a common criticism of rights that they are capable of appearing simultaneously on contradictory sides of a debate.[13]

The attraction of presenting the contest between the two in terms of abstract generalisations is, accordingly, very strong, in the hope that any point

[9] Tony Honoré, "Groups, Laws, and Obedience" in A.W.B. Simpson (ed.), *Oxford Essays in Jurisprudence, Second Series* (Oxford, Clarendon Press, 1973) at 1 – also in Honoré, *Making Law Bind* (Oxford, Clarendon Press, 1987) essay 2.

[10] R.W.M. Dias, *Jurisprudence*, 5ed. (London, Butterworths, 1985) at 498–501.

[11] John Finnis, "Comment [on Positivism and the Foundations of Legal Authority]" in Ruth Gavison (ed.), *Issues in Contemporary Legal Philosophy* (Oxford, Clarendon Press, 1987) at 69–70 – see also his *Natural Law and Natural Rights* (Oxford, Clarendon Press, 1980) at 16-9; and his "The Truth in Legal Positivism" in Robert George (ed.), *The Autonomy of Law: Essays on Legal Positivism* (Oxford, Clarendon Press, 1996).

[12] For a critical analysis of different forms of utilitarianism, see David Lyons, *Forms and Limits of Utilitarianism* (Oxford, Clarendon Press, 1965). For a pro-utilitarian summary of different forms, see J.J.C. Smart, "An Outline of a System of Utilitarian Ethics" in J.J.C. Smart and Bernard Williams, *Utilitarianism For and Against* (Cambridge, Cambridge University Press, 1973) – which also contains an extensive bibliography by Smart. See also, Jonathan Glover (ed.), above n5.

[13] Sumner, above n7 at 1. R.G. Frey, "Act-Utilitarianism, Consequentialism, and Moral Rights" in R.G. Frey (ed.), *Utility and Rights* (Oxford, Blackwell, 1985) at 61.

of conflict can be clearly presented without worrying about the lack of clarity among the particular contestants. But this strategy is unlikely to prove successful. How can we be sure that our abstract generalisations correctly represent the contestants, if we are not confident of pinning down a proper representative of either side? A more fruitful line of enquiry is likely to be the investigation of the contest among particular manifestations of each side. From this approach we can expect a more confident understanding of what the contest is about, and if we discern changes in the positions of either side, and if we discover that debate is fervently engaged in but never resolved we might learn more from this, than from resolving the contest by means of an artificial abstraction.

The approach to be adopted here will accordingly examine the work of some leading theorists: for utilitarianism, Bentham; and for rights, Rawls, Dworkin and Nozick. It would clearly be unfair to stage a final battle on the basis of these contributions. For quite apart from the one side outnumbering the other, Bentham does not possess the experience of the modern game that the others are familiar with, and the game play has developed considerably on the utilitarian side since Bentham. But it is not my purpose to stage a contest, and we shall subsequently anyway consider the more recent developments of utilitarianism. It is illuminating to consider Bentham at this point, not only because of his stature as the founder of modern utilitarianism and hence we get some raw insights into the purported distinctiveness of the approach, but also precisely because utilitarianism has developed subsequently so that we can also see in Bentham's writings some of the basic problems of utilitarianism laid bare. We shall subsequently take the opportunity of considering whether later utilitarians have successfully dealt with these problems.

As to the contributors to the rights side, the three chosen are the selectors' favourites when a contest between rights and utilitarianism is in the offing,[14] but again my purpose in this selection is not to field the strongest team available but rather to demonstrate how on closer examination these theorists have more in common outside the conventional rights-utilitarianism divide, and that in fact the approach taken by all four theorists to the common problems that they face unites them far more than it divides them.

Before proceeding to the detailed examination of these theorists, there are a number of general points that can be made which may help to dispel some of the confusion that has frequently troubled the discussion of rights and utilitarianism, and which may assist in clarifying the issues that concern us as we grapple with the detail of their contributions.

---

[14] Rolf Sartorius, "Dworkin on Rights and Utilitarianism" (1981) *Utah Law Review* 263, in Marshall Cohen (ed.), *Ronald Dworkin and Contemporary Jurisprudence* (London, Duckworth, 1984) at 206. Hart, EJP, 194.

2 SOME PRELIMINARY OBSERVATIONS

(1) The Moral Arena

The discussion of rights and utilitarianism ranges over issues in moral, political, and legal philosophy. Particular theorists may relate to concerns in any one or any number of these disciplines.[15] Bentham's utilitarianism was designed to embrace all three.[16] Rawls' theory of justice specifically excludes issues of general morality and is restricted to an examination of political and legal institutions.[17]

I want to characterise the discussion of rights and utilitarianism as essentially a moral one for two reasons. First, inasmuch as the discussion reaches issues in political or legal philosophy it does so in a way that relates to moral aspects of these disciplines. The theory of just institutions falls within political morality, and a discussion of utilitarian or rights-based perspectives on law involves an examination of the appropriate moral base for the law – using morality in the loosest sense possible of being concerned with determining what is the good, proper, or right way of behaving as a human. Secondly, the recognition of a moral characteristic to the discussion avoids unnecessary complications and can serve to simplify our enquiry.

For although the moral domain may be extensive and its remotest borders may not be clearly mapped, it is possible to locate a part of the moral territory which provides a clear arena in which rights and utilitarianism can be contested. Moreover, the features of this particular moral territory must be reproduced in any political morality or moral base for law, so that it is possible to confine our investigation to this moral arena on the understanding that it is possible, if considered desirable, to transfer our results to a political or legal arena – without becoming involved in controversies over the desirability of doing so.

---

[15] See nn 4–8 above.

[16] PML ch I:II-III. See also Amnon Goldworth (ed.), *Deontology* in the Collected Works of Jeremy Bentham (Oxford, Clarendon Press, 1983) (hereinafter, *Deontology*), which contains not only a more authentic text for Bentham's *Deontology* than that originally published and collaborated in by Bowring, (above n2) – see Goldworth's "Editorial Introduction" at xix-xxxiii – but also the texts of two versions of Bentham's unpublished "Article on Utilitarianism". Relevant references from these sources to the breadth of Bentham's concerns are given at nn 50 & 51 below. The view that Bentham's utilitarianism comprises a dual standard (community interest for political affairs, self-interest for private matters) put forward in David Lyons, *In the Interest of the Governed* (Oxford, Clarendon Press, 1973 – revised edition 1991) relies heavily on a particular exegesis of PML, and sits uneasily with a number of texts in *Deontology*: confirming the comprehensiveness and consistency of his utilitarianism (192, 318); indicating that "private deontology" operates in a residue determined by "the power of law and government" (249); emphasising that the act of the individual agent may have relevant consequences on the happiness of others (126, 191ff). For further discussion, see Ross Harrison, *Bentham* (London, Routledge & Kegan Paul, 1983) ch X.

[17] TofJ, 17, 108.

The appropriate part of the moral territory is that which covers how one individual deals with another. This much of the moral territory remains a constant part of any morality, no matter how much or how little emphasis might be placed on other features of the moral landscape – such as self-regarding duties, supernumerary duties, sexual morality, or the morality of institutions. And if we wish to consider political morality or the moral base of law, then this part of morality must also figure in our deliberations since the two disciplines that we extend our concerns to are faced with the same fundamental issue of regulating how one individual deals with another.[18]

A further factor confirms the appropriateness of choosing this particular moral arena for our investigation. The point at which rights and utilitarianism have regularly come into conflict has been precisely where one individual is to be treated at the extreme of being sacrificed for the greater good of others.[19]

(2) Moral Theories and Moral Approaches

The conflict between rights and utilitarianism which may occupy the moral arena selected may amount to a conflict between two moral *theories*, which

[18] This point may be made in a strong reductionist form, as Bentham, or Nozick, does: that everything in society is ultimately composed of individuals. (Bentham, PML, ch I:IV–V; Nozick, ASU 89, 90). But even in a weaker form which relies on the oblique concern of social institutions with individual relations it holds good. So, for example, Rawls may limit his concerns to the justice of institutions (n17 above), but these same institutions will have an impact on and regulate the relations between individuals, such as by imposing a minimum wage which regulates how a particular employer deals with a particular employee. See TofJ ss 18, 19, 51 & 52 for the general picture. On the justice of a minimum wage Rawls is rather evasive. Despite indicating that the difference principle can apply to "the distribution of income" (TofJ, 78), and maintaining the importance of the difference principle in assessing how various objectives continue to "promote the prospects of the least favoured" (318), when it comes to discussing wage levels (304–10) Rawls loses the option of a minimum wage by relegating "the precept of need . . . to the transfer branch", concluding that "it does not serve as a precept of wages at all." (at 309). This particular free-market orientation of Rawls' pay policy is not, however, a necessary outcome of his general approach to justice. Rawls himself recognises on the previous page that a just outcome may require that "the underlying market forces, and the availability of opportunities which they reflect, are appropriately regulated." (at 308).

[19] There is some variation in representing this point of conflict. Hart, it is submitted correctly, speaks of the (transitive) "sacrifice of some individuals" and "the imposition of sacrifices on innocent individuals" (EonB 96, 98 – cp EJP, 194), whereas others speak of the requirement of individuals to sacrifice themselves: David Richards, "Rights and Autonomy" (1981) 92 *Ethics* 3 at 19; Will Kymlicka, *Liberalism, Community and Culture* (Oxford, Clarendon Press, 1989) at 22. The hypotheticals discussed on the occasions of conflict consistently portray a transitive sacrifice of another (eg the sheriff executing an innocent scapegoat to prevent a riot – devised by Smart, as recounted in Eric D'Arcy, *Human Acts* (Oxford, Clarendon Press, 1963) at 2–4, referred to in general terms by H.J. McCloskey, "A note on utilitarian punishment" (1963) 72 *Mind* 599, and discussed in, eg, Smart above n12 at 69ff and John Finnis above n6 at 95ff; or, the surgeon extracting the kidneys of the alcoholic tramp – discussed in Hare above n7 at 132ff and below, ch IX:6) rather than the reflexive sacrifice by an individual of himself. The distinction is not merely grammatical. If I am under a moral duty to sacrifice myself it does not follow that you have the right to sacrifice me. (Consider analagously, a moral duty to give to charity.)

seek to provide an understanding and justification for determining particular conduct between persons as moral or otherwise. As such these theories seek not only to explain and justify, but also to deliver a practical moral *approach*.

It would be possible to seek to deliver a practical moral approach without being concerned about the theoretical considerations, and this is commonly done – for example, in taking a given set of traditional moral precepts and working out how they apply to different practical situations that are encountered. It would also be possible to devise a grand moral theory that was incapable of yielding a practical moral approach, being concerned solely with the abstract properties of morality rather than their practical realisation. Some moral theorising might have this limitation, and it might be considered a legitimate enterprise nevertheless to be dealing with the abstract qualities of morality. On the other hand, it would be possible to deride such theorising as being inadequate or at least incomplete if it is incapable of determining a practical moral issue.

In the case of the conflict between rights and utilitarianism, those who engage in the discussion are prepared to address practical moral concerns like taxation, court procedure, discrimination, killing, etc – and as part of the discussion are prepared to castigate the other side for failing to be able to reach a practical outcome, or the right practical outcome, on the basis of its theoretical approach.

The discussion is accordingly a comprehensive one in seeking to provide a moral theory that is capable of accounting for but also delivering a practical moral approach. For either side to triumph, it must achieve congruence between a coherent moral theory and a practical moral approach in the following respects:

(1) The moral theory justifies a practical moral approach – it provides a compelling reason for those subject to it to abide by that approach.

(2) The moral approach thus justified is capable of determining what is and what is not required, permitted, or otherwise encouraged by that practical moral approach – and what lies wholly outside its provenance.

(3) And in both the above respects the moral theory is sufficient, without recourse to an alternative or deeper theory, to provide a full justification for a complete practical moral approach that it is capable of delivering.

In short, we are looking for (1) justification, (2) practicality, and (3) sufficiency.

There is one major problem that arises from presenting the discussion of rights and utilitarianism in this way. Bentham's utilitarianism, and the natural rights he opposed it to, can both be regarded as moral theories, the latter as a representation of a theory of Natural Law.[20] However, rights in themselves

---

[20] Equally derided by Bentham – PML, ch II:XIV n para 6.

do not constitute a moral theory, though they may provide the conceptual apparatus through which a moral theory is expressed.[21] Since our modern champions of rights have discarded the Natural Law banner, what precisely provides for the theoretical underpinning of their use of rights becomes a significant question. Although some attempt will be made within this section to clarify in general terms how rights may be used within moral theory,[22] the full significance of this point can only be appreciated through a detailed consideration of the individual contributions to the discussion.

(3) Three Central Aspects of Morality

What can be said in simple and general terms about a practical moral approach which governs the dealing of one person with another? Three basic aspects of that standard part of morality can be readily identified, which it will be helpful to signify as M1 – M3.

M1 *Morality involves respect for the other.* This respect is mutual and reciprocal. In any moral conduct involving two persons (let us call them "the moral agent" and "the other"), the conduct prescribed will express respect for both parties in the present arrangement, and also allow for the same prescription to hold should the positions of the moral agent and the other be transposed. This is evidenced in the most elementary precept of morality, whether expressed as popular saw or Kantian categorical imperative: do as you would be done by. It is often linked to the enjoyment of equal status as human beings:[23] I as a human being can expect from you the behaviour that respects my humanity that you as a human are capable of giving – but by the same token equally worthy of receiving.

A number of further pointers to this elementary feature of morality can be briefly mentioned. We can distinguish a moral obligation from a legal obligation on the basis of this feature of mutual and reciprocal respect. For instance, it is possible to say of an enforceable legal but not of a recognised moral obligation that it is oppressive on the duty holder – which amounts to a negation of respect for the other. This may be the very reason for criticising the law as immoral, and may be the incentive for reforming the law (eg, the working conditions of children, the rate of interest on a loan, etc).

---

[21] See further, John Finnis, *Natural Law and Natural Rights* (Oxford, Clarendon Press, 1980) ch VIII, particularly at 198 and 210–1.

[22] See 2(4) below.

[23] See Amartya Sen, *Inequality Reexamined* (Oxford, Clarendon Press, 1992) at 130–1 – "Every plausibly defendable ethical theory of social arrangements tends to demand equality in *some* 'space', requiring equal treatment of individuals in some significant respect . . .". See also, Dworkin TRS, 180ff, works cited in n125 below – particularly (iv) at 10; and Will Kymlicka, *Contemporary Political Philosophy: an Introduction* (Oxford, Clarendon Press, 1990) at 4–5, 44. However, enjoyment of equal status should not be regarded simply as the product of egalitarianism – see Joseph Raz, MofF ch 9; and for a healthy dose of scepticism on the rhetorical uses of equality, see Peter Westen, "The Empty Idea of Equality" (1982) 95 *Harvard Law Review* 537.

Similarly, it would be possible to enjoin someone not to enforce his strict legal rights, where to do so would unfairly take advantage of the other (eg where the other has through no fault of his own undertaken a legal commitment on the basis of a mistake that the law does not recognise as vitiating the commitment, and performing that commitment will ruin him but failing to do so will not seriously affect the right holder), but we do not enjoin people not to enforce their moral rights. Rather, the position that would respect the victim of unfortunate circumstances at the expense of forgoing the enforcement of legal entitlement is regarded as the moral position: "You are strictly entitled to the money legally but I do not think it would be the right thing to take it." And a person with a moral entitlement[24] is encouraged to enforce it as being the appropriate conduct to respect all the parties involved.

A final pointer can be found in a jurisprudential observation. It has been suggested, and is plausible (however limited), that law can be analysed in terms of the expression of one human's sovereign will over all others. No such analysis has ever been suggested for morality, and on the basis of this first aspect of morality nor is it plausible.

M2 *Morality requires a denial of self-interest – in order to respect the other's interests.* This aspect of morality relates to its obligatory or normative nature. Morality is not a scheme that expresses how people behave in order to achieve mutual satisfaction of their wholly compatible interests, in which case the problems of morality would become merely coordination problems,[25] and a failure to resolve the problem would be described as inconvenient or awkward, but not morally wrong. The point is that the moral agent is faced with a choice as to whether to behave in a way that respects the other by furthering his interests or whether to further his own interests, and morality places an obligation upon him to deny his own interests for the sake of the other. If there were no possible conflict of interests in this way, there would be no need for the moral obligation.[26]

---

[24] It is important to distinguish an entitlement from a claim here. See generally, ch IV. More particularly, it should be noted that a moral claim may not lead to an entitlement because although justified in the abstract it is competing in concrete terms for a limited pool of resources which cannot sustain it alongside other competing claims which are given priority – see further ch V. In the present illustration a moral *entitlement* indicates a position that has been established after all the morally relevant factors affecting the appraisal of a moral claim have been dealt with.

[25] See Edna Ullman-Margalit, *The Emergence of Norms* (Oxford, Clarendon Press, 1977) at 77–8 & 101–2 – "In the case of co-ordination norms . . . in so far as conformity to them ensures the achievement of co-ordination, it is the interests of each and every one involved which are served by the conformity." (at 101).

[26] One of the strongest denials of a conflict of interest, and hence of the need for self-denial, is to be found in Bentham's *Deontology*, whose full title proclaimed: "Deontology: or Morality made easy: Shewing how throughout the whole course of every person's life duty coincides with interest rightly understood; Felicity with Virtue; Prudence extra-regarding as well as self-regarding with Effective benevolence." (119). However, within the work itself Bentham acknowledges the possibility of conflict of interests and self-denial (154–5, 179, 185), and develops a fuller account of "two branches" of self-interest, the one "*purely* self-regarding" and the other "in alliance with and acting in support of [extra-regarding interest]" (195). Bentham provides in the "Practical" section of his work a catalogue of self-regarding interests which may be the cause of

It may be objected that the self-interest that is denied is wholly illusory in that complying with the moral obligation will yield far greater benefit to the agent through his participation in the moral order that accords to him the respect that it requires him to grant to the other, than breaching the obligation. The objection is unsound for it treats the moral agent at the point of temptation to follow what lies to hand as an obvious convenience as though he were in the position of moral enlightenment, in which he could see the transient state of that temporary convenience and measure it as paling into insignificance relative to the great benefits of participating in the moral order. But the agent does occupy the former position, not the latter. And in that former position complying with the moral obligation does require a denial of self-interest.[27] So, we may neglect the promise we have made whose performance has become inconvenient, and breach a moral obligation for the sake of self-interest. Or, on a grander scale, we may neglect the interests of litigants in order to preserve a system of legal procedure that serves the self-interest of lawyers – to use an illustration that Bentham provides.[28] And if failing to comply with the moral obligation involves serving self-interest, then the corollary is that complying with the moral obligation involves a denial of self-interest.

This is not to say that people do not willingly, even happily, behave in a moral way. The force of the moral obligation is not to be regarded as the primary motivation for engaging in moral conduct, any more than the fear of punishment should be regarded as the primary motivation for engaging in lawful conduct. Nevertheless, just as the existence of a legal obligation indi-

evil doing to others, with the aim of furthering their avoidance (260–1). The view of Bentham's position obtained from these texts not only endorses the aspect of morality presently being considered but also damages fatally Lyons' enterprise, which seeks to construct a position for Bentham that embraces a natural harmonization of interests and non-egoistic motivation for man (above n16, at 18). For a critical account of Bentham's ambiguity on this issue, see Hanna Pitkin, "Slippery Bentham: Some Neglected Cracks in the Foundations of Utilitarianism" (1990) 18 *Political Theory* 104 at 117–21.

A similar switch from one form of self interest which disregards the interests of others to another that promotes them is evident in an essay by Joseph Raz, "Duties of Well-Being" in his *Ethics in the Public Domain* (Oxford, Clarendon Press, 1994) – hereinafter, EPD, ch 1. Although Raz indicates that a successful transition need not involve a sacrifice of well-being on the part of the agent (at 27 & 28), the agent must still deny or "abandon" the former self-interest.

[27] Lyons recognises that for there to be no conflict of interests in such a case, the requirement is "not simply that there are no real conflicts of interest, but that there never seem to be any to an agent who must make a relevant decision" (above n16 at 15). Derek Parfit, *Reasons and Persons* (Oxford, Clarendon Press, 1984) appears to recognise this point (at 120–1), but if so it would pose a serious obstacle to his view that rational enlightenment can be relied on as the basis for self-denial.

[28] The self-interest of lawyers was metaphorically incorporated as "Judge and Co" in "Principles of Judicial Procedure" in Bowring (ed.) above n2, vol II at 76. More particularly, Bentham targeted the "sinister" self-interest of Alexander Wedderburn, who had become Lord Chancellor, "whose interest it was, to maximize delay, vexation, and expense, in judicial and other modes of procedure, for the sake of the profit, extractible out of the expense." (PML, ch I:XIII n). Similarly, Bentham analyses the position of those who fought for the retention of the slave trade (*Deontology*, 334–5) as acting out of the self-interest "of the purse" – one entry in Bentham's catalogue of self-regarding interests (n26 above).

cates the possibility of men choosing to break the law, so too the existence of a moral obligation indicates the possibility of choosing to neglect the interests of the other that morality requires us to respect in preference to the pursuit of self-interest.[29]

It is as though our objector were analysing the position of a recidivist by examining the position of a law abiding resident of Mayfair. Yet in confusing the potential benefits of participating in a realised moral order with the actual position of the moral agent at the point of immoral opportunity, this objection does signal a further aspect of morality.

M3 *Morality promotes the fulfilment of both the moral agent and the other whose interests he serves.* Although morality may require the denial of self-interest by the moral agent, it is apparent from our consideration of the objection raised in M2 that morality does not do so at the expense of self fulfilment as defined from the moral perspective. This aspect is linked to the idea of mutual and reciprocal respect found in M1. Yet it is worth making as a separate point because it emphasises the purposive rather than the immediate experiential feature of morality, and it reiterates the enjoyment of equal status as human beings within that purpose.

If this aspect of morality were not present, then we would have a system that promoted the fulfilment of the one at the cost of depriving the other of fulfilment. The word we use for this is oppression, not morality. And again, we can call for the overthrow of oppressive laws, and deny a moral obligation to comply with them, or even assert a moral obligation to resist them,[30] for the very reason that such oppression is diametrically opposed to this aspect of morality.

But the sceptic may point out that what goes under the name of morality frequently appears to him to be oppressive in character, in denying fulfilment to the moral agent, or a significant proportion of moral agents under that particular scheme. There are in fact two objections here, but both can be met in a way that underlines the elementary nature of this general aspect of morality.

The first objection, that the moral system oppresses all those subject to it, is simply taking a critique of a moral system – possibly from the perspective

---

[29] Bentham expresses his concern (*Deontology*, 155–6, 305–6) that a person who had acquired mastery over the self interest that conflicted with virtue, to the point that "there exists no *call* to which any denial can be opposed", might be regarded as lacking in virtue because there arose no opportunity for denial of that self interest. Whereas, "the virtue, so far from being extinguished, has reached the pinnacle of perfection. . ." (156). Bentham suggests treating such cases as involving a "*self denial* in the character" (306).

[30] It may be a matter of degree as to when particular injustices reach the level of oppression, so as to provoke a moral reaction against compliance with the law, yet such a point can be recognised. Thoreau expresses the point elegantly: "when a sixth of the population of a nation which has undertaken to be the refuge of liberty are slaves . . . if [the injustice] is of such a nature that it requires you to be the agent of injustice to another, then, I say, break the law." – H.D. Thoreau, "Civil Disobedience" (originally delivered as a lecture in 1848) in *Walden and Civil Disobedience* (Harmondsworth, Penguin, 1983) at 389, 396.

of an alternative moral system based on different axioms – rather than identifying a feature of the moral system. So, for example, from the perspective of a humanist moral system, a religious moral system might be regarded as oppressive (and *vice versa*), but each of the two systems provides fulfilment on its own axioms to all moral agents.

The second objection, that the moral system oppresses a proportion of those subject to it, might be a partial repeat of the first objection, or more subtly it may be failing to recognise differentials that relate to the different roles that moral agents are capable of performing, so that the allocation of equal status as human beings is not impaired by different treatment that relates to the different roles that humans can perform, so long as fulfilment is equally attainable within those different roles.

Now this is not to deny the sceptic voice in asserting that such differentiation is nothing less than oppression concealed under the cloak of morality, but the existence of M3 as a general feature of morality is evident in the way that any such oppression has to be described in order to pass it off in moral clothing, as treatment that relates to the fulfilment of the particular agent in that particular role, rather than as treatment that is in some way unfulfilling whilst securing the fulfilment of others. So, women are seen as finding fulfilment exclusively in making a home for the family and do not require a higher education. Or, members of a particular ethnic group are regarded as congenitally unintelligent, and so should receive no education but find fulfilment in the menial work that lies within their capabilities.

(4) The Usage of Rights

There exists an uncertainty in the usage of rights in that rights can be used to express positions that have been worked out in accordance with normative principles, or non-normative policy implementations, or rights may be regarded as themselves constituting basic normative principles. For example, a legal right to a particular salary under a contract of employment expresses a position of the right holder that may be analysed in a number of ways.

The right to receive £x per month may be treated as a legal right on the basis of being found in an agreement that satisfies the requirements of the law of contract, and as such the right to £x can be regarded as expressing a position that is determined by the normative principles of the law of contract. It would also be possible to ask why the right holder was entitled to the particular sum of £x, for this is not derived from the principles of the law of contract. It might have been worked out by policy considerations relating to the relative status accorded to that job in relation to other jobs in the organisation, the market availability of persons to perform that sort of job, an assessment of the particular job holder's relevant skills and experience, etc, and as such the right to £x may well express a position enjoyed by the right holder that is the result of implementing one or more non-normative policies. On the other hand it would be possible for the particular sum of £x to have been worked out in accordance with other normative considerations found in principles favouring a minimum wage, or prohibiting sex discrimination. It may be the case that the law itself imposes a minimum wage from which the sum of £x is derived, or requires the payment of £x to the right holder, who is a woman, because the employer pays that sum to men doing like work, in order to avoid sex discrimination. If so, the right to £x again expresses a position that is worked out in accordance with normative principles, this time from employment law.[31]

Now if there were no legal requirements to pay a minimum wage, or to avoid sex discrimination, it might have happened that our right holder's contract stipulated entitlement to a lesser sum of £y, but those who took a moral perspective on a minimum wage or sex discrimination might still assert that the employee has a right to £x. This is now a moral right (rather than a legal one as before) which expresses the position of the employee as worked out in accordance with the normative principles of the particular moral perspective taken.

Having found a moral right for the employee in accordance with a particular moral perspective, it does not follow that the moral perspective taken is right-based.[32] The moral right is the expression of the moral perspective[33] not the basis for it – which might be anything: a religion, unarticulated tradition, social convention . . . even a utilitarian viewpoint.

But is it not possible for the moral right to be rights-based in the sense of expressing a position that is itself based on a right? So the right of this employee to £x might be derived from a right to a minimum wage, or from a right not to be discriminated against on the grounds of sex. But if these latter rights are the basis for the particular right to £x then they would need to constitute a normative principle rather than merely express one.

There is a crucial point to grasp here which is easy to lose amongst the varied usage of rights in legal and moral discourse. If we take an established

---

[31] It should be noted that the right may well express a position that expresses an amalgam of non-normative policy and normative principle. In the last example, the sum paid to male workers may be dictated by market forces, and the sum required to be paid to female workers is then derived from the interaction of those market forces with the prohibition against sex discrimination.

[32] The term is taken from Dworkin, TRS 171–3. For a helpful explanation of the use of the term, see Jeremy Waldron, "Introduction" in Waldron (ed.) above n6 at 12–4; and for further discussion see the essays by Mackie (above n6) and Raz (revised as ch 8 of MofF) also found in that anthology.

[33] Compare Raz's analysis of normative statements made from "the legal point of view", which he regards as analagous to statements made from the perspective of a particular moral outlook, such as vegetarianism (Joseph Raz, *Practical Reason and Norms*, 2ed. (Princeton, NJ, Princeton University Press, 1990) at 175–7); and also Neil MacCormick, *Legal Reasoning and Legal Theory* (Oxford, Clarendon Press, 1978) at 62 and Appendix thereto, "On the 'Internal Aspect' of Norms". Similarly, Feinberg, above n6, at 165–6 & 168–9, speaks of deriving moral rights from moral principles.

general right and recognise in specific circumstances a particular instantiation of it, then the process of recognition of that particular right may seem to involve a process of derivation from the general right, so that the general right is looked upon as being the basis for the particular right. This is, however, an error.

If the general right has been established, then the process of recognition of the particular instantiation of it only requires the operation of the normal rules of logical inference found in any valid syllogism. There is no call for the general right to provide any further basis for the particular right – the basis for the latter is already found in whatever constitutes the basis for the former.[34]

The confusion between a justificatory and an inferential relationship between rights is eased by the normative nature of the phenomena that lie within the relationship: rights express entitlements that are justified within the system or approach that recognises those rights. It is a simple matter to transfer the justification from the rights to the relationship between them, and then to conclude that the one right justifies the other.

Matters are worsened by the way that we speak about rights and in particular how we speak about reaching a conclusion that a right exists. If we talk about the "basis" for a right, then this might properly be regarded as indicating the justification for recognising the right, relaying a justificatory relationship between the basis and the right. However, it is also possible to relay a purely inferential relationship through regarding one (true) statement as the basis for making another, as in – "D has a contractual duty to pay P £1,000" so "P has a right to £1,000 from D". Here the first statement may be regarded as the basis for the second, in the sense that we can say that the second statement is true on the basis that the first statement is true. However, we are not here justifying the second statement but merely inferring it from the first, given our understanding of the correlation between contractual rights and duties. The point can be reinforced in this example by working the relationship the other way – "P has a contractual right to £1,000 from D" so "D has a duty to pay P £1,000". There would be a vicious circularity in claiming a justificatory relationship between the statements where the one statement was regarded as the justification for the other, and the other the justification for the first. But there is no circularity in recognising that the existences of two necessarily coexisting phenomena may be mutually inferred from each other.[35]

There is a further point to clarify before we extract ourselves from this confusion. It might be objected that the example just considered establishes an inferential relationship between statements concerning two coexisting

---

[34] If, on the other hand, the general right has not already been established in every instantiation which includes the particular right in question, then the recognition of that particular right must involve some further factor other than the general right, and again the general right cannot be regarded as the basis for the particular right. For further discussion on the different ways of deriving rights, see ch V.

[35] Eg, if you are my parent then I am your child, and vice versa.

phenomena (the correlative right and duty within a contract), but does not deal with the relationship involving one phenomenon that precedes another (the general right that is recognised before the circumstances for this particular instantiation of it even arise). Suppose B is the justificatory basis for a general right, GR, of which a particular right, PR, is a clearly recognised instantiation occurring some time after GR is established. The relationship between B and GR is justificatory. Because GR is justified (a recognised right), then so is PR. What is the relationship between GR and PR? Have we not concluded that PR is a justified right from GR, and hence must not the relationship be justificatory?

The answer is negative. We have done nothing more than in the earlier illustration, taking the *statement* that there is GR as the basis for concluding that there is PR, in a purely inferential manner given our recognition that P is an instance of G. The fact that PR occurs subsequently is only a historical accident. If the circumstances that give rise to PR were already in existence at the time of the establishing of GR, then PR would be established simultaneously with GR, and would coexist with it, and hence GR cannot be regarded as the basis for PR inasmuch as the basis for something must exist prior to its coming into existence, but rather B is the basis for both. If it so happens that the circumstances giving rise to PR occur after GR is established then this places a temporal space between their existence but not a logical one.

In other words, to speak of the one right being the basis for the other is at the most a form of shorthand for saying what can be stated more accurately as the basis for the one right is the basis for the other. Nevertheless, it is common practice to regard the more general right as in some way *normatively* prior to and hence more basic than the particular right,[36] an illusion that may be assisted by an *historically* prior enunciation of the more general right, as in a statute.

This same error occurs where the one right is a moral right and the other right is considered to be the legal right that is established in accordance with it. The moral right may be regarded as the basis for the legal right, but inasmuch as the moral right covers the same conduct as the legal right[37] then it cannot be the basis for the legal right, but rather whatever is the basis for the moral right may be the basis for the legal right which is identified with it. The process of identification is again nothing more than the application of standard rules of inference, and does not require the moral right itself to play a role in establishing the legal right. Of course, there is a need to accept that legal

---

[36] As in Hans Kelsen's famous hierarchy of legal norms: *Pure Theory of Law*, translated by Max Knight (Berkeley and Los Angeles, CA, University of California Press, 1967) at 221ff. In his discussion of the static and dynamic principles of authorising (at 195ff), Kelsen is unconcerned with the distinction explored here, between inferential and justificatory relationships between norms.

[37] Whether through the legal right being a particular instantiation of a general moral right, as with the two legal rights above, or because both moral and legal rights relate to the same subject matter (whether that subject matter is general or particular).

rights should be established where moral rights, or (more likely) moral rights of a particular type,[38] are recognised, but this adds a factor (or factors) extrinsic to the moral right to the basis for recognising the legal right, which now comprises the basis for the moral right together with the factor(s) that make it appropriate to establish a legal right in such a case. Again historical priority may lend an illusion of normative priority where the moral right has been recognised prior to the establishing of the legal right, such as where the moral right to equal pay for women is recognised prior to the legal right being established.

The convenient shorthand of rights usage may then put forward some rights as constituting basic normative principles, where in fact the true basis for the rights that these "basic" rights appear to authorise are to be found not in the so called basic rights but in the basis for those rights, and/or in other factors extrinsic to them.

In some respects the illusion is not only maintained by historical factors but also by an arbitrary breakdown[39] of analysis which leaves a right occupying the place of the basis of another right, where further analysis would reveal a different picture. So in the case of a legal right to £x under a contract of employment, it may be the case that the particular employee's right is an instantiation of a general legal right not to be given unequal pay as a woman, which is itself an instantiation of a more general legal right not to be discriminated against on the grounds of sex, which can itself be identified with a moral right not to be discriminated against on the grounds of sex, which may itself be regarded as an instantiation of a more general moral right to be given equal respect as a human being. In each case, the latter mentioned right may more readily be described as the basis of the former and give credence to the idea of a rights-based approach, if we fail to analyse each "basic" right as itself the expression of a position that has been worked out in accordance with particular factors that may on closer analysis constitute or contribute to the basis of the other right. Even in the last mentioned right of the above sequence, it is possible to seek a basis for it rather than treat it as itself basic. That basis, which may be found in an understanding of human existence and

---

[38] Hart's discussion of Mill's approach to those "particular moral rights in the recognition of which justice consists" (EJP, 189) is to be found in EJP, Essay 8 and EonB, ch IV.

[39] The breakdown is arbitrary with respect to analytical rigour. That is not to say that there might not be good reasons for stopping at that point in respect to other pragmatic considerations, such as wanting to know what the law is on a particular matter. In the illustration that follows, there would be no need to go beyond the first recognised general legal right to satisfy this pragmatic requirement, in say advising a client. There may be a need to go further to the general legal right found in statutory form, in convincing a court of the authority of the law. A historian may be directed by other pragmatic considerations to go further still. Where the pragmatic requirements of practical reason stop us at a particular point, that point may be described as an "exclusionary reason" in that it provides a sufficient reason for action in the terms of our system of practical reason (Raz, above n33 at 39ff, 62). However, the exclusion of further enquiry for the pragmatic requirements of practical reason does not preclude further enquiry to meet the concerns of analytical rigour.

the implications of that for the relations of humans with one another, may then constitute or contribute to the basis of the rights lower down in the sequence.

The usage of rights to constitute basic normative principles must then be regarded analytically[40] as an unacceptable solecism, which may rely on confusing historical account with normative analysis, and may depend on an arbitrary shutdown of analytical rigour. In every case, the error can be revealed by noting that the relation between the right that is described as basic and the right that it is described as being the basis for can at the most (where the derived right is necessarily recognised as an instantiation of the "basic" right) amount to a process of inference which relies on the application of logic and not on any intrinsic normative properties of the "basic" right.

Some of the insights on which these observations are based are evident in Hart's critique of Mill's conception of a moral right.[41] However, there are further implications that are missing in Hart's account. Hart recognises that a moral right based on a utilitarian perspective would merely be tautologous with utilitarianism,[42] ie is an expression of a position that is worked out in accordance with utilitarian principles. But Hart fails to generalise this for any moral right – that it is tautologous with the moral perspective that promotes it – and hence accuses utilitarianism of being unable to support "antecedent moral rights".[43] Whereas the more appropriate point to make is that utilitarianism is unable to support those moral rights which are worked out in accordance with other moral perspectives that are incompatible with utilitarianism – a point that could equally be made the other way round.[44]

Another important point recognised by Hart is that a moral right cannot be defined as the reason for a legal right, otherwise there would be no force in using the moral right to assert the need for creating the legal right since it would amount to the empty tautology that the reason for a legal right is the reason for a legal right, and therefore that there must be a recognition of "the importance or weight of the right identified as a [moral] right" as constituting the reason for a legal right.[45] It would be possible to discern compressed into Hart's phrase both the basis for the moral right and further extrinsic

---

[40] For its acceptability for purposes other than the analytical, see n39 above.

[41] EonB, ch IV.

[42] EonB, 94.

[43] *ibid*.

[44] Joseph Raz, "Hart on Moral Rights and Legal Duties" (1984) 4 *Oxford Journal of Legal Studies* 123 at 127–8 argues for the possibility of utilitarian moral rights. However, Raz suggests that utilitarian moral rights may conflict with utilitarian principles, which he explains on the basis of their prima facie nature. But this is to confuse the establishment of abstract rights on utilitarian principles with the rejection of particular concrete instantiations (again on utilitarian principles). There is no discord with utilitarian principles, but simply the point that the establishing of an abstract right does not amount to validating every concrete instantiation of it – see further, ch V.

[45] EonB, 94.

factors which evaluate that basis as being sufficiently significant so as to merit the creation of a legal right. But in any case it is clear that Hart is avoiding the error of treating the moral right itself as the basis for the legal right.[46]

However, Hart does not consistently avoid this error for in talking of "antecedent moral rights" he does postulate a type of moral right which is itself the basis, or "justification", for a legal right,[47] and as such Hart appears to be treating the right as itself constituting a normative principle. Nevertheless, this momentary vacillation does not prevent Hart from generally insisting on identifying the basis of the right rather than relying on the right itself in order to promote theoretical rigour, notably when insisting on an identification of the basis for universal human rights in "a theory of what individuals need and can reasonably demand from each other" and in finding rights theorists lacking in failing to provide it.[48] The lapse may accordingly be regarded as a slip into convenient shorthand rather than a considered analytical position, but the recognition of the ease with which the slip can be made should alert us when considering in greater detail below a conflict between rights and utilitarianism,[49] so as to ensure that we clearly grasp what exactly is signified by the conflict.

(5) Deontological and Teleological Approaches

It is an irony and something of an indictment of philosophical terminology that the term deontological, one of Bentham's many neologisms, which was thought apt by its author to convey ethics "in the largest sense of the word"[50] as capable of being approached by Bentham's distinctive utilitarian perspective,[51] has been turned against a utilitarian approach to ethics and used to narrowly represent an approach regarded as opposed to it.

[46] Raz's attempt (above n44 at 125–6) to rescue Mill's concept of a moral right at this point (though not at others) by modifying Mill's position that a moral right means there is a reason for a legal right to the proposition that the meaning of a moral right can be elucidated by showing that the statement of a moral right entails the statement that a legal right is justified does more than give Mill's argument the correct "logical form" (at 126), for it opens up the the possibility of finding the reason for the legal right beyond the moral right: the statement of the moral right is itself entailed by the basis for that moral right; the statement of the moral right entails the statement that a legal right is justified; therefore, the basis for that moral right entails the statement that a legal right is justified. Or, the basis for the moral right is the basis for the legal right, but not the moral right is the basis for the legal right. (For Raz's general position on rights, see n187 below.)

[47] EonB, 94 – cp at 95 "justifying them [legal rights] by reference to antecedent moral rights."

[48] EonB, 103–4 – cp EJP, 195–6, 221–2 and see also EonB, 95 for a general suggestion about the basis for the moral right in terms of individual good.

[49] Hart's slip, EonB, 94 & 95, is precisely in this context.

[50] *Deontology*, 124. It includes "the several fields of Ethics, meaning Private Ethics or Morals, Internal Government and International Law." ("Dedacologia: Art and Science Division", Appendix A in *Deontology*, 331). Cp para 83 of "Article on Utilitarianism" (*Deontology*, 318). For its derivation from the Greek, see *Deontology*, xix–xx, 249.

[51] Having as its objective "the sum of human happiness", "maximizing. . . happiness", "the maximization of well-being" – *Deontology*, 125, 249, 331.

This subverted use of the term is all the more awkward when it lacks a clear definition of its own status and seeks to find one in opposition to that approach from which it initially sprang. So, the utilitarian approach to ethics is designated teleological by Rawls, and the deontological approach is then explained as being non-teleological.[52]

Rawls expounds the essential difference between the two approaches in terms of a different emphasis over the relationship between the "two main concepts of ethics. . . the right and the good".[53] A teleological approach will identify the good, and seek the end of the maximisation of that good, and whatever is judged as realising that end is accordingly judged to be what is right. By contrast, a deontological approach will determine the right independently of an assessment of the good, and so may conclude that some action is the right one even if on a particular occasion it does not maximise the good.[54]

The distinction that is surfacing from this terminological diversion is composed of a number of elements, which are not necessarily connected.[55] First, there is the idea that a teleological or utilitarian approach in assessing whether an action is right by determining whether that action contributes to the maximisation of the good is concerned with the consequences of that action in a way that a deontological or non-utilitarian approach is not. Secondly, there is the relationship between the right and the good. Thirdly, there is the issue of the maximisation of the good. It will be helpful to clarify each.

(1) The Role of Consequences.

It is readily recognised that both teleological and deontological approaches to ethics are concerned with the consequences of human behaviour.[56] The

---

[52] Rawls, TofJ, 30: "deontological theories are defined as non-teleological ones" – following (see TofJ, 24 n11) William Frankena, *Ethics* (Englewood Cliffs, N.J., Prentice-Hall, 1963), 13–16, who states (at 14) that "Deontological theories deny what teleological theories affirm." The original corruption of Bentham's term seems to have occurred in C.D. Broad, *Five Types of Ethical Theory* (London: Routledge & Kegan Paul, 1930) – hereinafter, Broad, at 162 & 206–7, and sustained in W.D. Ross, *Foundations of Ethics* (Oxford, Clarendon Press, 1939) – hereinafter Ross, at 67–82. The views of these two authors are examined further in section 2(5)(3) below. However, it is worth stressing at the outset that Broad did not consider the distinction between deontological and teleological to be hard and fast, and regarded the two positions at their extremes "to be wrong, and to be in flagrant conflict with common sense." (Broad, 207–8, 221).

[53] TofJ, 24.

[54] TofJ, 24–5, 30 – again following Frankena (*loc. cit.* n52 above), though significantly Rawls does not make the point as Frankena does that the good is a non moral value (above n52, eg at 14).

[55] For the criticism that Rawls in fact attempts to make three separate distinctions turn on this terminological diversion, see Will Kymlicka, *Liberalism, Community and Culture* (Oxford, Clarendon Press, 1989) ch 3. The three identified by Kymlicka are: deontological/teleological; anti-perfectionist/perfectionist conceptions of the good life; equality of resource/welfare. Kymlicka considers that none of these issues is assisted by "the misleading language of the priority of the right or the good" (at 22). Here, we are concerned only with the first of the three distinctions.

[56] Rawls claims that an ethical doctrine that failed to take consequences into account "would simply be irrational, crazy." (TofJ, 30) Take as a simple illustration the morality of firing a gun

question arises as to how then any distinction between the two approaches is to be drawn in relation to consequences. Bentham thought that the great advantage of his utilitarianism was that unlike other moral approaches it permitted a scientific consideration of the morality of behaviour by measuring the incidence of what was to be valued (for Bentham, happiness) in the consequences of particular conduct and thus demonstrating the moral value of that conduct.[57] The distinctive role of consequences here does not lie in their being the location of some value on which basis it is averred that the conduct is moral, but in the idea that the consequences of conduct can be ascertained and assessed in order to measure the incidence of that quality which is capable of bestowing a moral value on the conduct. In other words, it is the prior use of consequences within an exclusive *method of assessing* the morality of conduct that makes them distinctive for utilitarianism. The utilitarian needs to know not merely that in some way acting morally will have a valuable consequence but precisely what valuable consequences his conduct will have in order to decide that he is acting morally.

The contrast is with an approach whose method for determining whether conduct is moral is not to rely on a prior estimation and evaluation of the consequences of that conduct but to see whether that conduct itself falls within a category that has been predetermined in accordance with the axioms of that moral approach as being moral or immoral.[58] So, for example, the axioms of the moral approach are found in the teaching of a religion which prohibits the speaking of falsehood, the conduct in question involves the telling of a lie which falls into this category, and therefore the conduct is determined to be immoral.

However, the absence of the moral value in the *method* of the non-utilitarian approach does not preclude it from the outcome or consequences. So for example, although pleasure may not form the test of what is moral, the furtherance of human happiness may still lie at the heart of moral conduct. Such an approach is compatible with the popular wisdom that those who seek pleasure end up miserable,[59] or found in the Judaeo-Christian teaching that

for pleasure in a field that I own, and try to determine the morality of this conduct (on whatever moral approach) without a consideration of the consequences (such as upon a party of schoolchildren who happen to be playing in the field, or upon my neighbours who are asleep in their beds at 3 o'clock in the morning. . .). See further, Finnis FofE, 82–84, and David Richards, "Rights and Autonomy" (1981) 92 *Ethics* 3 at 18. For further discussion of the arbitrary line between conduct and consequences in firing a gun, see Andrew Halpin, "Intended Consequences and Unintentional Fallacies" (1987) 7 *Oxford Journal of Legal Studies* 104 at 107.

[57] see ch IX:1.

[58] Bentham classified the competing options as Asceticism, which he in fact regarded as a corrupt form of utilitarianism (PML, ch II:IX) – seeking the maximisation of heavenly pleasure through undergoing earthly deprivations; and what he variously described as the Principle of Sympathy (PML, ch II:XIV) or the Principle of *Ipsedixitism* (*Deontology*, 304–5) – which amounts to regarding a doctrine moral because it upholds what is favoured.

[59] Subscribed to by Immanuel Kant, *Fundamental Principles of the Metaphysic of Ethics*, 1785, translated by Thomas Abbott, 10ed. (London, Longmans, 1969) at 13 [14].

calls for the avoidance of pleasure seeking in the moral life whilst maintaining the experience of pleasure as its outcome.[60]

It would indeed be difficult to deny that morality is ultimately concerned with the pleasurable outcome of the conduct it prescribes, without seeking to maintain the proposition that men can find fulfilment in unhappiness,[61] given our identification of the third aspect of morality, M3. In which case, the statement that what is moral maximises human happiness can be regarded as necessarily true in a trivial sense[62] – but not necessarily helpful in determining what does maximise human happiness, or what is moral.

Furthermore, the particular instance of conduct that appears to have unpleasant consequences and yet is to be regarded as moral in accordance with the moral duty imposed by a non-utilitarian approach still fails to make a sharp distinction in terms of consequences. For the perceived unpleasant consequences are merely those immediate and obvious, and there remain the wider consequences that may contribute to a net gain in pleasure. The point is that the moral duty in the non-utilitarian approach is imposed without concern to ascertain and evaluate all the consequences of that conduct, not on the basis that the outcome of the conduct does not matter.

The absence of a concern to *ascertain and evaluate* all consequences may be defended by arguments that are themselves outcome sensitive: (1) it is impossible to ascertain all consequences, so that any purported attempt to do so is arbitrary and biased, and may thus neglect other consequences that are significant; (2) the most significant impact each individual can have on the general good is by ensuring that his own behaviour is moral rather than by focusing on the remoter consequences of his behaviour in the actions of others; (3) the lapse from moral duty may have wider consequences than the immediate breach, in establishing a pattern of conduct or attitudes that will in general do more harm than the perceived good used to justify this particular breach.[63]

Nevertheless, it is common to cite Kant for the proposition that there can be a moral duty irrespective of the outcome of the conduct required by the duty, and then to use Kant's views as a deontological paradigm. Anthony

---

[60] Contrast "He who loves pleasure will be a poor man . . ." – Proverbs 20:17 – with ". . . in thy presence there is fulness of joy, in thy right hand are pleasures for evermore." – Psalm 16:11. See also, Herbert Spencer, *Social Statics* (London, John Chapman, 1851 – republished Farnborough, Gregg International Publishers, 1971) at 66–7: "It is one thing to hold that greatest happiness is the creative purpose, and a quite different thing to hold that greatest happiness should be the *immediate* aim of man."

[61] Derided by Bentham in his caricature of asceticism – PML, ch II:IX–X, where he points out: "Let but one tenth part of the inhabitants of this earth pursue it consistently, and in a day's time they will have turned it into a hell." (cp *Deontology* 313).

[62] Kant himself stated that the end served by moral duty embraced "the universal happiness of the whole world" – "On the Common Saying: 'This May be True in Theory, but it does not Apply in Practice'" in Hans Reiss (ed.), *Kant's Political Writings* (Cambridge, Cambridge University Press, 1970) at 65.

[63] See further, Finnis, FofE, chs IV & V. As Finnis remarks (at 119), "the effects of Socrates' refusal to participate in the liquidation of Leon of Salamis are still substantial, 2,400 years later."

Quinton does so in his entry for "deontology" in *The Fontana Dictionary of Modern Thought*,[64] and Rawls draws on Kant's views for the priority of the right over the good.[65]

A challenge to Kant's disassociation of right and consequence, whilst still maintaining a distinctive deontological approach, is attempted by Brand Blanshard,[66] who comments on "Kant, who tried disastrously to make right-doing independent of consequences".[67] However, within the course of a chapter Blanshard softens a deontological approach considerably,[68] and his retention of the use of "deontology" as a distinctive term could be easily discarded for more appropriate terms relating to the particular theorists under consideration – such as the "intuitionists".[69]

A more fundamental challenge would be to take issue with the conventional understanding that Kant did put forward a conception of the good that was disassociated from consequences. It may be the case that Kant, in insisting that the moral agent should act out of duty, was preoccupied with the moral agent not being *motivated* by a *self-interested* consideration of the consequences of his conduct,[70] but this is far from making a complete break with consequences. In particular, it is difficult to see how the moral agent is to derive his moral duty without a consideration of what consequences the conduct considered would have if acted on as a universal precept.[71] To take Kant's example, how do we decide that we are not content to allow everybody to make deceitful promises when in distress, without considering the consequences of such a practice? Kant may have rejected a role for the self-interested consequences of the agent, but that is not to reject a role for all consequences.[72]

Accordingly, the distinction between a utilitarian and non-utilitarian approach in relation to consequences is not as strong as it might at first appear: it is not a distinction that is based on whether a moral approach sets out to achieve a particular outcome (the happiness of mankind) or not, but a

---

[64] Alan Bullock *et al* (eds.), 2ed. (London, William Collins, 1988).

[65] TofJ, 31 n16.

[66] *Reason and Goodness* (London, George Allen and Unwin, 1961).

[67] *ibid.* at 147, occurring in ch 6, entitled "Deontology".

[68] Blanshard is close to the approach taken here in a number of respects – distinguishing between perceived and unperceived consequences (*ibid.* at 140, 148, 158); rejecting the absurdity of something being right though it does no good whatsoever (149–50); maintaining the connection between the right and the good (160).

[69] *ibid.* at 157.

[70] This concern is made explicit by Kant, above n62 at 64, in speaking of the moral agent's need "to ensure that no *motive* derived from the desire of happiness imperceptibly infiltrates his conceptions of duty." (original emphasis).

[71] See Kant, above n59 at 18[19] – 23[24].

[72] For further exploration of the idea that Kant's categorical imperative (in both of its first two forms) requires a *rational* assessment of the consequences of conduct as affecting all parties involved, see John Atwell, "Are Kant's First Two Moral Principles Equivalent?" (1969) 7 *Journal of the History of Philosophy* 273, which interestingly considers a Kantian approach to the problem of the sheriff contemplating using a scapegoat to placate a riotous mob.

distinction based on *the method* a moral approach employs in ascertaining whether conduct is moral where that conduct involves realising a particular outcome. Conversely, neither does the distinction lie in an imposition of duty on the one hand as opposed to the realisation of outcome on the other, for again in both approaches the differing methods may still lead to the recognition of moral duty.

With respect to their relation to consequences then, there must be grave doubt as to whether the use of the terms deontological and teleological for non-utilitarian and utilitarian approaches respectively is at all helpful, and concern that it is misleading. For denying the appellation teleological to non-utilitarian approaches may falsely suggest that these approaches are unconcerned with the outcome of moral behaviour, and denying the appellation deontological to utilitarian approaches may falsely suggest that these approaches are incapable of imposing any moral duty.[73] Nor does the use of these terms serve to clarify the real issue between these approaches at this point, which is what method we are to use in order to ascertain what conduct is moral.[74]

(2) The Right and the Good.

The second element of the purported distinction between deontological and teleological approaches is the relationship between the right and the good. If, as Rawls suggests, it is possible to give priority to the right over the good as his non-utilitarian theory of justice seeks to do, a number of points follow. The most obvious is that there may be a difference between what is regarded as right and what is regarded as good. It follows that on occasion what is regarded as good may also be regarded as wrong. And equally that what is regarded as right may also be regarded as bad. At this stage, unless we are prepared to justify a conception of the right that is indifferent to the good in the sense that we can, at least on occasion, hold something to be right though it does no good whatsoever, we have to admit competing conceptions of the good, so that on the occasions that what is regarded as right is regarded as bad from one point of view, it is also possible to regard it in some sense as good. We are then modifying our original statement to the form that the right must take priority over any particular conception of the good – which leaves open the possibility that at any given point there are other conceptions of the good which are not incompatible with the right.

Such different conceptions of the good may come about in a number of ways. There may be a variety of goods which are not commensurable in terms

---

[73] Although Bentham took pains to establish the connection between interest and duty, his utilitarian deontology was capable of recognising moral duties – and even creating the interest to conform to them through the imposition of a moral sanction – *Deontology*, 174–6.

[74] The point is nicely put by Bentham in discussing a theological, non-utilitarian approach to morality which would ascertain what was right by determining the will of God on the matter. Bentham objects that rather we are to ascertain what is the will of God by determining what is right – PML, ch II:XVIII.

of a basic good, so that different conceptions of the good are possible by making different selections from the goods available. Let us call these the variety conceptions of the good. There may be conflicting perspectives on what amounts to the good, yielding different conceptions in relation to whichever of the perspectives is taken. These we shall call relativist conceptions of the good. There may be a competition for the good that is available among those who are capable of enjoying it due to a lack of resources or opportunities making it impossible for all to enjoy the good to the same extent. This leads to the possibility of different conceptions of the good in accordance with whose interests are satisfied, or given priority. These we shall call subjectivist conceptions of the good.

The point is that if we want to characterise a moral approach as giving priority to the right over the good, but we are not prepared to acknowledge that something can be right even though it does no good whatsoever, then however we arrive at them we must be saying that there are conflicting conceptions of the good and that the right determines which conception to follow on any particular occasion. For if there were only one conception of the good, there would either be no need to give priority to either, or if we still insisted on giving the right priority over the good we would have to accept that the right did on occasion amount to what was of no good whatsoever.

But if the right is thus regarded as a balancing factor to ensure that the selection from different conceptions of the good is in some way appropriate, the question is on what basis the right can determine a particular balance to be appropriate. We can in fact see this sort of balancing function being performed in the avoidance of excess from among a variety of goods so that, for example, the good of exercise is not pursued without at times partaking of the good of rest.[75] Similarly, we might regard liberal tolerance as performing a sort of balancing function between relativist conceptions of the good. Or, distributive justice as performing the function between subjectivist conceptions of the good. In the first example, however, we would say that the pursuit of one good to excess makes it no longer a good – such as in the case of fanatical exercise leading to physical exhaustion or long term harm to the body. Here we might then say that the right does not so much take priority over the good as set the limits of the good.

It is tempting to see if the balancing of the other conceptions of the good can be treated in the same way. In the case of liberal tolerance imposing a limit on the unbalanced pursuit of one relativist conception of the good at the expense of other conceptions, it does so from the premise that different relativist conceptions of the good should be available to be chosen by those who

---

[75] The two goods selected here might be regarded as essentially conflicting, in that the unrestrained pursuit of the one will necessarily lead to the suppression of the other. Even where goods only conflict due to limited opportunity to select from among a range of possible goods, the selection of one at the expense of other possibilities can be regarded as excessive and no longer a good (eg, pursing one's career as a workaholic). The recognition of essentially conflicting goods inevitably leads to the requirement of some balancing factor.

pursue them: the good consists not merely in what is achieved by pursuing it but also in the fact that it has been chosen.[76] Therefore the imposition of one conception of the good can be resisted on the ground that this denies to it what is an essential aspect of its goodness, that it can be chosen from among other conceptions of the good. Here again, we might then say that the right, in the form of liberal tolerance, sets the limits of the good in that the exclusive[77] pursuit of a single relativist conception of the good makes it no longer a good.

In the case of distributive justice performing a balancing function between different subjectivist conceptions of the good, the idea that the right sets the limits of the good would have to involve accepting that one subjectivist conception of the good pursued in isolation – ie giving exclusive priority to the satisfaction of one person's interests at the expense of others' – turns what would otherwise have been a good for that person into something that is no longer a good.

It should be noted that we are talking here about recognising the limits of what is good, rather than establishing limitations on what good can be pursued. Rawls' conception of distributive justice does the latter, in terms of which goods have "value" or are "reasonable".[78] It is this possibility of assessing the good which produces for Rawls a priority for the right.[79] However, Rawls does not completely eschew the alternative view. He states on the following page that "bounds are placed upon *what is good*".[80] And in any case, Rawls' priority is not strictly the right over the good, but the right good over the wrong good – ie a balancing of goods, rather than displacing the good by the right.

We could press the former view further by arguing that the deeper premise of a system of distributive justice is that an individual can only enjoy good as a member of a community where both his good and the good of the other members of that community are satisfied. The satisfaction of the good of others, and others' satisfaction in one's own good, would then be an inherent feature of one's own good – from the perspective of distributive justice – which would be analogous to the essential aspect of choice in good as perceived by liberal tolerance. For example, the satisfaction of fulfilling one's desires to eat expensive food might be regarded as defeated if this were done at the cost of depriving others of food and causing them to starve.[81]

---

[76] See Joseph Raz, MofF – particularly at 424–9; and, "Free Expression and Personal Identification" (1991) 11 *Oxford Journal of Legal Studies* 303, also found in EPD, ch 6.

[77] Either due to the fact that it is imposed, where other conceptions would otherwise be available; or, due to the fact that this particular conception of the good itself excludes any alternative conception – this amounts to a more fundamental objection from the perspective of liberal tolerance, that this conception of the good is wholly unacceptable as a good – see Raz, MofF, 425–6; EPD, 152.

[78] TofJ, 31.

[79] *ibid.*

[80] TofJ, 32 (my emphasis).

[81] This might seem strained – until we sit the starving person at the dinner table next to the gourmet. An effective way of ignoring the claims of distributive justice is to ensure that one seeks

Whether or not the illustrations provided of the relationship between the right and the good are considered to be compelling in themselves, or sufficiently representative to base a general view of this relationship on, it is clear that inasmuch as we are not prepared to embrace the proposition that the right can consist in what is of no good whatsoever, then the right cannot be displacing the good, in the sense which taking priority over it would normally convey, and must in some way be performing a function on the good which leaves the good in some form or another in place. The idea of a balancing function which sets the limits on different conceptions of the good, which has been explored here, is merely one suggestion of how this function could be understood. The attractiveness, or otherwise, of this suggestion does not add or detract from the basic point that the identification of the relationship between the right and the good as one of the right taking priority over the good remains untenable.

If we turn to consider the other side of the purported distinction between deontological and teleological approaches, that the teleological or utilitarian approach does not give priority to the right but rather derives the right through the maximisation of the good, then we have reached the third element that we identified in the purported distinction. We can undertake the clarification of this third element, the maximisation of the good, whilst at the same time considering what role it plays in the relationship between the right and the good.

(3) The Maximisation of the Good.

The idea of deriving the right through a maximisation of the good does, as Rawls points out, hold a strong intuitive appeal and seems to be self-evident.[82] The most obvious point to make here is that if we have identified the good, the only reason for not maximising that good can be if there is some alternative good whose existence is threatened by the pursuit of the first good (unless, again, we are prepared to accept that it can be right to pursue what achieves no good whatsoever). From this observation two simple points follow.

First, if there is no reason for not maximising the good we have identified because there is no alternative good,[83] the concept of the right is redundant. We have simply the single good, which is what is worth pursuing; and since there is no alternative, that good is worth pursuing to the maximum. That it

the satisfaction of the good of others and others' satisfaction in one's own good within the limited society of those in a position similar to oneself: being careful who you invite to dinner.

[82] TofJ, 24–5.

[83] Technically, the argument that follows holds whether we are talking about on every discrete occasion, there only being the one good (allowing there to be other goods unique to other occasions); or, if we are talking about there being on all occasions the one good. It would also hold, therefore, if on one occasion it were possible to pursue independently and simultaneously different goods, since this would be equivalent to the different occasions with their unique goods occurring at the same time without affecting each other. However, this is all rather fanciful, due to the fact that we commonly experience the pursuit of one good on one occasion having repercussions on the pursuit of another good on another occasion.

is right to pursue this good to the maximum is inherent in its being the only good to pursue, and it is tautologous to say that the maximum good tells us what is right. At the most, the right can be regarded as synonymous with the good, but not derived from it, in a way that gives priority to the good.

On the other hand, if there is an alternative good whose existence is threatened by the pursuit of the first good we have identified, then this is a reason for not maximising that first good, and hence we cannot derive the right from the maximising of the good, nor give priority to the good in this sense.

The combination of these two points leads to the conclusion that whether there is one good, or more than one good, no sense can be given to deriving the right from the good, or of regarding the good as having priority over the right in this sense. The different conflicting conceptions of the good that we have identified above, in terms of a variety of goods, relative goods, and subjective goods, would indicate that it is difficult to argue for a single good, and the apparent plausibility of the utilitarian derivation of the right through a maximisation of the good is perhaps traceable to a readiness to overlook the fact that the good can signify different and conflicting things.

The tendency to identify a teleological approach with a single conception of the good[84] has an intriguing history. The two terms, "deontological" and "teleological", were employed by C.D. Broad due to his dissatisfaction with Sidgwick's classification of ethical theories which distinguished between "intuitionism" and "utilitarianism" whilst recognising that the latter nevertheless depended on the ethical intuition that pleasure and nothing else is intrinsically desirable. Broad's terms thus avoided the untidy and unhelpful need to distinguish between two types of intuitionism in Sidgwick's classification.[85]

For Broad, the distinction between the two categories that he labelled deontological and teleological was drawn on the basis of whether the approach was prepared to hold an action good irrespective of the consequences or was concerned to assess its goodness on its consequences.[86] I have already dealt with the role of consequences in determining the characteristics of ethical approaches,[87] and in any case Broad himself was not prepared to draw a tight distinction on this basis.[88] What is of more interest to our immediate concerns is that Broad did not consider that either category necessarily embraced a single good or principle of right, or a plurality. Both approaches could be "monistic" or "pluralistic".[89] However, he saw a tendency for teleological approaches to be monistic, and regarded universalistic hedonism as "a fairly plausible form of monistic teleological theory"; whereas he did not regard there to be a plausible deontological theory which could subsume all

[84] See, for a recent illustration, Samuel Freeman," Utilitarianism, Deontology, and the Priority of Right" (1994) 23 *Philosophy and Public Affairs* 313.

[85] Broad, above n52 at 206.

[86] Broad, 206-7 – cp 162.

[87] section 2(5)(1) above

[88] See above, n52.

[89] Broad, 207, 214–5.

principles of right under a single principle – though he thought that Kant's theory could probably be described as monistic deontological.[90]

Sir David Ross in his *Foundations of Ethics*[91] amplifies Broad's approach but makes the key distinction between deontological and teleological approaches turn on whether there is more than the single ethical principle that one should maximize the good.[92] Although Ross concedes "the natural wish to reach unity and simplicity in our moral theory", he rejects the notion that we should expect an ethical theory to be monistic, and argues that the facts indicate otherwise.[93] Among the further moral principles Ross recognises are those which are distributive in character,[94] and those which relate to other aspects of justice.[95] Yet even if it were possible to resolve all conflict and to identify some grand synthesising conception of the good, we would still not be able to make sense of the idea of giving *priority* to the good.

The question whether a utilitarian approach can produce a grand synthesising conception of the good will be examined in detail below, in considering Bentham's greatest happiness principle (and variations upon it). Before proceeding to a consideration of particular theorists, we can conclude our general observations by noting that the clarification of the second and third features of the purported distinction between deontological and teleological approaches weakens the distinction further. There are no grounds for drawing out the distinction in terms of a priority to be taken by the right or the good, as Rawls does,[96] because such a priority proves untenable on either side. What we are left with is the possibility of finding a different form for the conjunction of the right and the good: in a balancing of conflicting goods, or within a grand synthesising conception of the good.

Such differences that remain, in the method by which the right and the good are to be ascertained, or in the form in which the right and the good are to be discovered, may be regarded as significant. But the probing of these differences is not at all assisted by a specious distinction cast in an illegitimate use of terms, and it would be more helpful to abandon the use of the terms deontological and teleological altogether as a means of depicting how a utilitarian approach to ethics may be distinctive over other approaches.

---

[90] Broad, 215, 207.
[91] above n52.
[92] Ross, 67–83.
[93] Ross, 83.
[94] Ross, 69–75.
[95] Such as the duty to compensate for wrongdoing – Ross, 76.
[96] TofJ, 28, 31, 33.

IX

Rights, Utilitarianism and Morality 2 Four Theorists

1 BENTHAM

Bentham starts his *Introduction to the Principles of Morals and Legislation* with the justification for utilitarianism as a moral approach. The point about utilitarianism for Bentham was that unlike all traditional morality it was *scientific*:[97]

"... truths that form the basis of ... moral science are not to be discovered but by investigations as severe as mathematical ones, and beyond all comparison more intricate and extensive."

Yet however complex this science, Bentham's utilitarianism is constructed on the self-evident[98] axiom:

1 Happiness is desirable[99] for each man.

It is worth pointing out three further propositions that do NOT follow from this axiom:

2 Happiness is the only thing desirable.
3 The desirability of happiness takes priority over anything else.
4 The pursuit of happiness is the means to achieving happiness.

Taken together **2–4** may be regarded as representing a hedonistic approach, for which Bentham has been criticised.[100] The point may be made in passing

---

[97] Preface to PML at xvi. Cp Bentham's reference to "moral science" at the end of ch I.I, and contrast the "contrivances" of other moral systems in ch II.XIV.

[98] *ibid*. ch I.XI–XIV.

[99] Bentham expresses this in terms of mankind's "subjection" to pleasure (*ibid*. ch I.I), which holds sway even when man is unaware of it (ch I.I and XIII); and, obliquely, in the form of a challenge (ch I.XIV.10) to find an alternative motive to that of seeking pleasure and avoiding pain. He also describes "the greatest happiness" as the "universally desirable, end of human action" (n1 to ch I.I) – but this is a reference to the happiness of "all those whose interest is in question" which manifests an ambiguity that Bentham exploits without defending or even suggesting in its stronger form: that the happiness of all others concerned is desirable to each.

[100] I use hedonism in the broad philosophical sense as relating to any kind of pleasure (whether lofty or base), as opposed to the popular restricted sense relating to sensuous pleasures. Bentham himself did not use the term, toying instead with "eudaimonology" as an alternative for his

that it is fallacious to ground a hedonistic approach on Bentham's axiom, **1**. But this is not my present concern. For even if it is possible to justify the hedonistic approach, comprising **1–4** above, Bentham still has a problem in establishing the moral approach that he subsequently takes. For even if you accept **1–4**, it does NOT follow that the following two propositions hold:

5 Any other person's happiness is desirable.
6 The greatest happiness of the greatest number is desirable.

But it only follows that:

7 The greatest happiness of each man is desirable for each man.

Indeed, from **1–4** it follows that **5** *does not hold* unless you can show both of the following:

a The happiness of one person is only realisable in a situation where all other persons may also achieve happiness.
b The means for achieving the happiness of one person is to seek the happiness of others.

Together **a** and **b** can be regarded as the modifications on **4** that are required in order to reach **5**. If we had **a** alone this would be insufficient, for **1–4a** would only mean that coincidentally when A desired happiness that this was not incompatible with O achieving happiness, but this would not require A to be concerned with O's happiness. **5** would only occur if we also added **b**, where the realisation of A's happiness is bound up with his seeking O's happiness, since only then is O's happiness desirable for A on the premises we have accepted thus far.

However, if we accept **1–4ab** and hence **5**, this does not enable us to reach **6**. On the contrary, **6** now becomes incompatible with what has been already accepted, since the process of maximisation explicit in **6** implies a proportion (albeit a minimum proportion) of unhappy people, which contradicts **a**.[101]

"utilitarianism" but rejecting it as inappropriate for lacking suitable derivatives ("felicity" was also considered as a substitute for utility) – "Article on Utilitarianism", paras 29 & 35; *Deontology*, 300–2. For the reaction against Bentham's hedonism (in the broad sense indicated) from within utilitarian writing, see Smart, above n12, section 3.

[101] This is recognised by Bentham himself when considering the greatest happiness principle in *The Constitutional Code* in Bowring (ed.) above n2, vol IX at 6, where he points out that the form of the principle is required because of the competition and incompatibility between different persons' happiness – otherwise it could have been "the greatest happiness *of all*".

Lyons (above n16, at 68–9) makes much of this comment being found in the later *Code* and ties it in with a passage from Bentham's *Memoirs* (Bowring (ed.) above n2, vol X at 80–1), where Bentham remarks that he had been astounded at the hostile reception to his utilitarianism and had failed to account for it until "sixty years had rolled over my head". Lyons argues that it was the late dawning on Bentham of "the principle of self-preference", which is mentioned in this passage, that shed the light, and hence maintains that in PML and other major works Bentham retained a belief in the harmonization of interests and non-egoistic motivation for man. However, the passage in the *Memoirs* could be interpreted in another way, as indicating that what shed the light was not the awareness of man's selfishness, but the awareness that this also controlled those who purported to govern for the interests of others: "If self-preference has place in every human

The problem is insurmountable, for even if we modify **a**, so that it is not *all* other persons whose happiness must be compatible with A's happiness, we would have to modify **5** to: Any other person whose happiness is compatible with A's is desirable for A. And this would certainly not lead to **6**, but only to the proposition that the greatest happiness of those whose happiness is compatible with A is desirable for A. And we could only reach **6** on a hit or miss basis if it happened that A and his compatible hedonists were in the majority, which is far from grounding **6** as a general proposition.

In short, Bentham's reasoning fails on two counts in moving from his "scientific" axiom towards the general principle of utility: the greatest happiness of the greatest number.[102] First, it embraces a hedonistic fallacy (taking **2–4** to follow from **1**) in order to establish the hedonistic aspect of the general principle, and secondly it fails to address the dangers of egoism in the initial axiom **1**, which make it impossible to deal with the incompatibility of interests that are implicit in the maximisation found in the general principle, **6**, and which are also an aspect of morality, as noted in M2 above.

There still remains a further crucial problem for Bentham within **6**, the general principle of utility itself. For as it stands it is open to all the excesses of majoritarianism (or aggregationism),[103] and thus the happiness or other interests of O, if he happens to fall within a minority as against A and those whose interests are compatible with his, can be neglected at will. It is at this point that mention is usually made of the importance of rights, in order to secure the interests of individuals which would be neglected by this crude majoritarian model.

However, Bentham himself seems to have been aware of the importance of protecting individuals, which is apparent from his famous dictum:[104]

breast, then, if rulers are men, so must it have in every ruling breast." (at 81). Certainly, there are indications in the earlier works of Bentham's awareness of the self-preference principle – see n28 above.

[102] For various references to the principle, see above n51, n99 and also PML, ch 1 – and, for Bentham's own modification of the principle, see below n112.

[103] I assume for the moment that the persons who can contribute to the maximisation are living members of one community, in speaking of majoritarianism. That this was Bentham's perception is argued by Lyons, above n16. The point can still be made if the community of interests is extended to future generations (as Parfit does, above n27) in terms of aggregationism.

[104] The dictum is attributed to Bentham by John Stuart Mill, but is not to be found in these words in Bentham's writings – see L. Werner, "A Note about Bentham on Equality and about the Greatest Happiness Principle" (1973) 11 *Journal of the History of Philosophy* 237 at n4. Perhaps the closest to be found in Bentham's written words is "having exactly the same regard for the happiness of every member of the community in question, as for that of every other" – *The Constitutional Code* in Bowring (ed.) above n2, vol IX at 6. There remains some controversy over whether the dictum should be regarded as purely aggregative, or distributive in character. In considering this controversy, Werner places much reliance on a French text of Bentham's (found translated in Mary Mack, *Jeremy Bentham: An Odyssey of Ideas 1748-1792* (London, Heinemann, 1962) Appendix D, "Essay on Representation") in arguing that Bentham's concern was purely aggregative. Werner cites in isolation axiom V of that essay, which holds that two "operations" are equally meritorious where the one provides ten persons each with a single portion of happiness and the other five persons each with two portions of happiness. In itself this does seem striking evidence of a purely aggregative approach. However, the axioms enumerated

"everybody to count for one, nobody for more than one"

And the practical outworkings of his utilitarian reforming zeal similarly attest to his concern for individuals.[105] But this individualism cannot, as we have seen, be deduced from Bentham's "scientific" axiom, nor from the general principle of utility itself. The observation of Bentham's individualism and its uneasy connection with his hedonistic utilitarianism led early critics to suggest that there was another influence at work within his utilitarianism. Both Dicey and Stephen argued that Bentham was far more indebted to the common law tradition of respecting individual rights than he acknowledged.[106]

Spencer had the temerity to suggest that the principle of utility was in fact insufficient and subordinate to the principle that everyone has an equal *right* to happiness.[107] For this he was savaged by Mill in his *Utilitarianism*, where he writes[108] that the equal right to happiness:

". . .may be more correctly described as supposing that equal amounts of happiness are equally desirable, whether felt by the same or by different persons."

by Bentham here are clearly cumulative, and axiom VI commences with the conjunctive "But" which introduces the qualification that "a double quantity of the cause of happiness will not produce a double quantity of happiness, but much less." This text therefore, whilst evidence of an aggregative approach on the part of Bentham is not evidence of an aggregative approach which is exclusive of distributive concerns, but rather the aggregative approach is made compatible with distributive concerns by the assumption that a distributively neutral allocation (or "operation") will produce a lesser aggregation. There is further evidence that Bentham failed to see a possible conflict between aggregative and distributive concerns (or, less charitably, fixed his aggregative calculus so as to meet distributive concerns) to be found in his unpublished "Article on Utilitarianism" – considered at n112 below. Werner cites (in section II of his article) a similar illustration, provided by Thomas Perronet Thompson in his article in *The Westminster Review* of 1829 which draws from Bentham's unpublished manuscript, as further evidence of Bentham's *exclusively* aggregative concerns, but again it is evidence only of aggregative concerns and the fuller analysis of Bentham's original illustration (n112 below) indicates a compatibility with distributive concerns. If Bentham failed to appreciate the important distinction between having an equal opportunity to contribute to an aggregation, and having some share of the aggregation, then he fell victim to an error that others have readily succumbed to (see nn110–1 below, and text threat). But whatever the source of Bentham's theoretical confusion (for a general critique, see Pitkin, above n26, particularly at 107–8), his concern for the interests of all individuals rather than the interests of the privileged few has been evident to many (see authors cited at nn105–8 below). For example, although Spencer denied the adequacy of the greatest happiness principle, he was sure that it was being used to make the assertion "that all men have equal rights to happiness" (above n60, at 94).

[105] See F.E. Dowrick, *Justice according to the English Common Lawyers* (London, Butterworths, 1961) ch 6.

[106] Leslie Stephen, *The English Utilitarians* (London, Duckworth, 1900) vol I, 133–6; A.V. Dicey, *Law and Public Opinion in England* (London, Macmillan, 1905), 2ed. with Preface by E.C.S. Wade, 1962, at 168–71.

[107] Herbert Spencer, above n60, ch V:3. Spencer's starting point was "that human happiness is the divine will" (at 75), from which he derived the equal right to happiness (77), and as a necessary means to its accomplishment his First Principle: "Every man has freedom to do all that he wills, provided he infringes not the equal freedom of any other man". (at 103).

[108] John Stuart Mill, *Utilitarianism*, 1863 – in Fontana ed., Mary Warnock (ed.) (Glasgow, Collins, 1962) at 319 n2.

And as such is not anterior to the principle of utility, but "the very principle itself".[109]

Mill's defence fails on the grounds that his equivalence is false, for an equal right to happiness cannot be equated to having one's happiness measured on the same scale once it is taken into a majoritarianist or aggregationist scheme,[110] for this can disgorge individuals with no right to happiness. The fallacy, which has been repeated since Mill,[111] is to equate an equal opportunity for each to influence whose interests are respected, with an equal respect for the interests of each. It is like telling children that they can all say what game they would like to play, and then trying to convince those whose suggestion has not been accepted that they are still playing the game they chose. Or, to use a severer illustration, it amounts to a gang of terrorists drawing lots to determine which of their hostages is to be shot, and arguing that because each hostage is given one lot, the terrorists are showing equal respect for the lives of the hostages. Interests in the process of selection do not match interests in its outcome.

Mill's blindness to this flaw in his argument, and Bentham's own blind spot, can perhaps be attributed to the naive assumption that if only the happiness of every individual were taken into account then the happiness of every individual would be respected, which is a working assumption that one might make if one had not even got the first part of the aspiration established.[112]

---

[109] *ibid.*

[110] See for a general criticism of Mill's confusion over rights and utility at this point, Hart, EonB, 99–100.

[111] By Dworkin, below section 2. Also, Will Kymlicka, *Liberalism, Community and Culture* (Oxford, Clarendon Press, 1989), repeats the error that utilitarianism can be interpreted as "a theory of equal consideration" – one "way of spelling out the idea that from the moral point of view the interests of each person matter equally . . .". (at 26). Kymlicka (at 25–6 shows that the position is common to a number of authors, including Hare in Frey (ed.), above n7. Hare there states (at 107) that "to have equal concern for all people is to seek equally their good, *or to give equal weight to their interests* . . .". But the alternative I have italicised relates to the process of selecting whose interests are to be pursued, and cannot, therefore, be equated with the former alternative of equally seeking the interests (or good) of all.

[112] Looked at in this way, Bentham and Mill were seeking to establish a fully democratic society, at a time when this was a radical suggestion, and had not progressed to the more sophisticated problem of how to deal with the excesses of democracy. Bentham in fact briefly refers to the problems of majoritarianism in his "Article on Utilitarianism" (Long Version), paras 54–58, where he amends his greatest happiness principle to exclude "of the greatest number" on the ground that it would allow account to be taken of "no feelings but those of the majority" (para 54). However, Bentham is still arguing on an aggregationist basis that this would reduce "the aggregate stock of the happiness of the community". He is able to do so by staging an illustration where there is a majority of one in a group of 4001; and, by assuming (a) that there is a greater loss of happiness in the members of the minority for the related gain in happiness of the members of the majority, and (b) that to restore the members of the minority to happiness does not similarly result in a related loss of happiness to members of the majority. The "Article" is to be found in *Deontology*, at 283. For a critical account of the support for democracy by Bentham and James Mill, see John Plamenatz, *The English Utilitarians* (Oxford, Blackwell, 1958) at 184ff. Plamenatz considers the support is imbued with a pre-utilitarian English concern with the right to freedom: "if they had been, say, Chinese utilitarians, they might perhaps never have been moved to contrive a utilitarian argument for democracy." (at 192).

Although Bentham's arguments fail, and others within the utilitarian tradition have sought to improve upon them, it is instructive to note first how his enterprise as he envisages it operating possesses the aspects we have associated with a moral approach, and secondly how Bentham fails to satisfy the criteria we have identified for a successful moral theory. To identify clearly Bentham's failings is to have something by which to judge whether subsequent theorists, on either side, have succeeded.

First then Bentham's enterprise clearly does possess all three aspects of morality, M1–M3, if we take it operating in the way he envisages. His dictum on individualism clearly is intended to enshrine respect for the other – M1. And this taken together with the general principle of utility (proposition 6 above) is meant to combine fulfilment of the self with fulfilment of the other – M3. Also in Bentham's move from proposition 1 to proposition 6 there is required a denial of self-interest: that self-interest which would operate to maintain a mere maximisation of one's own pleasure (proposition 7).[113]

However, Bentham's enterprise fails each of the criteria we have identified for a successful moral theory: justification, practicality, sufficiency. His justification depends on a "scientific" axiom offering a pleasure motive, which cannot in fact sustain the moral enterprise that follows. Moreover, in working through his moral approach that general principle on which it is supposed to be based in practice proves insufficient, as is indicated by Bentham's own recognition of the dictum of individualism. Though even this is inadequate to ensure that each individual is given the respect that a moral approach requires.

2 DWORKIN

Rawls, Dworkin and Nozick have each in different ways produced moral theories based on rights in an attempt to redress what is seen as the failure of utilitarianism to accord proper respect to the individual. In this way the three theorists comply with the first aspect of morality, M1, in insisting that every individual should be given proper respect through the enforcement of his rights. Since these rights are in each case available to every individual, it also follows that M3 is satisfied. The compliance with M2 is usually more obliquely put in that the potential source of conflict for the rights of the individual is expressed as the interests of the state or general welfare, but even in such formulations it must follow that for the respect for others to be manifested in the enforcement of rights, those whose interests would be enhanced by the promotion of the contrary pull of general welfare (quite possibly the majority of people) must deny such self-interest.

---

[113] Seen in practical terms in the calls for reform Bentham made, such as that noted n28 above, which would require the denial of the self-interest of the lawyers in order to promote the maximisation of happiness for all concerned, including the litigants.

That each of these theorists seeks to establish a rights based moral approach to deal with the perceived deficiencies of utilitarianism is not startling. As we have seen, such a role for rights was suggested by Spencer as an immanent critique of Bentham's own theory, and the suggestion that Bentham was himself indebted to the traditional respect for individual rights found in the Common Law was made by Stephen and Dicey. The intriguing question to ask is how each of these theorists seeks to satisfy the criteria for a successful moral theory in a way that sets them apart from the failures we have noted for Bentham.

It will be convenient to first ask this question of Dworkin's theory, since he has attracted much criticism for failing to extract himself from the snares of utilitarianism. At the heart of Dworkin's theory lies the right to equal concern and respect, which is described as "fundamental and axiomatic".[114] This is Dworkin's basic formulation of M1, which gives rise to particular rights which can "trump" non-respecting considerations of general welfare[115] (ie where general utility would fail to respect individuals).

The first anxiety about the right to equal concern and respect is that it is so vague as to be meaningless,[116] so that any attempt by Dworkin to fill it out with a particular reference point is to be welcomed. Unfortunately, Dworkin's attempt to do this is done in the context of demonstrating how the right to equal concern and respect would modify a utilitarian system. Whilst being justified by the "most fundamental tenet"[117] of utilitarianism that each person is to count as one,[118] the right refines the calculation that a utilitarian would make to ensure that no person gets counted twice.[119]

The logical trauma that comes from following this reasoning, whereby one position U (the utilitarian) is based on the same premise as another position R (rights based) but the two conflict, so that R has to be used to correct the errors of U (ie R which is based on the same premise that led to the erroneous U is correct), might explain the readiness of critics to suggest that Dworkin's rights are contaminated by utilitarianism.[120] Perhaps Dworkin's position can be rendered more intelligible by recasting it as: the premise adopted by utilitarianism, that each person is to count as one, is not followed rigorously in conventional utilitarian calculations which erroneously allow an element of

---

[114] TRS, xv.

[115] MofP, 359.

[116] See Joseph Raz, "Professor Dworkin's Theory of Rights" (1978) 26 *Political Studies* 123.

[117] MofP, 362.

[118] *ibid*, 362, 371. At 360, Dworkin states that a "proper understanding of what utilitarianism is . . . will itself justify the right . . .".

[119] I ignore for present purposes whether Dworkin's approach to "double counting" TRS, 234ff is intrinsically sound. For comment, see Sartorius, above n14; Hart below n120; Dworkin's Reply below n121; and, Stephen Guest, *Ronald Dworkin* (Edinburgh, Edinburgh University Press, 1992) at 233.

[120] Sartorius, above n14; Jules Coleman, "Book Review: *Taking Rights Seriously*" (1978) 66 *California Law Review* 885 at 917; H.L.A. Hart, "Between Utility and Rights" (1979) 79 *Columbia Law Review* 845 in EJP, ch 9.

double-counting which offends that premise, and therefore the conventional method of calculation needs to be modified in order to discount double-counting in order to be faithful to the premise. But if this is the case, and this modified position represents Dworkin's rights, it is not the case that his rights are contaminated by utilitarianism but that they are utilitarian: they simply express positions that are a correct outworking of the utilitarian premise. In this case, Dworkin has added nothing to Bentham's utilitarianism with its individualistic dictum, and can be regarded as suffering from the same failings. In fact, as will be seen, in one respect Dworkin's theory is a lesser theory than Bentham's.

Dworkin has responded to the criticisms that his theory is entangled with utilitarianism by the suggestion that he has been misunderstood: the apparent contamination with utilitarianism arose from the fact that he was discussing rights in the context of a utilitarian society, and his observations are not accordingly general nor capable of providing a wider picture of his view of rights,[121] which is promised in a subsequent book.[122] But both the rebuttal of the criticism and the promise prove empty.

The rebuttal is empty because if Dworkin's rights do constitute an independent moral theory then it should be discernible in the analysis of any society to which it is applied. Dworkin's fundamental problem is not that his rights seem to take on a utilitarian tinge when applied to the analysis of a utilitarian society but that they are not discernible as an independent moral theory. Either this is because a utilitarian society fully embraces and exhibits Dworkin's rights – in which case the independent role for his rights as a trump against utility collapses as illusory (they simply express utility); or this is because in general Dworkin's rights fail as an independent moral theory and merely operate as an adjunct of whichever society they are applied to.

The promise is supposed to be delivered in *Law's Empire*, but far from establishing a general picture of his rights as an independent moral theory this book reinforces the view that his rights fail in this respect. In one sense the promise proves empty because Dworkin abandons rights in this book, or at the very least neglects them, in favour of a new abstraction, integrity. Certainly there is nothing in this book to mark a clear line betwen Dworkin's rights and utilitarianism in a way that his earlier writing failed to do.[123] And if, as it seems, all is now subservient to integrity, then rights too fall under its yoke.[124] But this is a yoke which can harness rights to the integrity of any particular society, so that again Dworkin's rights fail as an independent moral theory, and the "fundamental" right to equal concern and respect[125] does

---

[121] MofP, 370; "A Reply by Ronald Dworkin" in Marshall Cohen (ed.), *Ronald Dworkin and Contemporary Jurisprudence* (London, Duckworth, 1984) at 281–2, 289–90.

[122] MofP, 6; see also, 414 n16.

[123] Ronald Dworkin, *Law's Empire* (London: Collins, 1986) – hereinafter, LE.

[124] LE, 223.

[125] In another departure from his concern with rights, Dworkin explores the idea of equality in a number of essays and lectures: (i) "What is Equality? Part 1: Equality of Welfare" (1981) 10

nothing more than express the "equal" respect that one enjoys as a citizen of that particular society, and is subjugated to whatever differential roles that society might visit on its members.[126]

We may then conclude that Dworkin has failed to satisfy the criteria for a successful moral theory. His theory that is constructed on the "axiomatic", "fundamental" right to equal concern and respect turns out to have been built on an abstraction which provides no justification, practicality, or sufficiency for his theory as a *moral* theory, and his adherence to the premise that each is to count as one far from satisfying the aspects of morality is reduced to the proposition that everyone is to enjoy equal status as a member of a society – a society that is capable of denying the practical aspects of morality in just the same way as a society determined by Bentham's utilitarianism.

3 RAWLS

The stature of Rawls as a champion of rights against the excesses of utilitarianism has never been impeached by suggesting that he might be a covert utilitarian. Both Dworkin and Nozick pay Rawls homage as establishing the need for rights to protect the individual against the calculations of utility,[127] and

Philosophy and Public Affairs 185; (ii) "What is Equality? Part 2: Equality of Resources" (1981) 10 *Philosophy and Public Affairs* 283; (iii) "Comment on Narveson: In Defense of Equality" (1983) 1 *Social Philosophy and Policy* 24; (iv) "What is Equality? Part 3: The Place of Liberty" (1987) 73 *Iowa Law Review* 1; (v) "What is Equality? Part 4: Political Equality" (1987) 22 *University of San Francisco Law Review* 1; (vi) "Foundations of Liberal Equality" in Grethe Peterson (ed.), *The Tanner Lectures on Human Values*, vol XI (Salt Lake City, Utah, University of Utah Press, 1990). Gerald Postema has observed ("Liberty in Equality's Empire" (1987) 73 *Iowa Law Review* 55 at 57 n12) that within this body of work Dworkin drops the vocabulary of "trump rights", but considers that the same idea is to be found in the "special protection" Dworkin allows for certain fundamental liberties (see (iv) at 53), which are also referred to as "these important rights" (*ibid.*). However, the change goes further than a choice of vocabulary. Such rights are expressions of individual positions (see (ii) at 340–1), but positions *derived from* the conception of equality or liberty (for Dworkin the two are compatible) that is accepted (see (iv) at 7, 12, 24, 25, 47, 53). Moreover, Dworkin explicitly allows for differences in viewpoint as to which conception is adopted and hence which rights are required (*ibid.* at 7 & 53 – which speaks of "our political culture"). Although Dworkin claims in passing ((iv) at 13 n11) that his work on equality confirms "the methodological claim about rights" made in his earlier work, it is evident that the "fundamental and axiomatic" right to equal concern and respect (n114 above) has been replaced by the "foundational and universal" abstract egalitarian principle occupying a "fundamental level" from which "any plausible argument for rights" must be derived (iii) at 31–2, 34–5). These developments in Dworkin's work leave unanswered the fundamental question of what happened to taking rights seriously.

[126] That this might fail the aspirations or moral claims of some of the members of that society is a point made by Allan Hutchinson, "The Last Emperor?" and by Valerie Kerruish and Alan Hunt, "Dworkin's Dutiful Daughter: Gender Discrimination in Law's Empire" – both in Alan Hunt (ed.), *Reading Dworkin Critically* (Oxford, Berg, 1992). For a view that Dworkin's integrity is superfluous to the practices of an actual society, see Stanley Fish, "Still Wrong After All These Years" (1987) 6 *Law and Philosophy* 401, in *Doing What Comes Naturally* (Oxford, Clarendon Press, 1989) ch 16.

[127] TRS, 149; ASU, 183.

Rawls' well known complaint that utilitarianism fails to respect persons[128] has become the standard battle cry for rights theorists in the conflict with utilitarianism. However, in one respect Rawls is closer to Bentham than is Dworkin.

We saw that Dworkin's theory of rights proceeded from the premise of the right to equal concern and respect, and provided no anterior justification for his theory, or motivation for engaging in his moral approach. Bentham by contrast sought to establish his theory on the "scientific" observation of the human desire for pleasure, which is meant to provide both justification for his theory and motivation for following the utilitarian approach.

Rawls, like Bentham, provides a combined justification and motivation, in his use of rational self-interest through his device of the "veil of ignorance" in his *A Theory of Justice*. The particular principles of justice derived, maximum equal liberty and distributing resources to favour improving the position of the least well off, are intended together to secure the respect for and fulfilment of individuals in the aspects of morality we have identified.[129] The justification or motivation comes from making this moral approach desirable to every member of society by artificially making the positions worked out in a society guided by these principles to serve the self-interest of its members, in that these are the positions that the members would have determined to be in their own best interest from behind the veil of ignorance (where they did not know which positions they would actually occupy).[130]

In a sense then, Rawls' motivating force of rational self-interest is a more sophisticated version of Bentham's pleasure motive. But it fails for precisely the same reasons. Consider the propositions 1 to 7 met above in discussing Bentham's utilitarianism[131] and replace "happiness" with "the outcome of rational self-interest" in each of the seven propositions, and it will equally be impossible to derive proposition 6, which is required for Rawls' two principles of justice, and we will again end up in proposition 7. The sleight of hand which conceals this in *A Theory of Justice* is treating the people beyond the veil of ignorance as the people who stood behind it, so that it appears that each person is concerned with the interests of everyone else. However, if the force of rational self-interest can be conditioned by the circumstances prevailing on one side of the veil in order to artificially create concern for other people's positions, it can equally be operated to different effect by the circumstances on the other side.[132] A significant acknowledgment of this failing seems to have been made by Rawls in his later book, *Political Liberalism*,[133]

---

[128] TofJ, 27.

[129] M1 and M3 – it should be remembered that M2 can be derived obliquely from a rights approach (section 2 above).

[130] TofJ, 16–9.

[131] Section 1.

[132] A range of criticisms on this point are collected in Norman Daniels (ed.), *Reading Rawls* (Oxford, Blackwell, 1975) and usefully summarised by Daniels in his "Introduction" at xviii–xxii.

[133] New York, NY, Columbia University Press, 1993.

where he limits the scope of his theory of justice to a society that imbibes the liberal values on which it is founded.[134]

Even in this more restricted habitat, Rawls' theory of rights suffers from a number of flaws. Assuming for the moment the liberal premises required by Rawls, the principles of justice he derives are still sufficiently abstract as to cause problems in deducing particular individual rights. Is there anything within the principle of maximum equal liberty, or within the principle of distributing resources to favour the position of the least well off – "the difference principle", to ensure that the aspects of morality are complied with and that individuals are respected in concrete situations?[135]

In considering this issue we can concentrate on the second principle, for the first principle securing maximum equal liberty would by itself fail to establish a moral approach. Rawls' "basic liberties of citizens" would give, say, the victims of a policy which denied health care to anybody over the age of 65 the liberty to vote, seek public office, write to the newspapers, march in protest, believe and think strongly about the iniquity of the policy, possess pamphlets and own books decrying the policy, all without interference from the law.[136] But despite its priority in Rawls' scheme of justice,[137] the first principle would fail to condemn the policy as immoral; indeed, it would have nothing to say about it one way or the other.[138]

Rawls' formulation of the second principle, "the difference principle", possesses a number of problems when we are considering whether it succeeds in establishing a moral approach. The principle requires that, "Social and economic inequalities are to be arranged so that they are . . . to the greatest benefit of the least advantaged . . .".[139] The problems can be traced to a methodological flaw and an unspoken assumption.

The methodological flaw can be traced deep into Rawls' theory, but the fissure appears on the surface. The methodological basis of Rawls' approach is to take the least well off position and to consider all possible options for a particular social or economic arrangement in relation to that position, and to

---

[134] Brian Barry, "Good for us, but not for them" – review of Rawls' *Political Liberalism*, *The Guardian*, 14 August 1993, accuses Rawls of betraying the liberal cause and denying support to liberals in illiberal societies, such as China, of which he states, "The movement for political reform needed arguments of the kind Rawls offered [in TofJ]. It could not appeal to tradition or to values implicit in existing institutions." Cp Frank Michelman, "The Subject of Liberalism" (1994) 46 *Stanford Law Review* 1807, and Samuel Sheffler, "The Appeal of Political Liberalism" (1994) 105 Ethics 4, particularly at 20–22. See also, Barry's contribution to the debate on Rawls' political liberalism found in (1994) 7 *Ratio Juris* at 325: "In Defense of Political Liberalism".

[135] Rawls himself has a strange disdain for these, preferring to discuss the positions of "representative persons holding the various social positions, or offices, or whatever. . ." – TofJ, 64.

[136] Enumerated at TofJ, 61.

[137] TofJ, 61–3 & 541ff.

[138] Given that the grounds for according priority to maximum equal liberty assume the establishment of adequate economic and social conditions (TofJ, 542), it might be thought that this constitutes an unrecognised principle of justice prior to both the principles Rawls articulates.

[139] TofJ, 83. I ignore the further requirement of "fair equality of opportunity" stated by Rawls, since it adds nothing to the present discussion.

choose the option which provides the best deal for that position. The methodology is borrowed from Pareto economics, and proceeds on the intuitive appeal of adopting a policy that makes everybody happier: If everyone's position is improved, how can anybody complain?[140] Rawls' modification, of ensuring that the least well off position is favoured by the option that improves it the most, adds a strand of social justice to this intuitive appeal: If we are doing the best we can for the least well off in society, how can anybody say that we are being unjust?

The illustrations Rawls employs[141] in fact take it for granted that as long as we are looking after the least well off, everybody else will at least benefit to some extent (though not as much as some of them might if we neglected the least well off).[142] So the principle appears to combine the qualities of making everybody happier whilst keeping society just.

However, if Rawls' principle is applied to situations other than those considered by Rawls it can collapse because Rawls' presupposition about the link between improvements of welfare among the different groups in a society no longer holds. Parfit and Broome suggest practical situations where the options available include cases where one party need not always be in the worst off position,[143] which makes it impossible to apply the difference principle as formulated, and makes it questionable to apply it even in a modified form.[144]

The general point to be made here is that the difference principle as applied by Rawls takes a rather patronising attitude to the possibility of improving the lot of the least well off: it can only improve by the efforts of the better off, activated by self-interest in improving their own position, causing a trickle down effect of social improvement.[145] And even if we take into account that Rawls is applying his principle to a society that benefits from just institutions and equality of opportunity, and allow for the options that are to be considered in accordance with the difference principle as operating on a society that is already as just as it could be in the circumstances that prevailed before the change of circumstances that generated the options now under consideration, it simply is not the case that we can only imagine the possibility of improvement in the conditions of the least well off on the basis of a trickle down from

---

[140] For a general discussion of Pareto economics, see Jules Coleman, *Markets, Morals and the Law* (Cambridge, Cambridge University Press, 1988) ch 3.

[141] TofJ, 76ff.

[142] "It has been taken for granted that if the principle is satisfied, everyone is benefited." – TofJ, 80.

[143] Parfit above n27, 490ff.

[144] Broome shows, *ibid* at 492, that even if you modify the difference principle to select the option which allows for whichever is the least advantaged class in that option to be in a better position than the least advantaged class in any other option, this may cause injustice to a greater number of people in the class whose position has been worsened by selecting that option with them in the worst position.

[145] For a failure of the trickle down effect to deal with the housing problems of the poorest classes in the 1930s, see John Griffith, *Judicial Politics since 1920: A Chronicle* (Oxford, Blackwell, 1993) at 20.

the self-interested and self-motivated improvement to the positions of the better off.

Consider as just one example, a change in circumstances brought about by a widely available technological advance that could either be used to improve the working conditions of a workforce in a factory, or to improve the salaries of the directors. The opportunity is not brought about by any effort on behalf of the directors, such that requires motivation through additional incentives. It would be possible to transfer the whole benefit to the least well off. If the directors balk and refuse to introduce the improvement on the ground that there is nothing in it for them, the principle of justice is subverted by the exigencies of collective bargaining in order to determine who gets what share in the improvement of welfare.

The crack widens if we take a case where it is not assumed that the society is already as just as it could be. For in this case, it is easy to imagine a situation where the improvement to the least well off could be accommodated by them exchanging positions with the better off.[146]

And once we peer into the crack it goes deeper. There are three further practical difficulties in applying the principle. First, there is the arbitrariness of isolating a particular social or economic value, such as income.[147] The gains on net income produced by tax cuts will have an impact on the resources available for education or health care; the amount of government revenue spent on health care will have an impact on the amount of resources available for education. Who is to count as the least well off: those on a low income, the terminally ill, those requiring pre-school nurseries? The incommensurability of different aspects of social and economic welfare taken with the interdependence of their provision makes it impossible to objectively identify the least well off.[148]

A second further practical difficulty that is related to this is that it is impossible to tell what the outcome of the implementation of a chosen option will be in terms of improving the position of the least well off. To take the simplest of examples, income tax cuts favouring the least well off might have knock on effects which subsequently leave their overall welfare sadly diminished. In general, Rawls does not seem capable of coping with a society where its citizens are facing a general worsening of conditions.[149]

---

[146] This is not possible for Rawls in the case of an already just society since the improved position of the better off has been reached as a necessary condition for getting the least well off into the best position available for them.

Rawls does, however, allow for his principle to be applied to a society where we cannot be sure of its pedigree of justice – TofJ, 80. The relation to the situation of hypothetical equality is judged irrelevant *because it is assumed everybody will benefit from the application of the principle.*

[147] As Rawls does, TofJ, 78.

[148] The incommensurability problem has clear parallels in utilitarianism – on which see further Finnis, FofE, 86–94.

The political advantage of this fact is often exploited by politicians who agree to the desirability of one policy but point to the unfortunate impact its implementation would have on another facet of social or economic welfare that is dear to the heart of their audience.

[149] The recession free vision of Rawls' theory can perhaps be attributed to the link he makes between the realisation of justice and economic efficiency – see TofJ, 79 & 82.

A third related difficulty lies in the role Rawls allows incentive in his calculation of what options are actually available. The justification for initial
inequality is that the additional benefit held out to the one group operates as
the necessary incentive to activate their entrepreneurial skills in accomplish-
ing what leads to the benefit of all.[150] But there is in the nature of this exercise no way of telling what incentive is actually required because the incentive
will be claimed by those who have already achieved the gains as the fruits of
their entrepreneurial skills, and it will be impossible to assess what they (or
others) might have done without that particular incentive. It is not simply a
case of considering known available options as it might be with various different arithmetical ways of dividing a sum of money between different parties. This leads to the possibility of inequalities being justified by the appeal
to an incentive that nobody can demonstrate is necessary or not,[151] so that
the real options for improving the lot of the least well off are never known.

Finally, there lies within all that Rawls has to say on the difference principle an unspoken assumption. In a sense it is an assumption that slips
between the two principles of justice, but in a more fundamental sense it
undergirds them. In relation to the difference principle, there is an assumption that no matter how bad the position of the least well off, it is not critical so as to call for a major revision of our structure of society, but this cannot
be guaranteed by the difference principle itself which carries no safety net.
Rawls seems oblivious to this point perhaps because when he considers the
difference principle the position of the least well off is at least secured by their
enjoyment of equal liberty in accordance with the first principle.[152] However,
when considering the first principle the position of equal liberty is dependent
upon sufficiency of economic and social welfare.[153] There is then a prior principle required by Rawls' theory of justice, of establishing a sufficient level of
economic and social welfare. Or, to put it another way, his theory only applies
to a society that is already just in this respect.

We cannot therefore detect in Rawls' theory of rights satisfaction of the
requirement of justification on the ground of rational self-interest, since this,
like Bentham's pleasure motive, would end up defeating the scheme that
Rawls attempts to found on it. And even if Rawls reverts to an intuitive
appeal to the merits of his modified Pareto principle, we have found that it is
in practice incapable of doing anything more than expounding the practices

---

[150] TofJ, 78. Rawls does not claim that this actually is the case but that it must be the case if
the initial inequality is to be justified.

[151] A topical illustration is the justification given for the large increases in pay of the chairmen
of UK water and gas companies after privatisation. See, for example, *The Independent*, London,
22 November 1994, at 3, which contains a number of perspectives on the 75% pay rise given to
the chief executive of British Gas – described variously as "grotesque", "obscene", and a "highly
incentivised remuneration package".

[152] TofJ, 545. The weakness of a conception of liberty devoid of all material provision is considered more fully in section 4 below.

[153] TofJ, 542.

of a form of social welfare that can be practised in a society with very narrow and rather unusual social and economic parameters. And outside of these conditions, Rawls' principle is vague and illusory, capable of arbitrary application and the rationalisation of self-interest at the expense of respecting the positions of others. Moreover, many of these latter criticisms spring from the incommensurability of welfare and the impossibility of working out the full consequential impact of selecting a particular option, difficulties that are familiar for a utilitarian approach. Indeed, Rawls' recognition that under the right circumstances the difference principle is wholly compatible with the principle of utility,[154] and his characterisation of the difference principle as a "maximizing principle",[155] prioritising the position of the least well off but set in a situation where everybody's position will improve,[156] might lead us to conclude that Rawls has not so much abandoned utilitarianism as sought to modify it.

4 NOZICK

If our suspicions are that Dworkin might be[157] a covert utilitarian and Rawls a revisionist utilitarian, there is still unlikely to be even a whiff of a suspicion about Nozick. Nozick's conception of the minimalist state, justified to the extent and virtually only to the extent that it serves to uphold the property rights of its citizens, with a stigmatising of any redistribution of wealth to meet the welfare needs of others as tantamount to forced labour,[158] might seem so far removed from any conception of morality which shares the characteristic of respecting others (M1), and so remote from the possibility of even considering others as a contribution to any calculation of utility, that it might seem wholly out of place to mention Nozick except as the polar extreme to the views that we are considering.

However, what has made Nozick's theory of rights so significant is his claim that it has a moral justificatory force that sets it apart, not only from utilitarianism but also from the liberal welfare rights of Rawls. For Nozick, it is the exclusive attention paid to property rights that is capable of marking out the separateness of persons required to fully respect others morally, which guards against the excesses of utilitarianism and at the same time stands against liberal welfarism.

An obvious rejoinder to Nozick is that he has simply failed to consider other types of rights that might be as equally important as property rights,[159]

---

[154] TofJ, 82. See further, Scheffler's query, above n134 at 9.

[155] TofJ, 79.

[156] TofJ, 80.

[157] Or, might *have been* – in his earlier discussions of rights and utilitarianism.

[158] ASU – the last mentioned image is found at 169.

[159] Thomas Nagel, "Libertarianism Without Foundations" (1975) 85 *Yale Law Journal* 136 at 137–8; Hart, EJP, 207.

and that his view is therefore theoretically impoverished.[160] However, what is of more interest to our present enquiry is how Nozick seeks to establish a moral theory that justifies such a narrow approach. I will suggest that Nozick does in fact fail to provide a moral theory, in accordance with the criteria we have established. Nevertheless, some of the reasons why he fails are particularly illuminating.

The first reason is a flaw in arguing from the moral form to the sort of libertarian position that Nozick adopts.[161] Nozick concedes that he does not offer "a precise theory of the moral basis of individual rights"[162] but is content to argue from an acceptance of the idea of respect for individuals which is manifested in these individual rights.[163] At this point Nozick can be identified with Dworkin, who similarly argued from the "axiomatic" right to equal respect, but from this common starting point he takes a rather different direction.

Nozick does this[164] by linking his libertarian content to the moral form, on the basis that inherent in the moral form is the "distinctness of individuals",[165] and from this one may infer the libertarian constraint which upholds the distinctness of individuals by allowing them to lead their own lives.

There is so much assumption compressed into that last inference, but let us ignore it for the moment. Even if Nozick were right that it is this capacity to formulate life plans and live in accordance with them which gives meaning to an individual's life,[166] this "meaningfulness" is no more capable of establishing a moral theory than Bentham's happiness,[167] or Rawls' rational self-interest. A modified propositon 1 would still lead to a maximisaton of the prospects of one's own meaningful life plans (7). And what of those meaningful life plans that are frustrated by the disproportionate wealth that facilitates so many life plans, that is unfortunately owned by others? Far from providing us with "an argument from moral form to moral content",[168] the

---

[160] Nagel condemns Nozick for being "theoretically insubstantial" (*ibid.* at 137) and for "start[ing] from the unargued premise that individuals have certain inviolable rights" (138); Hart is more generous in conceding that "there is argument of a sort, though it is woefully deficient." (*ibid.* at 204). For a theoretically sophisticated defence of Nozick's starting point, see Horacio Spector, *Autonomy and Rights* (Oxford, Clarendon Press, 1992), discussed as an objective of the book at 7. Spector's approach is considered further below.

[161] Nozick's libertarianism is of a particular kind. Jonathan Wolff, *Robert Nozick: Property, Justice and the Minimal State* (Cambridge, Polity Press, 1991) identifies it with "rampant capitalism" – at vii–viii.

[162] ASU, xiv.

[163] ASU, 33–4.

[164] ASU, 34.

[165] The shifting epithet from Rawls' "separateness of persons" to Nozick's "separate lives" (ASU, 33) which leads on to the "distinctness of individuals" (34) can hardly be regarded as accidental.

[166] ASU, 48–50.

[167] Nozick himself suggests the comparison (ASU, 50): "Or, why not replace 'happiness' with 'meaningfulness' within utilitarian theory, and maximize the total 'meaningfulness' score of the persons of the world?"

[168] ASU, 34.

particular content Nozick argues for would be capable of wrecking the moral form.

The moral form bearing Nozick's content is nevertheless shored up by two devices: an historical justification for the existing distribution of property, and a peculiar conception of rights, both of which are employed to lend moral force to Nozick's content.

The historical justification of property becomes relevant because the undisturbed pursuit of meaningful life plans for Nozick involves the exercise of property rights,[169] and it would be difficult to sustain the morality of this if the property rights themselves had not been legitimately acquired. The second reason for Nozick's failure is then that his moral theory depends on finding a society whose distribution of property is historically pure, with titles notionally stretching back to an initial innocent acquisition. Since the title to property in most countries' histories is at one time or another written in blood, this might seem an insurmountable problem, and Nozick does not demonstrate the energy to overcome it.[170] More fundamentally, this makes any moral approach that Nozick is developing limited to a society which might have had such a pure history.

The other reasons for Nozick's failure that we shall examine relate to his peculiar conception of rights. The peculiarity does not lie in the pedigree – Nozick adopts his rights from Locke,[171] but in their fallacious use. The two reasons we shall give for holding Nozick's use fallacious are circularity and conceptual error.

The circularity is rather convoluted and is all but concealed by Nozick's facility for switching between the rights of two societies. The rights that Nozick borrows from Locke are in fact those rights that Locke posits in the State of Nature.[172] Whether Locke was correct in postulating a State of Nature with the particular characteristics suggested, does not matter for the present.[173] Let us go along with Nozick and take Locke's set of Nature rights, including the all important property rights. It is the exercise of these property rights that presents the practical possibility of choosing a life plan and making one's life meaningful.[174] But where do these rights come from? Nozick takes them from Nature. And where are these rights exercised? Nozick wants them exercised within Society, fully and without anything but the minimal restraint.

The confusion between Nature rights and Society rights is assisted by the Lockean way in which Nozick establishes a just society: men bargaining[175]

---

[169] ASU, 171–2. Contrast property rights as the foundation for a liberal welfare outlook: Waldron (1988) above n6; Hillel Steiner, *An Essay on Rights* (Oxford, Blackwell, 1994).

[170] ASU, 153.

[171] ASU, 10, 174–82.

[172] *ibid.*

[173] For an abrasive criticism of Locke's concern with property rights, see Bentham's "Article on Utilitarianism" in *Deontology* at 314–5.

[174] ASU, 49–50, 171–2.

[175] Even if only hypothetically – ASU, 293–4.

with the rights that Nature has bestowed to set up a social arrangement for their benefit. But even if the founders of the Society could have pointed to the property they owned within the new Society to be precisely the same as that they had enjoyed in Nature,[176] as soon as we move along several generations of citizens we find people owning property in accordance with the institutional structure of that Society and it is evident that the property rights can only be Society rights. These people never owned anything in the State of Nature, which is now only a dim historical recollection or myth. And there are now other people who do not own property at all: second children who have failed to inherit under the custom of primogeniture that prevails in the Society, those families whose lands had to be sold to pay off their debts when the harvest failed. . . In fact, the majority of the citizens of the Society are now without property and work as bondsmen or slaves for the propertied classes.

The argument that Nozick used to restrict the state to the enforcement of property rights on the basis that this is what ensured the distinctness of individuals in permitting them the practical possibility of choosing a life plan and making their lives meaningful can now be stood on its head. We have a large number of citizens in our Society for whom the necessary inferences from Nozick's premises about the distinctness of individuals and the meaning of life require a redistribution of property rights.[177]

Nozick avoids this conclusion by analysing the role of property rights in Society on the basis of how property rights were enjoyed in Nature.[178] The circularity of his argument can now be exposed: the institutional structures of society determine the extent of property rights – property rights determine the extent of the institutional structures of society. The circularity is concealed by Nozick's deployment of Nature property rights in the second statement, as standing outside of Society and thus breaking the circle. But the truth of the matter is that Nature stands so far removed from Society as to have no bearing upon it whatsoever.[179]

---

[176] This, of course, is insufficient to make the property *rights* the same: any more than the property rights in a book I am reading on an airline flight are the same in the jurisdiction I land in as they were in the jurisdiction I departed from.

[177] Even in their most abstract expression, ASU, 30–3, Nozick's premises would require this about-turn. Nozick argues that the permitted side-constraints on people's behaviour are an expression of a Kantian concern not to violate people by using them as means, and taking this categorical imperative Nozick uses it against any argument to improve the overall social good, which would amount to using people as means to that end. However, the unpropertied class in the condition that Society has reached have no possibility of a meaningful life and can only serve (as slaves or bondsmen) as the means to the ends determined by the propertied class.

[178] Similarly, the explicit rejection of welfare redistribution is made by Nozick at the point of considering the needs of members of the fledgling Society in relation to their Nature property rights (which all possess – such is the bounty of Nature), but at the same time he considers a redistributive function of protection *would* be justified – ASU, 26–8.

[179] Nozick's embrace of a Lockean romantic vision of Nature as "a state of perfect freedom to order their actions and dispose of their possessions and persons as they think fit. . ." (Locke's *Second Treatise of Government*, s 4 – in John Locke, *Two Treatises of Government*, edited by

The final reason we shall consider here for Nozick's failure is a conceptual error, which is profound in its consequences because it permits him both the means and the end of his objective: a right that asserts the distinctness of individuals without any reciprocal obligation to those from whom their distinctness emerges. Such a right is needed by Nozick in his deployment of Nature rights as providing a status for the individual outside Society in order to justify limiting Society's grip upon the individual, and also to express the position of the individual once recognised within Society as bearing no responsibility for the other members of it.

The right used by Nozick is, in Hohfeldian terms, a liberty,[180] or transferred to the terms of political theory, a negative liberty. It is asserted by the individual against Society to limit Society's restraints upon him, and then used within Society with no tie of reciprocity towards the other members of Society. This is the key concept of libertarianism, that liberty can consist purely in the absence of restraint and hence require no positive commitment to provide resources to enable the enjoyment of liberty – the positive liberty that welfare liberalism by contrast would require. Spector has recently advanced an intricate argument to support this libertarian position, which if successful would provide a moral justification for Nozick's enterprise. Despite its greater sophistication, Spector's argument reproduces the same basic conceptual error that lurks in Nozick's more brutal assertions.

We can flush the error out by considering it first in Hohfeldian terms, and then applying our findings to the grander scale of the concept of liberty within political theory. Liberties which we possess, say over our property, are constituted by the correlative duties in others.[181] And once we recognise these correlative duties as determining our liberty, we can only locate it *within* a society that imposes duties on others. And if we look to others to comply with those duties which ensure our liberty, there can be no objection in principle to our submitting to duties which ensure the liberties of others.

Even in Nature, the only liberty which might avoid this correlation would be a liberty over property which was so plentiful in the bounty of Nature that there was never any dispute as to who could enjoy it, and never any conflict over who was to possess which part of it.[182] However, it is difficult to imag-

---

Peter Laslett (Cambridge, Cambridge University Press, 1988) – quoted by Nozick, ASU, 10) perhaps colours his analysis with the assumptions that everyone has possessions to dispose of, and that Nature has the resources to sustain the pursuit of an unlimited number of life plans. This latter assumption seems to hold in the Utopia stage of his book – at 324.

[180] In that it permits the owner to do something over his property. Nozick's own reference to Hohfeld (ASU, 175) is rather muddled: he applies it to the liberty of using an unowned object, prior to it becoming owned through acquisition – but if the using of it is the process of acquisition, such a liberty would never arise, and we would do better to speak of a Hohfeldian power here.

[181] See ch II. Strictly speaking the liberty is constituted by the circle of protective claim rights and their respective correlative duties, which combine to prevent interference with that conduct over which the liberty is exercised.

[182] Locke places a proviso on his principle of acquisition of property in the State of Nature, that there should be "enough and as good left in common for others" (above n179, s27) –

ine this, even in the State of Nature, ever extending beyond the liberty to breathe the air. And certainly Nozick did not envisage this for his Nature property rights, for the mutual protective associations were called for in order to protect them.[183]

Nozick avoids the implications of this dependency of a liberty on correlative duties by characterising his rights as "side constraints" on other people's actions,[184] as though in some way the right (liberty) precedes and is the reason for the duties in others not to interfere with the right holder's position, rather than being constituted by them. This elevates the right to a "basic normative principle", in the sense we have considered and rejected above,[185] with a normative force independent of the correlative duties, so that it appears legitimate to require the right to be respected without considering any reciprocal ties that might flow from those duties.

The illusion is assisted by Nozick borrowing his rights from Nature, and giving them a semblance of priority in their presocial natural form. But wherever the rights are located they require the correlative duties by which they are constituted, so that even the liberty in its natural form (unless the liberty to breathe the air) would coexist with these duties in Nature. And whatever is the basis for the right (liberty) is necessarily the basis for the duties by which it is constituted, rather than the right itself being regarded as the basis for imposing the duties.

Nor can it be said the the presocial Nature right (together with its correlative duties) is the basis for the Society right, since this is only to repeat the error identified above[186] of treating a moral right as the basis for a legal right, rather than recognising that the basis for the moral right may be (in part) the basis for the legal right.

However the property owner's liberty is regarded (whether in Nature, or in Society – or, even, in Society derived from Nature), it cannot be treated, as Nozick treats it, as an independent justification for imposing duties, or "constraints", upon others. On the contrary, the liberty is dependent upon those correlative duties themselves being justified. And whatever is the basis for justifying the imposition of duties on others in order to secure my liberty, might then be regarded as the basis for imposing duties on me in order to secure their liberties. However this argument works out, I cannot rely on the liberty constituted by the imposition of duties on others, as itself the reason for my having no duty whose imposition would go to constituting the liberty of others.

---

considered by Nozick (ASU, 174–82) but not regarded by him as particularly significant (at 182). For criticism of Nozick on Locke, see Waldron (1988) above n6 at 280–3; Wolff above n161 at 27, 102ff.

[183] ASU, ch 2.
[184] ASU, 29.
[185] ch VIII:2(4).
[186] *ibid*.

This rather dense argument has a number of clear implications. In general, it indicates a significance for duties that has been denied them by an assumption of the priority of rights.[187] There are two further implications on the political plane. The first sounds like radical rhetoric: one cannot rely on the holding of property as itself a reason for withstanding the redistribution of property. More rigorously, that is to say that the basis for one person holding property may be the basis for denying the holding of property to another; but, the mere fact that the one person holds property is not in itself any reason at all for denying the holding of property to another; and moreover, it may be possible to see in the basis for imposing duties on others in order to allow the one person to hold property, that there might also be a basis for imposing duties on that person in order to allow others to hold property; and even, in failing to find a satisfactory basis for imposing duties on others in order to allow the one person to hold property, there might rather be a basis for imposing duties on that person in order to allow others to hold property. In short, the basis for property rights must be vindicated before those property rights can be asserted as the basis for any position of the right holder in relation to others.[188] If this point is cast as rhetoric, then it answers Nozick's rhetoric that the taxation of the propertied classes amounts to forced labour.

The other implication is directed towards political theory, in that the recognition of the correlative duties as constituting the liberty amounts to upsetting an independent notion of negative liberty. The negative liberty (freedom from constraint by others so as to be able to enjoy property) is now seen to be

---

[187] Joseph Raz has stressed the significance of duties in linking the importance of duties to the realization of individual well being and the interdependence of individuals in the moral context. (See EPD, ch 1, "Duties of Well-Being"; and, "Liberating Duties" (1989) 8 Law and Philosophy 3.)
    Raz does not pursue the present concern with viewing those duties in relation to their correlative rights, though it is compatible with his general position on rights: "'X has a right' if. . . an aspect of X's well-being (his interest) is a sufficient reason for holding some other person(s) to be under a duty." (MofF, 166 – similarly, "Legal Rights" (1984) 4 *Oxford Journal of Legal Studies* 1). However, the approach taken within this chapter makes a further clarification on Raz's approach. The treating of X's interest as the sufficient reason for placing the other under a duty could easily slip into the position of regarding X's right, which relates directly to his interest, as the reason for the duty on the other. However, this is unacceptable since the right cannot exist without the correlative duty/ies. Accordingly, a clearer statement for the definition of X's right would be ". . .if there is a sufficient reason for protecting X's well-being by holding some other person(s) to be under a duty." The "sufficient reason" can be equated with the "basis" for the right/duty(ies), in the sense discussed above (VIII:2(4)), and this reformulation of the definition avoids the suggestion that a right itself can be regarded as the basis for another normative position, which emerges in Raz's own discussion of rights – eg, "the fact that rights are sufficient to ground duties. . ." (MofF, 183). This aspect of Raz's position on rights has been succinctly criticised by Michael Perry, "Taking Neither Rights-Talk nor the 'Critique of Rights' Too Seriously" (1984) 62 *Texas Law Review* 1405 at 1407–8 n8.

[188] This statement should not be misread as denying the trivial truth that the right holder does have a position in relation to others. The point is that the holding of the present right is not a *basis* for the right holder's present position – so that it cannot be legitimately changed; nor the *basis* for any other position.

constituted by the positive liberty (provision of opportunities by constraint of others so as to be able to enjoy property).[189]

More fully, we can say that if the idea of negative liberty is to be realised at all, it requires two things: (i) the provision of resources (of which property is a paradigm), over which to exercise the liberty; and (ii) the provision of opportunities for enjoying the exercise of that liberty over those resources through the restraint of others interfering with those opportunities.[190] Neither is sufficient. For if we provide resources to A but take no steps to prevent others from interfering with A's enjoyment of those resources, then A has no liberty to enjoy his property. But equally, if we prohibit interference by others with A's behaviour in certain ways, so as to secure the opportunity of enjoying his property, but he has no property to enjoy, then A still has no liberty to enjoy his property in any meaningful sense. We might as well say that the law provides the homeless beggar with a perfect liberty to enjoy his swimming pool, since the law of trespass prevents any other person from interfering with his enjoyment of it.[191]

However, by now we have left an exclusive conception of negative liberty and embraced a conception of positive liberty. What our analysis leads us to

[189] For general discussion of negative and positive liberty, see David Miller (ed.), *Liberty* (Oxford, OUP, 1991). As well as Berlin's essay, this anthology includes two essays which are followed in some respects by the position developed here: Gerald MacCallum, "Negative and Positive Freedom" (1967) 76 *Philosophical Review* 312; Charles Taylor, "What's Wrong with Negative Liberty" in Alan Ryan (ed.), *The Idea of Freedom* (Oxford, OUP, 1975) 175. A particularly clear illustration of the congruence of Hohfeldian analysis and the conceptions of negative and positive liberty is provided by Tom Campbell, "Rationales for Freedom of Communication" in Tom Campbell and Wojciech Sadurski (eds.), *Freedom of Communication* (Aldershot, Dartmouth, 1994) at 21.

[190] Isaiah Berlin in his "Introduction" to *Four Essays on Liberty* (Oxford, OUP, 1969), at xxxviii–xl, clarifies his approach to negative liberty in a way that recognises these two elements. Berlin points out that if negative liberty consisted solely in an absence of frustration of (or, interference with – at 123) what a man is trying to do, then it could be attained, as by the Stoic, in not trying to do anything which another would interfere with. *A fortiori* it could be attained by not having the opportunity of doing anything in the first place. Berlin accordingly recognises that the idea of negative liberty also "ultimately depends. . . on how many doors are open, how open they are. . ." (at xxxix). The point in fact lies latent in Berlin's original formulation: "I am normally said to be free to the degree that no man or body of men interferes with my activity." (at 122). There is here not only a requirement of the absence of interference, but also of the opportunity for activity.
Nevertheless, subsequently in his Introduction (liii–lv) Berlin overrides the point in his insistence that the conditions for the exercise of liberty (including material provisions) are distinct from liberty itself: "If a man is too poor or too ignorant or too feeble to make use of his legal rights, the liberty that these rights confer on him is nothing to him, but it is not thereby annihilated." (at liii). This is clearly motivated by Berlin's anxiety that recognising the need for the provision of resources can become a license for paternalistic tyranny (at lv). However, Berlin confuses two distinct cases. Ignorance of one's rights may effectively prevent their exercise, but does not, it is true, annihilate them – they are there to be exercised, even for breaches that occurred during the period of ignorance. On the other hand, having no property does not merely prevent one from exercising property rights: one simply never has them. For further criticism of Berlin's position, see Jeremy Waldron, *Liberal Rights* (Cambridge, Cambridge University Press, 1993) ch 1.

[191] Berlin himself (above n190 at lv) speaks of "the freedom of the pauper who has a legal right to purchase luxuries" as a "fraud". But a fraudulent liberty is no liberty.

conclude is that the two cannot be separated.[192] Negative liberty in expressing A's freedom from interference is stating precisely what is required to constitute A's positive liberty to enjoy that over which he is subject to no
interference from others. And both assume that A does in fact have the
resources to enjoy.

The mistake of the libertarian is to take the existence of A's resources for
granted, and to focus instead on the negative aspect of A's liberty in terms of
the constraints on others to prevent their interfering with A's opportunities to
enjoy those resources.[193] This is made easier by considering a wholly abstract
notion of interference.[194] However, when a libertarian perspective is employed
in an attempt to provide a justification for rights, then some acknowledgment
must be made of the resources granted to A since it is these resources that are
the subject matter of the rights that it is sought to justify.

Nozick does this by referring to property rights. But we have seen that by
thus bringing the positive aspect of A's liberty into focus, it can be revealed
that there is not a basis for justifying those rights in their mere existence as
rights. Spector's more sophisticated argument for underpinning a libertarian
position,[195] recognises the importance of the positive aspect of liberty, but
keeps it firmly in the abstract. At the heart of his "deontological theory of
practical rationality" is the proposition that "each person's positive freedom
has distinct and unique worth".[196] But this is just an abstract equivalent of
Nozick's proposition that each person's property rights are to be valued.
Nozick's proposition is seen in a different light once we recognise that not
everyone may have these property rights. Similarly, if we provide a fuller version of Spector's proposition – "the positive freedom that each person may *or
may not have* has distinct and unique worth" – its absurdity becomes trans-
parent.[197]

---

[192] Berlin's attempt to do so is significantly treated as turning not on a logical distinction but
a historical one (*ibid*. 131ff): the positive aspect of liberty which deals with providing a man with
mastery over his own interests has historically easily been corrupted into providing a man with
what others have determined to be in his own interests.

[193] There is another historical feature to the purported distinction in that the physical provision of resources may be historically prior to the provision of all the opportunities to enjoy them.
But in that case the liberty enjoyed by A develops, and at any historical moment it is still composed of the negative and positive aspects – there is simply a danger of taking the positive aspect
for granted due to a confusion of the positive opportunity to enjoy the resources with the physical provision of the resources. But if the resources were at one point physically provided but
denied a full negative protection from the interference by others, then to that extent there was
lacking the positive opportunity to enjoy those resources.

[194] Hence the libertarians' concern over what exactly amounts to an interference with A – see
the discussion in Spector, above n160 at 25ff.

[195] *ibid*.

[196] *ibid*. 180.

[197] Spector does not consider the need to ensure that everyone possesses a substantive positive
liberty that is to be valued, but resorts to an individualistic conception of positive liberty (158–9)
to justify ignoring the point. However, permitting each individual to satisfy his own conception
of positive liberty does not preclude the need to ensure that each individual does possess those
resources which his particular conception of positive liberty requires. A value free positive liberty
might be one thing, an empty positive liberty is certainly quite another.

Our examination of Nozick's theory of rights may conclude with the finding that he fails to produce a moral theory, not simply because his attempt to provide a justification fails but also because he fails to provide a moral approach. The approach Nozick provides to enforcing property rights may be practical, to the extent that property rights are compossible,[198] but it is not *moral*.[199]

5 GENERAL COMMENTS

Leaving the conventional labels of rights theorist and utilitarian to one side, much can be said about what these four theorists share in common, and where they do differ it is not apparent that the difference is one that the conventional labelling can be based upon.

We can take what we have called the first aspect of morality, M1, which requires respect for the other, and call this *the moral form*. The requirement to respect others is the aspect of morality which addresses the moral agent, and the other two aspects we have identified effectively indicate what is involved for the moral agent (M2) and what is the outcome (M3) when he adheres to M1, so there is no harm in taking M1 as in a sense representative of morality. But it is a moral *form* only, since it is possible to argue for any number of contents to fill out the idea of what is involved in respecting another in the mutual and reciprocal manner that morality requires.

Each of our four theorists employs the moral form. Dworkin and Nozick, we have seen, start with it as self-evident or assumed. Bentham and Rawls do not start with the moral form but they quickly move towards it: Bentham by means of asserting the individualistic dictum, Rawls by means of the device of the veil of ignorance. The process by which each of these two obtains the moral form may have an initial appearance of justification but on closer examination, we have seen that this attempted justification fails. So we can say that in fact none of the four provides any justification for adopting the moral form. In effect, all four assume it.

But if the moral form is assumed, we have no basis for proceeding to an outcome of substantial morality, since we lack any particular justification for having the form of morality which might also inform us as to its content. That is to say that because we do not know why to respect each other (form), we

---

[198] See Hillel Steiner, "The Structure of a Set of Compossible Rights" (1977) 74 *Journal of Philosophy* 767. This does not follow merely because the set of property rights successfully identifies the ownership of each existing bit of property. There may still be conflicts over what different owners do with their different bits of property, as, for example, the law of nuisance demonstrates. For problems in expressing the law of nuisance in terms of rights, see N.E. Simmonds, "Epstein's Theory of Strict Tort Liability" (1992) *Cambridge Law Journal* 113 at 131ff.

[199] Hart comes close to the suggestion that Nozick is essentially dealing in *legal* rights: EJP, 205.

cannot know the answer to the fundamental moral question, how to respect each other (content).[200]

In effect, what each of the four theorists does in the absence of a justification for morality which could be followed through into a particular practical moral approach is to generate a further abstraction from the moral form in order to provide a general guide as to moral conduct. And if we overlook one or two differences in presentation, and allow ourselves to assume that other desiderata can be expressed in a lowest common denominator of pleasure,[201] we can express the four general guides in the following way:

(1) Maximisation of everyone's pleasure. (Bentham)
(2) Maximisation of everyone's pleasure so long as[202] everyone gets an equal chance. (Dworkin)
(3) Maximisation of everyone's pleasure so long as the pleasure of the worst off is maximised. (Rawls)
(4) Leaving everyone to maximise his own pleasure. (Nozick)

And if we insist on calling the first guide utilitarian,[203] there really seems no good reason why we cannot call the others reform utilitarian, revisionist utilitarian, and even anarchic utilitarian. For the serious point to be made is that all four of them in fact fail to provide a practical moral approach, which is capable of sustaining the moral form in providing respect to the other in all cases – in whatever terms that respect is expressed in each of the theories.

There is another common feature to these four theories. It can be said that all of them in failing to provide the justification for a practical moral approach resort to the established morality of a society in order to avoid their theoretical shortcomings. With some it is more open. Dworkin, through his use of "integrity", quite flagrantly adopts the established morality of a society as a

---

[200] I am not putting this forward as a necessary relationship between form and content (to know why a box has four sides and a base does not tell you what exactly to put in it). The use of form and content is little more than metaphorical. The point might as easily have been made by talking about the concept of morality with a contestable value element (see ch I:3(4)) of respect, but the tendency in practice is for theorists to discuss morality by positing the moral form, which has the great attraction of being assimilable to whatever moral content(s) might be favoured by the theorist's audience.

[201] If this is not the case, then Rawls would have to want to argue that maximum liberty and social and economic welfare is not pleasurable, or at least not the means of obtaining the most pleasure that we could be aiming for, and Nozick similarly with his meaningful life plan. In any case, the precise desideratum is of secondary importance. Substitute, if thought necessary, a more neutral term such as "interest" – as Bentham himself allows in *The Constitutional Code*, in Bowring (ed.) above n2, vol IX at 6. The fundamental point is how respect for the other is secured in relation to whatever desideratum is selected. The point is not affected by the particular desideratum chosen, as can be seen from our substitution of different desiderata in the seven propositions first applied to Bentham's happiness – above, sections 1, 3, & 4.

[202] It is not evident that this does anything more than make explicit what is considered to be implicit in Bentham's formulation – see above, section 1.

[203] We should recall that for Bentham utility was the promotion of happiness – *A Fragment on Government*, ch I.ILVIII n[*l*], in Bowring (ed.) above n2, vol I at 271–2; PML, ch I.II; "Article on Utilitarianism" para 27, *Deontology*, 299.

last resort to found his rights. Rawls, it seems, acknowledges in the end the need to ground his rights in a society that has adopted liberal values – to which we might add, and also possesses some rather peculiar socio-economic traits. Nozick was relying on an established set of property rights to found his meaningful life plans. And even Bentham, it has been suggested, in smuggling in his individualistic dictum, was actually relying on a society that had at least to a certain extent embraced the common law tradition for individual rights. So equally, if you want to label one of them a rights theorist, why not allow that all of them can be so called, in weaving into their theories the rights that express the particular outlook of some society (actual or imagined), that can then be accommodated within the abstract generosity of the moral form.

The conclusion we have reached with regard to all four theorists is that they have failed to provide a justification for a practical moral approach, and further, that they have failed to work out in practice a moral approach that retains respect for each individual. I have suggested that the common features of their reactions to these problems do more to group them together than to distinguish them on the basis of the conventional rights-utilitarianism divide.

6 THE WIDER DEBATE

It was noted above that Bentham cannot fairly be called upon as a representative of modern utilitarianism, and it would be wholly inappropriate not to consider the advances and modifications that have developed within utilitarianism since Bentham. Also, there has recently been a spate of utilitarian theorists who have attempted to capture the territory of the rights theorists by demonstrating that utilitarianism can itself provide the basis for rights as basic normative principles. In considering these further developments I shall adopt the strategy of using the results obtained from our examination of Bentham in order to test whether the development has made any significant progress.

There have essentially been two developments within utilitarianism itself.[204] The one has been to modify the maximand: pleasure has been replaced by choice. But we saw when we applied the results of our examination of Bentham to Rawls and Nozick that a substitution for Bentham's maximand did not affect the significance of the results for moral theory. So although this modification may alter the appeal of utilitarianism, it does not alter the inability of utilitarianism to justify a practical moral approach.

The second major development runs into the claim to be able to provide a basis for rights, and does merit more detailed consideration. This is the devel-

---

[204] See works cited at n12 above. Although these developments are usually represented as modifications to the utilitarianism of Bentham, we have noted that Bentham was himself open to modifying the description of the maximand (see n201 above), and further he displays at times in his reasoning a form of indirect or rule utilitarianism, such as when considering slavery – *Principles of the Civil Code*, Part III ch II, in Bowring (ed.) above n2, vol I at 344–5.

opment from act utilitarianism to rule utilitarianism, whereby the calculation of utility (in terms of happiness, choice, or whatever) is not done on the occasion of each separate act but in order to provide rules, by adhering to which the greatest utility is to be secured overall. Once utilitarianism can be used to establish a rule, and then a system of rules, it is a short step to locating within such a system those rights which appear to secure the respect for individuals that the crude act utilitarianism was incapable of securing. The view that this is possible in one way or another has been put forward by a number of authors,[205] and doubted by a similar number.[206] I do not want to become involved here with all the points that this suggestion raises, but rather to concentrate on how this suggestion might address the problems we have noted that Bentham faced in attempting to establish a utilitarian moral theory.

One point to reconfirm in the case of this more sophisticated utilitarianism which offers a second systemic level of moral reasoning to complement the first level of reasoning that is concerned solely with individual acts, is that the mere demonstration that the outworking of the second level system happens to coincide with positions that intuitively or otherwise we feel ought to be the subject of rights that have the force of basic normative principles, does not turn these rights into basic normative principles. For the rights that are produced in this way are merely *expressing* the positions of this system, without having at all influenced how these positions are reached.[207]

The obvious question to pose is how such second level utilitarian theories reach these positions, and whether it is possible to see the criteria for a successful moral theory met. The general point to be made is that insofar as each of these theories attempts to justify the securing of these rights positions by reference to the maximand of first level utilitarian reasoning it must inevitably fail for precisely the same reasons that Bentham was found to fail. For the qualification of the propositions that we have considered above, not only by any variation in maximand, but also by the addition of a rule formula, does not affect the basic flaw in reasoning that we have revealed. Add, for example, the rule formula, "Following the rules that produce the most . . ." to the commencement of proposition 1, and we again can only reach a similarly modified proposition 7 – not the required modified proposition 6, which would provide the basis for a second level utilitarian system.

On the other hand if the securing of these rights positions is justified by reference to a non-utilitarian moral principle of promoting respect for others, and the system is then adopted by utilitarianism on the understanding that such a system of rights will best promote the chosen maximand, then it is to the proposed moral principle that we must look in order to determine whether a sound moral theory has been advanced. The role of utilitarianism is

---

[205] See above n7.
[206] See above n8.
[207] See ch VIII:2(4).

rendered nugatory,[208] and amounts to nothing more than the trivial assertion that the greatest happiness (or whatever desideratum) will be secured by what is morally right.

It is possible for utilitarians to flit from maximand to moral principle and back to maximand in this way, apparently securing moral rights without ever endorsing any moral principle. It is illusory. The maximand cannot yield a moral principle, and the moral principle can at best only coincide with the maximand in a trivial manner. But the illusion can be strengthened by the facility of artificially upping the maximand, so as to endorse a particularly favoured moral principle, as Bentham himself recognised.[209]

As to the practicality of such an approach, the practical motivation to develop such a system varies amongst the authors of the systems. In some cases, it is based on psychology – we need such a system to psychologically motivate people who would otherwise fear that they might fall victim to a first level utilitarian excess, such as having one's kidneys forcibly removed to contribute to the greater welfare of two grateful recipients, who would otherwise die of kidney failure. In other cases, it is based on the uncertainty of getting the first level utilitarian calculation correct – how do we know that the maximand will in fact be increased from the two recipients' lives rather than from the continuation of the donor's life? And sometimes, an element of self-interest is acknowledged as possibly influencing the first level utilitarian calculation, which needs to be corrected by the standards enshrined in the second level system.

But if we recognise such failings at the first level, and if we also take into account that the modified proposition 1 which acts as the premise for the second level system is only capable of yielding a self-interested proposition 7, it is apparent that there is absolutely nothing in the second level to prevent the first level type of excesses reemerging in accordance with the interests of the architect or practitioners of the system. You can alter the psychological conditioning of the others (only the kidneys of a particular ethnic minority are taken whose life value is less than the recipients'[210]), or in some way avoid the psychological fear by manipulation of the information available (all the donors are stated to be the dead victims of car crashes). You can rationalise a build up of the maximand that is sufficiently clear to justify treating others in the way you see fit (it is obvious that the utility available from the continuation of the life of an elderly alcoholic tramp is less than that available from the lives of two young recipients in socioeconomic class A). You can cast

---

[208] There is no utilitarian *method* – see ch VIII:2(5)(1).

[209] eg, in general terms, *Deontology* 192ff; and for the particular illustration of tipping the maximand against the slave trade, see *ibid.* 334–5.

[210] This can minimise the dread among the majority population if properly handled in two ways: first, they have no fear for themselves since they are not members of the minority group; secondly, their revulsion at what is going on can be displaced by the understanding that the promotion of two more valuable life forms is a morally justified price to pay for the extinction of one lesser form.

doubt upon the irrational self-interest of others, whilst maintaining the objective rationality of your favoured option (it is irrational and selfish for the tramp to object and an admirable act on the part of the two recipients in undergoing major surgery which will contribute greatly to the general welfare of society).

We may accordingly conclude that also on the criterion of practicality such second level utilitarian reasoning fails, since it cannot secure in practice the *moral* requirement of respecting others. In essence, this is for the same reason as operated on the first level utilitarian reasoning. For even if we take a step up to the second level the same maximand is operating – no matter how refined its operation.[211] Furthermore, there is nothing in these approaches to suggest we should regard rights as basic normative principles that can in some way determine the positions that are reached. We have again only succeedeed in establishing rights that express positions otherwise determined. The moral form may again be subscribed to[212] but it is still not yielding a substantive morality.

7 CONCLUSIONS

(1) Utilitarianism

Our conclusion that the deficiencies of Bentham's utilitarianism as a moral theory have not been overcome by subsequent modifications to the utilitarian approach can be seen as demonstrating a flaw that runs to the base of utilitarianism, in its adoption of the interests of the individual as its starting point. However those interests are characterised (as happiness, welfare, realization of choice, or whatever) in a variant of proposition **1**, it is impossible to reach the proposition necessary for a moral theory that is capable of displacing the interest of the individual in order to recognise the interests of others – which is an essential aspect of any moral approach (M2).

The second flaw common to utilitarian approaches arises out of the first. In an effort to encompass the interests of others, the interests are detached from the individual and placed within a maximising proposition (**6**). As well

---

[211] It has been pointed out that if we adopt the first level premise as the reason for stepping up to the second level, there is nothing to stop us stepping down when convenient to do so – see David Lyons, above n6; and also Richard Brandt, above n7, ch 11, who acknowledges the force of Lyons' argument as applied to Hare's type of second level utilitarianism, though not to his own. In some cases manipulating the second level might be regarded as doing just that, but the stronger point can be made that it is possible to operate this manipulation whilst maintaining the second level form of reasoning by qualifying our rules and procedures in the second level system in a sufficiently sophisticated or devious manner.

[212] It is noticeable that the motivations for these attempts at second level utilitarian reasoning seem to invariably involve justifying a position that is accepted as intuitively moral. The background social order in the case of these theorists may then be regarded as a society which shares their moral intuitions.

as being unjustified by the starting proposition, this has the effect of render-ing a practical moral approach impossible since it may lose the respect moral-ity requires to be paid to others (M1) in the maximising aggregation.

The second flaw may be recognised, and combatted by utilitarians in one of two ways. One way is to deny the flaw and allege that the respect moral-ity requires to be paid to others is in fact fulfilled in the maximising process by counting each person's interests. But this we have observed is to confuse counting each person's preference as to which interests are to be respected, with respecting each person's interests. The other way is to argue by means of a development of rule utilitarianism, or indirect utilitarianism, for a system of morality in which the rights of each individual are respected. It is argued that this remains a utilitarian approach because it realises the maximisation of interests required by proposition 6. But such a system, we have observed, is either only coincidentally connected with utilitarianism and makes the whole utilitarian enterprise a redundant assertion of a trivial moral truth; or, it is derived from the utilitarian maximand, in which case it remains open to the same moral abuses that were identified with the simpler form of utilitari-anism.

We conclude that utilitarianism is not a moral theory, and is incapable of providing a moral approach. Bentham's own real concerns with the interests of others are evident enough, but it is also clear that to respect those interests Bentham has to distort, or at least expand on, his utilitarian precepts, through which he was perhaps more concerned with the enfranchising of other people's interests rather than ensuring their respect.

(2) Rights

The common recourse to rights as a means of ensuring that the moral require-ment to respect others is satisfied has been noted from early criticisms of Bentham onwards. But for each of the three modern rights theorists that we have examined in detail we have concluded that there is also a failure to pro-vide a moral theory, or to undertake a practical moral approach. We have also observed that the hard distinction frequently drawn between a utilitarian and rights based approach is unmerited. Indeed it is possible to see a common source of the failings of the utilitarians and these rights theorists, in that each of the latter, in the same way as the utilitarians, make their starting point for a moral theory the interests of the individual rather than the need for the indi-vidual to respect the interests of the other.

The strength of this tendency is perhaps due to the obvious presence of rights which promote individual interests in any moral system. However, we have observed that these rights cannot be regarded as themselves constituting basic normative principles, but rather as merely expressing such principles as the system adheres to. The error of treating the particular expression of the principle as itself the principle is aggravated when the expression selected is incomplete, as with a right which only expresses the position of one party to a relationship with other parties whose interests are also covered by the moral principle. And we have observed that redressing this error reinstates duties as enjoying an equivalent significance with rights.

If this is considered as reducing the importance of rights, to those rights which can be recognised as coexisting with the duties they involve, this is perhaps a step towards denying the rhetoric of rights but affirming the substance of those rights that remain. And in the moral arena at least, it is possible to see this as ultimately leading to the recognition of the substantial rights of others in a far more extensive manner.

(3) The Moral Conundrum

What can we say about morality itself from our examination of these theories? Perhaps it is possible to represent the failure of these theories in terms of a conundrum.

The moral conundrum is this. How can morality at one and the same time require self-denial (M2) and profess to be offering self-fulfilment (M3)? An attempt may be made to resolve the conundrum by arguing that the self denied in M2 differs from the self fulfilled in M3, in terms of irrational/rational, uneducated/educated, unenlightened/enlightened, etc.[213] But any such attempt faces two insoluble problems.

The one problem has already been mentioned. It is not possible for a person in the enlightened position to justify a moral requirement to an unenlightened person through a justification that depends upon the agent finding a particular quality in the conduct prescribed. It simply will not work: tell your unenlightened agent to seek happiness, say, and he will falsely attribute happiness to the conduct that his unenlightened reasoning falls upon.

The second problem has only been alluded to. If there is a basic uncertainty in the moral stature of man, which the suggested switch from a false self to a true self necessarily indicates, on what basis can we say that the moral agent considering his own conduct, or the framers of our moral system, are operating with sufficient moral stature to be trusted, rather than manipulating the result for their own ends? For in positing the two selves we are acknowledging the possibility of the "false" self operating out of a misguided self-interest which will trample over the legitimate interests of others. That this is a real problem is apparent not only from the conflicting assumptions made by the theorists we have examined about the appropriate lines to be drawn between legitimate self-interest and the denial of self-interest called for to promote the interests of others, but is apparent also from any brief consideration

[213] The sinister implications of this line of reasoning are presented by Berlin, above n190, at 132–4.

of the clashes of moral rhetoric found throughout history to the present time.[214]

The basic flaw revealed in both of these problems is the endeavour to found a morality upon man when the deeper premise of the moral enterprise is that man is not to be relied upon. Given this premise, if we construct a moral theory based on some attribute of man (the pursuit of happiness, welfare, etc) the moral enterprise is bound to fail for the very same reason as that for which it was required. If we value this unalloyed attribute, as the basis of our moral approach, what have we to say to the moral agent who insists on pursuing it relentlessly with no concern for the other? Abandon the premise, however, and the very reason for requiring the moral enterprise is gone. But if we have learned one thing from the conflict between rights and utilitarianism, it is that the moral enterprise, as we have identified it, has an extraordinarily strong hold.

The intractable difficulty of resolving the moral conundrum might be regarded as essentially a problem of rational humanism, for the problem as we have described it can be traced to the effort to locate *within man alone* not merely the basis for morality (the value of the self of agent and other), but also at one and the same time both the means for destroying it (the pursuit of self-interest by agent against the interest of the other), and the very same means of promoting it (the fulfilment of self through realisation of self-interest of agent and other). The conundrum remains intact.

The alternative should be briefly mentioned: the moral value of both agent and other as created by God, the means for destroying that value in the departure from God's creative purpose in the pursuit of self-interest, and the means of promoting it through the redemption of the fallen destructive self-interest in order to rediscover the compatible fulfilment of self within God's creative purpose.

This alternative is absent from the theories we have examined. Instead the search for moral theory is abandoned by the selection of a particular society (as best fits the moral intuitions and personal predispositions of the author) in which the various interests of its members are ordered in a practical scheme to which I adhere, and thus apparently subdue my own self-interest for the sake of the other members of that society – and also, more pointedly as a moral theorist, for the benefit of ceasing to question whether my own position and the positions of others within that society are fully moral.

And so the moral enterprise is located within a convenient filling out of the moral form, a convenience that does not ensure that moral respect is in practice accorded to all the members of that society. Or, the moral enterprise may seek a securer foundation than the wisdom of man, whose wisdom that very enterprise calls into question.

---

[214] For a number of illustrations in the recent UK legal context, see Griffith, above n145. For a variety of historical illustrations, see Spencer, above n60, particularly at 159–60, 430–1.

Part 5

Conclusion

X

Some General Reflections

Although it is possible to view the different studies on rights contained in this book as a series of self-contained enquiries on some of the many issues that can be found growing in or over the fertile field of rights theory, in this final chapter I want to suggest there are two basic issues that have been addressed by these studies, and briefly comment on how the contributions made to these issues have general implications for the use we make of rights.

The two basic issues addressed are: What is the nature of rights? and, How can we reason with rights? In the early studies the former issue is prominent. Part 2 of the book contains three studies aimed at developing Hohfeld's analytical insights on the nature of rights. Countering Hohfeld's neat array of four pairs of mutually-defining correlatives, I argue towards a fundamental analytical point with respect to the nature of rights: **A's right, even in the form of a liberty, cannot be regarded independently of the duty/ies on B that coexist with that right.**

This analytical point is introduced in chapter II by demonstrating that contrary to Hohfeld's assertion of a liberty enjoying an independent identity, it must be understood as being precisely constituted by the set of protecting claim-rights correlative to the duties in others not to interfere with the conduct over which the liberty is enjoyed.

This deals with the first of three potential challenges to the fundamental analytical point. In chapters III and IV two further challenges are met, arising from studies on two other concepts found in Hohfeld's scheme, whose analysis Hohfeld himself neglects:[1] power and claim.

The challenge from power does not come from Hohfeld's conception but from Hart's. Clearly if Hart were correct in identifying powers as the basic case of rights, and choice as the defining characteristic of power, the challenge to the fundamental analytical point would be irresistible. For even if the fundamental analytical point could be maintained in the cases of claim-rights and liberties, it would only operate at a secondary level, ignoring the primary level where the right holder's power holds sway. One of the main objectives of chapter III is to show that power cannot fulfil the role that Hart wants to give

---

[1] This is of course quite understandable, given Hohfeld's confidence in mutual definition of his concepts within the relationships of correlativity – see ch II:2.

it, and is (as was first suggested in chapter II) in fact an adjunct, although a very significant one, to rights in the form of claim-rights and liberties.[2]

The third possible challenge to the fundamental analytical point comes from claims, which are examined in chapter IV. For if the principal role of claims is to assert the value of the status or interests of the individual claimant, then this insight on the nature of a claim upsets the right-duty coexistence from within by making the dominant position the claim-right to which the duty answers. It would then be possible for A to assert his right logically prior to, and as a basis for, B's duty. The important finding in chapter IV in this respect is that not all claims can be identified with rights. What gives force to an individual's claim in the particular circumstances where it is equivalent to a right requiring a correlative obligation on B, is that it is a justified claim. Hence the mere assertion by the claimant is insufficient to amount to a right, and its *justification* as a right must regard not merely the respect that A is claiming but the wider cost of that respect on others, before constituting the claim as a recognised right coexisting with the necessary duty in B.

This provides a connection with the next set of studies in Part 3. The framework which is constructed in chapter V, and illustrated in chapter VI, looks more closely at the processes by which particular rights are justified. The forms of the rights studied here are not represented in Hohfeldian terminology, but in the vernacular language in which they are commonly expressed. The break with Hohfeldian conceptions here is significant, in underlining that their proper location is found in expressing the outcome (or a putative outcome) of litigation.[3] Hohfeld's conceptions can only represent the positions found at the level of dispute rights in the framework. The different notions of a right identified, their possible origins, and the relationships between them, link the instantiation of an individual's specific concrete right to wider considerations which can only be addressed by considering the different views on how conflicting interests can be resolved within society. This approach is wholly compatible with the fundamental analytical point, which denies the possibility of insulating an individual's concerns in the assertion of a right.

The main brunt of chapters V and VI, however, is to commence with treatment of the second basic issue. These chapters seek to investigate the particular ways in which reasoning with rights can become confused. Chapter VI provides practical illustrations of the use of the framework, and in chapter VII some conceptual parallels to these possible confusions are identified in the approach taken by Unger to rights.

---

[2] The power-based view of rights is also criticised in ch VII in considering Unger's view of rights.

[3] See ch II:8. Dworkin's failure to grasp the essential characteristics of Hohfeld's analysis (see ch II:2) leads him to erroneously portray Hohfeld's conceptions as participating in the processes at an abstract level through which competing versions of dispute rights can be formed, and to falsely depict D holding simultaneously a duty and its Hohfeldian negation, a liberty – *Taking Rights Seriously* (London, Duckworth, 1977) at 308. The error is, however, illuminating in drawing attention to the limitations of Hohfeld's analysis.

The two themes of the nature of rights and reasoning with rights, flow side by side in these chapters. For as we expound the different possible notions of a right, this necessarily has repercussions for what sort of statements purporting to be grounded on the recognition of rights are in fact intelligible. An overarching point may be introduced here, that in all cases a statement put forward as a valid inference to be drawn from the existence of a right cannot be maintained solely on the basis of the interests favoured by the right holder.[4] Contrary to Unger, the right holder does not shoot at will, but is given a gun whose range is limited to take into account the interests of others.

In Part 4 of the book, we move away from discussion of particular rights to the deployment of rights in general theory. In chapters VIII and IX we discover that rights theorists are using rights within general theory in much the same way as utilitarians make use of utility, to furnish a central part of their conception of society, specifically covering the moral aspect of society, without being able to justify doing so. The enterprise on both sides of the rights-utilitarianism debate collapses because of a failure to provide a foundation for the deployment of the moral form which would be capable of giving it a moral content.

More particularly this involves a failure to provide for the consideration of the other side of the rights relationship – at the concrete level, the position of the duty holder; at the more general theoretical level, the position of the other whose interests must be taken into account if the moral aspect of society is to be maintained.[5] The different devices employed by each of the four theorists examined, in their different ways derive a spurious conclusion from an individualistic premise.

This is dramatically so in the case of Nozick, who of the three rights theorists may be regarded as the most overtly individualistic. He is left asserting rights in one society with a concealed basis in an imaginary society in order to maintain the illusion of the individualistic origin of rights.[6] This illusion is seen to be common to other libertarian thinkers, who endeavour to assert on the level of general theory Hohfeld's flawed analytical position on privilege/liberty, in arguing for an independent conception of negative liberty.[7]

Within Part 4 the theme of reasoning with rights is developed further. The important finding here is that the solecistic expression of using rights as a basis for reasoning compacts and confuses an inferential process with a justificatory process and has to be replaced by a more accurate analysis: we may infer the existence of what necessarily exists alongside rights from the existence of rights, but only reason in a justificatory manner from the basis of rights. Since this basis is the basis not merely for the right but also for the

[4] See further at n8 below.
[5] See ch VIII:2(3).
[6] ch IX:4.
[7] *ibid.*

correlative duty, we reject again the suggestion that rights can be elevated to a prior status over duties, and maintain the overarching point that reasoning towards valid ethical conclusions depends on a consideration of the positions of each of the parties affected.[8]

All this suggests that when the heat of the debate over rights is at its strongest, it is easy to give exclusive focus to P's interests in the demand for their incorporation in a society that is presently ignoring them. But on a cooler analysis of the nature of rights the conflict is in fact between two different social conceptions of relations involving P and those whose own interests would be affected by the recognition of P's interests. Neither in the existing society that P attacks, nor in the visionary society that P commends, can P's obligations or rights be isolated from the rights or obligations of others.

In this way the fundamental analytical point can be regarded as something which has to be recognised at the level of general theory, concerning the nature of the relationship between rights and society. Rights express the resolution within society of situations of conflict between the interests of different members of society. If rights are asserted against established ways of resolving those conflicts, then the proclaimed rights equally express a resolution of conflicting interests, that necessarily draws us to take in the interests of both sides of the conflict in justifying a resolution in favour of the new rights.[9]

Given that the resolution of such conflicts of interests is common to all societies, this implication of the fundamental analytical point goes against those historical analyses of rights which portray them as emerging late in the development of western civilisation.[10] Rather it makes the case for recognising the

---

[8] The confusion between the inferential process and a justificatory process considered in ch VIII:2(4) is also found in a particularly strong form in Phillip Montague, "Two Concepts of Rights" (1980) 9 *Philosophy & Public Affairs* 372. Montague proceeds directly from establishing an inferential relationship between the existence of right and the existence of a duty, to asserting that the right is the justificatory basis for the duty – at 378. By contrast, an approach closer to the position maintained here is to be found in Robert Alexy, "Rights, Legal Reasoning and Rational Discourse" (1992) 5 *Ratio Juris* 143 – Alexy recognises the coexistence of rights and obligations (at 144), the distinction between rights and the basis for rights (at 145), and develops in his distinction between rights based on rules and rights based on principles something similar to the distinction between general concrete rights and abstract rights. The basic divergence is to be found in Alexy's view of the process of reasoning from abstract/principle rights (at 148–50) which is more formal and less open to conflicting conceptions of society than the view taken here in chs V and VI. Further support for the coexistence of rights and duties is to be found in the authors cited (though not accepted) by Montague at 376.

[9] There is nothing in this to suggest an "impartiality" or "fairness" in regarding the interests of both sides. The point is merely that the interests of both sides necessarily fall within the scope of the justification: the slave's interests in liberty can only be justified in justifying depriving the slave owner of property interests; the consumer's interests in protection from negligently manufactured goods can only be justified in justifying depriving the factory owner of interests in not being burdened by the expenses of quality control.

[10] Richard Tuck, *Natural Rights Theories* (Cambridge, Cambridge University Press, 1979); Otto Gierke, *Natural Law and the Theory of Society*, translated by Ernest Barker (Cambridge, Cambridge University Press, 1950).

existence of rights in all societies, even though possibly expressed in different ways.[11]

As to the significance of the modern preoccupation with rights, this would have to be understood in a rather different light: the use of rights to assert positions for the individual within a reformed society as against the positions enjoyed in established society, arose rather late in the day.[12] It is understandable that the reforming zeal which begot such rights, particularly given their characteristically abstract expression,[13] in the enthusiasm for proclaiming the interests that had previously been denied should create a blindspot to the interests that would now be subordinated. Rights are given a rhetorically elevated status and duties are forgotten, even though their coexistence is necessary for the rights that are being proclaimed.

It is possible to go further and suggest that what is revealed as a defective analysis of rights, also affects contemporary debates over the theoretical significance of rights, in which rights are commonly identified with an unbalanced individualistic approach to society, which must be rectified by a non-rights approach.[14] The better view would be that *any* approach may find expression in terms of rights, and we do not advance any debate by diverting attention from the issue of what right-duty relationships are appropriate, to a confused discussion over whether one side has, or should have, rights or not.[15]

---

[11] Cp ch IV:4. The case is forcefully made by Alan Gewirth, *Reason and Morality* (Chicago, IL, The University of Chicago Press, 1978) at 98–102; and Fred Miller, *Nature, Justice, and Rights in Aristotle's Politics* (Oxford, Clarendon Press, 1995) ch 4 – Miller provides at 93-108 a fascinating demonstration of how Hohfeld's conceptions can be found expressed in the Greek of Aristotle.

[12] The point that it is the emergence of rights as an instrument for challenging the established order that is characteristic of more modern Western societies is made by Eugene Kamenka, "The anatomy of an idea" in Eugene Kamenka and Alice Tay (eds.), *Human Rights* (London, Edward Arnold, 1978) at 6–9.

[13] See ch V n17.

[14] The obvious examples are the conflict between communitarian and liberal theories of society – for a discussion of the place of rights in this conflict, see Amy Gutman, "Communitarian Critics of Liberalism" (1985) 14 *Philosophy & Public Affairs* 308; and the criticism of a rights approach as being peculiar to certain dominant forms of Western liberal thinking, which can be countered by different cultural approaches – see Robert Cover, "Obligation: A Jewish Jurisprudence of the Social Order" (1987) 5 *Journal of Law and Religion* 65; Karl Klare, "Legal Theory and Democratic Reconstruction: Reflections on 1989" (1991) 25 *University of British Columbia Law Review* 69 (both excerpted in Henry Steiner and Philip Alston, *International Human Rights in Context* (Oxford, Clarendon Press, 1996) ch 4, which provides further discussion on this theme).

[15] So a communitarian approach can find expression in terms of rights, and the real issue is whether the rights in such a conception of society can be better argued for than the rights in a competing (liberal) conception of society. The debate cannot be conducted by alleging a blight on all rights and then pretending that rights are only to be found on the competing side of the argument. For an attempt to build a communitarian approach to rights, see Michael Freeden, "Human Rights and Welfare: A Communitarian View" (1990) 100 *Ethics* 489 – and for a broader discussion of the conflict between communitarianism and liberalism, see David Luban, "The Self: Metaphysical not Political" (1995) 1 *Legal Theory* 401. Similarly, alternatives to Western liberal culture may have in a number of respects an emphasis on social obligation that Western liberal culture ignores, but this will inevitably give rise to rights (although quite distinct ones) in the beneficiaries of such obligations – eg the greater duty on children to care for their parents in the

A full analysis of rights will inform our general legal, moral, or political theory. An impoverished analysis will distort our theory, and give credence to the sceptic's complaint that rights do not advance anything. Where rights do have value when fully analysed is to provide us with an understanding of the way in which the interests of individuals need to be justified as entitlements as against the interests of other individuals.

This may in turn spark calls for reform in alerting us to the unwarranted neglect of the interests of some members of society, and it will be possible to express our revolutionary conception of society in terms of rights – as much as the established order did so. But this leaves us with the question of where we get our understanding of the values that are capable of combining respect for different individuals within the community. If this book has advanced our understanding of rights at all, then it is clear that this is a question that a whole library of books on rights could not answer.

Gikuyu tribal culture in Kenya, discussed in Steiner and Alston *loc. cit.*, will coexist with the correlative rights in parents.

Bibliography of Works Cited

Robert Alexy, "Rights, Legal Reasoning and Rational Discourse" (1992) 5 *Ratio Juris* 143

James Allan, "Bills of Rights and Judicial Power – A Liberal Quandary" (1996) 16 *Oxford Journal of Legal Studies* 337

Aristotle, *Organon*, Loeb Classical Library edited and translated by Harold Cooke (London, William Heinemann, 1949)

—— *Metaphysica*, Loeb Classical Library edited and translated by Hugh Tredennick (London, William Heinemann, 1933)

John Atwell, "Are Kant's First Two Moral Principles Equivalent?" (1969) 7 *Journal of the History of Philosophy* 273

Randy Barnett, "Of Chickens and Eggs – The Compatibility of Moral Rights and Consequentialist Analyses" (1989) 12 *Harvard Journal of Law and Public Policy* 611

Brian Barry, "Good for Us, But Not for Them" – Review of John Rawls' *Political Liberalism, The Guardian*, 14 August 1993

—— "In Defense of Political Liberalism" (1994) 7 *Ratio Juris* 325

Hugh Beale and Anthony Dugdale, "Contracts between Businessmen" (1975) 2 *British Journal of Law and Society* 45

Jeremy Bentham, *The Constitutional Code* in John Bowring (ed.) (1838–43) vol IX

—— *A Fragment on Government* in John Bowring (ed.) (1838–43) vol I

—— *Principles of the Civil Code*, in John Bowring (ed.) (1838–43) vol I

—— *Memoirs* in John Bowring (ed.) (1838–43) vol X

—— *Of Laws in General* (ed. H.L.A. Hart) (London, Athlone Press, 1970)

—— *An Introduction to the Principles of Morals and Legislation*, 1781 (eds. Burns and Hart) (London, Athlone Press, 1977) – also (New York, NY, Prometheus Books, 1988)

—— *Deontology* in Amnon Goldworth (ed.) (1983)

—— "Article on Utilitarianism" unpublished text reproduced in Amnon Goldworth (ed.) (1983)

—— "Principles of Judicial Procedure" in John Bowring (ed.) (1838–43) vol II

—— "Dedacologia: Art and Science Division", Appendix A in *Deontology*

—— "Anarchical Fallacies" in John Bowring (ed.) (1838–43) vol II

—— "Essay on Representation", an English translation of the original French essay written in 1788, Appendix D in Mary Mack (1962)

Isaiah Berlin, *Four Essays on Liberty* (Oxford, OUP, 1969)

—— "Introduction" in Isaiah Berlin (1969)

Peter Birks (ed.), *Pressing Problems in the Law, Volume 1: Criminal Justice and Human Rights* (Oxford, Oxford University Press, 1995)

—— *Harrassment and Hubris: The Right to an Equality of Respect*, the Second John Maurice Kelly Memorial Lecture (Dublin, Faculty of Law, University College Dublin, 1996)

Brian Bix, "Conceptual Questions and Jurisprudence" (1995) 1 *Legal Theory* 465

Brian Bix, *Jurisprudence: Theory and Context* (London, Sweet & Maxwell, 1996)

Brand Blanshard, *Reason and Goodness* (London, George Allen and Unwin, 1961)

Robert Bork, "Neutral Principles and Some First Amendment Problems" (1971) 47 *Indiana Law Journal* 1

—— *The Tempting of America: The Political Seduction of the Law* (New York, NY, Macmillan, 1990)

John Bowring (ed.), *The Works of Jeremy Bentham*, 11 vols (Edinburgh, William Tait, 1838–43)

Richard Brandt, *Morality, Utilitarianism, and Rights* (Cambridge, Cambridge University Press, 1992)

C.D. Broad, *Five Types Of Ethical Theory* (London, Routledge & Kegan Paul, 1930)

W.J. Brown, "Re-Analysis of a Theory of Rights" (1925) 34 *Yale Law Journal* 765

W.W. Buckland, *A Text-Book of Roman Law* 3ed. revised by Peter Stein (Cambridge, Cambridge University Press, 1975)

Alan Bullock *et al* (eds.), *The Fontana Dictionary of Modern Thought*, 2ed. (London, William Collins, 1988)

Charlotte Bunch, "Women's Rights as Human Rights: Toward a Re-Vision of Human Rights" (1990) 12 *Human Rights Quarterly* 48

Tom Campbell and Wojciech Sadurski (eds.), *Freedom of Communication* (Aldershot, Dartmouth, 1994)

Tom Campbell, "Rationales for Freedom of Communication" in Tom Campbell and Wojciech Sadurski (eds.) (1994)

Joseph Chan, "Raz on Liberal Rights and Common Goods" (1995) 15 *Oxford Journal of Legal Studies* 15

Lynn Chancer, "Feminist Offensives: *Defending Pornography* and the Splitting of Sex from Sexism" (1996) 48 *Stanford Law Review* 739

Christine Chinkin, "Rape and Sexual Abuse of Women in International Law" (1994) 5 *European Journal of International Law* 326

—— "Women's Rights as Human Rights under International Law" in Conor Gearty and Adam Tomkins (eds.) (1996)

George Christie, "The Uneasy Place of Principle in Tort Law" in David Owen (ed.) (1995)

Marshall Cohen (ed.), *Ronald Dworkin and Contemporary Jurisprudence* (London, Duckworth, 1984)

Jules Coleman, "Book Review: *Taking Rights Seriously*" (1978) 66 *California Law Review* 885

—— *Markets, Morals and the Law* (Cambridge, Cambridge University Press, 1988)

—— "Tort Law and the Demands of Corrective Justice" (1992) 67 *Indiana Law Journal* 349

—— and Jody Kraus, "Rethinking the Theory of Legal Rights" (1986) 95 *Yale Law Journal* 1335

Walter Wheeler Cook (ed.), *Fundamental Legal Conceptions as Applied in Judicial Reasoning by Wesley Newcombe Hohfeld* (New Haven, CT, Yale University Press, 1919 – revised edition with new foreword 1964)

Arthur Corbin, "Foreword" to Walter Wheeler Cook (ed.) (1964)

Robert Cover, "Obligation: A Jewish Jurisprudence of the Social Order" (1987) 5 *Journal of Law and Religion* 65

David Crossley, "Utilitarianism, Rights and Equality" (1990) 2 *Utilitas* 40

Norman Daniels (ed.), *Reading Rawls* (Oxford, Blackwell, 1975)

—— "Introduction" in Norman Daniels (ed.) (1975)

Eric D'Arcy, *Human Acts* (Oxford, Clarendon Press, 1963)

David Daube, "Matthew v. 38f." (1944) 45 *Journal of Theological Studies* 177

Richard Delgado, "The Ethereal Scholar: Does Critical Legal Studies Have What Minorities Want?" (1987) 22 *Harvard Civil Rights – Civil Liberties Law Review* 301

R.W.M. Dias, *Jurisprudence*, 5ed. (London, Butterworths, 1985)

F.E. Dowrick, *Justice According to the English Common Lawyers* (London, Butterworths, 1961)

Ian Duncan Wallace, "Murphy Rejected: The Bryan v Maloney Landmark" (1995) 3 *Tort Law Review* 231

Ronald Dworkin, *Taking Rights Seriously* (London, Duckworth, 1977)

—— "What is Equality? Part 1: Equality of Welfare" (1981) 10 *Philosophy and Public Affairs* 185

—— "What is Equality? Part 2: Equality of Resources" (1981) 10 *Philosophy and Public Affairs* 283

—— "Comment on Narveson: In Defense of Equality" (1983) 1 *Social Philosophy and Policy* 24

—— "A Reply by Ronald Dworkin" in Marshall Cohen (ed.) (1984)

—— *A Matter of Principle* (Oxford, Clarendon Press, 1985)

—— *Law's Empire* (London, Collins, 1986)

—— "What is Equality? Part 3: The Place of Liberty" (1987) 73 *Iowa Law Review* 1

—— "What is Equality? Part 4: Political Equality" (1987) 22 *University of San Francisco Law Review* 1

—— "Foundations of Liberal Equality" in Grethe Peterson (ed.) (1990)

—— *Freedom's Law: The Moral Reading of the American Constitution* (Cambridge, MA, Harvard University Press, 1996)

John Eekelaar, "Families and Children: From Welfarism to Rights" in Christopher McCrudden and Gerald Chambers (eds.) (1994)

—— and John Bell (eds.), *Oxford Essays in Jurisprudence, Third Series* (Oxford, Clarendon Press, 1987)

Horst Eidenmüller, "Rights, Systems of Rights, and Unger's System of Rights" (1991) 10 *Law & Philosophy* 1 and 119

Richard Epstein, "The Utilitarian Foundations of Natural Law" (1989) 12 *Harvard Journal of Law and Public Policy* 713

—— "Subjective Utilitarianism" (1989) 12 *Harvard Journal of Law and Public Policy* 769

William Ewald, "Unger's Philosophy: A Critical Legal Study" and "Reply" (1988) 97 *Yale Law Journal* 665 and 773

Joel Feinberg, *Rights, Justice and the Bounds of Liberty* (Princeton, NJ, Princeton University Press, 1980)

—— "In Defence of Moral Rights" (1992) 12 *Oxford Journal of Legal Studies* 149

David Feldman, *Civil Liberties and Human Rights in England and Wales* (Oxford, Clarendon Press, 1993)

—— "Human Rights Treaties, Nation States, and Conflicting Moralities" (1995) 1 *Contemporary Issues in Law* 61

—— "Content-Neutrality" in Ian Loveland (ed.) (forthcoming)

John Finnis, "Some Professorial Fallacies About Rights" (1971–2) 4 *Adelaide Law Review* 377

John Finnis, *Natural Law and Natural Rights* (Oxford, Clarendon Press, 1980)

—— *Fundamentals of Ethics* (Oxford, Clarendon Press, 1983)

—— "Comment [on Positivism and the Foundations of Legal Authority]" in Ruth Gavison (ed.) (1987)

—— "On 'The Critical Legal Studies Movement'" in John Eekelaar and John Bell (eds.) (1987) – also in (1988) 30 *American Journal of Jurisprudence* 21

—— "The Truth in Legal Positivism" in Robert George (ed.) (1996)

Stanley Fish, "Still Wrong After All These Years" (1987) 6 *Law and Philosophy* 401

—— "Unger and Milton" [1988] *Duke Law Journal* 975

—— *Doing What Comes Naturally* (Oxford, Clarendon Press, 1989)

James Fishkin, "Utilitarianism Versus Human Rights" (1984) 1 *Social Philosophy and Policy* 103

P.J. Fitzgerald (ed.), *Salmond on Jurisprudence*, 12ed. (London, Sweet & Maxwell, 1966)

William Frankena, *Ethics* (Englewood Cliffs, NJ, Prentice-Hall, 1963)

Michael Freeden, "Human Rights and Welfare: A Communitarian View" (1990) 100 *Ethics* 489

—— *Rights* (Buckingham, Open University Press, 1991)

Samuel Freeman, "Utilitarianism, Deontology, and the Priority of Right" (1994) 23 *Philosophy and Public Affairs* 313

Peter French *et al* (eds.), *Studies in Ethical Theory* (Minnesota, MN, University of Minnesota Press, 1978)

R.G. Frey (ed.) *Utility and Rights* (Oxford, Blackwell, 1985)

—— "Act-Utilitarianism, Consequentialism, and Moral Rights" in R.G. Frey (ed.) (1985)

W.B. Gallie, "Essentially Contested Concepts" (1956) 56 *Proceedings of the Aristotelian Society* 167

D.J. Galligan, "Rights, Discretion and Procedures" in Charles Sampford and D.J. Galligan (eds.) (1986)

—— *Discretionary Powers* (Oxford, Clarendon Press, 1986)

Ruth Gavison (ed.), *Issues in Contemporary Legal Philosophy* (Oxford, Clarendon Press, 1987)

Conor Gearty and Adam Tomkins (eds.), *Understanding Human Rights* (London, Mansell, 1996)

Robert George (ed.), *The Autonomy of Law* (Oxford, Clarendon Press, 1996)

Alan Gewirth, *Reason and Morality* (Chicago, IL, The University of Chicago Press, 1978)

Allan Gibbard, "Utilitarianism and Human Rights" (1984) 1 *Social Philosophy and Policy* 92

Otto Gierke, *Natural Law and the Theory of Society*, translated by Ernest Barker (Cambridge, Cambridge University Press, 1950)

Jonathan Glover (ed.) *Utilitarianism and its Critics* (New York, NY, Macmillan, 1990)

—— "Persons, Justice, and Rights" in Jonathan Glover (ed.) (1990)

Amnon Goldworth (ed.), *Deontology* in the Collected Works of Jeremy Bentham (Oxford, Clarendon Press, 1983)

—— "Editorial Introduction" in Amnon Goldworth (ed.) (1983)

John Gray, "Political Power, Social Theory, and Essential Contestability" in David Miller and Larry Seidentop (eds.) (1983)

John Griffith, *The Politics of the Judiciary*, 4ed. (London, Fontana Press, 1991)

—— *Judicial Politics Since 1920: A Chronicle* (Oxford, Blackwell, 1993)

Stephen Guest, *Ronald Dworkin* (Edinburgh, Edinburgh University Press, 1992)

Amy Gutman, "Communitarian Critics of Liberalism" (1985) 14 *Philosophy & Public Affairs* 308

P.M.S. Hacker and Joseph Raz (eds.), *Law, Morality, and Society* (Oxford, Clarendon Press, 1977)

Andrew Halpin, "The Limitations of a Legal System" [1981] *Juridical Review* 29

—— "Intended Consequences and Unintentional Fallacies" (1987) 7 *Oxford Journal of Legal Studies* 104

—— "Good Intentions" (1987) 137 *New Law Journal* 696

R.M. Hare, *Moral Thinking: Its Levels, Method, and Point* (Oxford, Clarendon Press, 1981)

—— "Utility and Rights: Comment on David Lyon's Essay" (1981) *Nomos XXIV* 148

—— "Rights, Utility, and Universalization: Reply to J.L. Mackie" in R.G. Frey (ed.) (1985)

J.W. Harris, "Unger's Critique of Formalism in Legal Reasoning: Hero, Hercules, and Humdrum" (1989) 52 *Modern Law Review* 42

—— "The Privy Council and the Common Law" (1990) 106 *Law Quarterly Review* 574

—— "Murphy makes it Eight – Overruling comes to Negligence" (1991) 11 *Oxford Journal of Legal Studies* 416

Ross Harrison, *Bentham* (London, Routledge & Kegan Paul, 1983)

H.L.A. Hart, "Definition and Theory in Jurisprudence" (1954) 70 *Law Quarterly Review* 37

—— "Are There Any Natural Rights?" (1955) 64 *Philosophical Review* 175

—— *The Concept of Law* (Oxford, Clarendon Press, 1961) – 2ed. (Oxford, Clarendon Press, 1994), edited by Penelope A Bulloch and Joseph Raz

—— "Between Utility and Rights" (1979) 79 *Columbia Law Review* 828

—— "Utilitarianism and Natural Rights" (1979) 53 *Tulane Law Review* 663

—— *Essays on Bentham* (Oxford, Clarendon Press, 1982)

—— *"Legal Powers"* in H.L.A. Hart, (1982)

—— "Natural Rights: Bentham and John Stuart Mill" in H.L.A. Hart (1982)

—— *Essays in Jurisprudence and Philosophy* (Oxford, Clarendon Press, 1983)

Yasuo Hasebe, "Why the Japanese don't take rights seriously" unpublished seminar paper presented at Reading University, March 1990

Didi Herman, "The Good, the Bad, and the Smugly: Perspectives on the Canadian Charter of Rights and Freedoms" (1994) 14 *Oxford Journal of Legal Studies* 589

W.N. Hohfeld, *Fundamental Legal Conceptions* (New Haven, CT, Yale University Press, 1919)

Homer, *The Iliad*, translated by E.V. Rieu (Harmondsworth, Penguin, 1950)

Tony Honoré, "Groups, Laws, and Obedience" in A.W.B. Simpson (ed.) (1973)

—— *Making Law Bind* (Oxford, Clarendon Press, 1987)

David Howarth, *Textbook on Tort* (London, Butterworths, 1995)

Alan Hunt (ed.), *Reading Dworkin Critically* (Oxford, Berg, 1992)

Allan Hutchinson, "The Last Emperor?" in Alan Hunt (ed.) (1992)

—— and Patrick Monahan, "The Rights Stuff: Roberto Unger and Beyond" (1984) 62 *Texas Law Review* 1477

Catherine Itzin (ed.), *Pornography: Women, Violence and Civil Liberties* (Oxford, OUP, 1992)

Francis Jacobs, *The European Convention on Human Rights*, 1ed. (Oxford, Clarendon Press, 1975)

Tim Jewell and Jenny Steele (eds.), *Law in Environmental Decision-Making* (forthcoming, Oxford University Press)

W.J. Kamba, "Legal Theory and Hohfeld's Analysis of a Legal Right" (1974) *Juridical Review* 249

Eugene Kamenka, "The anatomy of an idea" in Eugene Kamenka and Alice Tay (eds.), (1978)

—— and Alice Tay (eds.), *Human Rights* (London, Edward Arnold, 1978)

Immanuel Kant, *Fundamental Principles of the Metaphysic of Ethics*, 1785, translated by Thomas Abbott, 10ed. (London, Longmans, 1969)

—— "On the Common Saying: 'This May be True in Theory, but it does not Apply in Practice'" in Hans Reiss (ed.) (1970)

Mark Kelman, *A Guide to Critical Legal Studies* (Cambridge, MA, Harvard University Press, 1987)

Hans Kelsen, *General Theory of Law and State* (Cambridge, MA, Harvard University Press, 1945)

—— *Pure Theory of Law*, translated by Max Knight (Berkeley and Los Angeles, CA, University of California Press, 1967)

—— *General Theory of Norms*, translated by Michael Hartney (Oxford, Clarendon Press, 1991)

Joanna Kerr (ed.), *Ours by Right: Women's Rights as Human Rights* (London, Zed Books, 1993)

Valerie Kerruish and Alan Hunt, "Dworkin's Dutiful Daughter: Gender Discrimination in Law's Empire" in Alan Hunt (ed.) (1992)

Elizabeth Kingdom, "Transforming Rights: Feminist Political Heuristics" (1996) 2 *Res Publica* 63

Karl Klare, "Legal Theory and Democratic Reconstruction: Reflections on 1989" (1991) 25 *University of British Columbia Law Review* 69

Albert Kocourek, *Jural Relations*, 1ed. (Indianapolis, IN, The Bobbs-Merrill Co., 1927)

Will Kymlicka, *Liberalism, Community and Culture* (Oxford, Clarendon Press, 1989)

—— *Contemporary Political Philosophy: an Introduction* (Oxford, Clarendon Press, 1990)

Edward Levi, *An Introduction to Legal Reasoning* (Chicago, IL, University of Chicago Press, 1949)

Geoffrey Lewis, *Lord Atkin* (London, Butterworths, 1983)

John Locke, *Two Treatises of Government*, 1689, Peter Laslett (ed.) (Cambridge, Cambridge University Press, 1988)

Ian Loveland (ed.), *Importing the First Amendment* (forthcoming, Oxford, Hart Publishing)

David Luban, "The Self: Metaphysical not Political" (1995) 1 *Legal Theory* 401

Steven Lukes, "Five Fables about Human Rights" in Stephen Shute and Susan Hurley (eds.)

David Lyons, *Forms and Limits of Utilitarianism* (Oxford, Clarendon Press, 1965)
"Rights, Claimants, and Beneficiaries", (1969) 6 *American Philosophical Quarterly* 173

—— *In the Interest of the Governed* (Oxford, Clarendon Press, 1973 – revised edition 1991)

—— "Utility and Rights" (1982) *Nomos XXIV* 107 – also in Jeremy Waldron (ed.) (1984)

Gerald MacCallum, "Negative and Positive Freedom" (1967) 76 *Philosophical Review* 312

Neil MacCormick, "Voluntary Obligations and Normative Powers", (an essay in two parts contributed by Neil MacCormick and Joseph Raz) (1972) 46 *Proceedings of the Aristotelian Society Supplementary Volume* 59

—— "Children's Rights: a Test-Case for Theories of Right" (1976) 62 *Archiv für Rechts- und Sozialphilosophie* 305

—— *Legal Reasoning and Legal Theory* (Oxford, Clarendon Press, 1978)

—— *HLA Hart* (Stanford, CA, Stanford University Press, 1981)

—— *Legal Right and Social Democracy* (Oxford, Clarendon Press, 1982)

—— "Rights, Claims and Remedies" (1982) 1 *Law and Philosophy* 337

—— "Reconstruction after Deconstruction: A Response to CLS" (1990) 10 *Oxford Journal of Legal Studies* 539

—— and Zenon Bankowski (eds.) *Enlightenment, Rights and Revolution* (Aberdeen, Aberdeen University Press, 1989)

Eric Mack, "A Costly Road to Natural Law" (1989) 12 *Harvard Journal of Law and Public Policy* 753

Mary Mack, *Jeremy Bentham: An Odyssey of Ideas 1748-1792* (London, Heinemann, 1962)

J.L. Mackie, "Can there be a Right-Based Moral Theory?" from Peter French *et al.* (eds.) (1978) in Jeremy Waldron (ed.) (1984)

—— "Rights, Utility, and Universalization" in R.G. Frey (ed.) (1985)

Catherine MacKinnon, *Only Words* (London, HarperCollins, 1994)

Kathleen Mahoney, "The Constitutional Law of Equality in Canada" (1992) 24 *New York University Journal of International Law and Politics* 759

Sir Henry Maine, *Ancient Law*, 10ed. with Introduction by Sir Frederick Pollock (London, John Murray, 1920)

Diana Majury, "Equality and Discrimination According to the Supreme Court of Canada" (1990-91) 4 *Canadian Journal of Women and Law* 407

B.S. Markesinis & S.F. Deakin, *Tort Law*, 3ed. (Oxford, Clarendon Press, 1994)

Andrei Marmor, *Interpretation and Legal Theory* (Oxford, Clarendon Press, 1992)

—— (ed.), *Law and Interpretation: Essays in Legal Philosophy* (Oxford, Clarendon Press, 1995)

H.J. McCloskey, "A Note on Utilitarian Punishment" (1963) 72 *Mind* 599

Christopher McCrudden, "Freedom of Speech and Racial Equality" in Peter Birks (ed.) (1995)

—— and Gerald Chambers (eds.), *Individual Rights and the Law in Britain* (Oxford, Clarendon Press, 1994)

Theodor Meron, "Rape as a Crime under International Humanitarian Law" (1993) 87 *American Journal of International Law* 424

—— "The Case for War Crimes Trials in Yugoslavia" (1993) 72 *Foreign Affairs* 122

—— *Henry's Wars and Shakespeare's Laws* (Oxford, Clarendon Press, 1993)

J.G. Merrills, *The development of international law by the European Court of Human Rights* (Manchester, Manchester University Press, 1993)

Frank Michelman, "The Subject of Liberalism" (1994) 46 *Stanford Law Review* 1807

John Stuart Mill, *Utilitarianism*, 1863 – in Fontana ed., Mary Warnock (ed.) (Glasgow, Collins, 1962)

David Miller (ed.), *Liberty* (Oxford, OUP, 1991)

—— and Larry Seidentop (eds.), *The Nature of Political Theory* (Oxford, Clarendon Press, 1983)

Fred Miller, *Nature, Justice, and Rights in Aristotle's Politics* (Oxford, Clarendon Press, 1995)

Martha Minow, "Interpreting Rights" (1987) 96 *Yale Law Journal* 1860

Phillip Montague, "Two Concepts of Rights" (1980) 9 *Philosophy & Public Affairs* 372

Nicholas Mullany and Peter Handford, *Tort Liability for Psychiatric Damage* (Sydney, The Law Book Company Limited, 1993)

Phillip Mullock, "The Hohfeldian Jural Opposite" (1971) 13 *Ratio* 158

Thomas Nagel, "Libertarianism Without Foundations" (1975) 85 *Yale Law Journal* 136

Robert Nozick, *Anarchy, State, and Utopia* (Oxford, Blackwell, 1974)

Frances Olsen, "Statutory Rape: A Feminist Critique of Rights Analysis" (1984) 63 *Texas Law Review* 387

David Owen (ed.), *Philosophical Foundations of Tort Law* (Oxford, Clarendon Press, 1995)

The Oxford Paperback Dictionary, compiled by Joyce Hawkins (Oxford, OUP, 1979)

The Oxford English Dictionary, 2ed. prepared by J.A. Simpson and E.C.S. Weiner (Oxford, Clarendon Press, 1989)

Derek Parfit, *Reasons and Persons* (Oxford, Clarendon Press, 1984)

Stephen Parker, "Rights and Utility in Anglo-Australian Family Law" (1992) 55 *Modern Law Review* 311

Michael Perry, "Taking Neither Rights-Talk nor the 'Critique of Rights' Too Seriously" (1984) 62 *Texas Law Review* 1405

Grethe Peterson (ed.), *The Tanner Lectures on Human Values*, vol XI (Salt Lake City, Utah, University of Utah Press, 1990)

Hanna Pitkin, "Slippery Bentham: Some Neglected Cracks in the Foundations of Utilitarianism" (1990) 18 *Political Theory* 104

John Plamenatz, *The English Utilitarians* (Oxford, Blackwell, 1958)

Frederick Pollock, *Jurisprudence*, 2ed., (London, Macmillan, 1904)

Gerald Postema, "Liberty in Equality's Empire" (1987) 73 *Iowa Law Review* 55

—— "In Defence of French Nonsense" in Neil MacCormick and Zenon Bankowski (eds.) (1989)

David Price, "Taking Rights Cynically: A Review of Critical Legal Studies" (1989) 48 *Cambridge Law Journal* 271

Anthony Quinton, entry on Deontology in Alan Bullock *et al.* (eds.) (1988)

John Rawls, *A Theory of Justice* (Oxford, OUP, 1971)

—— *Political Liberalism* (New York, NY, Columbia University Press, 1993)

Joseph Raz, "Voluntary Obligations and Normative Powers", (an essay in two parts contributed by Neil MacCormick and Joseph Raz) (1972) 46 *Proceedings of the Aristotelian Society Supplementary Volume* 59

—— *The Authority of Law* (Oxford, Clarendon Press, 1979)

—— "Legal Rights" (1984) 4 *Oxford Journal of Legal Studies* 1

—— "Hart on Moral Rights and Legal Duties" (1984) 4 *Oxford Journal of Legal Studies* 123

—— "Professor Dworkin's Theory of Rights" (1986) 26 *Political Studies* 123

—— *The Morality of Freedom* (Oxford, Clarendon Press, 1986)

—— "Liberating Duties" (1989) 8 *Law and Philosophy* 3

—— *Practical Reason and Norms*, 2ed. (Princeton, NJ, Princeton University Press, 1990)

—— "Free Expression and Personal Identification" (1991) 11 *Oxford Journal of Legal Studies* 303

—— *Ethics in the Public Domain* (Oxford, Clarendon Press, 1994)

—— "Duties of Well-Being" in Joseph Raz (1994)

—— "Rights and Politics" (1995) 71 *Indiana Law Journal* 27

Hans Reiss (ed.), *Kant's Political Writings* (Cambridge, Cambridge University Press, 1970)

Barney Reynolds, "Natural Law versus Positivism: The Fundamental Conflict" (1993) 13 *Oxford Journal of Legal Studies* 441

David Richards, "Rights and Autonomy" (1981) 92 *Ethics* 3

W.V.H. Rogers, *Winfield & Jolowicz on Tort*, 14ed. (London, Sweet & Maxwell, 1994)

W.D Ross, *Foundations of Ethics* (Oxford, Clarendon Press, 1939)

Alan Ryan (ed.), *The Idea of Freedom* (Oxford, OUP, 1975)

Sir John Salmond, *Jurisprudence* – see P.J. Fitzgerald (ed.) (1966)

Charles Sampford and D.J. Galligan (eds.), *Law, Rights and the Welfare State* (London, Croom Helm, 1986)

Rolf Sartorius, "Dworkin on Rights and Utilitarianism" (1981) *Utah Law Review* 263 – also in Marshall Cohen (ed.) (1984)

Linda Schwartzstein, "Austrian Economics and the Current Debate Between Critical Legal Studies and Law and Economics" (1992) 20 *Hofstra Law Review* 1105

Sir Stephen Sedley, "Human Rights: a Twenty-First Century Agenda" [1995] *Public Law* 386

Amartya Sen, "Rights and Agency" (1982) 11 *Philosophy and Public Affairs* 3

—— *Inequality Reexamined* (Oxford, Clarendon Press, 1992)

Samuel Sheffler, "The Appeal of Political Liberalism" (1994) 105 *Ethics* 4

Stephen Shute and Susan Hurley (eds.), *On Human Rights: The Oxford Amnesty Lectures 1993* (New York, NY, Basic Books, 1993)

N.E. Simmonds, "Epstein's Theory of Strict Tort Liability" (1992) 51 *Cambridge Law Journal* 113

—— "The Analytical Foundations of Justice" (1995) 54 *Cambridge Law Journal* 306

A.W.B. Simpson (ed.), *Oxford Essays in Jurisprudence (Second Series)* (Oxford, Clarendon Press, 1973)

J.J.C. Smart, "An Outline of a System of Utilitarian Ethics" in J.J.C. Smart and Bernard Williams (1973)

—— and Bernard Williams, *Utilitarianism For and Against* (Cambridge, Cambridge University Press, 1973)

Torben Spaak, *The Concept of Legal Competence*, translated by Robert Carroll (Aldershot, Dartmouth, 1994)

Horacio Spector, *Autonomy and Rights* (Oxford, Clarendon Press, 1992)

Herbert Spencer, *Social Statics* (London, John Chapman, 1851 – republished Farnborough, Gregg International Publishers, 1971)

Jane Stapleton, "Duty of Care and Economic Loss: A Wider Agenda" (1991) 107 *Law Quarterly Review* 249

Jenny Steele, "Scepticism and the Law of Negligence" (1993) 52 *Cambridge Law Journal* 437

―― "Assessing the Past" in Tim Jewell and Jenny Steele (eds.) (forthcoming)

Henry Steiner and Philip Alston, *International Human Rights in Context* (Oxford, Clarendon Press, 1996)

Hillel Steiner, "The Structure of a Set of Compossible Rights" (1977) 74 *Journal of Philosophy* 767

―― *An Essay on Rights* (Oxford, Blackwell, 1994)

Samuel Stoljar, "White on Rights and Claims" (1985) 4 *Law and Philosophy* 417

Julius Stone, *Legal System and Lawyers' Reasonings* (Stanford, CA, Stanford University Press, 1964)

Nadine Strossen, *Defending Pornography: Free Speech, Sex, and the Fight for Women's Rights* (New York, NY, Scribner, 1995)

Robert Summers (ed.), *Essays in Legal Philosophy* (Oxford, Basil Blackwell, 1968)

L.W. Sumner, *The Moral Foundation of Rights* (Oxford, Clarendon Press, 1987)

Cass Sunstein, *Democracy and the Problem of Free Speech* (Riverside, NJ, Free Press, 1993)

―― *The Partial Constitution* (Cambridge, MA, Harvard University Press, 1993)

C.F.H. Tapper, "Powers and Secondary Rules of Change" in A.W.B. Simpson (ed.) (1973)

Charles Taylor, "What's Wrong with Negative Liberty" in Alan Ryan (ed.) (1975)

H.D. Thoreau, "Civil Disobedience" (originally delivered as a lecture in 1848) in *Walden and Civil Disobedience* (Harmondsworth, Penguin, 1983)

Richard Tuck, *Natural Rights Theories* (Cambridge, Cambridge University Press, 1979)

Mark Tushnet, "An Essay on Rights" (1984) 62 *Texas Law Review* 1363

Richard Tur, "The Leaves on the Trees" [1976] *Juridical Review* 139

―― "The Notion of a Legal Right: A Test Case for Legal Science" [1976] *Juridical Review* 177

William Twining and David Miers, *How To Do Things With Rules*, 3ed. (London, Weidenfeld and Nicolson, 1991)

Edna Ullman-Margalit, *The Emergence of Norms* (Oxford, Clarendon Press, 1977)

Roberto Unger, "The Critical Legal Studies Movement" (1983) 96 *Harvard Law Review* 561

―― *The Critical Legal Studies Movement* (Cambridge, MA, Harvard University Press, 1986)

―― *False Necessity, Part 1 of Politics* (Cambridge, Cambridge University Press, 1987)

―― *Social Theory: Its Situation and Its Task, A Critical Introduction to Politics* (Cambridge, Cambridge University Press, 1987)

Sir Paul Vinogradoff, "The Foundation of a Theory of Rights" (1924) 34 *Yale Law Journal* 60

―― *Common Sense in Law*, 3ed. revised by H.G. Hanbury (London, Oxford University Press, 1959)

Georg Henrik von Wright, *Norm and Action* (London, Routledge and Kegan Paul, 1963)

Jeremy Waldron (ed.), *Theories of Rights* (Oxford, OUP, 1984)

―― (ed.), *Nonsense upon Stilts* (London, Methuen, 1987)

―― "Nonsense upon Stilts? – a reply" in Jeremy Waldron (ed.) (1987)

—— *The Right to Private Property* (Oxford, Clarendon Press, 1988)

—— "When Justice Replaces Affection: The Need for Rights" (1988) 11 *Harvard Journal of Law and Public Policy* 625

—— *Liberal Rights* (Cambridge, Cambridge University Press, 1993)

—— "A Right-Based Critique of Constitutional Rights" (1993) 13 *Oxford Journal of Legal Studies* 18

L. Werner, "A Note about Bentham on Equality and about the Greatest Happiness Principle" (1973) 11 *Journal of the History of Philosophy* 237

Peter Westen, "The Empty Idea of Equality" (1982) 95 *Harvard Law Review* 537

Alan White, "Meaning and Implication" (1971) 32 *Analysis* 26

—— "Rights and Claims" (1982) 1 *Law and Philosophy* 315

—— "Reply to Professor MacCormick" (1982) 1 *Law and Philosophy* 359

—— *Rights* (Oxford, Clarendon Press, 1984)

—— "Do Claims Imply Rights?" (1986) 5 *Law and Philosophy* 417

Glanville Williams, "Language and the Law" (1946) 62 *Law Quarterly Review* 387

—— "The Concept of Legal Liberty" (1956) 56 Columbia Law Review 1129 – also in Robert Summers (ed.) (1968)

Jonathan Wolff, *Robert Nozick: Property, Justice and the Minimal State* (Cambridge, Polity Press, 1991)

Index

'A superb account of cloak-and-dagger religious intrigue in Tudor England . . . describes a John le Carré-like world . . . *God's Traitors*, with its crisp prose and punctilious scholarship, brilliantly recreates a world of heroism and holiness in Tudor England' **Ian Thomson**, *Financial Times*

'Truly excellent . . . *God's Traitors* crosses the divide between popular and academic history. It raises issues of some real historical importance, not least of how much archival material, more often glimpsed than analysed, might still be out there which has things to tell us about the period but which is often excluded from mainstream versions of it' **Professor Michael Questier**, *Spectator*

'Detailed and absorbing . . . *God's Traitors* is both a dramatic and thrilling story of fear, faith, courage and deceit and an important exposé of the terror of life as a Catholic in Elizabethan England' **Anna Whitelock**, *New Statesman*

'In the quality of her research and sensitive handling of issues that remain raw to this day, Jessie Childs succeeds in evoking "the lived experience of anti-Catholicism" as few have done before' **John Cooper**, *Literary Review*

'A fine book: extraordinarily learned, exciting . . . beautifully written . . . remarkably fair and astute' **Professor JJ Scarisbrick**, *The Weekly Standard*

'Wonderful – both scholarly history and Tudor espionage thriller' **Simon Sebag Montefiore**

'In considering the fundamentalisms of today, it's as well not to forget our own gruesome and intolerant past, and Childs has employed her impressive research skills and storytelling verve to bring that past vividly to life' **Virginia Rounding**, *Daily Telegraph*

'A rollicking story . . . engaging history and a cracking read' **Melanie McDonagh**, *Evening Standard*

'Ingeni⌐ ⌐ ⌐ ⌐ of plots, intrigues, gracious stately homes ⌐ with consum-
mate r⌐ ⌐nt

'Excellent . . . Childs has written an engaging history of English papists, filled with memorable episodes. It poses a number of good questions about liberty and security' **The Economist**

'A riveting account of resistance in an age of intolerance, *God's Traitors* brings alive the story of the men – and remarkable women – of a defiant family' **Leanda de Lisle, author of *Tudor: The Family Story***

'Fascinating . . . What makes Childs's book different is that she concentrates . . . on the stay-at-home English Catholics who were obliged to negotiate their divided loyalties in these trickiest of times' **Kathryn Hughes**, *Mail on Sunday*

'A vivid, sometimes even humorous picture of devout Catholics keeping up appearances' **Daisy Dunn**, *Daily Mail*

'Superb and groundbreaking . . . A superlative, flawlessly written book . . . This is a book about saints and traitors, certainly; but above all it is about the strengths and frailties that made these people human. They have had to wait a long time, but at last they have found a historian who offers them both justice and dignity' **Mathew Lyons, author of *The Favourite: Ralegh and His Queen***

'There's micro history and macro history – and then there's the rare book that takes a seemingly small subject and lets it lead to wider issues. Minutely researched and vividly readable . . . manages to explore big questions still relevant today: belief and politics, security versus liberty' **Sarah Gristwood**, *BBC History Magazine* **Books of the Year**

'Jessie Childs shakes off a sense of Reformation familiarity by focusing on one family, the Vauxes, who will not forsake their Catholic faith; with this concentrated human dimension, the suffocating fear, the concealment, the imprisonment and torture, is given fresh life, and makes the dilemma even more acute' **Sinclair McKay**, *Telegraph* **Books of the Year**

'A splendidly evocative portrait, not just of a family, but of an anxious, even paranoid age' **Dominic Sandbrook**, *Sunday Times* **Books of the Year**

'A gripping tale of spies and skulduggery . . . *Gods Traitors* is thought-provoking and timely' **Ben Macintyre**, *The Times* **Books of the Year**